FINANCE MASTERS

A Brief History of
International Financial Centers
in the Last Millennium

FINANCE MASTERS

A Brief History of
International Financial Centers
in the Last Millennium

OLIVIER COISPEAU

Maverlinn Ltd, UK

 **World Scientific**

NEW JERSEY · LONDON · SINGAPORE · BEIJING · SHANGHAI · HONG KONG · TAIPEI · CHENNAI · TOKYO

Published by

World Scientific Publishing Co. Pte. Ltd.
5 Toh Tuck Link, Singapore 596224
USA office: 27 Warren Street, Suite 401-402, Hackensack, NJ 07601
UK office: 57 Shelton Street, Covent Garden, London WC2H 9HE

British Library Cataloguing-in-Publication Data
A catalogue record for this book is available from the British Library.

The cover image is based on the video showing folding instructions and tutorials freely given by Won Park online.

FINANCE MASTERS
A Brief History of International Financial Centers in the Last Millennium

Copyright © 2017 by World Scientific Publishing Co. Pte. Ltd.

ISBN 978-981-3108-82-0

Desk Editor: Sandhya Venkatesh

Typeset by Stallion Press
Email: enquiries@stallionpress.com

Printed in Singapore

ABOUT THE AUTHOR

Olivier Coispeau

As an economist and investment banker, Olivier engineered numerous industrial partnerships, led complex industrial projects in various financial hubs and closed M&A transactions for international industry leaders, foundations and governments, especially in the financial institutions, energy and transportation sector. He worked for strategy consulting firms and financial institutions notably for JP Morgan, Clinvest, and Schroders between Europe, the USA and Asia.

He is also a specialist in investment and previously co-headed funds in Europe. He is the co-founder of Maverlinn, a strategy and growth acceleration advisory firm. Aside from advising on industrial projects, he dedicates spare time to working in less favoured areas on responsible leadership. He spent many years in emerging countries advising industry leaders on development and growth acceleration.

He studied economics and finance at Stanford University, Paris-Dauphine University, and Institut d'Etudes Politiques de Paris. He taught economics for several years at the Paris-Sorbonne University and authored many publications. He is a frequently invited guest speaker at finance and strategy forums.

ACKNOWLEDGEMENT

This short essay originates from a fortuitous speech delivered in the city of Dalian, China in June 2012. On short notice, my colleagues and I were invited to meet a German delegation led by Senator Frank Horch, Vice Mayor of Hamburg, one of the famous German seaports and former state-city "Freie Hansestad". We gathered at the China Shipping Container Lines headquarters where we were welcomed by CSCL Deputy Managing Director, Zhao Hongzhou. My short "impromptu" speech was related to some salient events of our European medieval seaport history, considering that some facts captured from this distant past might cast some interesting light at a time of accelerated change for China, and in particular for the city of Dalian. I enjoyed going where my path took me across centuries along the merchant routes, and it triggered a desire to grasp a more con-sistent view on the landscape I could see emerging from my investiga-tions. My intention was then to try to connect, from the economist point of view, the dots across time and geography on the conditions that once made the economic success of visionary free ports on the North and South of Europe, leading to their dominance in international sea trade and in international finance.

The further extension of this first work owes much to meeting Serge Kebabtchieff, the charismatic President of the "Editions Eska" (Paris), who kindly encouraged me to publish an essay on the emergence of International Financial Centres after we jointly attended the July 2012 Paris Europlace finance forum. The shadow of the 2008–2009 financial crisis was very palpable and many of the bankers and government officials attending the conference were preoccupied by possible shock wave replicas of this global financial tsunami and their possible devastating impact on the world economy. The project was strengthen by my desire to provide a series of almost independent but connected chapters illustrating the salient points which led over centuries and geographies to the emergence and persistence in difficult times of leading international financial centres, which have proven to be at the core of the development of modern finance. This would also connect, as a side reflexion with my personal experience of working on finance hubs in Europe, Asia, and the USA. Therefore, this idea encouraged me to focus on a simple book of modest nature which may be read as a popular primer accessible to a broad audience. My editors Rajni Nayanthara Gamage and Qi Xiao at World Scientific (Singapore) also kindly mentioned they were very supportive of the idea at a time where I was slightly hesitant to continue.

This essay is based on early personal research made on the conditions underlying the emergence of international financial centres and an extensive canvassing of professional and academic literature. My friend Seamus Grimes, Emeritus Professor of Geography at the Whitaker Institute, National University of Ireland, Galway, has generously shared time, insights, and materials. He also made always useful suggestions and helped correct a number of mistakes, although the remaining ones are solely mine. There will never be enough words to thank the economists, the geographers, and the historians who have dedicated their lives to make this short synthesis possible. Hundreds of thousands of pages have been written without any doubt, and much of that had already been done by very gifted and talented people. Therefore, my initial and primary goal remained to try to identify more specifically salient factors in the development of international financial centres since their emergence in late medieval times and put them in perspective on a millennium. One of the challenges has been to reconcile the various interpretations of distant events and include the most recent, and sometimes controversial, findings — for example, the emergence of economic geography or the causes of defining events in the destiny of leading hubs. The decision to work on a compact and abridged format became obvious to facilitate a quick introduction to this rather dense topic and highlight key learning points. This choice would indeed have some adverse consequences as such a format may not suit the needs of those willing to go deeper into more historical details, especially since the simplification of history may, from time to time, take from our understanding of the complexity and breadth of the situations of the time. Hopefully, the compiled bibliography may provide, to those willing to go beyond the following chapters, an opportunity to do so. I hope that the reasons for focusing on key success factors in the emergence of almost a millennium of finance masters will remain a sufficient motivation for the readership to accept the limitations of this somewhat difficult but deliberate trade-off.

The logical next step beyond the pleasure of the historical narrative was to focus on understanding why a series of small random events can produce large consequences for economic geography and is also crucial to understanding why underlying differences in natural geography can have such large effects: that cried out for a theoretical framework to be tested for in the labs, not to forget that "one must avoid the development of a complex mathematical apparatus whenever it is not strictly indispensable".[1] People like Paul Krugman from the City University of New York, or Masahisa Fujita from the Kyoto University, have done that very well already with cute mathematical models and plain language explanations, capable to position more precisely verbal arguments and prove that their implied conclusion is not only a matter of rethoric. As a result, a new school of economic geography has emerged since the 1990s. Their work together with those of many other economists is a path to better understand the geography of the world economy, across centuries, both between and within nations — and how it engages in a process of "self-organisation" in which more or less symmetric locations can end up playing very different economic roles.

Olivier Coispeau
London, November 2015

---

[1] Maurice Allais *Nobel Lecture*, 9 December (1988).

FOREWORD

This is a remarkable account of the historical circumstances, the geographical context and the many institutional factors which gave rise to the emergence of international financial centres over the past 900 years.The author's range of knowledge is reflected in the following texts mentioned in the book which made important contributions to the development of the financial sector: Leonardo of Pisa's Liber Abaci (The Book of Calculation) published in 1202; Francesco di Balduccio Pegolotti's professional handbook in 1340; Marco Polo's Marvel of the World, also known as *The Million Lies Marvels* on his travels in Asia 1276-1291; Ibn Battuta's The Rihlah or The Travels1304-1368 and John Wheeler's A Treatise of Commerce in 1601; De La Vega's Confusion de Confusiones, the first account of a stock exchange in 1688; Pierre-Joseph Proudhon's Manuel du Spéculateur á la Bourse in 1857; Louis Bachelier's PhD dissertation Théorie de la Spéculation in 1900; and more recent key contributions such as articles by Black and Scholes (1973) and Merton (1973) on pricing options and other derivative securities.This more recent work by Myron S. Scholes and Robert C. Merton, which is seen as having some impact on the reckless trading before the 2008 crisis,resulted in them sharing the 1997 Nobel Memorial Prize in Economic Sciences.

Referring to De La Vega's sometimes 'confusing' account of business practices in 1688, Coispeau points out that the main financial contracts currently traded, such as forwards, call and put options, and futures were already in use in Amsterdam at this time. In addition to providing an

insightful explanation of how technological innovations have revolutionised financial trading in recent years, this book provides an invaluable and
necessary context for a deeper understanding of the historical evolution of
innovations in financial transactions, explaining among many other things
some of the earliest attempt to model risk-taking when cargoes were being
transported through pirate-infested seas. It also explains how risk taking
in more recent times has become increasingly challenging to evaluate
because of the difficulties associated with monitoring transactions being
conducted by sophisticated computer programmes in milliseconds, and
which are also open to attack from software viruses.

In addition to providing background to key historical publications in
the history of finance, the book also chronicles the development of key
landmark financial instruments. Among these are the following: the first
bill of exchange in the 13th century; also in the 13th century,the introduction of sovereign debt to provide funding for military adventures; in the
1300s, Venice was the first state to issue the prestiti, which could be called
the first Eurobond; in 1309, the first bourse was opened in Bruges; the
1345 banking collapse was likely triggered by Edward III's defaulting on
his debt to the Lombardy bankers in 1342; in 1455, the use of the holding
company was perfected by the Medici bankers; in Pingyao, Shanxi
Province, Lei Lutai converted his Xiyuchen Pigment shop into the
Rishengchang Draft Bank, the first institution to issue cheques in 1823;
the lottery is said to have been invented by Benedetto Gentille in 1610; in
1688 Llyod's coffee shop in London witnessed the first days of the
world's best known insurance underwriting company; in 1752, Benjamin
Franklin founded America's oldest insurance company; on May 17, 1792,
leading New York merchants signed the Buttonwood Agreement which
committedthem to trade securities only between themselves; and in 1863,
Edward A. Calahan invented the first stock price ticker tape.

To explain the widening gulf that emerged over time between economics and ethical considerations, Coispeau points to the influence of
David Ricardo, but his historical analysis also points to the greatly
reduced influence of religion in the business world and particularly in the
financial sector in recent times. Without specifically setting out to do so,
Coispeau's history provides a rich background to the significant role
played by religion in the earlier stages of financial history. Among the

topics he deals with are the central role of Catholic teaching on usury, the Catholic church as a major entity dealing with banks and other financial institutions, and the role of Jesuit education in developing leadership. He refers to the positive role played by Thomas Aquinas in the 4th Latern Council in 1215 on the morality of usury. After 1236, the use of sea loans went into decline when they were condemned by Pope Gregory IX's as usurious. An important reason of the prevalence of Jewish bankers in the Christian world was because the restriction on usury did not apply to them. Despite the church's significant sanctions against usury, Lombardy bankers gradually replaced Jewish money lenders in the 13th century. A positive spinoff for civilisation in general arising from their fear of being declared heretics by the church for practising usury was the willingness of Italian bankers to build beautiful frescoed churches all over Florence and in other Italian cities.

For many readers, the most fascinating part of the book will be the last section which provides important insights into the 'Great Recession'. If, according to Coispeau, it took scholars 500 years to fully understand the nature of the 14th century banking collapse, one wonders how long it will take us to fully appreciate the significance of these recent catastrophic events. Without seeking easy scapegoats, Coispeau draws many lessons about the dangers posed by a highly complex financial system that is increasingly dependent on sophisticated algorithms and information technology, to the point where risk taking is becoming more robotic, depersonalised and removed from ethical frameworks.

Although the book's primary objective is not to explain the background to the most recent global financial crisis, the historical perspective helps us realise that while not being new historically, the world then and now are different places in different times, particularly in terms of technology developments. The recent economic crisis which in no small way was caused by the reckless use of financial models and instruments such as derivatives, with scant regard for the lives of the millions who were subsequently negatively affected, reflects a financial sector that has become disembedded from its historical roots and empirical foundations, and indeed from whatever ethical practices that were once associated with it. The book really takes off to another level when the discussion turns to the Great Recession. No longer are we looking at the evolution of finance

with the detachment of many centuries, but we are now involved in issues
that have cost many people dearly, and while the technical discussion is
masterful, the historical foundation on which it has been built helps us to
realise that only some aspects of this crisis were original.

More than anything else, the author lays down clear markers for
urgently needed progress in ethical guidelines if financial centres are to be
sustained into the future. It is a masterful treatise on the absolute requirement of trustworthiness as a basis for the development such centres,which
draws on the lessons of many historical failures to establish such a foundation. If financiers and merchants had to face the threat of real sanctions for
practices such as usury in earlier times, the effectiveness of media exposure of corrupt practices and significant fines imposed on those found
responsible in recent years have been far from effective because of a significant disconnection between ethical standards and what has deemed to
be acceptable behaviour by many. While regulators and those responsible
for setting ethical standards continue to scramble to keep pace with the
rapid pace of technological change in the sector, the need for ethical training within the financial sector's workforce remains paramount. For students of the business world, and particularly for those who use their
expertise in the complex world of financial transactions, this book provides an invaluable and indispensable source to rediscover those lessons
from history which can help restore credibility to their profession.

Seamus Grimes
Emeritus Professor
Whitaker Institute
National University of Ireland, Galway

INTRODUCTION

"Go with me to a notary, seal me there
Your single bond; and, in a merry sport,
If you repay me not on such a day,
In such a place, such sum or sums as are
Express'd in the condition, let the forfeit
Be nominated for an equal pound
Of your fair flesh, to be cut off and taken
In what part of your body pleaseth me."[2]

About 2.8 million years ago, our remote human ancestors were an insignificant species living in a corner of East Africa.[3] One hundred thousand years ago, at least six different species of humans inhabited this planet. The Cognitive Revolution, about 70,000 years ago, enabled less than a million of *Homo sapiens* to conquer the world and drove all other human species to extinction. One of the distinctive features of *Homo sapiens* is its ability to adapt to new situations by learning and implementing more

---

[2] William Shakespeare, *The Merchant of Venice*, Act 1, Scene III.
[3] Dr. Yuval Noah Harari, A Brief History of Humankind, *Department of History, Introduction*. The Hebrew University of Jerusalem, (2012).

advantageous behaviour, and this is often accomplished by several components of the brain working together to solve the problem. As humans, it took us about 3 million years to grow from a few thousand individuals to a billion (1815), and it only took us 200 years to grow from 1 to 7 billion.[4] In the middle of this expansion, money started to play a significant role in human relationships as far as the 7th century A.D. and only became a discriminating social factor in the last millennium or so. It gradually became clear that one of the distinctive rights of humans is the right to own and trade property in a reasonably free environment. Securities started to be traded by investors on listed exchanges for just 400 years, with rice futures trading originating from the 17th century in Japan. Connecting the dots across centuries is a delicate exercise as culture, psychology and physical circumstances were very different one century after the other. In addition, narrating the epic saga of the mega financial companies led by a small circle of adventurous medieval merchants through the influx of precious luxury goods without understanding the frugal life of the massive part of the population farming in the countryside may lead to an incorrect perception of the medieval economy. Poverty was common in this subsistence economy, and focusing only on the rich and powerful would bear the risk to provide too idealised a representation of the economic reality of the Middle Ages. However, one cannot help thinking that a shared idea of trust, respect and ambition between the men of the same "nation", motivated those who were instrumental in building great economic centres, strong financial hubs, dedicated in spite of the Brownian movements of history, to serve beyond the limitations of their own lives for the development of a better world. Some simple metrics must be kept in mind, the size of "planet finance" in 2014 can be estimated by the total amount of assets under management worldwide — about USD 294 trillion, almost three times the consolidated GDP of all countries of USD 107.5 trillion (in terms of purchasing power parity).[5] Sovereign debt

---

[4] Pr. Yves Coppens, Collège de France, Interview with O. De Lagarde, France Info, 31 January (2014).

[5] PPP exchange rates help to correct distortions that can arise with the use of spot market exchange rates in international comparison. The idea originated with the School of

which has been a major factor behind the emergence of financial hubs is currently estimated worldwide USD 59.7 trillion: combining the debt of the United States, Japan and Europe together accounts for 75% of total global debt, and coincides with the location of the leading financial hubs in their capacity to raise funds.

In the 5th century A.D., the Athenians were wealthier than the Spartans. Athens was a city-state open to the sea with a port, merchants and a powerful navy whilst Sparta, another powerful Greek city-state, laid a strong emphasis on military training and frugal living. Foreigners were not very welcome in Sparta, the city-state was in constant conflict with its local peers notably Athens and Corinth. Neighbouring Messenians were conquered, enslaved and each year Sparta would solemnly declare war against them making the murder of Helots[6] a permissible act. This much feared and disciplined city was located in the most fertile Eurotas valley of Laconia in the southeast Peloponnese but was landlocked. Continued Spartan ambitions in other parts of Greece, Sicily and Asia Minor were the cause of political instability and rampant conflicts. Sparta was certainly a feared model but not a very attractive one: as a result, it was much poorer than Athens. Spartan culture would be remembered as a brutal and merciless one in which citizens were compelled to serve from their childhood a totalitarian state, Athens, as a democracy and a free market for brilliant intellectuals and a human testimony to cultural achievements. The radical opposition between Athens and its nemesis Sparta deeply influenced political thinkers, early economists and generations of rulers. Plato, Aristotle and Plutarch discussed this contrast at length, and the reference to the antagonism of these political models continued over 1,500 years. As humans, we already know as a prerequisite, that brutal discipline and order comes with a price incompatible with freedom, a condition for the development of a creative, flexible and harmonious society. Finance has all over this journey relied on trustworthiness, which is not only synonymous with the resilience of ethics in difficult times but also

---

Salamanca in Spain during the 16th century and was developed in its modern form by Gustav Cassel at the end of WWI.

[6] Messenian inhabitants, enslaved by Sparta.

benevolence, justice and an uncompromising search for excellence. Ethics means aiming to live "a good life with and for others in just institutions".[7] Those who have played with different formulations, or chosen to ignore this, have always experienced severe psychosociological hurdles leading ultimately to political chaos, collateral damages and finally the disintegration of their own culture. As far as the Roman Empire was concerned, merchants were not highly regarded and were often treated with contempt compared to those in charge of governing the Empire. This has laid a deep and lasting footprint on the relationship between business and power, especially in Southern Europe. This heritage has been the cause of centuries of misunderstanding between politics and economics, and we still pay the price for what should be now be labeled as a necessary but archaic step in the evolution of our species.

Universities sprang up in the late 12th and 13th centuries largely in response to the recovery in the West of Aristotle's works on logic and should be now called the sciences. Coincidently, Venice started to emerge in the 12th century as the leading trading and financial hub in the fragmented Mediterranean area, following the great schism of the 11th century which led to Byzantium challenging Rome. Since then, the most influential cities of this world have been quietly but fiercely competing in a merciless race for wealth and for sea trade domination. The smartest rulers of the most advanced state cities quickly realised that trade, and the capacity to establish enforceable contracts for the delivery of goods, would only be a first step in their quest to establish a long standing dominance over international economy. Becoming a key international financial hub would be even more lucrative than trading. Many of these ambitions have been disrupted by bitter internal feuds or wars, as the route for becoming finance masters has been paved with obstacles for many of the aspiring candidates. But those with a clear vision and a strong determination have often been paid back handsomely, especially when the geographical location of the city was favourable to the development of financial services. These centres developed through the professionalism of their key constituent, their rulers and the merchant bankers, who emerged as a combination of money-changers, bankers,

---

[7] Ricoeur, Paul, *Oneself as Another*, Chicago: University of Chicago Press (1992).

merchants, partners or agents in land or sea trade, all without one of these activities being clearly predominant. However, what made a merchant and later a banker successful was his firm capacity to anticipate what was going to sell or disappear from the markets; were vair linings still fashionable in the North of Europe, or was it rather the sable trimmings? The correct choice made a cargo, or a loan, either a profit or a loss. Information was very much at the core of business, and those business gatherings at the largest European fairs provided unique opportunities to meet colleagues and customers and learn about the true market needs.

Although there does not appear to be a universally accepted definition of financial hubs under the term "international financial centre" (IFC), such places are known to be high density specialised business centres, hubs of expertise for wholesale finance, that genuinely serve clients from all over the world in the provision of the widest possible array of financial services necessary to support trade and international business. Adam Smith just posited the phenomena of specialisation and exchange as an expression of a "propensity in human nature ... to truck, barter, and exchange one thing for another," effectively shifting the focus to wealth creating specialisation as a consequence of exchange. To qualify as genuinely international, financial centres have been generally requested to offer a concentration of at least five critical value added activities including: financing of foreign trade, currency exchange, international fund transfers, foreign borrowing and lending and foreign investment. They perform medium-of-exchange and store-of-value of functions similar to money and focus like a magnifier, pure trading energy capable of activating and fueling the transformation of the world from a timely concentration of expert resources and cutting edge infrastructures. Therefore, they propel the emergence of a specific type of urban community and dedicated infrastructure with a broad opening to the outside world. It is no coincidence that a number of fast moving emerging cities have openly set ambitious agendas to become the world financial hubs of the 21st century. In the light of the brief and bright history of IFCs in the face of 7 million years of human or pre-human existence, it seems quite appropriate to reflect upon the conditions that made the fortune of these world financial hubs since they started to shine from European medieval fairs about 900 years ago.

Pre-modern IFCs flourished across Europe, the Middle East and coastal Africa, under the umbrella of the Roman Empire — which also traded with Persia and the Orient. As Rome's power waned after the Germanic invasions of the 5th century, its control of sea also receded. The strategic shipyards of Ravenna and Misenimum fell into disrepair and the Pax Romana on sea became a memory as piracy took its rights again in the Mediterranean. The Vandals crossed the sea, through Spain, established a virtual pirate kingdom centred on Carthage and a strong war fleet of nearly 120 vessels capable of sailing to Rome. As a result, IFC trajectories were nearly extinguished between the 5th and 11th centuries A.D. but they were revived with the commercial revolution of the High Middle Age. This revolution was the result of an influx to Europe of luxury goods, such as spices, silk, precious stones and slaves, coming from the East of the Mediterranean first and from the sea routes leading to India, Asia and the Americas later after a perpetual state of war in Europe led navigators to seek new and safer routes for their ships. In the 10th century, Europe was still socially, culturally and economically backward, overtaken by a still solid Byzantine Empire, the flourishing world of Islam, albeit showing the first signs of political division, and further East, virtually unknown, the magnificent Song dynasty in China. But a century later, Medieval Florence, Venice and Genoa organised as state-cities were at the frontier of capitalism between the mid-12th and the early 16th century. Certainly, key reasons for their phenomenal economic development were the progress made in technology, trading, finance and shipping. This was also the result from an economic perspective of the opening of their markets to the outside world with a desire to create the best conditions to facilitate and benefit from trade, sometimes at the price of wars and severe internal feuds. This open ended model sets a sharp contrast with the development of China under the Ming dynasty which discouraged merchants from developing relationships with the outside, and emphasized a self-centred development. As colonial empire-building and industrial development took off in Europe, large financing needs arose triggering the need for large cross-border specialised financial firms and trading platforms to emerge. A rich trail of economic history helps us to understand where IFC come from and how the most astute managed to become excellent and therefore dominant trading places. Getting back to the early days of capitalism in the Middle Ages, it is enlightening to understand how the early financial centres managed to establish dominant positions in Europe, as standalone entities. It is especially fascinating to better observe how a handful of free entrepreneurial medieval cities led by visionary, ambitious and sometimes merciless rulers managed to dominate the key trading routes, especially on sea since many overland routes were disturbed by wars, and subsequently ruled over the financial routes of Europe and beyond for centuries.

As of today, the dots can be connected and some intriguing conclusions can be drawn looking back at the patterns of IFC formation, only that history will not always repeat itself and this is definitely the salt and pepper of proactively inventing our future. However, spanning over almost a millennium, the critical components of successful marketplaces including stability, trustworthiness and safety have remained decisive and permanent building blocks. This is something that must be meditated on in the light of Montesquieu's candid remark that the natural consequence of commerce is to lead to peace.[8] This enigmatic sentence can hardly be understood in an historical perspective without the subsequent explanation that trade interdependence between nations is definitely a stabilising factor and therefore a factor of peace within the framework of rational economic games, and not by the virtue of commerce itself as it shall be later seen.

From a patchwork of kingdoms, counties and free cities, most of them mostly agrarian, with limited exposure to the outside, and some becoming lively urban centres open to foreign merchant, financial flows in the 11th century concentrated on places such as peasants markets, and later large fairs carefully sponsored by the rulers and the Church to encourage and facilitate business. They were in the most physical sense, "free places" where people could merrily gather from time to time, to trade and also entertain themselves. The schedule of large markets and fairs was aligned with Christian religious events and festivals, which often connected with ancient pagan rites. This also explains why the Church played a significant role in their organisation. The exchange was based primarily on

---

[8] Charles de Secondat and Baron de Montesquieu, *The Spirit of the Laws* ("*L'esprit des lois*"), Book XX, Chapter II, (1748).

farming products, then in the High Middle Ages on precious goods such as silk fabric, furs, spices and wine. The discovery of gold and silver in the New World later added a completely new monetary dimension to international trade. This busy heterogeneous world of eminent and humble European merchants gathered and traded from markets to fairs sometimes only through trusted intermediaries (*"certi missi"*). As a result, an increasingly complex web of financial services, initially based on trade, developed including currencies exchange and credit instruments, such as letters of credit. From the 11th century onward, the motto *Deus enim et proficuum* ("For God and Profit") began to appear in the ledgers of the catholic Italian and Flemish merchants. The separation between trade and finance then occurred in the 13th century and the emergence of merchant banking powerhouses in Italy, allowed finance to gradually become an autonomous discipline.

Almost 900 years later, safer sea routes and technology helped market operators migrate their physical trade to heavy duty vessels, high speed telecommunications networks and computer infrastructure. From the Great Depression to the New York terrorist attacks of September 2001, the market capitalisation of the Dow Jones industrial doubled every decade on average, with a simultaneous acceleration of the trading volumes, doubling every 7.5 years then every 2.9 years before the Great Recession of 2008–2009, a path comparable to the Moore's law in semiconductors. Today, the heart of stock exchange infrastructures consists mostly of virtual places embedded in silicon stored in dark refrigerated vaults, their half-human half-cybernetic brains being disseminated within an even more international pool of users. In the background of the finance cobweb, high speed networks form the secured nervous system of IFC where more sentient machines and scattered expert clusters have replaced the previous human operated stock exchanges. In the 20th century, markets became by themselves listed and tradable financial assets, and in the 21st century machines are likely to handle, on their own, the most sizable part of trading. Defining the geographical frontiers of IFCs is becoming more complex as networks are abolishing traditional borders, but the control of its key constituents will continue to be for sure a challenge to leadership and sovereignty. Several of their key constituents will continue to be unrelated to finance, talents on the one hand and the capacity to physically deliver goods and services on the other hand will be critical to ensure dominance. Diversity will continue to be necessary to regenerate business models.

After the first wave of stock exchange mergers rocked the market in 2006 starting with the Chicago Board of Trade (CBoT) gobbling up Chicago Mercantile Exchange (CME), protagonists paused for about four years, until late 2010, when Singapore Exchange Ltd (SGX) and Australia's ASX Ltd said they were in merger talks. Then Deutsche Börse AG and NYSE Euronext confirmed they were also in merger talks, a few days after London Stock Exchange Group Plc and Canada's TMX Group Inc. announced they would also merge. In the meantime, Brazil's BM&F Bovespa SA and Shanghai Stock Exchange are expected to form a joint venture. In 2013, BATS and Direct Edge merged to become tougher challengers to NASDAQ. This wave of mergers is part of the latest deal-making frenzy in a consolidating industry of international markets often thwarted by regulatory hurdles. There has been a drop in number of exchanges in the mature U.S. and Europe markets, while there has been a rise in emerging Asian markets. In North America, for example, there were over 60 exchanges in the 1930s, while there was only a half of that number in recent years. But there has not been a subsequent concentration in liquidity, and there has been a significant development of non-transparent alternative trading systems. The choice of venues for large scale IPOs illustrates vividly the competition between financial hubs, even if underwriting fees are not a vital constituent of their revenues. The impact of listing prominent world companies cannot be underestimated on the brand image of a hub. As strategic alliances and new technologies are remodeling the structure of the world most powerful stock exchanges, a condensed, and necessarily abridged, overview of the IFC development can perhaps help better understand what is at stake for the world of finance, and for us, users, moving forward in this new digital millennium.

CONTENTS

About the Author   v
Acknowledgement   vii
Foreword   xi
Introduction   xv

**Chapter 1 From the Annual Fairs of the 11th Century to Early
International Banking**   1

The Merry Fair of St Giles as An Early Model
   of a Multinational Trading Centre   2
The Champagne Fairs, the Leading Trading Hub
   in Europe   10
The Ascent of Lombard Merchant Bankers   26
The Banking Disintegration of the Mid-14th Century   37

Chapter 2 The Domination of the Mediterranean Region   47

Lombard Finance and the Turbulent Medici Era   47
The Rise and Apogee of Venice, the Lagoon City   57
Opportunites Beyond the Known World   68
Landing in another World   76

**Chapter 3 The Shift Towards the North of Europe
in the 16th century** **83**

The Ascent of the Flanders, with a Little Help
from Columbus 83
The Revenge of "La Superba", the Turbulent Italian
City-State 93
The Orange Revolution: The Opportunistic Rise
of Amsterdam 103
Secondary Places, including the Much Specific
Case of France 117

**Chapter 4 The Transatlantic New Financial Order
in the 18th Century** **133**

The Steady Emergence of London as Europe's
Finance Centrepoint 133
The Takeover of the First Place by New York 148
The Need of an Asian World Class Financial Centre,
after the Second World War 168
Medieval Japan: A Secluded Archipelago Split
in Internal Feuds 169
Vertical and Horizontal Challenge: New Geographies
and New Industries 180

Chapter 5 Pools, Bots and Trolls **201**

The Importance of Being Networked 201
The Derivative Revolution 213
Welcome to the Machine 221
Barbarians at the Gat.Exe 239

Chapter 6 Uninvited Guest to the Party **245**

Mirror, Mirror or the Tyranny of Index Rating 245
Gambling "Financial Centres": Place Your Bets … 254
OFCs Revisited 268
Trustworthiness from the Early Days of Finance
to the 21st Century 278

Conclusion **295**

Maps **303**

Graphs **309**

Acronyms **313**

Bibliography **315**

    Further Reading 321
    Other References 332

Index 335

Chapter 1

FROM THE ANNUAL FAIRS
OF THE 11th CENTURY
TO EARLY INTERNATIONAL
BANKING

The decline of the Roman Empire in the 5th century A.D. meant the gradual disappearance of most of its trade and the feudalisation of economic and social relationships. In the Roman dominated Europe, the Latin *"feria"* was synonymous with holy or free day, and is the origin of the word "fair." Each feria was a day when a large number of people would take time to gather, worship and trade. This explains that in the Middle Ages the Church was so active in sponsoring such events as it was not only an opportunity to worship and state its importance in society by ruling and customs, but also a significant source of income. Sunday grew to be a popular day for markets and fairs. Folks could attend church and then stroll in the market to trade, entertain themselves and socialise. The fair represented for the people a break from regular life and hence from regular purchase. Until Copernicus (1473–1543), most merchants took for granted that the Earth was flat, but their main problem with that theory was the fact that explorers had yet to reach the edge of the world and avoid being swallowed by the Great Abyss. Plato and Pythagoras had earlier mentioned the possibility of a spherical shape, but it was not until the Portuguese navigator Ferdinand Magellan circumnavigated the world in the 16th century, funded by the Spanish Crown, that the matter was really settled for good. This changed the world and it changed international trade.

The Merry Fair of St Giles as An Early Model of a Multinational Trading Centre

It seems reasonable to assume that International Financial Centres started an early primitive life in the 11th century at an annual "free fair" most likely in Winchester (Wessex, England) in a peaceful place only half a kilometer from the North Oxford city walls. Winchester began as a Roman town: Venta Belgarum was built about 70 A.D., and was made a civitas or regional capital, the fifth largest city in Roman Britain, but when the last Roman soldier left Britain in 407, Winchester seemed to have been abandoned and deserted, until the Saxons arrived in the 6th century to revive it, and renamed it Venta Caester, then Wintanceaster. The earliest official reference to the fair comes from The Session Rolls of James I where it is recorded that a gentleman named Thomas Cantyn was fined six shillings for swearing six insufferable oaths at the parish wake, but unlike the annual fairs of Nottingham and Hull, its ancestry cannot be traced back to a Charter fixing in the Medieval calendar. This southern English place was an important wool trade center at the time of William the Conqueror. It was really after the Norman conquests that fairs became of capital importance in England. As markets grew bigger, fairs attracted even more people from greater distances and more importantly foreign merchants. There were many opportunities to trade and equally large opportunities to have a merry time as "strange beasts and birds, apes, bears and ferrets were also brought for sale to St. Giles' Down". When the fair was nearing a close, the much awaited entertainment appeared: freak shows, parading giants, dwarves and faeries, menageries of unseen animals, magicians, musicians, farces and puppet shows, pigs solving amazing questions of fortune or arithmetic, astronomical clocks fascinated the audience. The rapid and ephemeral assembly of the fair created a unique and extraordinary economic momentum requiring the services of every carpenter of the county, and the participation of builders, agents, bailiffs, auctioneers, accountants, surveyors and cooks among many others. There was certainly a darker side to the fair as thieves, crooks, beggars and prostitutes also congregated. Hygiene was generally poor during this time and the incredible reports from autopsies performed by practitioners showed the prevalence of parasites, infections and wounds of all types with direct consequences on life expectancy of the population at large.

It was a characteristic of the fair that it was open for business to all comers and free from restrictions that applied to foreigners in most market towns regulated by guilds. The fair is likely to have started when Walkelin, the first Norman bishop of Winchester and chaplain of William the Conqueror, procured from William Rufus[1] the grant of a fair on the vigil, feast and morrow of St. Giles, to be held 'on the Eastern hill of Winchester', the summit of a Chalk Spur, which falls steeply to the east bank of the River Itchen. King Henry I extended the fair time for further five days in exchange for lands taken from the bishopric. Six additional days were granted and Henry Plantagenêt, early in his reign, doubled the number of days allowed by his grandfather. The Winchester fair was located in Walton Manor on the St. Giles' hill churchyard outside the city's eastern suburb. The fair, possibly the largest in Europe, was a much awaited and very popular event. It was held every year from 1096 in September for only 16 days. During this time, all other trading in Winchester ceased, and the Bishop received the revenues normally due to the King. Such fairs were distinguished from markets by merchants buying and selling with each other rather more than selling to ordinary customers. They were more specifically distinct by their legal privileges including their own laws, their own courts and their own armed protection for merchant travellers, as their vicinity also attracted outlaws and robbers, a prevalent problem plaguing trade. During the time of the fair, every function of civic government and the regulation of trade was transferred to the Episcopal officials. Grants of fair franchises by the King were highly regarded as a very valuable privilege; the Augustinian friar who had been the King's jester received his charter of the St. Bartholomew's

---

[1] William Rufus was the son of William the Conqueror, who died in 1100, shortly after Walkelin (1098).

fair in Smithfield, in 1133.[2] Records exist of 2,800 grants of franchise markets and fairs between 1199 and 1483.

Winchester city, well placed on the Itchen river navigable by small craft to the foot of St. Giles Down, home of the eponymous fair, had a convenient opening to the continent through Southampton. It was not too near the coast, and was astride an important route from the Midlands to the sea. The special advantages of the location turned out to generate a cusp in the market potential function that determined the optimal fair location choice. It was not so much considered a grave problem that Southampton could be occasionally a cause of annoyance as the municipal authorities of the port had it in their power, if they desired, to hamper the fair of St. Giles by offering counter attractions to traders. By 1200, Winchester had a Mayor to handle the delicate relationships with the seaport. They were complicated and a matter of subtle diplomacy between the Bishop of Winchester and the city of Southampton. The streets and other open spaces of Winchester accommodated a complex and continuously changing system of markets. Merchants from all over England, and from overseas including Ireland, the Low Countries, Gascony,[3] Spain and Provence, came to the annual fair of St. Giles. They were greeted and recognised upon their arrival and their signature reflected their financial credit. Recognition would indeed lead to trustworthiness, a cornerstone in the development of financial hubs. The most important of the English traders came from London and their absence from the fair was regarded as a grave misfortune. The presence of foreigners attending the fair was awaited but as business was still very fragmented and individual, no corporate name had emerged yet from these commercial gatherings. In the 13th century, under the later Angevins, the St. Giles fair was established as one of the four great fairs of England also including Boston, St. Ives, established in 1110 by Henry I, and Northampton, which is indeed one of the most important fairs in Europe during the reign of Henry II. These fairs had so much economic significance that special courts were established within the fairs to hear merchant disputes which emphasised the

---

[2] The fair was terminated in 1855 after degenerating into debauchery and public disorder.
[3] The Duchy of Gascony extended across the South West of France. The English Royal family held possession of the territory from 1154 to 1450 after the marriage of "Aliénor of Aquitaine" to Henry Plantagenêt of England.

need of a prompt, fair and effective justice in resolving merchant issues. At the opening of the fair, a proclamation was read by the steward of the Lord of the manor, who was also the Lord of the fair and market, and was acting, as the proclamation's read, "on his Majesty behalf". The proclamation intended to define the rules of the fair and contained the expected code of conduct for all the participants, including the penalties applied to those who do not comply with the code. It prohibited quarrels and fights and asked the participants to trade in an open and fair way so that "none buy or sell in corners, back sides or hidden places upon pain of forfeiture of all such goods and merchandise bought and sold and their bodies to imprisonment".[4]

Since the early 17th century, the prevailing view has been that fair courts enforced a body of law based on autonomous merchant principles, the *Lex Mercatoria*. Supposedly, this law differed from the municipal laws of existing jurisdictions in that it was created autonomously by merchants and expressed their customs, reflecting unwritten usages rather than the written command of a sovereign legislator. The *lex mercatoria* established convenient procedures to govern commerce across political borders. The law merchant thus was supposedly representative of a new legal order, free from the control of local laws and local Lords. The actions of the St. Ives court, a small village in Huntingdonshire, are uniquely well documented,[5] and show that the "law merchant" was not involving merchants under a single and autonomous body of principles, but was embodied in the emerging common law. Interestingly, this matter would be debated again 730 years later for the regulation of algorithmic agents operating on the financial markets. At the St. Ives fair, one of the English centres for cloth trade, the court decisions were largely under the authority of the King and his Lord, the Abbot of Ramsey. The merchants did participate in the establishment of legal principles, the resolution of disputes and

---

[4] Another example of this proclamation since Henry Stanley, Lord Strange, 4th Earl of Derby, first proclaimed the Charter in 1593, can be found at the historic market town of Broughton-in-Furness (Cumbria, United Kingdom) http://www.cumbria.gov.uk/news/Archive/2006/july/31_07_2006-102439.asp.

[5] Fourteen of the fair court's annual plea rolls dated between 1270 and 1324, recording the administrative business of the court as well as the cases argued before it are preserved in the Public Record Office and the British Museum.

the enforcement of the fair court's judgments. But this challenges the view that the merchants of the Middle Ages were using as an exception a parallel private legal system. Commercial customs and substantive laws varied significantly across towns and fairs, and did not constitute a coherent legal order. However, the incentive for a prompt and fair enforcement of the court decisions was also rooted as a significant source of income for the Ramsey Abbey. This emphasizes the need for a swift and fair commercial justice based on the sovereign authority, which took notice of mercantile customs, and did not place contradictory demands on merchants trading across jurisdictional lines.

As a result, Winchester's early economic importance secured many privileges for the citizens from the Crown. By the 14th century, Winchester was near to being autonomous, appointing its own officers, collecting its own dues and holding its own courts. However, this was only to hide a profound decline accentuated by the pestilence of 1362, and a civil war between the King and his barons led by Simon De Monfort. The city was pillaged in 1365 and many Jews were killed. The city successively lost its status as a national administrative centre, as a royal residence, and as an international, and even as a regional market especially as London grew bigger and became the new capital of England. A sure sign of this decline was the transfer of the Royal mint from Winchester to London in the mid-13th. It is probable that the fair of St. Giles had reached its high-watermark of prosperity under the Angevin Empire ruled by the house of Plantagenêt. The Plantagenêt Empire was the improbable result of the incredible efforts of Foulque Nerra, the "Black" Count of Anjou the audacious calculation of William the Conqueror, the wisdom of William X of Aquitaine and the human experience of Edward the Confessor, the last Saxon king to rule in England. One can try to imagine what Europe would be today if the fortune of the Plantagenêt family had lasted.[6] The civil troubles of the Barons' Wars caused in the 13th century by the Baron's opposition to King Henry III's costly policies, disturbed trade. Later, the outbreak of the Gascon war was a critical period in the history of the fair: gross receipts soon diminished by one-third, earmarking the permanent decline of the fair. This was

---

[6]Favier, Jean, The Plantagenêts: Origin and Destiny of an Empire, XI–XIVe, Fayard, 6 October (2004).

further aggravated by the years of Great Pestilence (1349, 1362), as the total gross receipts of the fair continued to fall. A sure sign of the fair's degeneration was that numerous properties around were derelict after foreign merchants ceased to visit it.

In Germany, the first Frankfurt trade fair documented in the writings of Elieser ben Nathan of Mainz, one of the foremost rabbis of his time, goes back to the Assumption holiday in the year 1150, and the first highly official Frankfurt Autumn Trade Fair was approved in a letter by the Emperor Frederick II. "We, Friedrich, Roman emperor chosen by God, King of Jerusalem and Sicily, hereby make known to the world by way of this writ that we, in unity and each as individuals, will provide special protection for each and every person travelling to the fairs of Frankfurt. We demand that no person shall be hindered or harassed in any form during his or her travels to and from the fairs. If anyone should dare to counteract this demand, let be known that this person shall reap the wrath of Our Majesty. Our Majesty's seal shall serve as assurance for the commands of this document" 11 July, 1240. At a time when the roads were not safe, the imperial letter would make clear that travellers and merchants to the fair would be under Frederick's sovereign protection and there would be military retaliations if some parties tried to harass or rob the participants. The concern to create a safe and trusted environment at the highest level of the state was certainly one of the early critical conditions to foster a "safe harbour" for business. German and foreign merchants visited the place and exchanged currencies and goods produced in all parts of Europe and the Mediterranean region. Among the variety of items traded early in Frankfurt in all directions, textiles, weapons and spices always played a crucial role. The Frankfurt fair is thought to have been first created as a harvest market to sell the local agricultural surplus. An autumn fair is mentioned from 1227 and later a spring fair from 1330, to take advantage of the declining Champagne fairs in France. The free Imperial City of Frankfurt, under the Hohenstaufen emperors, was declared the first trade fair city in the world, endorsed through an Imperial Privilege as it attracted business from the Baltic to the Mediterranean. The Römerberg, the "roman mountain", was the place where the trade fairs were taking place and occasionally the site of all kind of festivities, including celebrating the coronation of the Holy Roman Emperors. It indeed experienced a strong growth and became increasingly of national importance. Later, the Frankfurt fairs of the 14th century did not only offer consumer goods but also a growing number of religious manuscripts composed by monks. When Gutenberg invented movable character printing in 1445, the book trade started and with it, the first book fair took place in 1480 which is still making the international reputation of Frankfurt today.

Other successful fairs developed in the ancient seaport city of Lübeck and in Leipzig in the 12th century where fairs have been taking place near the river Pleisse. Lübeck city was originally founded on a strategic and relatively safe island at the meeting place of the rivers Trave and Schwartau by Count Adolf II of Schauenburg and Holstein in 1143. A large fire on the Lübeck peninsula almost changed the course of its development, but the city was revitalised by Henry the Lion, Duke of Saxony in 1159, and quickly developed into a significant trading centre for the Baltic Sea region. Merchants flocked from Saxony, Rhineland and Westphalia. In 1161, the Duke opportunistically negotiated a partnership with the Scandinavians of Gotland Islands, further opening the reach of the city down the Neva river to Novgorod. Wine, salt and furs were shipped from here, amongst other goods. Being recognised as a free Imperial City in 1226 helped Lübeck achieve substantial political power and independence. The only obstacle to its prosperity were the Danes, who under King Waldemar II occupied the city from 1201 to 1227. With their departure after the Battle of Bornhoved in 1227, any final obstacles were removed. German cities achieved domination of trade in the Baltic with striking speed over the 13th century. This is the time when Lübeck developed its trade with the Hanseatic League[7] and became a reputed commercial center on the Baltic coast of northern Germany, as it was centrally and conveniently placed with respect to all the other Hanseatic towns and cities. The city smartly managed to secure direct

---

[7] In the middle of the 12th century, North German seafaring merchants joined together to form the Hanseatic League ("Hansa" in German), a broad commercial community designed as a "super Guild" to pursue their shared economic interest. Throughout the North Sea and Baltic Sea region, up to 200 cities were members of the League, as were several leading trading houses. For over 400 years, the Hanseatic League played a major role in shaping economies, trade and politics before losing its significance in the mid-17th century.

access to the Baltic Sea through a series of acquisitions of properties up to the mouth of the river Trave. Due to its privileges and its status as the "leading city of the Hanseatic League," Lübeck at once assumed a dominant position in the federation of cities and exerted its influence on the Baltic, just as Venice and Genoa exerted their control over the Mediterranean. At its peak, the Hanseatic League encompassed over 60 cities from Tallinn to Bruges, able to form contracts and liable as joint debtors for the offences of individual members. The major difference with Italian cities is that Lübeck imposed on itself a stringent self-discipline to remain peaceful with neighbouring cities. In 1375, the Holy Roman Emperor Charles IV granted Lübeck the prized title of 'Glory of the Empire': only four other cities, Florence, Pisa — connected to Florence by the Arno river, Rome and Venice, shared it. However, the lights of the city would never reach the magnificence of its Italian peers. In the 15th century, the Hanseatic cities would mutually strengthen each other; a ship from Lübeck to Danzig would not only carry its own cargo but was also commissioned to transport freight for other members of the league and save precious resources. The use of the *Sendeve* commission not only saved time and money but also constituted a first step toward partnership. This capacity to join forces in reciprocal services became a distinctive feature, and a long lasting success factor of the Hanseatic team spirit. Hanseatic registered partnerships were obliged to split up to half of the proceeds with the merchant in charge of the ship due to much more difficult navigation conditions in the Baltic than in the Mediterranean. With the Hanseatic League's decline in importance in the 16th century, Lübeck's predominant role in northern Europe came to an end after 300 years. The strong competition of other cities in particular those of the Nurnberg merchants which, despite stringent and prevalent protectionist regulations, developed an effective international land-based network competing with Hanseatic cities, in Geneva, Lyon, Warsaw, Sevilla and even Brescia, diluted the Hanseatic networks and the power of its leading Baltic cities.

A more careful analysis of the emergence of leading medieval fairs highlights the fact that a strategic geographic positioning, quality of the legal framework, convenient facilities offered to participants and benevolence from incumbent princes, abbots or bishops provided a significant competitive advantage in the development of the fairs beyond the borders of their original counties, at a time when roads or canals were not very safe and were slow for travellers, especially merchants. Competition from Nurnberg, Bavaria, a free imperial city by the end of the 13th century, with Hansa cities in particular provided both an accelerator for efficiency and "creative destruction" as the fate of Lübeck has shown. Nuremberg soon was, with Augsburg another free city member of the Swabian league, one of the two great trade centres on the route from Italy to Northern Europe.

The Champagne Fairs, the Leading Trading Hub in Europe

The Champagne fairs seem to have been held since the year 427, according to the writings of Sidoine Appolinaire, Bishop of Troyes. For sure, they are much older than the establishment of the French monarchy. The Gallo-Roman city Augustobona (Troyes) was strategically located on the famous Roman Agrippa way, which connected Boulogne a French city situated on the English Channel to Milan in Italy. Since the 10th century and until 1285, the Counts of Champagne, managed to rule their county as sovereign princes in a state of quasi-independence to the French King. In the 11th century, under the protection of Thibaud I, a dynamic Jewish business community settled in Champaign. The situation of the Jewish community had always been fragile in the Middle Ages: they were needed due to usury laws but were socially unwelcome. Attracted by the success of the Champaign fairs, the region became the most important Jewish community in France and made a decisive contribution to the development of trade and finance. The fairs held in French Champagne and Brie developed gradually on a European scale as early as the 12th century and became an important economic center for cloth and clothing, ironwork, woodwork, wool, agricultural implements and food, changing the structure of Europe's traditional farming economy. They became the main mart for international trade, and the hub of local and international commerce. Merchants had been accustomed to making profits of 3–4% annually in hard cash and goods trading here. There was a circular self-reinforcing process in which the decision of merchants to come to this place with good access to customers, colleagues and suppliers actually improved the market or supply access of other producers in that location, thus generating significant economies of scale even in the context of imperfect competition. These fairs offered a smooth transition from the semi-annual fairs to widescale or wholesale trading. One of the drivers of this evolution was the development of transportation and logistic services associated with safe delivery, storage and conservation of large quantities of goods in warehouses and depots, such as the Hanseatic depot. These permanent facilities as intermediate points of transit contributed to the decline of semi-annual fairs as such events were no longer a required path to trade. This change was undoubtedly facilitated by increased and improved transportation that enabled the movement of large quantities of goods across land or by sea.

The nearby Clairvaux Abbey, a Cistercian monastery founded in "Val d'Absinthe" later renamed "Clair Vau", was once an unsafe and improper place for farming situated between Champagne and Burgundy. Under the leadership of St. Bernard in 1115, the Abbey was founded with a few monks from the Citeaux Abbey and it became the political and religious center of Christian Europe. The Abbey's comforting presence and prestigious influence created a favorable environment for the development of business in this area. The Count of Champagne, Thibaud II, the Great, a close friend of St. Bernard, protected the Abbey and enlarged its domain. Thibaud even contemplated spending the last years of his life in the Abbey as a Cistercian monk. At the death of its founder in 1153, the Abbey had also gained a considerable economic influence beyond Champagne with a farming domain of 355 hectares and 1,853 hectares of woods.

With Clairvaux nearby, the Champagne fairs were a key economic hub opened to professional merchants. They were organised in a series of six round the year fairs, each lasting over six weeks. They were precisely located in Champagne cities throughout the year's calendar: in 2nd January (in Lagny-sur-Marne), the Tuesday before Mid-Lent, i.e., between 26th February and 1st April (in Aube-sur-Bar), in May, the Tuesday before Christ's Ascension (in Provins), in 24th June, the "fair of St. John" (in Troyes), on 14th September, the fair of St. Ayoul (in Provins), on 2nd November the "fair of St. Remi" (in Troyes). Each fair was followed by a break for merchants before moving on to the next fair.

A round of six fairs organised as a clever network of tightly connected Champagne cities gradually became an economic hub connecting the Northern (Low Countries and Germany) and the Southern European (Italy and Spain) economies. This cycle of permanent fairs represented a significant competitive advantage over other medieval fairs. Each of these fairs was an ephemeral city of stalls and barracks built in the vicinity of a permanent one. It is no coincidence that these cities had a good hinterland in the form of waterways (the river Seine and the Marne), and were connected to the large ancient Roman routes, the Via Agrippa from Milan to Boulogne and other main Carolingian roads. The Count of Champagne and Blois, Thibaud the Great, also a renowned poet, was capable of attracting, as early as 1137, a large crowd of merchants from Europe after establishing a "Conduit des Foires", the most feared passport protecting merchants travelling to Troyes against those who would dare attack them. Count Thibault II also provided the necessary infrastructure for the fairs including storage, hospitality, such as the Hôtel-Dieu in Provins (Ile-de-France), covered markets ("granges aux Dimes") and reliable weighing and measuring instruments for the merchants to run safe and trusted businesses. The development of such institutions had a decisive positive influence. As early as 1148, when moneychangers from Vézelay were robbed on their way to the Provins fair by a French nobleman, Count Thibault II wrote to the regent of France demanding that the moneychangers be compensated and declared, "I will not let take place with impunity such an injury, which tends to nothing less than the ruin of my fairs". The King of France, Philippe Auguste, later endorsed this example by providing additional protection to those travelling to the fair of Troyes.

Although the main reason for medieval fairs was trade and commerce, again every fair was an opportunity of merry making. Singers, musicians, fire-eaters, sword swallowers, ropewalkers and fools were among the people who made a living travelling from one fair to another performing their arts. Fairs would often coincide with major medieval sports events such as the much prized archery tournaments. They were also the occasion of medieval popular games and competitions such as wrestling, strength contests, and jousting events. Rare and impressive animals from remote countries were displayed and performed tricks; the most popular being dancing bears, smart pigs and clever monkeys. This highlights that serious trading had been since the early ages closely intertwined not only with religion but also with popular entertainment. While the lower and middle classes were able to enjoy loudly the annual fairs and engage themselves in haggling and bargaining, for members of the upper classes, such behaviour was considered inappropriate. Noblemen would rather use an agent or a proxy to engage in trade during the fairs.

Each fair in Champagne was precisely organised and would last three to six weeks. It was once established that in Provins more than 3,000 craftsmen gathered by streets or district. Typically, the first eight days would be dedicated to registering the merchants, organising the trade stalls and storage. The next 10 days will be about the trading of cloth and fabric, the next 10 days about the trading of furs and leather, the next 10 days about various bulk goods including spices or precious stones, the remaining 14 days will be dedicated to the settlement of all trades before the fair officially closes. The taxes levied on the trade were stable and light, especially on the trading of animals. The local currency, the "Denier Provinois", also had a good reputation and was welcomed all over Europe, which certainly provided a distinct competitive advantage. The foreign merchants especially enjoyed this pragmatic and transparent policy designed by the Counts of Champagne to facilitate trading and make their presence at the fairs an enjoyable and lucrative experience. Trade was carefully regulated and enforced by the powerful merchant guilds. Originally, a body of rules and principles were laid down by merchants in Europe to regulate their dealings, and it consisted of usages and customs common to merchants and traders in Europe with slightly local differences. It was enforced through a system of merchant courts along the main trade routes as the international law of commerce. It emphasised contractual freedom, alienability of property, while shunning legal technicalities and deciding cases according to what is equitable and good (*"ex aequo et bono"*). Fair courts originated from the problem that civil law was not responsive enough to the growing demands of commerce: there was a need for quick and effective jurisdiction, administered by specialised courts. The guiding spirit of the merchant law was that it ought to evolve from commercial practice, respond to the needs of the merchants, and be comprehensible and acceptable to the merchants who submitted to it.[8]

---

[8] United Nations, UNTERM http://unterm.un.org/dgaacs/unterm.nsf/0f99a7d734f48ac385 256a07005e48fb/c9fb3dc687d144ef8525757000716fcf?OpenDocument.

By the 1170s, the Counts of Champagne had supplemented ordinary public legal provision at the fairs by appointing special security officials called fair wardens ("gardes des foires"). The "Defense of the fair" allowed merchants to recover their due, and faulting debtors were not allowed to come back to the fair. There were special fair courts where dishonest traders were tried. At markets, punishments for the guilty included a day in the stocks or pillory, being pelted by passers-by with rotten vegetables and fruits. A butcher convicted for cheating customers might be grossly pulled through the market on a sledge with a piece of stinking meat around his neck. The fair was also fiercely protected from unregistered outsiders, and foreign merchants would typically need to wait for hours before registering and being authorized to enter the fair to trade.

Safety and justice were of paramount importance and were presumably key success factors in the ascendency of the fairs. The counts of Champagne ensured, sometimes in person, that merchants were secure, enforcing private property rights, the rights of humans to use specified goods and to exchange them, through their own law courts, employing wardens to police the streets, and cooperating with municipal and ecclesiastical officials to guarantee security in the fair towns. Special "fair wardens" were appointed as early as the 1170s, with policing, regulatory and jurisdictional powers at the fairs, and later to exert pressure on foreign jurisdictions to enforce the safe conduct of the fairs. In addition to rendering justice, the counts would also guarantee on their ruling authority the loans that the merchants made at the fairs to clients from whom obtaining payment might be difficult due to their high status or privileged position. A fundamental reason for preference and success of a system of strong private property rights is that private property rights protect individual liberty. The rulers of Champagne made sure that trade contracts would be enforced and operated through an effective four-tiered system of public law courts which judged lawsuits and officially witnessed contracts with a view to subsequent enforcement. Public alternatives to the princely court system did exist, the four fair towns of Champagne had privileges for operating municipal mayoral courts, and the Church provided another set of public law courts offering contract enforcement at the fairs. Some monasteries, such as the Abbey of St. Pierre or the Priory of St. Ayoul were granted the capacity to render justice during the fairs. The later had jurisdiction over Provins and its surroundings for the first seven days of the annual autumn fair. Ecclesiastical tribunals also offered contract enforcement to foreign merchants visiting the Champagne fairs in a wider European forum.

The availability of such a rich set of legal instruments created a favourable environment for international trade. The strongest evidence for the competing courts system's effectiveness is that foreign merchants liked to use various courts, and especially the municipal ones. This was another way to create this unique and trusted business environment in the Champagne fairs, since jurisdiction competition created incentives for courts to provide impartial judgments. The Jours de Troyes was the highest princely court in Champagne, and was a tribunal which judged important cases as a court of first instance. It also heard appeals from lower tier courts. The second tier consisted of the courts of the four bailiffs which judged cases involving high-status parties including foreign merchants. The third tier consisted of the courts of the provosts, who rendered justice to commoners. Finally, the lowest tier of the princely justice system consisted of village courts operated by appointed mayors.

The visionary management of the rulers of Champagne, supported by Philippe Auguste, King of France, provides a vivid example of the role of the political authorities in delivering the needed institutional framework for this trading centre to flourish. The Counts were capable of showing their commitment to investing and contributing to the development of a local high quality infrastructure, including canals, storage, fortifications and hospitality for the merchants. Above all, inspiring a stable and cheerful atmosphere of business confidence was essential as they guaranteed security, property rights and contract enforcement, regulated weights and measures, supported foreign merchant lenders against politically powerful debtors, and provided a level playing field between all merchants.

The Champagne fairs then became more established as larger and continuous trading events in the 13th century, and the French Champagne fairs became a major trading hub in Continental Europe. There were hundreds of smaller scale fairs in Europe but until the 13th century, no other regional hub in Europe was capable of matching this cleverly designed environment and of shining as a well-recognised place for trade. The success of the fair was often attributed to the Counts ability of applying public order to business.[9] For sure, the counts of Champagne had a vested interest in creating a favourable environment for business to flourish. They provided the fairs with a police force, the "Guards of the Fair", who heard complaints and enforced contracts, excluding defaulters from future participation; weights and measures were strictly regulated. Trade in itself was not a sufficient condition for success, as respect for the merchant commitments was carefully monitored to enforce a safe trading environment. The Italian merchants from Asti were the first ones to cross the Alps in the 13th Century, and very soon followed by the Tuscan (from Siena, Florence and Lucca) and Genoese merchant bankers attending the Champagne trading fairs. However, the earliest evidence of a massive presence of Italian traders in fairs of international significance relates to trade events held in the French region of Languedoc.

The last Count of Provins, Robert III, the Fat, started to levy heavier taxes on the participants in the fair. This led to civil unrest and riots culminating in 1279 with the murder of the Mayor of Provins, Guillaume de Pendecoste, who had ruled that the working day should be increased by 1h without compensation. The decline of the Champagne fairs may be related also to the unpopular monetary reform of Louis IX in 1265, but most probably started with the death in 1274 of the latest Count of Champagne, Henry III, who left Jeanne de Navarre as his sole heir. The marriage of Philippe the Fair, King of France with Jeanne de Navarre in 1284, sealed the subordination of Champagne to the French Royal Domain in 1285 including the disappearance of the trusted Champaign currency, "Denier Provinois". Economic incentives were threatened by the takeover, and a decisive piece of the leadership of the fair venture was taken apart. The new French King, Philip IV, the Fair, had decided to centralise the French monarchy and levied more tax to finance its dynastic wars. To appropriate the wealth built around the fairs, he needed a firmer grip on Champagne itself, this would help in expanding its military and fiscal capacities. To fulfil this objective, King Philip did not hesitate to start a war with Flanders,[10] despoiling Flemish merchants, extorting heavy

---

[9] Favier J, *Gold & Spices: The Rise of Commerce in the Middle Ages*, 1st Ed. US: Holmes & Meier Publishers Inc. (1998).

[10] France invaded Flanders in 1297.

tax payments, incarcerating Lombard merchants, and barring exports of raw wool and undyed cloth from France. This sounds like a reminiscence of the past royal misconduct in the years 1080, when French King Philippe I did not hesitate to rob the foreign merchants who came to attend fairs between Paris and Orleans. The price to pay for this drastic change of policy — centralization — not to say nationalism, and for upsetting foreign merchants, was certainly a rapid and permanent decline of trade at the Champagne fairs within 15 years of their coming under French central governance. Some corrective actions were taken by the French crown after important foreign merchants deserted the fairs, but the reputation of the place was already spoilt. King Philip also realised that the Templars, whose order was founded in 1119 in Jerusalem to protect pilgrims possessed financial resources of such magnitude that he decided to dissolve it. As a military and religious order Templars were financially active internationally, with more than 9,000 centres and two headquarters, they were known as safe custodians for deposits, made loans on their own resources, carried out transfer of funds and had great moral authority, earning them the trust of the people. King Philip, in fear and envy of their wealth, condemned those in charge to be burned at the stake with the prime objective of appropriating all of the order's riches. This political coup on two pillars of the French economy created a shockwave which probably left a deep suspicion of the predatory intentions of the French crown. In the meantime, another reason for the acceleration of the decline of the fair was the recognition that the financial instruments for credit and currency exchange ironically developed at the fairs themselves finally made them less necessary to conclude trade. Finance had just started to become more autonomous, thus dematerialising trade across Europe.

It also became obvious that as Blanche d'Artois, widow of Henry III, Count of Champagne, remarried Edmond of Lancaster, son of Henry III of England, this marriage would start a long era of English presence and unrest in Champagne. The Hundred Years' War began in 1337,[11] it was

---

[11] The Hundred Years War was a series of wars from 1337 and 1453, on both land and sea, arising primarily from the political and dynastic conflicts of the Kings of England and France. It was fought mainly in France but also engulfed Brittany, Scotland, the Iberian Kingdoms, the Netherlands and other countries.

going to last longer than 100 years. Around the same time in Italy, a series of wars disrupted the trade routes that connected Italian cities with France. Land or canal transportation which was already slow and risky became even more expensive, due to the multiplicity of tolls, and also quite unsafe. For 1,000 years, from around 800 to 1815, tolls were collected on the Rhine River in Europe. Each of the 64 tolls conducive of royalty stacking[12] on the cargo ships sailing the Rhine river in the 14th century, were set to maximise revenues oblivious of the consequences not only on river traffic but also on their own revenues until they got finally removed.[13] The inflation of tax and transportation cost choked the natural north–south routes for trade. As a result of geopolitical unrest, and as the sea ships were becoming more reliable and the acts of piracy better controlled, the Genoese and Venetian merchants felt it was now time to innovate in opening up direct sea routes connecting Italy with Flanders, bypassing Champagne and therefore diminishing the importance of the fairs. Long distance sea fares soon represented a cost of no more than 10% of the total shipment compared to an unpredictable 30–60% by land. The German merchants did their best to promote to their Italian counterparts another attractive Eastern route through the Simplon and the St. Gothard pass in the Swiss Alps; the traditional traffic through the routes of the Grand St. Bernard pass and Cenis pass both collapsed. All the equilibrium of the European North South traffic had shifted East through Switzerland or through sea routes. The last important group of Italian merchants left the Provins fairs in 1350, after which the Champagne fairs retained only regional significance. The Champagne fairs thus have a central role in the understanding of the institutional foundations of market-based economic activity. All these changes accelerated the obsolescence of the old trading model especially as some other cities willingly became new trading hubs. Lombards, and especially Florentine merchant bankers, so-called as their activities were a mixture of trade, finance and production, made their first appearance in the last centuries of the Middle Ages. They led the development of medieval finance as they attended the fairs. Aside from the largest

---

[12] Formalized by Augustin Cournot (1801–1877) and Carl Shapiro (1955).
[13] Quoted by Jean Tirole in his Nobel Prize Lecture delivered on 8 December 2014 at Aula Magna, Stockholm University.

international hubs, Paris, as a financial place gained a significant role in dealing with roughly half of the financial settlements.

The growing economic activity at the end of the Middle Ages, led to an increasing need for money exchange, supply of good money and the conversion of coins. The monetary supply was not only needed for the large amount of trade carried out by the small circle of powerful merchants who were at the foundation of the commercial revolution, but also by the immense population of small rural merchants negotiating here a basket of fruit, there a rabbit skin or a tired piece of cloth to survive in the hope of establishing themselves in a small shop. Because of the different currencies used throughout Europe, all the wholesale merchants carried a small set of coin balances for weighing coins to determine their value. This was a complicated business. A decent training in algebra and geography were needed to avoid being fooled: one had to learn the basics with a notary or a vicar before finding an apprenticeship. Money changers were soon holding and transferring large sums of money all over Europe and extending loans to merchants. All merchants were involved in finance — as givers of credit, as receivers of credit, or usually as both. As the demand increased, so did the number and sophistication of services. The nature of merchant banking makes it difficult to list precisely who was a genuine banker making profits mainly from cambium and who was primarily a trader "buying low and selling high".[14]

Common financial activities came to include granting loans, investing, as well as most of the deposit, credit and transfer functions of a modern bank. The question of defining interest, a word derived from the Latin *"intersum-esse"* to designate the licit difference between the principal and repayment of a loan, remained a major obstacle to the growth of finance. Economy was still very much an emerging science: medieval universities had only four faculties: theology, law, medicine and philosophy,[15] which gives an indication of the limited bandwidth through which the world was perceived at the time. The ban on usury by the three major monotheistic religions, Christianity, Islam and Judaism, although Jews

---

[14] A famous comment made by Bardi's agent Pegolotti.

[15] Immanuel Wallerstein, *World Systems Analysis: An Introduction*, page 3, Duke University Press, 27 August (2004).

were not forbidden to loan money at interest to Gentiles, an ethnonym that commonly means non-Jew, did much to complicate and obscure medieval financial practices. The Catholic Church's ban on the charging of "oppressive and excessive interest" on loans, i.e., the exaction of interest or of any specified return beyond the principal value of a loan, was inspired by several writings of the time. Pierre Lombard, a leading theologian, explained in 1150 in his "Livre des Sentences" ("The book of final sentences"), which was a basis of the scholastic education, that usury is a proxy to stealing money. The Papal legate, Robert of Courçon, an English cardinal, would call for a council on this *turpe lucrum*,[16] with the intention to eradicate it from the Christian world. The interpretation of the Deuteronomy verses 23:19–20[17] remained a problem for centuries, although Exodus 22:25 sheds a very different light on conditions of lending money based on social responsibility and compassion "If you lend money to one of my people among you who is needy, do not treat it like a business deal; charge no interest". The ban on interest, which was justified by a theological argumentation based on fraternity and natural moral law, found solid support in secular power up to the time of Charlemagne and remained absolute until the 12th century. However, "friendly" loans, which had nothing to do with friendship, proliferated especially for small amounts. The Church directive on usury cannot be understood in terms of the significance of how great fortunes were outrageously build in the 13th and 14th centuries at a time where the utmost poverty was still plaguing Europe. In the 18th century, when Adam Smith was writing about the introduction to the Wealth of the Nations, he vividly recollected of something that he saw among people living in the poor highlands of Scotland, who were so desperately poor that mothers found themselves in the horrifying position of trying to decide which of their children will get to eat because there was not enough for all of them for a day. This was probably at the root of the moral concern of Adam Smith, perhaps this point has not been highlighted enough in what we owe him in the understanding of

---

[16] Enrichment without work.

[17] "You may charge a foreigner interest, but you may not charge your brother interest, that the Lord your God may bless you in all that you undertake in the land that you are entering to take possession of it."

social interactions. Some of the most elaborate thinking about the foundation of modern capitalism, and in particular the nature of contracts, free markets, interest, wages, and banking that developed after the Reformation was actually articulated centuries before Adam Smith, by the school of Salamanca and in the writings of Spanish Catholic scholastic thinkers of the 16th and 17th centuries.[18] The theoretical framework of our modern economy came from a long maturation process which was crystallised both by the Italian medieval commercial revolution and by the Victorian industrial revolution. It would not make sense to say that one was more important than the other.

As this usury restriction was not applicable to Jews, most bankers and financiers in the Christian world were Jewish. However, the medieval rabbinical attitude toward lending money on interest to Gentiles was very conservative, restricting it to scholars or to cases where it was absolutely necessary for livelihood. Ultimately, the widespread demand for credit and the profitability of such business made it universal among Jews. Mordecai B. Hillel of Germany (b. 1298) wrote that "there is no profit in any form of commerce like that to be made in lending money". It was reported that in 1196 the Abbey of St. Benigne in Dijon (Burgundy, France), borrowed 1,700 pounds from a Jew at the rate of 65%. For 11 years, the Abbey could not pay anything on the loan so that the debt had grown to an exorbitant 9,825 pounds. In Marseilles, the Abbey of St. Victor in 1185 owed 80,000 sous to Jew usurers and granted them some property, which would have included churches in payment. To avoid the "scandal" of Jews owning churches, the bishop of Antibes assumed the debt himself.[19] This unhealthy situation based on the lack of supplier competition, the prevalence of short term credit and the belief that money was just a neutral medium, would certainly lay natural grounds for a strong resistance against interest payment. Just as Jews lent money to Gentiles, they also frequently borrowed money from them, also on interest.

---

[18] Theologians such as Francisco de Vitoria OP, Martín de Azpilcueta, Juan de Mariana SJ, and Tomás de Mercado OP, anticipated many of the claims made by Smith two centuries later.

[19] Quoted by Norman Roth, Professor of Jewish History at the University of Wisconsin, Madison in Jewish Money lending http://www.myjewishlearning.com/history/Ancient_and_Medieval_History/632-1650/Christendom/Commerce/Moneylending.shtml?p=3.

A close examination of medieval trades shows that numerous significant credit-based trades were not bearing interest. Hence, pragmatism and
common sense called for a fair compensation for the risk of lending
money *periculum sortis*, and a compensation for the opportunity cost of
lending money without using it for other fruitful purposes *lucrum cessans*.
Therefore, other forms of reward were created, in particular through the
widespread form of partnership called *"commenda"*, possibly inspired by
Islamic merchants, but the most effective way to circumvent Church law
was international money exchange. As a result, the Florentine merchant
bankers were almost sure to make a nominal 8 to 30% return on their
loans, but this would be before taking into account solvency risks. The
"commenda" practice grew out from the cases when a wealthy merchant
carried on his sea trade not by himself but through his trusted representatives who were called *"tractators"*. As these travelling *"tractators"* performed the whole business, the merchant being only the capital-owner, it
became necessary to make the *"tractator"* economically interested or no
market incentive would be provided for rendering the service; accordingly he used to get his reward as part of the profits of the trade made on
behalf of the merchant. Finding the right *"tractator"* to do the business
as a business partner was of the essence. As a *"tractator"* became successful in trade, he had his own capital put into the business, and becoming the chief partner of the enterprise negotiated not with one partner
capitalist but with several, who contributed capital to this business getting for that a part of the profits. Thus this form of equity partnership
grew up, where only one of the partners was the active merchant, while
the other or several others only contributed the capital and received for
the "loan" a part of the profit. This sort of finance is very close to the
contribution of limited partners to a private equity fund today. This form
of capital investment was found already in the late part of the 10th century, but became a very common credit bargain in the 11th and 12th
centuries. It was considered so legitimate that in year 1206 Pope
Innocent III issued a decree in which the Ecclesiastical Courts keeping
the dowries of orphans according to wills, were advised to invest this
money with some reliable merchant to get the usual "reward". The
"commenda" continued to be investigated by moralist and churchmen in
the following centuries on the grounds of being possibly rampant usury

but it remained permissible. Some limitations to the freedom of the "*commenda*" contract were introduced late in the 15th century so as to secure a just relation of creditor and debtor: first, the creditor had no right to require his capital back; second, the debtor had the right of redemption if he wanted it; third, the charges should not be above the average rate; fourth, the charges should be attached to a property which by its nature is a source of permanent income. It must be remembered that this doctrine was formulated when money was just a metallic medium for exchange and factors of production were land and labour. In 1202, Leonordo of Pisa, commonly called Fibonacci, wrote an influential treaty on financial engineering, Liber Abaci (*The Book of Calculations*). His work not only introduced Hindu–Arabic numbers to Europe but also calculated the present value of alternative cash flows in addition to developing a general method for expressing investment returns, and solving a wide range of complex interest rate problems. Further progress in mathematical finance was complicated as St. Thomas Aquina born in 1225 addressed the sin of usury in the Summa Theologica (II-II.78), arguing against the charging of any amount of interest, as a sin against commutative justice. However, he made a tenuous but decisive opening towards the legal acceptance of interest which can be found in the scholastic usury Doctrine. The reason, stated by Thomas Aquina was very simple: if loans took the form of a partnership, the owner of the money, the creditor shared the risks of the enterprise and therefore was entitled to its profits. This was going to draw a much clearer line between loan sharks and risk takers.

More difficult was actually the day-to-day interpretation of such economic nuance in the Middle Ages quite unregulated banking practices and sometimes poorly educated ecclesiastic rural staff of the time. When the Aquina doctrine was formulated, there were no banks, where one could go, to deposit one's money and get quietly a safe annual return: one may make a great profit but one was always running a risk of losing all. The earlier fourth Lateran Council in 1215 addressed the problem with an effort to differentiate simple interest from the "oppressive and excessive interest" that was charged by some merchants or intermediaries. The Council stated that those found guilty of such practices were to be removed from contact with Christians until they made restitution. The full understanding of the sentence is important as it aims at prohibiting excessive interest, making an explicit distinction between excessive and moderate interest. Works of Orcagna, Andrea di Cione, the most prominent Florence painter from the 14th century and several Flemish artists vividly show usurers suffering chastisement in Hell. In the 14th century a less rigorous conception was developed and the greater part of both canon and civil doctrines, though maintaining the distinction between loans for consumption and loans for production, accepts for the latter lending at interest in three cases: (i) the creditor would need to accept illiquidity due to the assignment of his funds in the form of a loan, (ii) he would receive no income for his loan (iii) he would be exposed to a risk of default. However, in the daily life of the time, many documents show that the assessment of usury has too often been interpreted in too radical a way, as the understanding of economics was still limited at the time, leading in the absence of nuance to the full prohibition of interest. From time to time, it would also serve dubious strategies in providing a convenient excuse for a debtor to default, on the ground that he had been the victim of usury practices. A complaint lodged in 1275 by the inhabitants of the city of Nîmes, in France, to the seneschal of the King of France, revealed that they disputed the redemption of a loan based on a 256% interest rate,[20] thus emphasising that in these times of scarce money supply, loan sharks were certainly a problem susceptible of social unrest. Similar situations led the Kings of France to establish as a rule an official interest rate of 33.5% which was unfortunately seldom respected as a common practice.

The final blow to the old view on interest payment was dealt by the establishment of "*moutas pictatis*", small banking institutions established by the Franciscans to provide loan accommodation for the poor and free them from greedy private usury. This first institution was established in Griefo in 1463, the second in Perugia in 1467 with the Pope's approval. To further clarify the matter, Pope Leo X after the Fifth Lateran Council on 4 May 1515, proclaimed with the bull Inter Multiplices, that the charging of interest on loans in order to cover the cost of administration

---

[20]Pierre Racine, The commerce of money in the Middle Ages, Emeritus professor, University Marc Bloch, Strasbourg, France, working paper, Clio, November (2002).

was morally permissible. It specifically allowed *monti di pietà* to charge the debtors an amount destined to cover the legitimate costs of the transaction, stimulating the development of catholic financial institutions and a strong competition with the Jewish money lenders. All this would be beneficial to the structuring of sounder financial services and resulted in a decrease in the cost of credit. During his reign, Pope Pio V (1566–1572) approved a mortgage prototype known as *censo costitutivo*, which was a carbon copy of the Genoese *compere* system. Legitimisation under canon law of the financial use of bills of exchange would only occur in 1745, when Pope Benedict XIV's encyclical (Vix pervenit) admitted the legality for anyone to apply a moderate interest charge on loans. Today the permissible level of interest is still regulated in many developed countries; "loan sharks", illegal money lenders who charge very high interest rates, are still considered penal criminals and subsequently punished by laws.

The tension related to usury, and by extension to interest in general, and the Church doctrine probably came from the Decretals issued in 1234 by Pope Gregory IX confirming the Third Lateran Council's decree of 1179 that had excommunicated usurers and refused the unrepentant burial in consecrated ground. It required princes "to expel usurers from their territories and never to readmit them". This prescription was deeply rooted in the Aristotelian belief that "the most hated sort (of money-making), and with the greatest reason, is usury, which makes a gain out of money itself, and not from the natural use of it". As for non-Christians, usury was prohibited in both the Pentateuch and in the Quran. Thus, loan contracts which openly requested the payment of interest are rarely encountered from the 13th century. Custom would shed a useful nuanced light on the business perception of the practitioners as loans were definitively needed to fuel the delicate wheels of the commercial revolution. The financial solutions adopted were of two main types: monetary contracts and instruments of credit. Therefore, many merchant contracts would include the payment of a lump sum for the risk associated with defaulting and sometimes the final repayment amount would be written on a separate document, including the time value of money — a typical practice in Genoa, which remained not precisely known as most of the documentation was destroyed for the previously explained reason, to be found guilty of usury.

The Ascent of Lombard Merchant Bankers

The end of the 11th century and beginning of the 12th brought a moderate resurgence of business and trade, mainly in Venice, Pisa, and later, Florence, between Italian cities specializing in trade and Constantinople — and by extension the Orient. The supply to Italian seaports of strategic shipping provided a significant advantage to Italian merchants; alum from Asia Minor, silk and dyes, not to mention spices, slaves and other precious goods. The historical role of ports as young shoots around which cities grew explains why most large cities today are ports. The growth of international commerce in these cities led to the revival of banking. Merchant banking was predominantly an Italian business, emerging towards the end of the 12th century out of the trade with the Fairs of Champagne. The word 'bank' comes from the Italian, named after the '*banco*' or wooden bench on which merchants traded. Bankers did not work in a workshop as did the craftsmen, but behind a table set up in the market square. If a banker could not meet his financial obligation, the bench would be broken to inform on the situation ('*banco rotto*', the origin of "bankruptcy"). Banking was taking place in an environment where coinage in Europe was fragmented, extraordinarily complicated and heterogeneous, due to debasement[21] and the frequent issue of new coins, not to mention the counterfeit ones circulating in the market. Debasement was a plague and the root cause of not only economic problems but also social unrest and the rampant corruption of local governments. Currency crimes were widespread and ranged from counterfeiting to clipping, to washing, melting and trafficking in coins. The multiplicity of coins generated instability but made the fortune of money changers. In many areas of Northern or Southern Europe, barter was still a common practice; marten fur would be

---

[21] Reduction of the metal content, especially the precious metal, in a currency. In France, the silver currency went through 123 debasements between 1285 and 1490. Of these, 112 reduced the silver content of the currency by more than 5%. The single largest debasement reduced it by 50%.

conveniently exchanged for wine or olive oil. It also explains why for centuries the world finance was fascinated by gold, or sometimes silver, a reference which is tangible, trusted and quite simple to understand. Even fineness, a measure of the proportion of pure gold or silver in a bullion bar or a coin, was easily understood. Venice continued to use the badly debased remnants of the Carolingian coinage system until 1193. After the influx of silver used to pay for the crusaders' ships, Venice took the radical decision to mint a new large scale strong silver currency, the Grosso or "Matapan" composed of 98.5% silver. Florence followed a few years later with its own silver currency but the city financial elite was not fully satisfied by this decision and sought to show its ascending power. The answer came as a new strong gold currency, the Florin, minted in 1252: it was the first gold coin since the *solidus* of the Roman times and soon became the reference currency in finance. The initiative was quickly followed by the Genoese gold Ducat; both received an extraordinary warm welcome in Europe. France and England disliked the idea to leave the privilege of gold coins to the Italian city states, one of the most popular legacy of the Roman Empire. Both kingdoms minted gold coins in 1257 and 1266, but mostly for international publicity, as these precious metal currencies were hardly available for trade. Most of the coins used in the Middle Ages were made of silver, as Western Europe could not mine enough gold to mint coins. This idea of a finite reserve to mint coin remained persistent up to the 21st century.[22] The Florentine currency well-accepted all over Europe featured the lily of Florence on one side and the lamb of St. John the Baptist on the other. It contained 3.53 grams of 24 carat gold. At today's gold prices, it would have been valued at about €120. For a few Florence merchants, finance actually started to develop into a business in its own right.

As the "commercial revolution" was slowly spreading in medieval Europe, the campaign against usury vigorously renewed and culminated in 1311 with the Council of Vienna's decree of excommunication for all "magistrates, rulers, consuls, judges, lawyers, and similar officials" who

---

[22] In April 2011, Forbes quoted Gavin Andresen, chief scientist of the Bitcoin Foundation, saying, "Bitcoin is designed to bring us back to a decentralised currency of the people," and "this is like better gold than gold."

"draw up statutes" permitting usury or "knowingly decide that usury may be paid". The Council added that, "if anyone falls into the error of believing and affirming that it is not a sin to practise usury, we decree that he be punished as a heretic". However, as seen before the sin of usury was becoming highly judgmental and subject to misinterpretation. However, the diaries and family records of even the most avaricious Florentine merchants reveal that they had to be always cautious and creative to avoid colliding with the stringent Church laws. A new generation of businessmen was ambitious, often greedy, and came from Alba, Asti, Chieri, Milan, Venice, Piacenza, Bologna, Florence, Lucca and Siena; they were known collectively as "Lombards", and represented a small circle. These Italian "moneychangers", who often operated abroad grouped in a single guild organization. The guild was regulated by by-laws for the protection of its members' rights and had accredited consuls to the town authorities where the fairs were held. The exchange market was complex due to the multiple currencies and operated properly only when supported by a network of information and agents as widespread and reliable as possible. The rise of the *banchieri de scripta* (moneychangers) in the world of finance was accompanied by that of a category of merchants attending the international fairs. These were the "merchant bankers" (mercanti banchieri), so-called as their activities were a combination of trade, finance and production. Although they represented only a handful of wholesale traders, they were soon to become the most dynamic businessmen in Italy and beyond, with the most important transactions of the time in their hands. The expression "merchant bankers", which definitely originates from Italy, is deceptive: it does not relate to our contemporary meanings of "bankers" or "investment banks", except that merchant bankers are dedicated to financial investments and use capital resources belonging mainly to other providers. The very roots of this new type of merchants lie in Tuscany in the late 13th century and led to the development of companies known as "compagnie di negozio", the financial vehicle preferred by merchant bankers.

Besides currency exchange, merchant bankers played a significant role in dematerialising large transactions in their books, as a safe way to avoid carrying impractical bags of coins. The four essential financial instruments used by the Italian merchant bankers at the beginning of the modern age, included: (i) the bill of exchange a promise to repay a certain amount of money in a different location, in a different currency and at a future date, which was the most flexible and widely used despite its then limited negotiability; (ii) the bill of lading negotiable to order by endorsement or to bearer, (iii) shipping insurance, (iv) public debt securities of various forms (bonds, perpetuals, etc.) existing in a somewhat primitive form, were to take on distinct features from the 17th century onwards. Each of these four instruments had a decisive impact on changing economic life as they managed to make possible the circumterrestrial circulation of capital invested in trade, shipping and state finance, first on the basis of business relationships and then on gradually organised securities markets. It was almost a natural consequence of their success that the Italian companies' considerable financial resources and international prestige brought them to the attention of the rulers and in particular English Kings, who, during the second half of the 13th century, having pressured their Jewish money lenders, could hardly count on loans from them.

This probably explains why during the 13th century Lombard bankers from the north Italy, gradually replaced the Jews in their traditional role as money lenders to the rich and powerful. However, Lombards were not only concerned with the fate of their soul but also by their social reputation, as usury could give them a very bad name. They needed to atone for their sins and be seen doing so. This explains why they built so many chapels and churches and became fervent patrons of religious arts. A special attention was paid to architecture as this would ultimately be the best way to share the enjoyment of magnificent constructions, display their wealth and express their power in a socially acceptable way. An interesting parallel can be drawn with the contemporary quest of social responsibility; however, the wiser preachers of the 15th century would warn those who made great gifts to charity on the basis of pride rather than a true desire to contribute to the common good, but this was by no means a condemnation of becoming wealthy. The suspicion of usury soon remained a convenient way for the most powerful and dishonest princes to evade their obligation to repay their debtors, and this means of extortion became unfortunately common practice under the cover of Christian feelings until the lenders' confidence broke, and money became scarce.

As the "annuity" market developed, suspicions arose that the annuity contract was *de facto* usurious. Pope Innocent IV declared that annuities were not, and were legitimate contracts of sale, provided that the annual payments were based on 'real' properties.

The leading Bardi, Peruzzi, and Acciaiuoli family banks were all founded in the 1250s. This small circle of powerful families had developed special skills to survive political conflicts and even later emerged from the Plague relatively unscathed. Their early successes were due to a combination of business acumen, good management skills, wealth, political connections, strength and diplomacy. In the 1290s their businesses had turned into mega companies: they had grown dramatically in size and rapaciousness, and were reorganised, by the influx of new partners. These were "Black Guelph" noble families, of the faction of Northern Italian landed aristocracy always bitterly hostile to the government of the Holy Roman Empire. The Guelph League, centred around the powerful Este family of Ferrara, launched a series of wars throughout Europe, against the then-existing trends toward the establishment of European nation-states, in order to consolidate an ultra-feudalist, usurious world order. After the killing of both Manfred and Conradin Hohenstaufen in 1266, the Black Guelph unleashed chaos, economic ruin, and the rising power of a group of "Lombard bankers".

The sophistication of financial instruments probably had an adverse impact on the medieval fairs as gathering to clear transactions was less necessary. Venetian and Florentine merchant bankers offered to do it in travelling, and in spreading innovation, such as letter of exchange in 1291, and talents all over Europe. This wave of innovation dematerialised trade and rendered the presence of merchants at Champagne fairs less necessary as trade could be now safely conducted through trusted intermediaries. This is only an assumption as the important merchants who frequented the Champagne fairs, especially Lombards, liked to trade both in merchandise and money rather than specialising in one or the other. Machiavelli describes how by 1308, the Black Guelph ruled everywhere in northern Italy except in Milan, which remained a close ally of the Holy Roman Empire. Surprisingly, Florence in spite of its ingenuity and industrial strengths never became an international financial centre, possibly as a consequence of its federal and eclectic nature.

The city founded in 59 A.D. under the first Caesar's consulate[23] had managed to get its independence from the Empire and from the papacy in 1100, Florence was a "Commune" but not in the contemporary meaning; the city was definitively a city-state. Little has been left on how the city was actually governed except that 12 consuls were in charge of its destiny. Without clear leadership, Florence was too busy dealing with bitter and continuous internal feuds between families jockeying for power, keeping itself independently ruled as a commune resisting princely rule and disputing local leadership with neighboring cities. Its closest geographic rival was chiefly Pisa the sea port at the mouth of the Arno connected to Florence by road and barges, and its outport, Porto Pisano through which Florence was obliged to operate using Genoese shippers or use the busy network of canals to ship fine cloth to Aigues-Mortes (France), Lyon (France) and the North of Germany. Situated on the main route down the centre of Italy, linking the rich northern plains to the seat of power in Rome, Florence was well placed to flourish. The city's primary resource was its abundant Arno river which provided power and water for industry and access to the Mediterranean Sea for international trade. Another great source of strength was its smart merchant community, which set about transforming a local wool industry into an international business by importing large quantities of quality wool, from England and later Spain, to manufacture the fine cloth that was in demand all over Europe. This business was concentrated in the narrow Calimala road, home of about 20 workshops and warehouses. The Florentine merchants imported high quality crude wool from Spain and processed it entirely in the city. Then silk processing, "imported" from Byzantium,[24] took over the "Art of wool" after the Black Plague, together with velour, considered the most luxurious cloth in the High Middle Ages. The Emperor of Byzantium had developed Thebes and Corinth as unique silk processing centres since the 6th century, but when

---

[23] Some ancient story would even take the foundation of the city to the conspiracy of Catilina in 62 A.D.

[24] The silk monopoly in China and Persia had been broken earlier in the 6th century by the Byzantine empire through industrial espionage and smuggling silkworms and potted mulberry shrubs.

Roger II of Sicily launched attacks on those centres, he brought back to Palerma skilled silk craftsmen in 1147. This opened up new markets as a number of those craftsmen migrated to Lucca and later to Florence in the 13th century.

Compared to the other cities of the North of Italy, Florence was traditionally a Guelph city loyal to the Pope and not a military power. The city dealt with external conflicts with mercenary armies, often poorly organised and busy to find one assignment after the other, creating conflicts of interest from time to time. Florence was then a narrow city, filled of fortified places, sporadically agitated by unrest and violence between Guelph and Gibelin factions; setting city districts on fire and looting would be the ultimate way to defeat rival families. Another reason, as we shall see later, may be that the Florentine financial elite was not as successful as the Venetian one who had steadily managed to establish its dominance on Florence patrician families issued from the key commercial guilds. As its finance power finally became stronger in Tuscany, its emergence was unfortunately disturbed by a series of catastrophic events in the first half of the 14th century. The ingenious development of bills of exchange in Florence and the invention of double entry bookkeeping, led to the development of banking as a way of paying debts without the risk of having to transport cash, then as an acceptable scheme for evading the Church's usury laws, and finally as a means of extending credit. Clever accounting practices enabled Florence bankers to evade usury. What may be identified as excessive interest on a loan was presented in the accounts either as a voluntary gift from the borrower or as a fair reward on capital employed for the risk taken.

The archives of a well-known businessman of the time, Francesco di Marco Datini of Prato, born in 1335, provide an outstanding account of his progression from goods trading to finance. Following a year of apprenticeship to a merchant in Florence, Datini set up his own business in Avignon, the French home of the papal court. For over 30 years, he traded in religious, military and precious goods. Having made his fortune, he returned to Florence to become a merchant banker, opening additional offices in Pisa, Genoa, Barcelona, Valencia, and Majorca and engaging correspondents in Bruges and London. One of his business associates concerned about his intention to open a local bank in Florence wrote that he "risked the ruin of his reputation as a merchant by entering this business, since no banker could avoid usurious contracts". At the end of the 14th century, Datini was managing from his hometown Prato an amazing portfolio of nine principal partnerships: he was associated with Lotto Ricci trading in "Florentine goods", with Tuccio Lambertini to run three shops of fine clothing and shoes, with Gherardo Guidalotti to sell salt in the Rhône Valley, and with Nastagio di ser Tommaso to trade a variety of goods in Avignon and the Rhône Valley. It is no surprise that these partnerships were strengthened not only by friendship but also by family alliances. Typically, a merchant banker did not specialise exclusively in finance and was also a trader well positioned to buy low and sell high on the markets in a timely manner. His capacity to swiftly mobilise the needed financial resources would be a great advantage to act quickly on the market. Great Italian bankers such as the Bardi and the Peruzzi, also traded in wool, cloth, wine, and lead, and were not above trading in horses. As large merchant banking fortunes accumulated, those merchant banking houses became super companies seeking even larger financial transactions, and it seems only natural that they turned towards sovereign credit. However, these firms represented a narrow, although bright, segment of the prevailing rural economy. The principal Italian companies were invited to provide the monarchy with credit, which was substantial, and in the form of advances backed by customs revenues or in exchange for advantageous trading terms. In the early 14th century the Compagnia dei Bardi had offices in Barcelona, Seville and Majorca, Paris, Avignon, Nice, Marseille, London, Bruges, Constantinople, Rhodes, Cyprus and Jerusalem. The total staff of the firm can be estimated to be between 100 and 120 split in about 25 branches. The business had greatly benefited from bankruptcy of the Riccardi in Lucca (1294), the Ammanati and Chiarenti of Piosta, and the Buonsignori in Siena (1298). However, the failure of the company of the Great Table[25] had spillovers all over Europe and a disastrous trailing impact for centuries in its hometown. It is reported that a French satirist of the 15th century had marvelled at the

---

[25] The *Gran Tavola*, was the largest sienese bank in the Middle Ages founded in 1255, part of the Bonsignori family, with main branches in Pisa, Bologna, Genoa, Marseille and Paris.

ability of the Lombards to do business without money. The superiority of the companies was also palpable in their capacity to better train their staff. Around 1340, Francesco di Balduccio Pegolotti an agent who served the Bardi family from London to Cyprus, composed a professional handbook of practical advice for merchants on customs, facts and figures chiefly for the use of the Bardi staff. Pegoletti so described in detail the 188 different sort of spices, the lay out of the key trading cities, the type of currencies and the standard of weights, measures and coinage, the fees payable to intermediaries and of course the applicable taxes and tariffs. This insider view was meticulously revised and updated several times for about 15 years after each of his business trips, and contained all about what a prudent merchant would want to know before engaging into trade.

Despite the ban on interest or usury, no medieval European government could function without borrowing, given that its powers to levy taxes and exact rents was limited, especially while it was often engaged in costly military adventures. The financiers of the leading Italian cities developed what became a system of municipally funded perpetual debts, based sometimes on forced loans, *prestiti*, *prestanze*, or *luoghi* in Venetia, whose interest charges were financed by additional taxes on salt in the Rialto market, and on the weight-house or alternatively by floating debt in the form of "voluntary" short term loans in Milan. Even if forced loans were not very popular, citizens preferred them to direct taxation, because subscribers received both interest income and an asset tradable on the secondary market. In this case, the payment of interest was legitimated by the fact that forced loans were an obligation put on all citizens to defend their state. The renewal of the campaign against usury in the early 13th century explained the growing popularity of the *rente*, to finance municipal needs in the north of Europe, especially in France and Flanders. Such instruments unknown in Roman law, were based on the Carolingian census contract that many monasteries had long utilized in order to acquire bequests of lands, on condition that the donor receive an annual perpetual usufruct income from the land, in kind or in money.

Public finance and therefore sovereign debt became a topic of considerable importance in Europe. It was Florentine companies, the Guidi and the Frescobaldi, who financed Philip IV of France in his attempt to conquer Gascony and Edward I of England in his defence of it in the 1290s. The relationship between the Edward of England, Edward I, II and III, and the successive "bankers to the Crown", namely the Ricciardi of Lucca (1272–1294), the Frescobaldi of Florence (c.1294–1312) and the Bardi and Peruzzi (to 1345), also of Florence show the defining influence of Florence merchant bankers in the early development of international finance and European politics. The details of the development of sovereign credit under the three Edwards revealed that the King's relationship with Compagnia dei Bardi was more like a current account with an overdraft facility rather than a series of separate bond issues. Interest charges had to be disguised to circumvent the Church prohibition on usury, but the King could likely borrow at 15% annualised interest when his finances were stable but rates could increase over 40% during difficult times, most notably during wartime.[26] The transnational nature of the crown financing highlights the already high degree of internationalisation of medieval finance in Europe.

By 1325, the Peruzzi bank owned all of the revenues of the Kingdom of Naples (the entire southern half of Italy, the most productive grain belt of the entire Mediterranean area); the Peruzzi recruited and ran King Robert of Naples' army, collected his duties and taxes, appointed the officials of his government, and above all sold all the grain from his kingdom. One illustrious partner of the Compagnia dei Peruzzi was "Meissei Domnedio", the Lord himself, who got attributed one share of capital, together with the corresponding dividends which were distributed to charitable organizations. On the other side of the spectrum, in France, the infamous "Biche et Mouche", Albizzo and Musciatto Guidi, the two Francezi brothers of San Giminiano, had their "banc" in Paris, to better abuse Philip the Fair, acting as the ones in charge of the kingdom's finance. They arrogantly built one of the largest fortunes in Paris before falling into bankruptcy and had their franchise replaced by the Peruzzi's. This lesson that French public finance could be a target of choice for brash

---

[26]Adrian Bell and Chris Brooks, *Center for Economic History*, University of Reading, United Kingdom.

financiers was not forgotten and unfortunately repeated itself in the 18th century with catastrophic consequences.[27] Mirabeau[28] famously noted in a speech delivered in 1790 after the French revolution that "Public debt was the germ of freedom as it destroyed the King and the French monarchy, but we need to pay attention as public debt accumulates, to ensure that it does not destroy the nation and the freedom it brought us."

Given its political importance, the development of the sovereign debt market was a very lucrative trade. The merchant bankers certainly needed to evade shared suspicions of usury, and this explains why so many artworks and religious buildings, were commissioned by those 15th century bankers, constantly worried about their salvation and their reputation. And again, Florentine finance consistently demonstrated its innovative ability in creating the Monte delle Doti (Dowry Fund), a social insurance system fund set up in 1425 as part of long term voluntary lending to government. This fund provided finance capital needed to start a family and reduced the large stock of debt from the Monte Comune. It was a success until 1530 as the investment became gradually more popular than Monte Comune shares in terms of yields and market risk. Concerns about salvation and stiff competition among the wealthiest families to show off their status by creating the most beautifully frescoed chapels, contributed in turn to the rich beauty of the city, and therefore to the common good. Beyond its merchant bankers ingenuity and capacity to become a dominant financial centre, it seems that the city was busier preparing for its real mission, which would be to lead Europe from the Middle Ages to a new brilliant era; the artists, architects, scientists, thinkers and political figures who led the Renaissance were all born on the fertile soil in and around Florence, within the same century: Masaccio, Donatello, Ghiberti, Brunelleschi, Verocchio, Leonardo da Vinci, Botticelli, Ghirlandaio, Michelangelo, Lorenzo the Magnificent de' Medici and Machiavelli, just to name a few. Compared with Genoa or Venetia, the Medicean Florence

---

[27] John Law's Compagnie du Mississipi saga is narrated in Chapter III, Section 4.

[28] Mirabeau (1749–1791), Honoré Gabriel Riqueti, comte de Mirabeau was a Jacobin leader of the early stage of the French revolution, favouring a constitutional monarchy. He is remembered as an eloquent orator but was unfortunately involved in numerous financial scandals.

government would never have the legitimacy and as a consequence the ability to commit to honor its debt (probably due to exogenous factors), a key criteria for gaining recognition as the reference financial place to deal with. Self-proclaimed International Financial Centres were never really convincing in the world of finance where trust, expertise and stability are the ultimate reserve currency. Almost at the end of the Middle Ages, the first International Financial Centre, Venetia, finally emerged slowly from a strong and sometimes violent competition with three neighboring major Italian cities, Genoa, Florence and Milan.

The Banking Disintegration of the Mid-14th Century

The 14th century was especially a bad time for humanity, only echoed by the repeated horrors of the 20th century. The first half of the century brought catastrophic strains to the emerging European emerging economies. Over 50 years the following prominent companies disappeared: Riccardi (1294), Bonsignori (1298), Scali (1326) one of the oldest and strongest Florentine company, Bardi and Acciaiuoli (1343), Peruzzi (1346) and many others. Although agricultural productivity had increased, population growth had exceeded the limits of the agricultural economy of subsistence by 1300. Part of the problem was that the soils were exhausted and the world climate began shifting again in the mid-1200s. The Baltic sea froze, mountain glaciers expanded at several locations, including the European Alps, and average temperatures cooled slightly in what is called the Little Ice Age,[29] shortening the growing season. The situation was so threatening in the Alps that villagers summoned the Bishop of Geneva to perform an exorcism of the dark forces presumed responsible. Patterns of rainfall changed dramatically: it rained much more, with more frequent storms involving strong winds and floods. Agriculture became unsustainable in far Northern Europe, and in the rest of Europe agricultural productivity dropped significantly. Making matters even worse, a wave of epizootics destroyed much of Europe's livestock, depriving the population from much needed meat and dairy supply.

---

[29] Volcanic eruptions just before the year 1300 possibly triggered the expansion of Arctic sea ice, setting off a chain reaction that lowered temperatures worldwide.

In an agrarian economy this was poised to have catastrophic conse-quences, and the worst happened. The Great Famine (1315–1317) and the Black Plague in its various forms (1348), with a first outbreak of the dis-ease in Messina (1347) both devastated Europe in the first half of the 14th century decimating 30–60% of its population. First of all, with an expanding demography, floods and climate change, and soil exhaustion, crops failed. Simultaneously as the epizootic destroyed much of Europe's livestock, subsistence became more difficult. Famines were of regular occurrence in the 14th century; the Great Famine left a deep footprint on the European society[30] and led a million people to starve to death and a million others to migrate to other countries. Lower living standards due to the Depression, resulted in a much meager diet leading to a general degra-dation of the health condition of the European population and a loss of resistance to virulent pathogens. And then, the "Black Death" stroke. Then, the plague spread at a striking rate of around 30 miles in two to three days. It is possible that what we call Black Plague was more likely a viru-lent form of anthrax, or an Ebola-like virus transmitted person to person rather than through flea infested rodents.[31] Death was expected always in medieval times but it used to strike the children and the poor first. The Black Death was striking randomly, spreading from person to person, deci-mating cities, villages, convents and garrisons. Neither the Kings, nor the Church could do anything against it until the disease ran short of victims.[32] The certainty of the established order tilted and was replaced by the belief that now everyone was responsible of her/himself. The population decline was roughly uniform throughout Western Europe, with the Italian popula-tion falling from 10 to 7.5 million, France and the Netherlands from 19 to 12 million, Germany and Scandinavia from 11.5 to 7.5 million and Spain from 9 to 7 million. The largest percentage drop was in Great Britain, where the number of inhabitants fell from 5 to 3 million in this period. It is

---

[30] The story of Hansel and Gretel originates from this time.

[31] Christopher Duncan and Susan Scott, *Biology of Plagues: Evidence from Historical Populations*, University of Liverpool, Cambridge University Press (2005).

[32] Part of the European population may have been naturally protected by the mutated CCR5 gene.

generally assumed that the European population at the time was about 80 million. The Black Plague had killed an estimated 50 million[33] in Europe, roughly the third of the population living from Iceland to India, showing that the catastrophe was truly of extraordinary significance, even compared to the cumulated atrocities of the First and the Second World War. The population of Florence for example fell from 90,000 to 50,000. The plague erupted with a case-fatality ratio of 30–60%, killing a few million people in a few hours after a period of 3–7 days incubation. The disease settled and resurfaced virtually every decade in several waves, of lower consequences than the initial one, but possibly caused by the zoonotic bacterium *Yersinia pestis* that circulated among small animals and in particular wild rodents and their fleas. Rats lived in great number and density aboard the long haul ships, which now travelled at a speed of 40 km per day, and spread into remote seaports and households. In between, the Hundred Year War (1337) erupted between France and England further disrupting already difficult economic conditions due to climate change and epidemics. With the vast loss of life brought about by these catastrophic events due to the lack of knowledge to implement effective countermeasures, production slowed, food supply diminished, and prices soared. In France, the price of wheat increased fourfold by 1350. The plague disorganised the economy and life in every county, city and village, as people fled the Black Death. Most people believed that massive illness was a punishment of God for their sins. However, despite the profound personal tragedies created, it managed to create new opportunities for the survivors, and by the end of the century, the economy was back on its feet even stronger than before.[34]

The Acciaiuolis, the Bonaccorsis, the Cocchis, the Antellesis, the Corsinis, the Uzzanos, the Perendolis, the Peruzzis and the Bardis family banks, along with other smaller banks in Florence and Siena in particular, were all founded in the years around 1250. Florence was in the 1290s the site of a dynamic banking industry. These institutions led by "Black Guelph" noble families grew dramatically in size and ambitions. Most of these houses jockeyed for a bright spot on the lucrative sovereign credit

---

[33] World Health Organization.
[34] Georges Duby, The Middle Ages, Pluriel Hachette, p. 425 (1987).

market, in exchange for the pledging of royal (or papal) revenues. They continued lending their money to the King on demand deposit, despite the increasing risk of the Crown default, as they needed the royal license for the export of wool. This unhealthy practice of rampant corruption propagated to other sectors of the economy. The resulting credit expansion increased money supply on the basis of a mismatch between short term and long term resources. The Ricciardi of Lucca, first collapsed as the result of a "credit crunch" mainly caused by the unexpected outbreak of a war between France and England. The Frescobaldi were forced out of England in 1312 by Edward II's political opponents although they may have managed to minimise their financial exposure before their expulsion by seizure and looting. Edward III, a better ruler than his father, owed large sums to the Bardi and Peruzzi in the early 1340s, it was then no wonder that the most prominent lenders of the time experienced difficulties and three powerful Florentine banks, the Bardi, Peruzzi and Acciaiuoli, collapsed in the 1340s, together with the Siena banks. Since they also held money on deposit from other wealthy families throughout Italy, their failure spread financial loss in a systemic way. By 1342, England's budget had become so intertwined with its debtors, that the Lombard merchants contemptuously spoke of the King of England as "Messer Edward", complaining that they "shall be fortunate to recover even a part of his debts". Edward III's national budget was in the hand of either the Bardi or Peruzzi. Edward III had imprudently financed the war against France through usurious loans underwritten by the Florentine mega firms of the Bardi and the Peruzzi, which were secured on the expected revenues from a tax on wool. Rather than paying interest on his debts, Edward III gave the Bardi and Peruzzi large "compensations" for the hardships they were supposedly suffering in supporting his budget; this was in addition to assigning them his wool revenues. The primary conditionality of the loans was the pledging of royal revenues directly to the Lombards — a clear sign that the monarchs were fragile and lacked national sovereignty. Edward likely revolted against the brutal conditionalities of his creditors by defaulting on their loans starting in 1342, which resulted in seizure and looting the revenues of his kingdom by the people of the Bardi and Peruzzi banks. Edward III true debt was likely below 20,000 pounds when he defaulted, it was then certainly not the fundamental cause of the banking disaster of 1345, but likely the trigger. In Florence, public debt had been financed by speculative new loans created out of nowhere by Florentine banks. Neapolitan princes' massive withdrawal of funds fuelled a general crisis of confidence, causing a bank run and most of the banks to fail. In the absence of lender of last resort, liquidity was a recurrent problem as soon as the environment became more challenging, no one would be available to help through the wave of the monetary crisis, and contagion will reach the whole economy. As money was usually tied up for a long time, a cash crisis could have devastating impact, especially since communication to manage financial exposure all over Europe was not always reliable and information not always properly consolidated. It was certainly difficult for these early transnational banks to have a global perspective on their investing and financing activities, thus leading to great instability in the event of a crisis. However, the surviving Peruzzi account books reveal an enormous accounting undertaking to capture the entire European operations, and reflect the intrinsic limitation of the information technology of the time. These internal books show that the firm was regularly reorganised and newcomers were brought in, not only for their money but also for their own talent and prestige; this helped cushion the Peruzzi Company against the black or white strife in Florence during those years. Europe's difficulties and English crown partial default were certainly not the only reason for the difficulties of the Florentine banks which had likely already reached the limit of their capacity to manage the complexity of a European banking business and keep control of their international operations at a time when communications were still taking a long time. Most probably a huge international "bubble" of currency speculation amplified by the new merchant banks from 1275 through 1350 had also led the early medieval monetary system to uncontrollable instability with the exception of the much smaller Hanseatic League centres of Germany who had never allowed the Lombards to enter their cities. For a long time, there was no economic definition of what a bubble was, and it was even disreputable in academic circles to discuss the matter, the substituting Dutch term "Windhandel", wind trade, was used during the Tulipmania in the early 1630s, sharing the reference to thin air but did not fully capture the phenomena.

When the Bardi defaulted, the bankruptcy conditions were set by the justice of the time: 46% of the money deposited was given back to the creditors in the form of paper later negotiated on the market with another haircut, meaning that the cash equivalent would only be 30% of the deposits at the end. On the Peruzzi side, the total loss was about 80% of the deposits. As could be expected, bank failures were extremely detrimental to deposit-holders and undermined the trust in the Florence banking system. This episode which peaked in 1345 was worse than a crash as it led to the financial disintegration of the medieval financial system, as a result "all credit vanished together". In medieval times, in the event of a crash, no central bank would be capable to intervene as lender of last resort and the emerging banking market would not be regulated. Only the limited speed of communication between cites, by horse or waterway, will slow down the propagation of the crisis but may not prevent it from spreading like a wildfire, the economy would literally stop like a dead engine: capital vanished, stores and workshops closed, fairs dwindled, revenues and consumption collapsed. It took economic scholars nearly five centuries to understand the theoretical causes of this process, and articulate policies to restart economic growth. Many places paid a long-lasting token to these tragic times: as an example, after the pestilence of 1362, the annual fair of St. Giles, once the most important in Europe came to be of little more than local importance. Before the end of the Middle Ages and the beginning of the Enlightenment, the exchanges were punctuated with the organization of village markets (mostly based on barter and self-consumption) and gradually larger fairs. Such large regional fairs, such as the international fair of Champagne in France, were key in connecting the major European cities and organised as the most important occasional location for structured trade. The emergence of stronger cities in a still very rural society and the migration of population from the countryside to such cities was a sure sign of the acceleration of the European economic history. It can be seen that large cities have swallowed the smaller rural markets near their large fortified doors, both in Europe and in the Islamic world. In China which already had significant indirect trade connections with Europe to sell silk, spices and other precious goods, markets were organised differently at the center of rural local clusters developing at the circumference of a local circle where farmers could easily walk back and forth during the day to sell or buy goods. Small markets were prevalent and large regional fairs and exchanges were almost absent. The emergence of a class of powerful merchants was lagging behind Europe as the imperial regulation was strictly controlled and corseted exchange. Similarly, the imperial power was not willing to facilitate the emergence of guilds and mega trading companies which may have ultimately challenged its absolute power. The contacts with the outside world were not encouraged but may have occurred as early 200 A.D. A handful of Parthian adventurers and then merchants travelled regularly through the Silk Road from 130 A.D., when the Han dynasty officially opened trade with the West[35] to procure good horses, and set up a stallion breeding station, through technology transfer, to equip its cavalry. It is also probable that the route declined by the end of this dynasty in the 2nd century, but reopened gradually. For centuries, it was not only a conduit for silk and other precious goods, but also for invaders, travellers, missionaries spreading ideas and slowly interconnecting continents through more than a dozen communities. Even if some embassies were dispatched from China to connect with the West, they generally failed to do so, people from one end of the Road to the other scarcely met as cargo went through many intermediaries anxious to protect their fractional knowledge of the Road. Therefore, China continued to develop in virtual isolation from the rest of the world. When the Byzantine Empire fell to the Turks in 1453, the Ottoman Empire closed the Road and cut all ties with the West, forcing the merchants to take to the sea to ply their trade, thus initiating a series of expeditions beyond the known world.

From a regulatory perspective, the economic history of the Middle Ages can be summarised in Europe as a balance of power between the Church and the State, with the Church slightly more powerful. The ideal was a vision of order maintained by a harsh but benevolent Chivalry, inspired by the Church for the good of the people. After the Great Schism, which tore the church apart in 1378 when three popes claimed the seat of

---

[35] The history of the Silk Road pre-dates the Han Dynasty: the Persian Royal Road, which served as one of the main arteries of the Silk Road, was established during the Achaemenid Empire (500–330 A.D.).

Peter, creating two papacies in Rome and another in Avignon, the balance between the Church and the State was broken in the face of an unsustainable gap between ideal and reality. The nation-state came to hold sway, breaking the power of the Church, taxing, regulating, controlling and wreaking devastation through virtually continuous war on land or at sea for the redefinition of the European borders.[36] War has been with us since the dawn of civilisation and no human group phenomenon has been more constant and unfortunately rational. The wars of the calamitous 14th century were very disruptive as they frequently occurred but they did not cause a great deal of direct devastation: armies were small and professional, and hostilities were intermittent. But they resulted in strengthening the power of the winners; France consolidated its power on winning the Hundred Years' war, England after the War of Roses and Spain became one of the strongest monarchies in Europe following the unification of Castile and Aragon and the expulsion of the Muslims. Both the English and French monarchs proceeded to tax the Church, which brought them into a collision course with the Pope. The end of the 14th century is not by coincidence a turning point for European culture and demography. It marks the recovery from this transition reflected by the dark early years of the century and the stronger development of a healthier European economy.

In spite of this disastrous but pivotal century, one of the greatest achievements of the collapse of the banking system, was certainly the spontaneous development of short and risky financing circuit — private shared equity would be a good definition. English businessmen of the time called this "sleeping partnership", meaning that one partner freely brought finance with a view to developing its capital, and another one brought professional expertise with a view to taking advantage of his knowledge, the agreement was based on mutual trust and understanding: a notary and a fishmonger would jointly invest in a fishing boat and share the proceeds 50/50 or 75/25 for a number of years with the fisherman in charge of the

---

[36] Werner Sombart in Der Moderne Kapitalismus (1928), emphasized how the medieval society was characterised by a quasi-perpetual state of war, which created the need for the financing of a huge public debt which represented up to 75–80% of European public budgets in the 18th century.

boat who otherwise would never have had the money to run his own ship. As confidence increased in these partnerships, their duration increased together with their scope. This would have extraordinary consequences for economic development and the understanding between agents both at the microeconomic and macroeconomic level, and this is what is being rediscovered today with microfinance in emerging countries and beyond.

Chapter 2

THE DOMINATION OF THE MEDITERRANEAN REGION

Lombard Finance and the Turbulent Medici Era

A century of plague, hunger and war had dramatically changed the face of European markets and relationships between supply and demand. Located as northern and southern "feeder" hubs, Venice and the Baltic hubs clearly benefited from the tragedy of the Black Plague (1347–1352) which devastated Europe and killed 30–60% of its population. The "inland" was severely devastated and the waves of the pandemy accelerated the decline of the fairs of Champagne, in France. In spite of the disappearance of its prominent bankers struck by the crisis, life and business continued in Florence. There were still only two parties in Florence, like in other cities of the North and centre of Italy: Guelph, an allusion to "Otton the Welf", the unfortunate candidate to the imperial crown, and Gibelin, an allusion to Waiblingen, the name of the castle of Frederic II. The Guelphs were loyal to the Pope, the Gibelins, were supporters of the German emperors. There was no serious philosophical divide between the two parties but there was hatred: their organisation was changing according to family feuds, new alliances and divergence of interest. It resulted in clustered cities and sporadic fights, brutal murders and destructions involving an extraordinary violence between the Guelphs and Gibelins factions. Florence was in the middle of such violence, so that in 1257, the Gibelin parliament of Florence decided that this unmanageable and doomed city must, just like Carthage, disappear. The city was saved thanks to the courage of some Gibelin partisans but the decision was made and promptly executed to flatten the Guelfe districts, and the *popolo* a new communal management structure was formed. In spite of the search for a pacified political climate, violent conflicts continued to erupt and shook the structure of the Italian cities: Guelfes against Gibelins, White against the Black later. The Black were mostly joined by the newly emerging families; Spini, Peruzzi, Medicis supported by the Angevins loyal to the Pope. After the Gibelin victory of 1260 in Florence, almost nothing was be left of the Guelf party, except its financial power which even fragmented was still palpable outside of the city. For a century almost, the city of Florence was back to its favorite culture of violent and cruel political games; this turbulent sociological environment deeply impregnated the style of the state-of-the-art financial culture of the 14th century in Europe. Such was the context that banking developed in Florence due to the ingenious development of bills of exchange, first as a way of settling accounts without handling cash, then as a means of extending credit, which was mostly short term at this time, and finally as a means of evading the Church's inconvenient usury laws.

What caused the Peruzzi bankruptcy is the Company's loss of profitability which occurred gradually over a decade from 1325. It seems that the main reasons for this erosion were the perpetual wars in which Florence was involved, the more challenging geopolitical context in Europe, such as the Hundred Years War or the peasant revolts in Flanders, and the lack of management acumen and personal ethics of the senior management who took control following the death of the firm's visionary leader Tommazo Peruzzi. As the Florentine supercompanies were trailing hundreds of smaller services companies in their shadow, their crash in 1345 was systemic and triggered a massive economic crisis. It left a vacuum later filled by the Medici family, and friends,who ruled Florence for almost 400 years. The Medicis did not win Florence easily, as the linage of the clan was not as clearly established as its rivals. The family originated from the patrician class not from the nobility. As the Latin aphorism by Gratian reads: "Seldom or never can a man who is merchant be pleasing to God." It is then not surprising that another of Florence's greatest son, Dante Alighieri's (1321), became so critical. In his Divine Comedy, the merchant represented by Geryon is "that loathsome counterfeit of fraud", who has the outward features of kindliness, mildness and honesty but is fashioned with a serpent body, rapacious claws and a scorpion tail, perching on the cliff wall high above the abyss of hell. As such the Medicis were the first princely dynasty to win their status not by warfare, marriage or inheritance, but through commerce. In 1373, Foligno di Conte de' Medici complained bitterly about the modesty of the family means. A tax assessment of 1363 revealed that two Medici family members were even less well-off than many city shopkeepers. The first Medici to get a princely title or rank was registered only in 1569, centuries after the Estes, Gonzagues or Sforzas just to mention a few illustrious families of the time. The Medici family dominated Florentine politics for two and a half centuries and got its genes mixed with those of most royal families in Europe. As parallel to its development in the finance sphere, the family presided over a cultural achievement that is equalled only by Athens in the golden age. The ultimate beneficiary of Medici patronage was Michelangelo, who shared both the Medici instinct for making money and the Medici determination to ignore it. Machiavelli who did not like the Medici clan, and did not hide from it, clearly reported that they were a "family of usury" who managed to build their wealth stealing the properties of the monks near Arezzo. The Medicis were initially foreign currency dealers of doubtful reputation, member of the Arte de Cambio, seated at benches behind tables next to the wool market. Later it seems quite certain that the Medici family built its fortune on usury, and its derivative products, rather than trading cargoes from one continent to another. Maritime insurance, that the Medici family mastered, was considered a well-accepted means of financing in Florence, decades before it became common practice in Genoa.

It was in Rome in 1395 that Giovanni di Averardode' Medici, known as Giovanni di Bicci, founded his own money changing business, together with Benedetto Bardi, and started to make serious and respectable money. The history of the Medici Bank has come to light through the 1950 discovery of the Medici Bank's confidential ledgers ("libri segreti") in Florence's Archivio di Stato. The secrecy of these ledgers again betrays the non-public nature of bankers' activities, as well as the desire of many customers of Italian banks to deposit their money in secret accounts. The discovery of the bank books provide us with an in-depth unique understanding of how the Medici Bank operated in the 15th century. These books show that Giovanni was well organised, meticulous and kept an excellent record of his trades. The Medici Bank did not initially accept demand deposits. At first, it only took time deposits, which were actually true loans from the customers to the bank. Giovanni was also determined and finally convinced the papacy to give him some business. Issuing bills of exchange was another important part of his trade, and a convenient way for merchants to transfer money and obtain credit. After developing what had become a respected Roman bank, he decided to set up a branch in Florence and in Venice. Like other ventures of the time, the Banco Medici was also involved in a wide range of trading activities that included such diverse goods as almonds and four-poster beds; the most profitable areas were high-quality foodstuffs (spices, citrus fruits, olive oil), luxury items (woollen and silk cloth, jewels and precious metals), and raw materials (fine English wool, Tolfa alum for textile). The bank also managed three manufacturers of wool cloths and silk fabric (velvets, brocades, taffeta). In the 15th century, the Genoese provided the Medici who had received from the Pope the concession for the alum[1] mines, with the ships they lacked and purchased lots of alum destined for the English wool industry. The mines, a windfall for the ailing papal finances, were discovered in the Tolfa Mountains near Civitavecchia by Giovanni da Castro, the owner of a dyeing workshop in Constantinople expelled and ruined by the Ottomans. He was on his way to the papal court when he noticed the possibility of rich deposits, and brought the news to Pope Paul II who handsomely rewarded him. By this time, alum ranked among the more precious and strategic cargoes traded across Europe, valuable enough for English privateers to seize ships carrying it and taking it to home ports, where it was sold to the booming cloth industry in Britain.

---

[1] Alum was a strategic commodity for textile, leather work, medicine and even the Venetian glass industry. Alum was the only substance known at the time to have the ability to fix natural dyes to fabrics.

After the Great Schism, which tore the church apart in 1378, creating two papacies in Rome and Avignon, Giovanni and his son Cosimo completed the masterstroke by becoming the Holy See's sole banker in 1420 after the reunification of the papacy of 1415. By far, the best customer of the Italian banking and mercantile companies was the Church. No wonder that so many of the Italian merchants, and in particular the Medicis, became the estimated patron of arts and architecture which at the time were mostly religious. Giving back in the form of sponsoring religious architectural projects or artistic masterpieces was then seen as a very decent way of moderation and spiritual discipline, which also had the merit of clearly positioning by their magnificence the high rank of the donor. Besides building the Florentine financial power, it is probably less known but equally defining in the Medici family history that they contributed towards building one of the most extraordinary art collections of Europe. If Florence could not claim the title of international centre, there is no doubt that it won a worldwide recognition for becoming one of the most extraordinary international art centre ever under the stewardship of the Medicis.

In 1400, the Medici clan was constituted of nine distinct branches closely connected to each other. By 1420, Cosimo de' Medici had taken over the family business which was flourishing but tainted with serious usury and corrupt practices. When Cosimo de' Medici was arrested in 1443 by the Albizzi and Strozzi rival faction in Florence, upset by his growing influence, he narrowly escaped death and was exiled for ten years, to Venice where he managed to get control of a Florentine party working for his return. After exulting on his victory, Albizzi realised that they would need to face an unforeseen hurdle: the Medici money would not continue to flow into the Florence economy as it was either embedded in architecture for centuries or away from Florence. Rinaldodegli Albizzi and Strozzi's inability to balance the economics of the city led to their disgrace and exile: Cosimo de' Medici was recalled with honors in 1434. That very year Machiavelli would emphasise that the city of up to 120,000 inhabitants would not continue to be a republic anymore and would elect to become a tyranny in the hand of its Medici ruler. There would be no mercy, for those who tried to go against the Medici family, they would be ruined and disgraced, but their lives were spared. Following the Plague of

1348 and the epidemics of 1400 and 1417, the population of Florence fell to its lowest point in two centuries to less than 40,000 people. Depopulation and troubled public finances were dramatically underscored in 1423.

The founder of the Medici dynasty, Giovanni deiBicci, a skillful banker and intelligent businessman, thoughtful and reserved, lived in sober way and did not distinguish himself in dress or lifestyle. Although he had no interest in public appointments, he accepted to be *"Priore"* (Prior) in Florence on three occasions. Beneath a veil of apparent disinterest, he concealed a tenacious and ferocious intelligent mind to accumulate wealth, so that the family patrimony might become an instrument of political power in his hands and in those of his successors. The bank quietly developed under the rule of Cosimo dei Medici, the elder of Giovanni's two sons, Florence's most important patron of the arts, and had branches in Geneva, Bruges, London, Avignon, Lyon, Rome, Venice, Ancona, Pisa and Milan. Another mega trading company successor to the defunct Bardi and Peruzzi was born. In just a few years, Cosimo absorbed the majority of the 39 Florentine banks, which had begun to disappear in 1425, while his father was still alive. The Medici seemed to have perfected the use of the holding company to protect their international network in case of default of one of their branches and invested in lucrative industrial side businesses. Each of the branches was a limited partnership, so the main bank did not have unlimited liability for the debts of the branches, but the head of each branch was handsomely incentivised to develop profitable business for the family. The end of this arrangement in 1455 was possibly one of the factors leading to the eventual demise of the bank. With up to nine branches and many correspondent banks all over Europe, the Medici bank was probably the most powerful multinational organisation of its time, investing in multiple areas, serving the greatest multinational entity, the Church and acting as the leading private patron for arts and sciences.

In 1464, Piero succeeded his father Cosimo as *pater patriae* of the Republic of Florence, on what had become an informal hereditary charge. However, the Medici company's golden years had already passed with Cosimo's death. Five years later, on his death, the leading citizens of Florence invited Piero's son Lorenzo, aged only 20, to occupy the same informal position. He not only inherited the political prestige of his grandfather but also the fabulous wealth of the Medici business. In 1771, after the election of a new Pope Sixtus IV, fortune turned again the wheel of the Medici bank which lost its business with the Holy See awarded to the Salviati and the Pazzi families. The Pazzi conspiracy hatched in 1478, nearly ended his rule, killing his brother Giuliano but Florence stood up and remained loyal to the Medici. By nightfall, three of the Pazzi[2] conspirators who attempted to end the Medici rule, together with Francesco Salviati, the archbishop of Pisa in his ecclesiastical attire, were hanged at Florence's government palace, the Signoria. The Pazzi family was banned from Florence and their assets confiscated. The Pope then excommunicated Lorenzo and tried to persuade the King of Naples, Ferrante, to mount a punitive expedition against Florence. This led to a two year war with the Papal armies and the Kingdom of Naples. In 1479, Lorenzo *il Magnifico* secretly left for Naples and brought back peace to Florence after broking a peace treaty with Ferdinand I, King of Naples. Lorenzo aware that he needed to consolidate his new friendship and reconcile with the Pope, offered him the Renaissance which spread all over Italy and sent him the best Florentine painters, Botticelli and others to decorate the Sistine Chapel. In 1480, he established in Florence a Council of 70 members to assist in the government of the Republic, but then removed the management of public finance and the capacity to appoint new Lords. "One of the most powerful remedies that a prince has against conspiracies is not to be hated by the people generally" warned Machiavelli.[3]

Florence remained united and calm until Lorenzo's death in 1492 but on the financial side, the disastrous management of the Medici company by Tomaso Portinari led to the insolvency of several branches. Compared to his father and grandfather, Lorenzo showed less moderation in his lifestyle, and was more attracted by politics and ostentatious expenses. He dedicated much of his time expanding the incredible art collection of the family started by his father and neglected the family business. Some of these

---

[2] The Pazzi were a family of ambitious Florentine bankers in Rome from noble origin. They formed allies with Pope Sixtus IV, who was at odds with the Medici over the acquisition of the Imola city. A loan from the Pazzi bank allowed the pope to purchase strategic land and cities in exchange for granting the Pazzi a monopoly on valuable mines.

[3] Niccolò Machiavelli, *The Prince*, Chapter XIX, Mansfield translation, University of Chicago Press: Chicago (1998). He dedicated this book written after 1513, to the Medici family in an effort to demonstrate his support, but without success.

collections are still visible in the Uffizi and at the San Lorenzo library. As a result, developing Florence as a financial centre was certainly not a priority for Lorenzo, the family banking business became remotely managed and some costly mistakes were made by the foreign branches which were taking more independence under Lorenzo's lax management. The traditional vertical tied organisation of the family clan, changed to a more horizontal solidarity between peers of the same generation, neighbourhood, spiritual alliance and friendship, way beyond the ancient family lines. Nevertheless, the new masters of Florence were capable of following Italian merchants all over Europe with loans and credits. Loans were negotiated with "disgraceful bank managers" who, in order to make themselves "important," as Lorenzo the Magnificent bitterly remarked, hardly care about business integrity. The Medici bank would arrogantly prosper in merchant banking on an operating model close to modern holding companies until it suffered in 15th century the same fate as its illustrious Florentine predecessors. Each Medici branch was a legally independent entity whose capital was distributed amongst the Banco Medici in Florence, the limited partner, and one or more local shareholders, one of which was branch manager. Total share capital, excluding non-distributed profits, amounted to 88,000 florins, 78% of which belonging to the Medici family and the remaining 22% in the hands of local partners. From 1460, the bank's profitability was flat, in 1465 the Lyon subsidiary experienced serious problems, and in 1478 the London branch went bankrupt. The roots of the general economic and bank crisis that ruined the Medici Bank resemble those of 14th century Florence. Artificial credit expansion resulting from bankers' misappropriation of client deposits gave rise to an artificial boom fed by the increase in the money supply and the seemingly "beneficial" short-term economic impact of a large scale Ponzi scheme. Things started to turn sour for the Medici family, when Lorenzo, behaving like a royal omnipotent, and somewhat corrupt, ruler of Florence, raided the *Monte delle fanciulle*, a municipal saving fund created for the payment of all the daughter dowries in Florence. The dowry fund was a unique saving vehicle allowing a father to make a deposit guaranteed by the state for a fixed term — either seven and a half or 15 years. At maturity, if the nominated daughter survived and married, and the marriage was consummated, a specified amount would be paid to the girl's husband; otherwise, the deposit reverted to the commune.

This was insufficiently attractive, but when the terms were improved in 1433 and payment was promised to the father in case the daughter did not survive, investors responded with enthusiasm. Dowries signalled a family's place in society: it was a public and tangible sign of family status and expectations to continue occupying a rank among other comparable families. In that respect, marriage in Florence and elsewhere in Europe was an important and rather formal institution. In 1485, due to public finance problems, the fund paid only one fifth of the dowries, the reminder was registered on a special interest paying account of 8% per year, later reduced to 3%. Despite good intentions, the fund's financial problems appeared soon after its creation, casting serious doubts on the probity of the management of public finances. The Florentine marriage market and public finance were indeed very much interconnected as it became difficult to separate the dowry fund accounts from the city general expenses.

When the King Charles VIII of France invaded Florence in 1494 and confiscated all Medici property as a compensation for the Medici bank failure in Lyon, the whole family was thrown out of Florence again leaving the Bank in a state of bankruptcy. In the same year, all the branches were dissolved: burdened with debts, and deprived of management, they fell one after the other. The fall of the most prominent Florentine bank had as a proximate cause, what already happened a century previously with its predecessor bankers in the very same city. Finance stumbling once again on unmanaged credit expansion, triggering not only a run but also a departure of talent. It definitively ruled out the capacity for Florence to become a financial centre of international standing. As history would tell, the end of the bank was not the end of the Medici history. Their power in Florence, and beyond, spanned almost 400 years. Most of their wealth was invested in collections, art pieces and architecture. Ultimately, the Medicis were possibly more interested in power than money: two Medicis became popes (Leo X and Clement VII), two became queen of France (Catherine and Marie) and three became dukes (of Florence, Nemours and Tuscany). The Medici's unique patronage of Italian arts and sciences, associated with their political flair, was later to be leveraged as a defining Italian artistic contribution to the French Enlightenment.

Two hundred and sixty kilometers North East on the Adriatic Sea, Venice was in a position to attract the East Mediterranean trade and the skills of the Florence bankers. Its victory against the Genoese navy in 1381 during the Chioggia war created the much awaited opportunity for the most Serene Republic[4] to narrowly take the lead, but the fierce rivalry between Venice and Genoa on sea continued to rage until it reached its climax in 1390s. In the meantime, the Republic of Genoa went bankrupt, and the most urgent task was to rescue it. The efforts of the eight patricians who gathered the Wednesday morning on 2nd March 1408 in the great hall of the Casa di San Giorgio situated within a stone's throw from the Ligurian Sea would not be vain as we shall see later. At least one of them, Rabellas de Grimaldis, was a member of a dynasty which survived beyond the coastline of Italy.[5]

Like rival Genoa — "La Superba", the lagoon city is a port, carefully organised for the exchange of goods. It benefited from a strong industrial base for high quality silk cloth, glass industries and metal work — and a dynamic Lombardy as its hinterland. The merchants were trading everyday the large quantities of goods shipped toward the double Rialto plazas, one of the most reputed exchanges in Europe. Nearby the bankers ("*banchieri*"), in their narrow offices were gathering the transactions and organising the international payments and trade financing with the sophisticated instruments that also later made the fortune of Genoa in the 16th century. Venice, the lagoon city, had become the most important foreign exchange and trading city of the Mediterranean in the 15th century, and most of the rates were expressed in Venetian ducats, which had become the international trading currency. The key place for arranging such business was the house of the merchants, in the midst of the Venetian financial district at the south end of the Rialto bridge. Across the Grand Canal was the *FondacodeiTedeschi* built in 1228, where the increasingly important German merchants, with their supplies of central European gold and silver, were based. This special hostelry maintained by the Venetian Republic, managed by a superintendant accountable to the Senate, was a smart way to not only welcome German merchants but also control them. Visitors were only allowed to import products from their own region and purchase goods brought by Venetian merchants from

---

[4] Venice was formally known as the Most Serene Republic of Venice.
[5] See Chapter 6 "Gambling centers", on the foundation of Monaco.

overseas. No Venetians were allowed to compete with them in their own territory and any infringement was severely punished. The trading activities were highly specialised by type of goods (currencies, gold, silk cloth). The sophistication of the pepper or precious spices trade, for example, clearly differentiated from the domestic daily trade or local barter of cereals. This commerce was exclusively held by a well-defined group of large merchants trading bulk. The areas of trade specialisation were changing frequently, according to incoming opportunities. The domination of Venice lasted until it lost its leadership on the trade with the Eastern Mediterranean (Levant). However, international finance in Venice, as everywhere else in Europe, was still largely controlled by Florentine practitioners.

The Rise and Apogee of Venice, the Lagoon City

Venetian history is bound to the sea: the lagoon city emerged from the sea, and its wealth and power came from the sea, which was indeed the primary cause of the prominent political and economic standing the Republic achieved over centuries. The close relationship between the city and the sea was since the early Middle Ages symbolised in the *Sposalizio del Mare*, or Marriage to the Sea, a religious ceremony whereby the Doge sailed out into the Adriatic, surrounded by a procession of boats, offered prayers and later threw a ring into the water, signifying the marriage of the city to the sea. Furthermore, the city enjoyed a privileged and strategic geography on a major ancient route from Constantinople to Western Europe that went through the lagoon, up the Adige River into the Alps, over the lowest crossing point of the entire central Alpine mountain, at the Brenner Pass culminating only at 1,372 m, and down into the Rhine and Danube basins.

"La Serenissima" was first a swampy backwater inhabited by modest but bold fishermen, sailors and salt marsh workers, built partly on natural islands and partly on reclaimed and man-made islands. The Roman historian, Titus Livius accounted for a fleet of pirates led by Cleomynes, son of Cleomenes II, King of Sparta, wandering in 302 A.D. in the North of the Adriatic for looting. They landed in what would become Venice. The invasion was fiercely repulsed by the early Venetian inhabitants (Venetes) who managed to capture some of their invaders' boats later displayed as trophies. This alliance with and fight against sea and mud has forged this unique temper of the Venetian people, similar characteristics can be found in the foundation of Amsterdam, another great financial centre. Founded in the 5th century in the shadow of the Byzantine Empire, Venice benefited early from trading rights along the Adriatic coast and as soon as it started to become independent from the Empire, the city was wise enough to invest in the construction of a large and advanced state-owned navy. Charlemagne recognised Venice as a threat equal to the plague of Vikings raids in Northern Europe, and unsuccessfully tried with his son Pépin, King of Italy, to bring Venice to terms with his Empire. After helping defeat Charlemagne in battle and repeatedly helping Byzantium in its battles with the Arabs, Venice was granted *de facto* independence in 814. In 828, merchants from the lagoon stole the full relics of the Evangelist Mark from Alexandria in Egypt and sailed back home where a predecessor of today's St. Mark's Basilica was built soon afterwards. Following this accomplishment, Venice gained an immense prestige in Christianity and was awarded full independence by the Golden Bull of 992. The city then benefited from political and military independence from the rest of Europe under the protection of the powerful byzantine Emperor Nicephorus. Conveniently located midway between Constantinople (the gateway to the East) and Western Europe, Venice was uniquely positioned on the Adriatic on the most commercial routes of the time.

From the 9th century, its fleet provided all along its long history a significant competitive and military advantage and proved instrumental in building a visionary policy of state mercantilism *"avant la lettre"*. When Venice started to expend its reach, it first grew in areas neglected by the Western empires. The profound influence of sea commerce upon the wealth and strength of countries was clearly seen before the true principles that govern its growth and prosperity were detected.[6] In the 11th century, the city sent out military missions to subdue the nests of pirates which infested the Dalmatian coast and strengthened its control of strategic merchant sea faring routes. It positioned Venice as a pivotal city from the Adriatic to the Mediterranean and opened an era of stability favourable to the development of commerce. One of the defining event of the 10th

---

[6] Mahan, *The History of Sea Power on History 1660–1783*. Dover publications (1987) (p.1).

and 11th century was the reconquest by the Byzantium and Venetian navy of the main Mediterranean shipping routes and of the Arab possessions surrounding them. Merchant ships sailed within sight of land and navigation was too dangerous at night, Arab control of Syria, Cyprus, Crete and Sicily allowed Arab pirates to plunder the Aegean and Ionian coastlines and seas, making Christian shipping unsafe in the main routes of the Mediterranean waters.

In 1000, Constantinople was Christian Europe's richest and largest business centre. Its population of roughly 300,000 was as large as the combined populations of the next 10 largest cities in Christendom. By 1082, another Golden Bull granted Venice duty-free access to 23 of the key Byzantine ports and property-right protections from the caprices of corrupt Byzantine administrators. Most importantly, the Venetians were given buildings and wharfs within Constantinople to pursue their trade and establish their own Quarter in a more comfortable way. About 20,000 Venetian merchants settled in this quarter to develop a flourishing business, which would later lead to serious political tensions between Venice and Constantinople and the ultimate reason for the Venetian-led Fourth crusade. From its strategic trading point midway in the Mediterranean, Venice freely connected Europe with Africa and Asia Minor and the city's merchants were at home everywhere in the known world. Byzantium was then the door to Asian trade and supported the development of the Venetian sea hegemony which would help undercut the overland routes occasionally disrupted by wars, then controlled by Swedes and Russians along the Volga river. Venice kept its leadership as a hub for long distance shipping in the Mediterranean, the Black sea and along the Atlantic coast of Northwestern Europe. Then the city continued to grow in power and importance after the sack of Constantinople by crusading forces. This campaign orchestrated by the Venetians, wholly independent from the Empire, was planned to retaliate against 10,000 Venetian merchants being taken as hostage for ransom by the Byzantine Emperor and the subsequent genocide of Italian merchants in the Galata district in 1182. On 12 April 1204, 41st Doge, Enrico Dandolo, predecessor of Doge Ziani, ordered his galleys beached under the walls of Constantinople and urged his men to enter Constantinople by force. The city fell and was sacked by the crusader armies and in the upheaval that followed, Venice grabbed a vast swath of colonies. Through the resulting partition of former Byzantine lands, Venice acquired several new territories throughout the Aegean, Eastern Mediterranean and BlackSeas including the islands of Crete and Euboea, all of which helped to strengthen Venice's control on the commercial routes that passed through these waters. Venice set up a powerful administration to rule its new colonial empire, and made sure that the chief administrators of each territory, drawn from Venice patrician elite, would be properly compensated and incentivised for their performance and their loyalty. The Lagoon City continued to focus on building the known world most powerful military navy in its Arsenal, then the largest industrial venture in Europe, and managed to militarily overtake its rivals Florence, Siena and Genoa. The later was probably Venice's toughest competitor as it had direct access to the sea but the beginning of the Hundred Years War disrupted its main market, France, leaving Venice with the capacity to take the lead as an international financial centre. It took some time for Genoa to develop new commercial links with Spain and in the meantime Venice benefited from its alliance with Southern German provinces to develop its trading position across Europe. In the north, the development of Central Europe mining positively contributed to the development of the South German — Venetian alliance, symbolised by the magnificence of the Fondaco dei Tedeschi built in 1228,[7] as the headquarters of the South German merchants in Venice situated on the Grand Canal near the Rialto bridge. Conversely, the German alliance also opened the doors to the wealthy Hansa cities of the North of Germany and to the great northern European rivers, Vistula, Oder, Neisse and Weser, and obviously the Rhine. All of them opened for navigation and the transhipping of goods from Italy. Venice as a state-city was not only in a capacity to trade — marble, spices and slaves from central Europe — but also to make war as needed, and its hegemonic vision for a dominant position in wealth accumulation was quietly supported by a stable and powerful family oligarchy ruling over a strong political consensus on the future of the city. A pillar of the Venetian oligarchical system, sometimes improperly called Republican, is the *fondo*, the family fortune. The continuity of the family

---

[7]And rebuilt between 1505 and 1508 as a three level building facing a central courtyard after a fire destroyed it, with a façade on the Canal Grande frescoed by Titian and Giorgione.

fortune which often earned significant money through usury, war and looting was seen to be even more important than the continuity across generations of the family that owns the fortune. In Venice, the largest *fondo* was the endowment of the Basilica of St. Mark. This *fondo* was administered by the procurers of St. Mark and closely associated with the Venetian state treasury. The fortunes of the great patrician families were tightly associated around this central *fondo*, and if a patrician passed away without heirs, his fortune was transferred to this *fondo* to the benefit of the entire city.

The Venetian head of state, the Doge, more a magistrate than an absolute sovereign, was elected by the Venetian people only in the loosest sense before 1036. The Doges had come from one of three families, had absolute power, and could appoint their own successor. The massive expansion of Venice's trade after 1082 led to great political reforms, in particular, the end of a *de facto* hereditary Doge in 1032, the establishment of a parliament or Great Council in 1172. By 1192, the Doge could hardly do anything without the approval of an elected parliament, the Great Council, placing power primarily in the hands of the most influential families including the Mocenigo, the Cornaro, the Dandolo, the Contarini, the Morosini, the Zorzi and the Tron. The Great Council appointed all public officials and elected a Senate of 200–300 individuals and also chose the Council of Ten, a secretive group which held the most power in the Venice government. And this organisation was continued during the late Middle Ages and the Enlightenment. Compared to the colourful but tumultuous political life in Genoa, Venice was a model of social stability and political efficiency. There were several factors responsible for this situation: wealth was more equitably shared between citizens, merchants were involved in the government of the city in a fair way; the economic activity was dependant on a large portfolio of activities which would insulate the economy from the downturn of one's specific business.

Venice controlled the Papal credit, and had a significant influence on the continuing hostilities between the Papacy and the Holy Roman Emperors. In the 1180s, Doge Sebastiano Ziani, 42nd Doge of Venice tried to reconcile the two leaders of Christendom, Pope Alexander III and the Holy Roman Emperor, Frederick Barbarossa, the grandfather of Frederick II supporter of the Ghibelline Octavian antipope (Victor IV) elected in 1159.[8] Ziani who supported the Pope, helped Frederick's fleet in the siege of Ancona and on 24 July 1177, managed to mediate peace between the two leaders of Christianity in Venice. Incidently, Venice managed to get Emperor Frederick to agree to withdraw his standard silver coinage from Italy, and allow Italian cities to mint their own coins. Over the century from the Peace of Konstanzin 1183 which recognised Venice's autonomy to the 1290's, Venice established a quasi-monopoly in trading in gold and silver coin and bullion throughout Europe and Asia. Venice patricians managed to break and replace the European silver coinage of the Holy Roman Emperors, the Byzantine Empire's silver coinage, and eventually broke the famous Florentine "gold florin" after the 1340's financial blowout — which bankrupted all the Lombards but the Venetians bankers.

The city managed to expand its commercial reach by opportunity, becoming a key trading power, during the Fourth Crusade. In 1202, the crusader leaders had committed to pay to the Doge for the Venetian fleet service to Jerusalem 85,000 silver marks finding that they finally could not honour all of their commitment, due to fewer participants than expected. The crusaders accepted the suggestion that in lieu of payment they assist the Venetians in capturing the byzantine port of Zara, in vassal Dalmatia. In 1204, the majority of the crusade army was diverted to Constantinople, and eventually ended up capturing and sacking the city for their Venetian masters creating the Latin Empire of the East on the ruins of the Greek Empire. The booty, in loot and in territorial conquest was enormous and was a decisive factor in the emergence of the Venetian commercial power. This advance in the Mediterranean triggered several wars with Genoa, the arch competitor of Venice for sea supremacy. By the late 13th century, Venice was feared and recognised as the most prosperous city in all of Europe. At the peak of its power and wealth, it had 36,000 sailors operating 3,300 sail ships, largely dominating Mediterranean exchange. Defending their commercial routes and privilege meant stiff relationships with other Italian city-states, including wars as necessary and tactical alliances. Venice's state arsenal was justly feared and famous

---

[8]To be precise, not accounting for antipope Victor IV of 1138 because of that antipope's short tenure.

all over Europe. It was first conceived simply as a simple ship workshop, but in the 14th century it increasingly took on the functions of a veritable shipyard, especially for big merchant galleys[9] that could also be employed for war, and light galleys. The Venetian arsenal, like the Turkish one, included all the phases of production, from making sails to manufacturing gunpowder. The methods used in the construction of warships anticipated the industrial revolution, in terms of standardisation of production and control over labour. This was clearly the result of government intervention and a policy decision of Venice to establish a discriminating advantage on strategic sea roads.

Venice was also the first state to issue government bonds to its citizens in the same way modern governments issue bonds, to finance their budget. The Venetian *"prestiti"* were the first Eurobonds and if any rating agency had been around in the 1300s, they likely would have been the first AAA-rated government bonds, much needed to finance wars and assess the dominance of the city. Public finance was based on forced bonds and consolidated funds, *"monte"*. These were mostly loans to finance Venice's expansion that had been consolidated into permanent state debt. Holdings in the debt received regular payments of interest, and could be sold on the open market for such securities. The Venetians were the first to develop such an institution. Venitian *"prestiti"* were forced perpetual bonds, with a yield, subscribed in proportion to Venetian citizen's wealth assessed in the city registers, with no specific maturity date, but initially for a short time. In 1262, the Venetian government acknowledged its momentary in capacity to repay creditors, all loans were eventually transformed into long-term loans and the Great Council committed certain tax revenues to the regular payment of 5% annual interest. No physical bonds were issued, but all the perpetuities were registered through the Loan Officers, the *Ufficiali degli prestiti*. An important reason for their success was both their liquidity and fungibility as claims on these bonds could be sold and transferred to others who then enjoyed all the privilege of the previous owners. From time to time, the Venetian government would recall them and repaid the principal. The bonds, which were popular among the

---

[9] A large, usually single-decked medieval ship of shallow draft, propelled by sails and oars and used as a merchant ship or warship in the Mediterranean.

Venetian nobility, had a status of privileged reserve assets and they were used as endowments for charities, or dowries for daughters upon their marriage. A number of happy foreigners were also authorised by the Great Council to hold the bonds. The prestige attached to these assets and their sense of scarcity positioned them as Europe's most exclusive saving products. The largest part of the international business of the Venetian and other Lombard merchant banks was carried out thorough bills of exchange, a synonym for promises to pay. This rather simple instrument involved through the intermediation of a bank, a creditor providing local currency to the debtor in return for a paper bill stating that a certain amount of another currency was payable in relation with a trade at an agreed date, often at the next fair. The repayment was usually in a different currency, so the parties could easily incorporate the price of lending money, an interest payment and an arranger fee, circumventing nicely the church prohibition on usury. In a volatile monetary environment, this business could become treacherous and lead to a financial melt-down comparable to the one which ruined the Florentine bankers in 1345.

For international business, the Florentine florin had become the most common currency, and also served as the primary unit of papal accounting. Venetian merchants needed to mobilise large sums of money carrying great risks that could be rendered in any way by the hours in the commercial centre of Rialto of Venice. Thus, a specific investment structure was designed that enabled short-term partnerships for a trade and through which any Venetian with a little money could have a share. The merchants also pushed for remarkably modern innovations in contracting institutions. Known as *Colleganza*, the limited-liability partnership opened the door for a brand new type of a simple but effective stock market that facilitated large-scale mobilisation of capital for risky long-distance trade. It certainly was one of greatest innovation in business structuring and the direct precursor of the great joint stock companies of a later period, the Dutch VOC or the British Honourable East India Company. Profit was typically split as follows: 3/4 for the sedentary merchant contributing the capital and 1/4 for the travelling merchant, in charge of the cargo. If losses were made, these come out of the sedentary merchant's capital. If the losses exceeded this capital, as would be the case if the travelling merchant incurred large debts overseas, then the sedentary merchant's obligations were limited by his initial investment in the venture. When the travelling merchant came back, the accounts were settled and the joint stock company was dissolved. Over time, a group of extraordinarily rich merchants emerged and in the almost four decades following 1297 they used their resources to entrench and block political and economic competition, not only in Venice but probably beyond in nearby competing cities. In Venice, they made parliamentary participation hereditary and erected barriers to participation in the most lucrative aspects of long-distance trade. This 'oligarch' society has been documented in a unique database on the names of 8,103 parliamentarians and their families' use of the Colleganza. In short, long-distance trade first encouraged and then discouraged institutional dynamism and entrepreneurship with consequences for the revenues of trade and the distribution of wealth and power.

Venice established its leadership in international commerce thanks to both the capability of its merchants and the presence of its navy and soldiers. Strict navigation regulations provided that only Venetian vessels could ship spices to the city harbour. Venetian galley convoys were recognised at sight and respected on sea. The city was known to be a safe and reliable hub for re-exporting goods all over Europe. This leadership premium was definitively leveraged by the shrewd and capable emissaries of the lagoon city strategically positioned all over the key trading centres of the time. From the 13th century onwards, Venice imposed its monopoly over salt trade in the Adriatic, subjecting the coastal towns producing salt to its close control. Salt was exclusively imported by Venice and redistributed via excise men to both Venetian subjects and neighbouring states. The hegemony exerted over the strategic salt trade was the result of a deliberate military policy to control both supply and demand on the salt market and corner it as necessary. This policy became the model on which "Venice had deliberately ensnared all the surrounding subject economies, including the German economy, for her own profit; she drew her living from them, preventing them from acting freely. The 14th century saw the creation of such a powerful monopoly to the advantage of the city-states of Italy that the emerging territorial states like England, France and Spain necessarily suffered the consequences."[10] In Venice, the promulgation of

---

[10] Fernand Braudel, *Civilization and Capitalism, 15th–18th Century: The Perspective of the World*. Century, Harper & Row, Vol. III (1982).

the Capitulare Navigantium[11] and the reorganisation of the galley trade towards an organisation of publicly owned galleys that were auctioned off to private operators (i.e., the wealthiest families) dramatically reduced the economic competition faced by the most powerful families, competition both from commoners and from less-powerful nobles. However, it is likely that communal ownership of galleys not only expressed the solidarity of the Venetian nobility but also strengthened that solidarity in adversity. It came immediately after the political closure was tightened with a series of laws creating the Venetian nobility. Those excluded from the nobility did not give up and discontent continued to accumulate to the point where the political elite realised that their position could be jeopardised and turn into a bitter internal feud. In 1310–1311, the political merchant elite co-opted its most powerful opponents by inducting them into the Great Council ("the Enlargement"). However, the real ruling power would remain in the exclusive newly self-appointed Council of ten. Putting a lid on internecine rivalry and keeping trade as their absolute priority allowed Venice's oligarchs to keep cooperating so that they could exploit the rents from long-distance trade well into the 16th century. In the 14th century, they rather focused on providing innovative solutions to the financial problems of their time, such as the large price fluctuations and availability of strategic commodities; this resulted in the creation of the Wheat Chamber and the Salt Office, which led to establishing two funds, acting as state policy arms that guaranteed the regular supply of wheat and salt to the city.

Venice patricians were very aware of the surrounding competition and almost obsessively put all their efforts in focusing on the trade of the highest value added products of the time such as spice or bullion. In the 15th century, Venice's market share represented a bit less than 50% of the pepper trading and possibly jumped to two-third of the market a century later. Pepper also called the "grain of paradise", was bought, or more precisely exchanged for other goods, in West Africa first and then in India and not only used as a condiment but also to preserve food and for medical

---

[11]A law introduced in 1324 that forbade any merchant from shipping goods with a value in excess of his assessed wealth, thus keeping only a close circle of wealthy patricians in long-distance trade.

purposes. The net profit on imported spices could be between 1 (pepper) and 30 (nutmeg) times their acquisition price. Other valuable spices included cinnamon, ginger, mace or cloves. While big returns could be made, there were also big risks. Death abroad from illness, shipwrecks and piracy were common. Weather delays could also erase the profitability of a cargo, especially if the wind window had shifted. Furthermore, investing in a fleet of large ships including crew and maintenance was not for every Venetian family. This is why the "*Colleganza*", the ancestor of private equity or syndication was such a defining innovation.

The Lagoon City was one of the three city-states in Italy (Florence in 1252, Genoa in 1253 and Venice in 1280), capable of the early reintroduction of gold money as a currency into the Italian peninsula eight centuries after the fall of Rome. Just as most of the 14th century, exchange rates were expressed in Florentine florins, so most of the 15th century rates were denominated in Venetian ducats. Struck in near pure gold, the design of the Venetian gold ducat, or zecchino, remained unchanged for more than 500 years, from its introduction in 1284 to the conquest of Venice by Napoleon's troops in 1797.

For all these reasons, Venice managed to be recognised as the very first real International Financial Centre in Europe, meaning a trusted and attractive place to do business, with an influence that will go far beyond the borders of the city state. However, international finance in Venice, as everywhere else in Europe, was still largely controlled by Florentines who mastered the financial know how. Florentine financial hegemony managed to survive in the 15th century even after the industrial and commercial base for it had gone. Venice's decline started as both Ottoman power and strong European competitors emerged. The wealthiest Venetian nobility had managed to protect itself so well from outsiders that it became entrenched, complacent and incapable of injecting the needed dynamism to innovate and keep the lead. The talents capable of leading the development of the international sea faring venture would not dare waste their time in a city in which there was so little to gain. Both the economic and the political game was closed and under the absolute of the dominant oligarchy. Furthermore, the Venetian navy started to be dominated by more powerful vessels incorporating the latest technical navigation innovations. The maritime strength of the Ottoman Turks would eventually weaken the Venetian hold on the Mediterranean and break their monopoly in the 17th century. A final weakness of the Venetian state was probably the profound division between its entrenched oligarchs on the one hand and, on the other hand, the mainland and its local élites. Venice ceased to exist as an independent state after its conquest by Napoleon Bonaparte in 1797 and the Austrian takeover of the Lagoon City under the Treaty of Campo Formio.

Opportunites Beyond the Known World

Some 200 years following Alexander the Great adventures in the East, there was no sign of China in the knowledge of the classical world. It was all part of a separate and virtually unknown world. Until the 1st century A.D., sericulture was not known by the Roman, but oddly in Rome women wore silk traded from the mysterious Seres people from the land of Serica, the land where silk was produced.[12] From its beginnings in the Western Han (202–209 A.D.) until its height in the Tang dynasty (618–907), the Silk Road had well established commercial connections between the Mediterranean and Asia. The Road followed in fact no single route and was series of routes connecting East to West according to the political situation, the seasons and the quality of the settlements. The "Description of the world" narrating the travels to the East of Marco Polo born in Venice in 1254, at the zenith of Venetian power, provided the revelation of the existence of another world. Marco's account should have been a shock to his contemporary fellowmen, but nobody seemed particularly influenced or impressed. The book was a success but probably regarded as no more than a fantasy, comparable to the epic wandering of Odysseus, cursed by Poseidon for ten years, narrated in Homer's 1178 A.D. Odyssey. From 550 to 1250 A.D., the lack of curiosity and knowledge of the world beyond the horizon was prevalent. It is also probable that Polo did not want to release too many details — including the use of chopsticks, and possibly deliberately omitted to narrate critical and detailed observations as knowledge was considered strategic to the success of remote trading

---

[12]Little is known about Seres, coincidently in Chinese, 絲 (s●) refers to silk as well as fine thread and thread-like objects such as fibre, wire or string.

expeditions. The 13th century introduced a dramatic change in the perception of earth and revealed that the world had expanded, in the most irreversible way; international relationships, and in particular merchant relationships, entered a new era of profound changes until the end of the 15th century.

In the 12th century, already a mysterious letter began to circulate in Europe. The first authentic mention of Prester John is to be found in the "Chronicle" of Otto, Bishop of Freising, in 1145. It told of a magical kingdom in the East that was in danger of being overrun by infidels and barbarians. This letter was supposedly written by a Christian King known as Prester John who had converted to Nestorianism.[13] There were over 100 different versions of the letter published over the following few centuries. Most often, the letter was addressed to Manuel of Constantinople, the Byzantine Emperor of Rome, Frederick I Barbarossa, Holy Roman Emperor and other princes though other editions were also often addressed to the Pope or the King of France. Although there seems to be some scepticism, many raised unreasonable expectations about this kingdom, comprising the "three Indias", but India was a very vague notion in the Middle Ages: "vice-free peaceful kingdom", where "honey flows in our land and milk everywhere abounds." The Pope sent Philippus, one of his friends, for him, the Portuguese also went for him, and countless other explorations had the same objective of reaching and discovering Prester John's Kingdom that had rivers filled with gold and was the home of the Fountain of Youth. Throughout the centuries, editions of the letter kept getting better and more interesting. The kingdom would be presumably located in Kara-Khitan,[14] in Jordan, in Armenia, at the foot of the Caucasus or even in Abyssinia. The letters are probably Nestorian[15] forgeries. Either way, this enigma profoundly affected the geographical knowledge of Europe by stimulating interest in foreign lands and sparking expeditions outside of

---

[13] The doctrine based on the belief that Jesus existed as two persons, the man Jesus and the divine Son of God, rather than as a single unified divine person.

[14] A nomadic empire situated in Eastern Mongolian, using many elements of the Chinese Liao dynasty culture and conquered by the Mongolian empire in 1218. Little remains known about their civilisation.

[15] The Nestorians are followers of Nestorius (c. AD 386–451), who was Archbishop of Constantinople. Nestorianism was considered a heresy by the Roman Catholic Church.

Europe. Vasco de Gama even carried with him letters of introduction to this supposed Christian ruler. The legend lived on as cartographers continued to include Prester John's Kingdom on maps through the 17th century.

In the late 13th century, most of Europe knew nothing about the East, except for myths based on classical fragments and what was extrapolated from Christian teachings or the Prester John story. A few cartographers, including the author of the famous Catalan Atlas of 1373, benefited from Polos observations and had most likely managed to assimilate Marco's work. This would decisively influence long haul navigation, and many navigators would review Polo's accounts including Columbus who carried a copy of the travels of Marco Polo on his journey to the New World. As a brief encounter between East and West on sea, it was probably the Chinese Yuan ships of this era that Marco Polo caught sight of, consisting of four-masted high sea junks. They were much larger than most of the ships cruising in the Indian sea at the time, specifically the dhows, and capable of handling a crew of 1,000. The Yuan (Mongol) dynasty of the 13th and 14th centuries maintained a large high sea fleet, and had defined a policy of sending imperial emissaries to Sumatra, Ceylon and southern India to establish influence, and Yuan merchants gradually took over the spice trade from the Arabs.

But all this information would remain dormant, almost in indifference, just like Polo's return to Venice after travelling East for almost 25 years dealing with the Great Khan and exploring unchartered territories. Venice remembered that strangely dressed people went to their Venetian family Mansion in the district of San Giovanni Crisostomo struggling to get recognised and to speak proper Italian. Coincidently, as Polo was on his journey back home, Kublai Kahn passed away: the Silk Road got cut by tribal rebellion reclaiming their territory. Three years after returning to Venice, Marco Polo assumed command of a Venetian galley in the war against Genoa. He was captured in 1496 or 1498 and jailed in Genoa. While being there, he met a fellow prisoner, the Arthurian adventure writer Rustichello of Pisa. When prompted, he dictated his adventures to Rustichello who probably incorporated tales of his own as well. A Genoese-Venetian peace treaty in 1299 allowed Marco Polo to return home. Polo's account, was originally written in *lingua franca* by Rustichello who acted as a kind of ghost-writer. They were titled "Books of the Marvels of the

World," but are better known in English as "The Travels of Marco Polo." The book was a huge success, though many readers questioned Polo's reliability, possibly leading to the book's popular Italian title, "Il Milione," short for "The Million Lies." This may explain why the Polos, dubbed as odd but entertaining fellows, never got properly honoured for their explorations by the sceptical Patrician families of the Lagoon City. However, they may have influenced Venetian finance with their account of paper which caught on Europe in the years after their return. Polo stood by the book, however, and went on to start a business, marry, and father three daughters. When Polo was on his deathbed in 1324, visitors urged him to admit his book was just fiction, to which he famously proclaimed, "I have not told half of what I saw."

Another great adventurer, the Moroccan Muslim Ibn Battuta (1304–1368), who travelled mainly to Muslim countries with Muslim governments in Africa, Persia, India and the Far East, wrote a detailed account of his travels and narratives of life in the East (*The Rihlah*, or *The Travels*). Among other things, he specifically narrated the profitable practice of credit at the court of the Kings: "Every person proceeding to the court of the King of India, Sultan Muhammad Shah, must need have a gift ready to present to him, in order to gain his favours. The sultan repays him for it with a gift many times its value. When his subjects grew accustomed to this practice, the merchants in Sind and India began to furnish each newcomer with thousands of dinars as a loan, and to supply him with whatever he might desire to offer as a gift or to use on his own behalf, such as riding animals, camels and goods. They placed both their money and their persons at his service, and stood before him like attendants. When he reached the Sultan, he received a magnificent gift from him and payed off his debt to them. This trade of theirs was a flourishing one and brought in vast profits."

In the early Middle Ages, European civilisation was easily overtaken by the magnificent Song Dynasty in China and in the refined Byzantine Empire, the flourishing world of Islam, albeit showing the first signs of political division. In Carolingian Europe, forms of credit were still primitive until the beginning of the first Crusade, when the expansion of trade and contact with the Byzantine and Arab worlds, favoured the development of financial innovation. Only in the 16th century, with the disappearance of the Byzantine Empire and a weakening Ottoman Empire, Europe was able to compete with the China of the Ming dynasty. The Chinese world was dominated by a veneration of the past and the constant reference to traditional models, whilst in Europe there was business and political support to find new trading routes and acceptance of ideas coming from outside. Despite the wars and the epidemic diseases, the final centuries of the Middle Ages in Europe were characterised by an inventive spirit that was made up, rather than by a series of epoch-defining events, by the efforts of artisans, merchant bankers and artists who on a daily basis sought to improve the efficiency of their work and gradually broaden their ambitions in terms of scientific knowledge, economic footprint, cultural reach and military strength. Over time, it was the sum of a series of small-scale advances that was to be in the end of extraordinary importance.

In 1405, about 6,200 nautical miles away from Venice, close to a place Marco Polo had been travelling, an army of shipbuilders and scientists near Nanjing, was preparing China for the greatest sea adventure of the Ming dynasty. The Great Ming Armada was preparing for the first of its seven diplomatic journeys as far as West Africa, at the time the Venetian were consolidating their power in the Mediterranean. All the ships of Columbus and Da Gama combined could have been stored on a single deck of a single vessel of this fleet that set sail under the command of Admiral Zheng He. According to reasonable expectation, there should have been a wealth of records by contemporaries. But apart from a few records by Zheng's followers about their personal experiences and anecdotes by some Ming scholars, the Ming government from Manchu origin, and officials of the time paid very little heed to it.

The greatest seafarer in China's history, Zheng was not even a Han Chinese. Born Ma He, he was a Central Asian Muslim from the mountainous heart of Asia, several weeks travel from the closest port. He grew up speaking Arabic and Chinese, learning much about the world to the west and its geography and customs. Zheng was the son of a rural official in the Mongol province of Yunnan, taken captive as an invading Chinese army overthrew the Mongols in 1382. Ritually castrated, he was trained as an imperial eunuch and assigned to the court of Zhu Di, Prince of Yan. Within 20 years, he had become one of the prince's chief aides, a key strategist in the rebellion that who would lead his Prince in 1402 to usurp the throne as Chinese emperor Yong Le (1402–1424), born Zhu Di. The third Ming emperor was unique in the annals of Imperial China for he pursued an active maritime policy to explore Southeast Asia and the Indian Ocean. Renamed Zheng after his exploits at the battle of Zhenglunba, near Beijing, he was chosen in 1405 to lead one of the most powerful navies ever assembled in human history. Over the next 28 years (1405–1433), Zheng He commanded seven fleets that visited 37 countries, through Southeast Asia to faraway Africa and Arabia. In 1420, the Ming navy dwarfed the combined navies of Europe. Although all the conditions were met for Nanjing to become a strong shipping, financial and trading hub, it mostly remained a political power city, capital of the Empire throughout ten dynasties. The imperial city design purposefully served as the blueprint for the Beijing Forbidden City. Most of the «Great Treasure» fleet was built nearby at the Dragon Bay shipyard near Nanjing. The treasure ships equipped with nine masts and manned by 500 men, set sail in July 1405, they were over 300-feet long and 150-feet wide, the biggest being 440-feet long and 186-across, capable of carrying up to 1,000 sailors, displaced no less than 10,000 tons and had an aspect ratio (width to length) of 0.254; in other words, they were wide and bulky. The ships made a massive difference with the frail 135-feet Venetian galleys. Alongside from the treasure ships, the admiral's great fleet also contained a variety of other, specialised vessels: "equine ships",[16] warships, supply ships and water tankers. The objective of the Emperor Yong Le was to boost his damaged prestige as a throne usurper by a prestigious display of China's might abroad, sending spectacular fleets on great voyages and by bringing foreign ambassadors to his court. However, as the new emperor was wary of a possible power struggle from an emerging sea aristocracy, he decided to put foreign trade under a strict imperial monopoly by taking control of overseas Chinese trade thus restricting the emergence of a class of powerful sea merchants. The emperor was probably concerned that too wealthy a class of merchants would ultimately be tempted to challenge is power in favour of a political order more inclined to focus on the development of trade and innovation than on Court etiquette.

---

[16] Ships designed to carry horses.

Zheng He's imperial first fleet was truly extraordinary as it included almost 28,000 men on 317 ships. Loaded with Chinese silk, gold and silverware, copper utensils, and porcelain, the junks visited ports around the Indian Ocean. Here, Arab and African merchants exchanged the spices, ivory, medicines, rare woods and pearls so eagerly sought by the Chinese imperial court. The fleet sailed along China's coast to Champa close to Vietnam and, after crossing the South China Sea, visited Java, Sumatra and reached Sri Lanka by passing through the Strait of Malacca. On the way back, it sailed along the west coast of India and returned home in 1407. Envoys from Calicut in India and several countries in Asia and the Middle East also boarded the ships to pay visits to China. Zheng He's second and third voyages taken shortly afterwards, followed roughly the same route. In the fall of 1413, Zheng He set out with 30,000 men to Arabia on his fourth and most ambitious voyage. From Hormuz, he coasted around the Arabian boot to Aden at the mouth of the Red Sea. The arrival of the fleet caused a sensation in the region, and 19 countries sent ambassadors to board Zheng He's ships with gifts for Emperor Yong Le. In 1417, after two years in Nanjing and touring other cities, the foreign envoys were escorted home by Zheng He. On this trip, he sailed down the east coast of Africa, stopping at Mogadishu, Matindi, Mombassa and Zanzibar and may have reached Mozambique. The sixth voyage in 1421 also went to the African coast. Emperor Yong Le died in 1424 shortly after Zheng He's return. In 1421, China capital city moved from Nanjing to Beijing, far from the sea. The emperor successors felt the expeditions were harmful to China, fearing opening up too much to the unknown world, and discouraged further endeavours. Was there any chance that the Chinese Emperor heard that Tamerlan was preparing to invade China just before he died in 1405. This invasion plan which followed the Turko-Mongol conqueror's destruction of Delhi in 1398 could explain the Imperial decision to keep a stealthier profile and confine trade to the borders of China. The Chinese world was then dominated by a veneration of the past and constant reference to traditional models, whilst in Europe there was business and political support to find new trading routes and acceptance of ideas coming from outside. Yet, in 1430 Admiral He was sent on a final seventh voyage, as the new emperor decided to stop long haul exploration. Now 60 years old, Zheng He revisited the Persian Gulf, the Red Sea and

Africa. He possibly died on his way back in 1433 in India, or chose to finish his days in one of the Muslim seaports that he had previously visited. Seven times, from 1405 to 1433, the treasure fleets set off for the unknown, bringing back to China a vast web of trading links — from Taiwan to the Persian Gulf, preparing for the development of what could have possibly been a very powerful international financial and trading centre. However, the Hongxi Emperor ended further expeditions and left the Great Fleet rot in its Nanjing harbour. The long haul expeditions of Zheng He, who was himself a eunuch, were strongly supported by eunuch administrators in the court and bitterly opposed by the Confucian scholar bureaucrats. The completion of the internal Chinese Grand Canal was perhaps also seen as a better and safer use of Chinese scarce resources at this time compared to expensive and potentially dangerous long haul expeditions to the unknown world, especially since China had more to fear from land invasions than maritime intrusions.

In a remotely connected world, the fall of Constantinople, the trading gate to Asia, to the Ottoman Turks in 1453, jeopardised the trade of spices and silk with remote Asia. This awkward situation led the Portuguese fleet to investigate other sea trading routes as the overland was becoming unsafe. Columbus, a Genoese who had learned sailing in the Eastern Mediterranean, tried to interest the King of Portugal to back him in opening new navigation routes to the West of Asia but ended up serving the King of Spain, after gaining the support of Queen Isabella of Castile. Instead of reaching Japan, as he had intended, Columbus landed in the Bahamas Islands on the morning of 12th October 1492, which he mistakenly thought was "the Indies". Columbus would maintain, despite mounting contrarian evidence, that these territories were part of Asia.

Zheng's ships had probably been burnt and sunk decades before, just after his last voyage and the Xuande Emperor made every effort to "systematically destroy all official records of the voyages." The Chinese navy collapsed, and by 1503 it was down to one tenth of its Early Ming size. The anti-maritime league grew more powerful at the court and made its power known through imperial edicts. By 1500, it was made a capital offense for a Chinese to go to sea in a ship with more than two masts without special permission. A ruling of 1525 authorised the destruction of larger classes of ships. China entered an isolationist phase quite similar to that which closed Japan for two centuries. The navy and Chinese-borne overseas trade had by then disappeared. The imperial administration's attitude led during the Ming period to a decline in knowledge in scientific disciplines including mathematics and astronomy, aggravated until 1567 by the prohibition of maritime trade with abroad. All of this made China very different from other civilisations. Even when the state did not take the economic initiative, it oversaw, regulated and repressed. The emperor's authority should not have to depend on goodwill, the right attitude, or personal virtue: it depended on the careful monitoring to ensure that his power could never be put at risk. Despotisms abounded in Europe, too, but they were mitigated by law, by the authority of the Church, by territorial fragmentation, and within states, by the division of power between the various centres and local seigneurial authority. If the talented people were unhappy or persecuted, they would pack and move to another place. The history of time provides an interesting indication of the way power and strategic information were intertwined in ancient China. The early astronomical water-powered monumental and rather precise clocks of the Tang and Sung dynasties were imperial pieces reserved for the exclusive use of the emperor and his astrologers. The court treated time and knowledge of time as a confidential aspect of sovereignty, not to be shared with ordinary people. Compared to Europe, the China clock technology initially advanced, but later lagged behind since there was not a wide popular use of clocks to stimulate progress and foster innovation.

In spite of what had been decided by China's rulers of the time, Zheng He explorations remain an extraordinary accomplishment for all of mankind. As the Ming imperial court chose to keep away from international trading, Malacca, on the Malayan peninsula, Zheng He's most important port after those in China, became in the 15th century the hub of a prosperous regional trading network that extended across Southeast Asia and up to China. No doubt the vision of the imperial Great fleet anchoring in the port of Malacca must have changed their perception of the world forever.

Landing in another World

In 1513, the Portuguese landed on "Lintin island", near Guangzhou, China, in a Chinese junk coincidentally leased from Malacca, and erected a stone marker claiming the land for the King of Portugal, much to the displeasure of China which expelled the delegation in 1521. In 1557, the Portuguese merchant fleet established a trade base with China and Japan in Macau; it became an active seaport for both Chinese and Portuguese merchants conveniently located in front of Guangzhou, on the North–South route from Japan to Malacca. Lisbon negotiated leasehold for Macau in return for tribute paid to Beijing and established a walled village there. It cost about 600–800 gold florins to reach Cathay, the ancient name for China, but the journey was long: no less than 300 days of sea, almost a year with the necessary stops. The coming of European traders stimulated the Chinese Hokkien trading communities in Luzon (Philippines) and Nagasaki (Japan) but due to the indifference and lack of support of the China Ming emperors, they would end up serving the interest of either the Spanish or the Dutch.

Macau quickly became a prosperous trading seaport. Not so far way, Goa already functioned from 1510 as the capital of Portuguese India, next to the Daman and Diu enclaves located on the Arabian seacoast. Another chapter of the relationships between East and the West had just started. However, the domination of the Portuguese navy would always suffer from the lack of control of a consistent network of choke points in maritime commerce. Although they would patrol the South China sea, the strait of Malacca and the West coast of India for domination, the Portuguese were never in a position to prevent Muslims shippers from cargoing pepper and fine spices from the Moluccas to the strait of Sundas, from Atjeh (Northern Sumatra) to the Red sea and Alexandria where the Venetian merchants carried their trade throughout Europe. Gradually, the Portuguese lost their outpost to the attacks of the VOC, the Dutch East India Company, with which they fought every possible battle to bar their Asian and European competitors from the spice trade culminating with the Dutch occupation of Bantam (Indonesia) in 1662. Another commodity, already popular in Constantinople, was quickly expanding and changing social habits and lifestyle in Europe after being traded along the ancient arteries of the Levant: the commerce of coffee beans stretched from Mecca to Aleppo and then on to Baghdad and Mosul to the east and Alexandria and Cairo to the west. The English and Dutch became the main European coffee traders in the 17th century purchasing their coffee from transhipment ports on the West Indian coast in Gujarat or Malabar where they had permanent facilities. Pockets of free merchants survived in some safe areas: the Coromandel (India) merchants prospered, but their cargo were taken care of in the shadow of the dominant power of both the Dutch East India Company, and EIC, the British Honourable East India Company. Force was never the best long term option as it focused even more local energy to find alternative solutions: when the Dutch tried to compel Malabar pepper growers to bring their cargo to Cochin, they only fostered the revival of the Calicut free port, Cochin's historical rival. And when alternative shipping solutions were made available on the Coromandel coast, this new offer made the fortune of the English, the French who were confined mainly to their small outpost in Pondicherry, and other Asian shippers.

The ancient walled city of Pingyao in Shanxi Province founded in the 14th century can hardly be called an international financial centre. It offers however an interesting perspective on the early days of merchant banking in China, and beyond, due to its position on the path of the Silk Road. The city built behind thick walls was once the banking centre of Ming and Qing Imperial China, where the first Chinese banks originated. China, is well known for its notable financial history; paper money was first used under the Song dynasty in China some 500 years before it became a practice in Europe, in the form of letters of credit for transfers over large distances; an invention that was probably spurred by the Silk Road trade, as merchants used it as a convenient way to trade until 1450. The first draft bank (*"piaohao"*) originated under the reign of Emperor Daoguang (Qing Dynasty) when Lei Lutai, born in 1770, converted his modest Xiyuchen Pigment shop into the Rishengchang[17] Draft Bank, which specialised in exchange and the remittance of funds. It was the first institution to issue cheques in 1823. Nevertheless, just like its illustrious Italian predecessors 6,000 miles away, the firm expanded and managed around 100 branches in China. The practice of bank drafts, caught on in the city of Pingyao and it became the banking centre of the Qing Dynasty (1644–1911). There were 32 *piaohao,* with 475 branches covering most of China, some of them even had sub-branches in foreign neighbouring countries including Russia, Mongolia, Japan and even the Malay

---

[17] Sunrise Prosperity draft bank.

Archipelago. At the time Chinese bankers were held in lower esteem than peasants and tradesmen, and junior staff loyalty was ensured by keeping clerks in the Pingyao residence for the first three years of their apprenticeship. During this time, they were banned from marrying and could only visit their family if one of their parents passed away. Finally, a crisis of confidence in those banks resulted in a run of silver. With the 1911 revolution and the beginning of the first Republic of China, the draft banks floundered and fell, with their unwillingness to adapt or, at least, being very slow to adapt to the changing financial mandate in modern China. Subsequently, the government withdrew its remittance business, as currency unification removed the need for silver trade between cities.

Developing international trade across China was inconvenient as the Chinese imperial administration requested that foreign trade should be held only at the port of Canton ("Guangzhou"). A single location was easier to levy and collect taxes on the goods traded, monitor foreigners and control trade. Foreigners sailing to China were allowed to reside only on the island of Macao as they awaited favourable winds to sail back home. The real issues for the British therefore became not opium but freedom to trade. In China, opium was like spices a normal item of use and trade for centuries before the 1840 war, and for many decades following the Nanjing Treaty.[18] Not until the later 1790s did the imperial administration start to worry about its growing and adverse use. In the 1820s, China began to prohibit opium imports, though the bans failed to stop Chinese people entirely from growing or buying it in increasing quantities. The official concerns were the impact of opium consumption on work and the payment in silver made to foreign merchants for opium, and thus possibly leaving China. However, most of the money earned by merchants from the opium trade was reinvested in Chinese tea, rhubarb and silk which were in high demand in Europe, especially Britain. Bringing back tea rather than silver was a much more lucrative trade. When MacCartney headed the first British embassy reaching Beijing in 1793, to convince the Chinese emperor to open northern port cities to British traders, to diversify trade

---

[18] Opium was in normal use even in Europe for a long time, especially in the form of laudanum, and was routinely used by many personalities, including Premier Gladstone in Britain and Chancellor Bismarck in Germany, and it was seen no worse than gin or tobacco.

besides opium, and allow British ships to be repaired on Chinese territory, he hardly realised that he was dealing with the most luxurious court of all Chinese history. Even, the generosity of the British presents brought to the Emperor appeared insignificant beside the splendours of the imperial court. The Empire was governed by extremely strict and detailed rules and procedures, and in the Chinese official world, every tiny or trivial ceremonial detail mattered as an indicator of power and status. Emperor Qianlong refused any trade, regarded the embassy as a tributary mission, the only diplomatic system acceptable for imperial China, and ordered MacCartney to perform the kow-tow.[19] He urged him to deliver the following message to King George III: "We possess all things. I set no value on objects strange or ingenious, and have no use for your country's manufactures — Curios and the boasted ingenuity of their devices I prize not." He warned that any British vessels putting ashore in any other point other than Canton would be expelled. For Britain, winner of Waterloo and commanding the most powerful navy in the world, this was resented as an unforgivable outrage. The Chinese empire MacCartney visited had been the most populated country and the world richest economy for about two millennia. In the following two centuries, all of that would be changed: China would be semi-occupied, pauperised and torn by civil war and internal feuds.

Two Scottish merchants and adventurers, William Jardine and his partner James Matheson owned Jardine Matheson & Co, known as "the Firm", that was the largest importer of opium into China. Jardine once wrote to a missionary boarding his ship: "We have no hesitation in stating to you openly that our principal reliance is on opium…[which] by many is considered an immoral traffic, yet such traffic is so absolutely necessary to give any vessel a reasonable chance of defraying her expenses, that we trust you will have no objection." Tea, silk, cotton and opium were traded through different routes between China, Britain and India, and contributed as a significant source of revenues for the British Empire. Competition was fierce and in order to win the race to delivery, the firm took delivery of the first of many steamships in 1835, in order to stay one step ahead of

---

[19] Act of supplication made by kneeling and knocking his head to the floor which was required for foreigners to be made in the presence of the Chinese Emperor.

its rivals. From 1834 onwards, the Qing government itself debated the legalisation of opium, but ultimately decided against it and appointed Commissioner Lin Zexu to eliminate the trade in China completely. Lin's diplomatic counterpart was Charles Elliot, British Chief Superintendent of Trade in China, who became involved in extraterritorial disputes and ultimately banned all trade with Canton in 1839, including a blockade of foreigners in Canton. This was the final escalation before the war. When the Royal Navy having advanced up the Yangzi, was on the brink of storming Nanjing, China's ancient capital, both sides signed the 1842 treaty. China agreed to open four more ports; to having foreign consuls stationed at each; and to treating British and Chinese officials as equals. The Chinese would also pay a sizeable indemnity; and the British got the rock of Hong Kong, where they would be able to maintain merchants under the control of their own magistrates. Opium was not even mentioned in the treaty, but was mentioned as the responsible for a war. The fate of Hong Kong is known as it came under British stewardship becoming one of the most successful financial centres in Asia. The war can probably be simply interpreted as the result of an asymmetry of culture and interest: it was not imaginable for the Chinese court to recognise, given the customs of the time, that there could be any other issue in the demand of the Son of Heaven, and the outrage felt by British supremacy, the leading economic power after Waterloo, that China could persist in restricting their irresistible desire to freely develop their lucrative trade. What remained worrisome is that within 16 years of the 1842 Treaty of Nanjing, China abolished the opium import restrictions. By 1860, and much more so by 1900, the Chinese were growing at home many times as much opium as the British, or anyone else, could import, and they kept on doing it, in increasing quantities and virtually throughout all the wars and revolutions of the 20th century.[20]

---

[20]Gelber Harry, cf bibliography (2006).

Chapter 3

THE SHIFT TOWARDS
THE NORTH OF EUROPE
IN THE 16th CENTURY

The Ascent of the Flanders, with a Little Help
from Columbus

From 1500 to 1550 onward, the loss of Venice domination on Levantian trade, the repeated piracy attacks on northern fleets and merchants in the Mediterranean from 1570,[1] and the arrival of the Spanish and Portuguese precious metal from South America to Flanders and Brabant turned the wheel. Although in sheer numbers, they were not great, the Portuguese played a role that is not to be underestimated in Bruges first and then later in Antwerpe: this included merchant traders, representatives of the Portuguese King and courtiers. During the course of the 15th century, two regions in Europe, the north (Flanders, Brabant) and the south (Mediterranean Italy) started to fight for

---

[1] Northern competitors ousted traditional suppliers from their old market area and enjoyed a period of formative industrial growth long before colonial markets became a significant source of income.

dominant business influence all over Europe. The merchant banking Italian communities in Paris and London were dependent on those in Bruges — which logically became the key place for the financing of the fast growing business in northern Europe. Since the early 11th century, Bruges' direct entrance to the Zwin, the bay facing Bruges, had been disappearing due to the natural accumulation of sediment. As a consequence, Bruges could have quickly lost its function as a seaport in which international trade activities used to take place. Fortunately, the particularly violent storms of 1134 managed to protect and renew its connection with the Atlantic. This natural benefit revitalised city life and industries, recalling the golden age of three centuries. Bruges became one of the best wool manufacture region in Europe.

As seen in a number of international financial centres, the prosperity of a hub is intimately linked with its interaction with different cultures capable of fostering a rich dialogue and unlocking innovation. The [French] Burgundian brought this foreign contribution in Bruges, as before them, the two main powers, Flanders and Brabant, only stirred up uninspired political fragmentation of this region. The dukes of Burgundy unified and reorganised the political system, and built one of the ducal palaces in Bruges. This caused and encouraged cultural and artistic activities around the ducal court, courts of the magnates who were familiar with Burgundy's French style of rule, and courts of senior clergymen. The level of this cultural prosperity was the highest in the contemporary northern Alps. The manufacture of woolen cloth had shifted within southern Netherlands. No longer was it concentrated in the great cities of northern Flanders including Arras, Lille, Cambrai, Tournai or Ghent and Ypres. Similarly, the diamond cutting industry which greatly contributed to the fame of the city developed from the decline of Venice which formerly had a monopoly of the diamond trade. Bruges had a long standing trade relationship with England and Scandinavia, it was the first city to create a *bourse*; in reality a simple meeting place for merchants dealing in money and bills of exchange; not yet a real exchange, but still the beginning of one of the most important institution in price discovery of financial assets and in confronting offer and demand. Antwerp later moved this idea forward to create a real exchange and quotation platform for merchants.

Bruges situated at the end of the northern trade route from Venice, gradually took the lead as the pre-eminent diamond-cutting centre and the city reputation only increased in time. The first arrival of Genoese merchants in 1277 meant that the city acted as a hub between the Atlantic and the Mediterranean. No sooner had spice been first imported from the Levant, enormous inflows of capital activated banking in Bruges. The first bourse was opened in 1309, and Bruges became an international centre with the most elaborate money market and trading tools in the Low Countries during the 14th century. However, when the Zwin channel which gave Bruges access to the sea and prosperity started silting, the Bruges money market and the city's fortune began to decline, especially as Antwerp, situated only 90 km east was offering better communications and exchange, and new more effective diamond working techniques. The Bruges state became hostile to banks due to a frightening increasing number of bankruptcies and recurrent accusations that money-changers picked and culled coins. Money-changers "favored debasement whenever their cash reserves were running low because of a crisis in the money market," whereas the authorities preferred monetary stability. The climate was particularly hostile for foreign merchants who, between 1484 and 1488, were asked to either move out of town or resettle elsewhere.

Antwerp became a natural choice for the shift, stimulated by the presence of a dynamic Sephardic Jewish community which had returned to Northern Europe after the Spanish and Portuguese expulsion in 1490 and contributed to opening up the precious stones industry and the sugar trade. Antwerp became independent from the Duchy of Brabant in the 13th century. In 1356, the city was annexed to the County of Flanders and lost very many privileges, partly to Bruges' advantage. Fifty years later the political and economic tide turned again and the run-up to the city's Golden Age started and it turned into a world class metropolis: it became home to hundreds of merchants, tens of guilds and several trading houses. Antwerp was a centre of trade for craftsmen, particularly those in the luxury arts, such as jewellery, sculpture, fine metalwork and tapestry. The city protected by canals as a line of defense was located on one bank of the river Scheldt, and linked to the North Sea by the Westerschelde estuary. Great storm floods made the Scheldt more accessible, enabling shipping traffic to flourish. Sailing a large ship on the Scheldt was quite technical as sailors needed to keep aware of tides, mud flats and salt marshes. However, the city became the larger port for the trade of pepper and cinnamon two precious spices in Europe, thanks to Portuguese importation from the Azores, the Canaries and Madeira, and the western coast of Africa. It also became the capital for trading sugar in Europe, which was still considered a spice. A powerful Antwerp–Lisbon partnership created even more favourable condition for the emergence of a new international trading centre. The regulatory environment in Antwerp was much less strict than in other cities and this led to easier interactions within guilds and across industries. The city was for this reason a desirable location for craftsmen and traders. In 1501, the King of Portugal Manuel I chose Antwerp as the market for the spices his ships were beginning to bring from the West Indies. In Antwerp, syndicates of merchant bankers competed for spice contracts, paying in advance for spices to be delivered when the fleet arrived. From 1503, the re-export of Asian spices from Lisbon to Antwerp was working very well at the expense of the Italian spice business, and in particular that of Venice. In 1515, Antwerp opened a Bourse, in a dedicated building where locals and international traders could gather to conduct business and where regulation was kept to the minimum. It was a large success, and by 1531 an even better Bourse was built outside the city. Traders were then not obliged to trade commodities directly; they were buying and selling rights to commodities, mostly through contracts for future delivery structured as bills of exchange: Trading of finance products had taken over trading of physical products.

In the 1520, the trade was so profitable that half of the revenues of King John III of Portugal came from the re-export of spice to the north of Europe. In Antwerp, merchant bankers continued to compete fiercely for spice contracts, paying in advance for cargoes to be delivered when the fleet arrived. The long delay between the setting of the purchase price and delivery, together with the volatility of prices, made these contracts highly speculative, but they were opportunistically splitting the risk between hedgers and final risk takers. As a consequence, a vigorous commodity forward market grew up, trading not only in spices but also in other commodities with volatile prices, such as grain, salt, and herring. Optional contracts allowing the buyer (or the seller) to cancel the acquisition (or the delivery) of a cargo were frequently used and early foreign exchange volatility based instruments became very popular. Trading in commodity derivatives took place in the context of a widespread gambling climate including lotteries and wagers of all kind. But this would not last for too long before Venice took the necessary steps to re-establish its power on the spice market. Venice strategists made a number of tactical moves to control important secondary routes in Europe, such as Marseille (France) and facilitate the development of a secondary route which would gradually erode the Portuguese position. The Ottoman Turkish Empire under Soliman the Great, worked hard to reestablish its dominance and built another secured spice route with the city of Aleppo as a secondary hub, where the Venetians readied the shipping of goods to Europe.

The Pagaddertorens, little octagonal towers built in the 16th century, were located in the corners of rich Antwerp merchant homes as watchtowers. At the top was a platform with a panoramic view of the river. The watch had to announce ships arriving on the river carrying rich cargoes of spices and silks. The well informed merchants then hurriedly bought stocks of these ships on the Antwerp stock exchange, making fortunes by advance knowledge. The Escaut region became Europe's most active trading centre for silk cloth, delicate glass, books, fine metal work and diamond cutting. By the mid-1500s, ten jetties and eight inland ports were built to facilitate and accompany this growth. Antwerp had become "the centre of the entire international economy, something Bruges had never been even at its height."[2] The city had successfully started new intermittent fairs which gradually extended themselves to make a complete round the year cycle replacing the illustrious fairs of Champagne. It attracted numerous merchants and, in particular, the English cloth merchants and those coming overland from Western Germany, around Cologne. The English cloth exporters, 'the Merchant Adventurers', many of them London Mercers, were not allowed to sell English woolen cloth in Flanders, but were permitted to do so in Brabant. Therefore, they began to settle agents in Antwerp between fairs. As a result, a considerable cloth dyeing finishing industry grew up around the city of Antwerp, the finished goods being later sold to the West of Germany and the Northern European market. The city gave them privilege and a convenient location in which to settle and organise their trade. With the export of unfinished and undyed wollen white cloth, the national industry of England increased so as to represent

---

[2] Braudel, Fernand. *The Perspective of the World*, 1985 (Book 3), The Wheels of Commerce (Book 2), Civilization & Capitalism, 15th–18th century, University of California Press, First Edition (1992, Originally published in 1985).

a very significant part of the Antwerp economy. These exports became critical for the English economy and London became the principal harbor for cloth export to Antwerp for at least half a century. For this, Napoleon Bonaparte would famously declare that "Antwerp is a pistol aimed at the heart of England".

The Portuguese too were early in setting up a permanent base in Antwerp and started to trade wine and sugar, uncut diamonds directly shipped from India then gold from the New World and ivory from Africa. Portuguese traders settled in Antwerp, were buying German copperwares for the African trade from the 1470s, and silver for Asia after 1504; they sold sugar and spices from Atlantic islands and the Indian Ocean. The Germans continued to bring their metal products (copper and silver) there. The only known merchant company of Germanic origin that competed in size with the Italian companies, was the Great Ravensburg Trading Society founded by Henggi Humpis in the Imperial Free City of Ravensburg in 1380, at a business crossroad near Lake Constance and the Alps. For 150 years, the company made a name all over Europe first in operating paper mills and extended its business to other areas including the trading of precious metals. The company was not more specialised than its Italian or Hanseatic counterparts, as an early intuition of modern portfolio theory, diversification of business was of the essence in the Middle Ages. In 1494, the Fuggers sent their first deliveries of copper from Hungary to the Portuguese crown in Antwerp. By the beginning of the 16th century, the two annual fairs held in Antwerp, the Pentecost Fair in spring and the St. Bavo's Fair in August, were even more popular than the city's Friday markets.

Antwerp also had a policy of religious toleration, which attracted a large business minded and dynamic orthodox Jewish community. Trade was expanding in Antwerp but finance remained securely in Bruges, where exchange rates continued to be fixed daily on the Place de la Bourse, under the control of the Florentine consular house. Payment continued to be arranged in Bruges, just as goods had been previously delivered in Bruges, but paid for at the Champagne Fairs. From the end of the 15th century onwards, Genoese merchants came down to reside in Antwerp after the decline of Bruges and formed a Nation. In 1532, the Emperor Charles V recognised the Genoese Nation in Antwerp. It became one of the most powerful trade communities. The lottery as an instrument of public finance management reappeared in Flanders after being banned by the Church in 1215 (Ghent, Utrecht and Brussels, the later even guaranteed safe conduct for the participants coming out of town). For almost 100 years, Antwerp remained the commercial capital of northern Europe, until the religious and political events of the 1560s and 1570s intervened. The city managed to develop differentiating competitive advantages, first in introducing a real bourse, which was held in a dedicated building with real quotations, second in creating a well-regulated legal environment, third in offering a new generation of financial instruments — in particular, price for future delivery (futures) on commodities quoted spot every day and short-term sovereign loans. Forward contracts were particularly suitable to bills, e.g., the round-trip or *ricorsa* bills, which embedded differences in interest rates. Merchant bankers who had cash available and an in-depth understanding of the market were keen to arbitrage positions on the difference between the spot and the future price. The use of forward contract was often seen as an attempt to manipulate the market, especially since these early "Futures" were not as standardised and liquid as the one we use today. As far as sovereign loans were concerned, the catastrophic experience of early merchant bankers did not bring much moderation to the sovereign loan practices, and the mistakes made in Florence by the Bardis, Peruzzis and later the Medicis were repeated, resulting in the Habsburg bankruptcies and the implosion of the Fuggers of Augsburg. Like their Italian counterparts in other countries, the Fuggers managed to understand the needs of the Count of Tyrol, Frederik IV of Habsburg who was perennially short of money and seized the window of opportunity. They became famous in 1488 when Jakob Fugger, the Younger, financed a loan of 150,000 florins to Sigismund the Münzreiche of Tyrol, and as a collateral he received a mortgage on the mine of Schwaz and then over the entire silver production of the Tyrol. If the loans were not repaid on time, the Fuggers were to receive the Tyrolean silver production due to the Archduke. The Fugger family extended further monies to the Habsburg as they were pressed for more loans. The mine of Schwaz, in Tyrol, was the world's most important silver mine of the time, employing up to 11,000 miners. Around 1500, more than 85% of the silver traded in the world was mined there. When significant copper deposits were found in Neusohl in central Hungary, the Fuggers were immediately interested. This time, the case was more difficult as the Hungarian court was not very keen on embarking with German partners. Finally, with the assistance of a local business partner of Polish origin capable of convincing the Hungarian court, the Fuggers managed to win the case to build and operate the largest copper production centre at the time in Europe. The Fuggers who started out as wool merchants and traders of spices between their city and Venice, ended up rivalling the Medicis, as one of the prominent investors and bankers of their time. They focused on financing exclusively the Habsburg but were unfortunately great supporters of the disastrous economic policy of Charles V of Spain, which led them close to financial disaster in 1557, after Philip II of Spain issued the first state bankruptcy decree. They managed to recover some of their money but lost an overall 8 million florins, which was a considerable part of their gains as a merchant house.

German, Genoese and Spanish financiers, involved with precious metal and with the Seville–Antwerp trade, joined in lending to governments, during this long time of economic expansion. Antwerp entrepreneurs lent extensively to the English, Portuguese, Spanish and French governments. The first sign that the expansion of Antwerp would not go on forever came in the 1550s when the French, Spanish and Portuguese monarchies all declared that they could no longer consider the repayment of the capital of the loans made to them. Despite this situation, Antwerp remained the key financial centre in Europe in the following years. Antwerp was the greatest clearing house for international payments, but it was not the only one. In the south of Europe, Genoa was still very active, and gained even more traction at the end of the 1590s when the money market in Antwerp began to collapse. The crisis of the late 1550s hit English woolen cloth industry very seriously, hitting Antwerp's transformation industry and sea trade. In the three decades that followed the mid-century boom, the English connection with Antwerp was weakened and then completely broken. After 1572, Antwerp's commercial attractions faded rapidly. The politico-religious struggle between Catholic Spain and Protestant Holland sealed the faith of the city, as it became the capital of the Dutch revolt. In 1577, the sack of Antwerp by the Spanish army, the Spanish Fury, included the plundering of many of the foreign merchant warehouses which cut their losses and left Antwerp never to return. After the fall of the city in 1585, Antwerp again came under the rule of Philip II. When the

Dutch rebels took control of Zeeuws-Vlaanderen, a strip of land on the left shore, and closed the Scheldt river for shipping, cutting Antwerp off from the North sea in 1585, the glorious time of Antwerp as an international financial centre ended: the Dutch succeeded to divert the lucrative trade of Antwerp to Amsterdam. The third default by the Spanish state in 1596 provoked a wave of bankruptcies in Spain itself and in Antwerp. This final crisis definitively sealed the faith of the sea-city back from being the commercial world's centre to an inland port for two centuries. In 1601, John Wheeler's "A treatise of Commerce" was almost simultaneously released in London and Middleburgh (States of Zeland) as a defence of trade. Its publication was prompted by some earlier pamphlets from the Hanseatic merchants who may have seen the ambitions of English trading companies as a threat to their monopoly. As the secretary of the Merchant Adventurer Society, the strongest of the regulated trading companies, from 1601–1608, Wheeler is an advocate of regulated trade, a lobbyist and opinion leader targeting a large audience of gentry-investors, politicians and gentlemen-adventurers. One of the salient features of his book is to depict Antwerp and the Low Countries in a very poor light. The book, together with the rather monopolistic Hanseatic pamphlets of the time, held a specific place in terms of the debate on trade and investment principals during the early 17th century, and fuelled a vigorous debate on the best place and conditions to handle international trade.

Behind the scene, the evolution of the medieval society was also supported by a less visible and equally powerful cognitive revolution. François Rabelais, a French physician and humanist born in 1494, the author of the comic philosophical masterpiece "Pantagruel and Gargantua", wrote that a well-structured mind was better than a full mind, "Wisdom entereth not into a malicious mind, and that knowledge without conscience is but the ruin of the soul". Old-fashioned scholastic pedagogy is ridiculed and contrasted with the humanist ideal of the Christian prince, widely learned in art, science, and crafts and skilled in knightly warfare.[3] The diffusion of this knowledge owes much to the creation of new schools and colleges which offered the opportunity to access a new form of education better suited to fit the challenges of the Enlightenment as "the proper education of youth

---

[3] Encyclopedia Britannica, on François Rabelais.

will mean improvement for the whole world".[4] In 1548, 10 members of the recently founded Society of Jesus opened the first Jesuit school in Sicily at the invitation of citizens of Messina to educate their sons in the humanist mode. The Jesuits who had been trained outside Italy, especially in Paris, realised that they had learned some pedagogical principles practically unknown in Italy and that allowed students to make fast progress. The project was a resounding success, within a few years some 30 additional primary and secondary schools were created. In 1585, a school in Macau; and at about the same time they founded in Japan an art school in which local painters were introduced to Western techniques. The Jesuit education differed in many ways from the teaching in the monasteries of the Benedictines in the Middle Ages, and from the great Dominican and Franciscan teachers at the medieval universities. Jesuits formally designated the staffing and management of schools the primary ministry of the order, after initially imaging themselves as a corps of itinerant preachers and missioners. They actually set about creating such institutions and assumed responsibility for their continuance over time. These schools were not primarily intended for the training of clergy but for ordinary boys and young men who envisaged a worldly career in these times of radical change in the world economy. The humanist education showed appreciation for classic Greek and Latin literature and eloquence as its primary focus on the one hand, but on the other hand for a more "practical" education in commercial skills or in sciences as needed to accompany the commercial revolution. The Jesuits saw the boundaries between these two fundamental streams and reconciled in Jesuit humanist education what was needed for the world emerging from the englightment with the intellectual rigor and professionalism of the scholastic system. Even if the Jesuits, were not the only ones to contribute to the transformation of formal schooling in Europe at the time, it is probably fair to recognise that no group in the church, or in society at large, had ever undertaken an enterprise on such a grand scale in which these educational factors coalesced.

Aside from the education factor, Adam Smith later stated that the almost simultaneous discovery of America and of a passage to India were

---

[4] Pedro Ribadeneira S.J. (1527–1611) explained the purpose of the new schools in a letter to King Philip II of Spain.

the two most important economic events at the end of the Middle Ages and disturbed the established order of Italian trade in favor of the Spanish and Portuguese. But Italy reacted quickly to this game changer and reorganised its transnational trading model until it finally had to yield to the Dutch and English trading powerhouses. The brilliant development of networks of seafaring commerce also came with a very dark side: slavery, genocides, bacterian invasion, brutal cultural domination together with the supply of goods on which indigenous populations would become dependent such as alcohol.

The Revenge of "La Superba", the Turbulent Italian City-State

The dispersal of commerce in Europe was then very considerable, but sea trade remained the leading indicator of prosperity of the most influential cities. Since the 1560s, trading had confirmed its nomadic DNA, traders had been moving from Antwerp to regional trading centres including Seville, Rouen, London, Liege, Aachen, Cologne, Frankfurt, Middelburg, Emden and Hamburg as well as Amsterdam. It was by no means clear which if any of these places might be heir to Antwerp. Genoa, located on the quite inaccessible mountainous coastline of Liguria situated north of Italy close to the French border, was a savvy maritime empire but its merchants were not primarily interested in finance. Capital of Liguria in northwestern Italy on the Tyrrhenean Sea, the city state was squeezed on a tiny strip of land between the Alps and the Apennine mountains and the sea. Rainfall can be abundant in this part of Italy as the proximity of the sea and mountain creates an orographic effect. Due to geography, agriculture was more difficult because of the mountainous surroundings and the city always had less manufacturing activity than Venice. However, it was well known as the Italian Riviera where the combination of the Alps and the Mediterranean produced unexpected palm trees, citrus fruits and olives sharing the terraced growing space with more common northern species like chestnuts.

A first settlement was founded around 2000 A.D. by the Phoenician mariners who sailed in from Tyre in Phoenicia. They came through from Corsica and settled with the Ambrones tribe, one of the earliest ancestors of the Celts from Iberia. They remained a fiercely independent population, living mostly from piracy and were occasionally employed, as mercenaries. Above all, Genoese were excellent sailors. Along the marine routes, they used many innovations in navigation, such as the compass, the sextant, newer sails and rudders, the knowledge of astronomical navigation at night, modern cartography including the earth's spherical shape. The oldest sea charts in existence, linked to the emergence of the compass, are of Genoese origin. The earliest examples date from the late 13th century. Their navigation maps showed Mare nostrum ("Mediterranean basin") drafted with minute details, considering the knowledge available to the mapmakers at that time. A well-known Genoese reference chart is one drawn by Battista Agnese in 1544. The Genoese also mastered the sea loan or *foenus nauticum*, whose origin can be traced back to antiquity, as it is already mentioned in the Code of Hammurabi in 2250 A.D. The sea loan was the earliest instrument that attempted to separate sea casualty risk from other business risks. This was a debt instrument used to finance maritime commerce that was repayable only upon the safe arrival of a ship or cargo: if the ship or cargo were lost, the loan was forgiven. The sea loan was in widespread use in Genoa in the 12th century before becoming available in other seaports. Short haul navigations typically bore rates of 10%–20% per annum, while rates to more distant risky destinations in the Levant could be as high as 50%. Genoese merchants used this instrument to routinely finance the purchase of goods shipped overseas: the loan would be repaid on the return of the ship for small distance or on the arrival to destination for long distance trips. This instrument, including some interesting variations such as the *bottomry* or *pignus* loan, was a popular means of investment in Genoa, since yields were attractive for private investors. In 1236, the sea loan was condemned by Pope Gregory IX's as usurious, which led to its decline and to the development of the *cambium nauticum*, a variation of the former, disguising interest in the use of different currencies.

The Genoese preferred expanding method was the foundation of overseas commercial seaports building a private harbour with customs duty, a shipyard, a Genoese district and then gradually taking financial and political possession of the whole town. Genoa also had a rich history of being independent and of being taken over by larger empires such as the Romans, the Fatimid Caliphate, and also of seeding new cities such as Marseille in France. Echoing its turbulent past, the development of Liguria's capital city Genoa did not grow on a straight path: it went through two long-run expansion phases (roughly from 11th to late 13th century, and then from 16th to mid-17th century) interrupted by about two centuries of decline and then stagnation. The first expansion cycle took place right after the foundation of the Commune of Genoa (end of 10th century). Around 1000, Genoa took almost every Aegean island and city: from Rodhis to Smirnes and Samos. In 1098, Ligures organised the expedition leading to the first Crusade under the patronage of the most powerful Genoese family "Embriaci", whose members also played notable roles in the Holy Land Crusades in the 11th and 12th centuries. Guglielmo Embriaco and his brother Primo de Castello sailed for Jerusalem in 1099 and participated in the capture of the city. At the siege of Acre, King Richard I, the Lion Heart, fighting side by side with the Genoese army, placed England under the patronage of the Genoese Patron, the young warrior St. George of Cappadocia. He also took from the Genoese banner its Red Cross and placed it at the centre of the national flag of England. After three centuries of continuous expansion of its military and trade empire, Genoa dominated the two other rival state-cities: Venice and Pisa and became the hub between Northern economies (e.g., Fairs of Champagne, Hansa) and Southern markets (e.g., Byzantium, North Africa).

Beginning with the first crusade (1096–1099) in the Middle Ages, crusaders poured into the port of Genoa from England, France and other Western European areas. Genoese vessels transported the crusading armies to Antioch or Acre in the Holy Land. In return for their ferry services, the Genoese navy was handsomely compensated and granted trading privileges among the Christian controlled areas of the East. The Fourth Crusade and the sack of Constantinople by the Latins in 1204 resulted in a new distribution of power in the Aegean. Islands like Chios, Mytilene and others, passed into the control of the Genoese. Following the Fourth crusade, the Genoese merchants established a settlement in Constantinople and obtained in 1303 the privilege of building a fortified wall around their commercial district which was crowned in 1348 by a surveillance tower *Christea Turris* called "Galata",[5] on the hill of "golden-horn" of Istanbul, at the junction of Bosphorus until they surrended the keys of their city to the Ottomans in 1453. Genoa only became an important financial centre in the early Quattrocento with the establishment of a new institution bound by secrecy and strict rules: The Bank of St. George. Casa delle compere e dei banchi di San Giorgio, the world's first modern, public bank would survive for nearly 400 years and be reminded as the inventor of many of the financial instruments that are still practiced today. The city acquired an international status in the middle of the 1500s when Genoese merchants displaced the Fuggers from Augsburg, successor to the Medici after 1394, as the principal bankers of the Spanish court. Their money was needed in the first place for the maintenance of the Spanish troops in the Netherlands. The third and last war between Venice and Genoa in 1378–1381 led to some clarification: the Venetians dominated the routes to the East, leaving room to the Genoese for growth in trade with the West. Both centres equally traded with the North of Europe. Venice and Genoa competed and fought for leadership on overseas routes. Even Marco Polo was captured and jailed by the Genoese navy in 1398. Both city states shared institutions and legitimacy which gave them the power to rule the sea. Florence's elite continued to influence the north of Europe. The medieval Italian finance triad led by three extraordinary city states: Venice, Florence and Genoa left a very deep footprint on the history of financial centres with a strong international character, but each in a very distinctive way. Genoese merchants, although generally eclipsed in the 15th century by the Venetians, still maintained a strong presence in the south of the Iberian Peninsula, at Malaga, Seville and Lisbon. Lisbon and then Seville were excellent choices as they became key centres for growth in the second half of the century and even more in the 16th century.

Genoa already had a complicated and agitated history, which made it less interventionist than Venice as it was busy dealing with its internal quarrels. Protected behind a natural curtain of rocks, Genoa remained a republic for most of the Middle Ages. However, its turbulent nobility and

---

[5] This new tower replaced in a different location, closer to the sea, the old tower of Galata, an original Byzantine tower destroyed in 1203, during the Fourth Crusade of 1202–1204.

commoner factions were often busy with internal feuds and the city had been in fights with neighboring cities for decades. Family and clan factions were particularly bellicose, closed to foreign influence and generally difficult to deal with. The Alberghi, coalitions of families adopting a common name for the purpose of mutual defense, were always involved in a fight in some corner of the city. The factions even built internal city partitions and established controlled districts. Initially, aristocratic clans cooperated together and supported the emergence of the "social capital" that fostered the set-up of institutions and contracts aimed at channeling investments in crusades and distant trade. But, at the turn of 13th–14th century, these informal rules also undermined the Genoa's public institutions and its way of enforcing property rights and contracts. The state of Genoa was then less interventionist because it was more "factious and unstable," as Machiavelli noted in his "Istorie fiorentine". Unable to create a sufficiently open and stable environment for trade, Genoa was eclipsed by Venice. In spite of this chaotic situation, Genoa was still a very busy city, trading, shipping and controlling a naval empire. Before anything, the Genoese were master sailors and traders, it seems that the city was very focused and had little interest in producing the famous painters or poets that other rival state cities were so proud to honour. Since 1261, the Genovese navy had gained control of Constantinople, the largest city in Europe and, thus, the trade in the Black Sea. Genoa's merchants quickly developed markets at key ports on this sea. They exported wine, olive oil, and wool to the area, and imported furs, corn, spices and Persian goods. Since 1339, in an imitation of Venice, Genoa had a Doge running the city with the most influential families which unfortunately could hardly live in peace. Given the political environment, the office remained stormy until in 1396 the ruling Doge surrendered to the King of France in search of a neutral peacekeeper. Political life in Genoa was agitated and no fewer than thirteen uprising and revolutions took place between 1413 and 1453.

Despite the previous dominance of Antwerp, Genoese shipping companies managed to consolidate their influence and in due course redirected their vessels to safer and familiar waters, Genoa instead of Antwerp. Many businessmen in Genoa operated not only in shipping or finance, but also diversified their trade in the manufacture and sale of silk fabrics. The genius of 16th century Genoese finance was to use the silver inflows from the New World to make profits, through their deep expertise in matching complex international monetary and commodity flows, in interest rate spreads and trading bills of exchange. The main beneficiaries of Genoese loans were the Kingdom of Spain and its dependencies. Genoese short-term loans were granted to Spain via special contracts called *asientos*, which contained precise details of the terms and conditions including the guarantees offered to the creditors, and where and when repayment would be made, usually in tranches. Typically, these *asientos* were used to cover treasury shortages or for the transfer of funds from one part of the vast Spanish empire to another, with a one or two year maturity and backed by public revenues. The problem remained with the recurring default of the Spanish state, although it was always resolved by the conversion of floating debts of fairs into consolidated irredeemable debts (*juros*); the savings invested in the *asientos* were frozen and not convertible into money without major losses to the investors, mostly German bankers, rather than the Genoese who were mostly acting as intermediaries.

The Spanish sold silver, on the spot market, to the Genoese merchants in exchange for future delivery of gold in Antwerp; the gold was used to pay Spanish troops fighting in Flanders and the Low Countries. The cost to the Genoese of delivering gold up north, through bills of exchange, was a fraction of the cost and risk of physically shipping it from Spain to Antwerp. The Genoese merchant bankers acquired this strength through "increasing returns to scale in international financial services". Genoese silver was then shipped on Genoese vessels to Venice and from there to the Far East to settle a trade deficit. In exchange, the Genoese received bills drawn on Antwerp where they were used to buy gold. The time difference between the various positions was set through the use of credit, and final positions were settled during the fairs. Aside from its bankers' skills in mastering international financial settlements, Genoa had set up two institutions which anchored its reputation as a European centre-point for finance: the Casa di San Giorgio, and the related Banco di San Giorgio. The consolidation and unification of debts started in 1274 and was renewed in the years 1303, 1332, 1340, 1368, 1381, 1395 and 1407, with the appearance of the compere[6] of San Giorgio.

---

[6]In Genoa, single loans and the funds into which they were consolidated became known as compere. In other Italian cities, they would be named monti, depositi, prestanze, etc.

The opening of the Genoese public banks, a century and a half before other Italian cities and two centuries before the rest of Europe, acted as an important driver for the city's financial development. The *Casa di San Giorgio*, a financial institution, in fact a sovereign debt fund, was created in 1407 to consolidate the Genoa's public debt. San Giorgio's shareholders acquired all previous debt issues of the Republic of Genoa and used what today would be called a convertible bond, i.e., a bond which converts into equity when certain conditions are met. The *Casa di San Giorgio* administered the banco in its own name and at its own risk through trusted administrators chosen from top functionaries in the *Officium*, as the Casa was also called. The *Banco di San Giorgio*, opened for business on 2nd March 1408, it was a public bank with the primary mission of facilitating the management of the San Giorgio's shares, called *luoghi*. It was the first bank in Italy to offer deposit taking, clearance and lending services and the second of that kind in Europe. The bank's foundation was linked to the geopolitical crisis of the time: Genoa's public debt was escalating following the wars with Venice, the lack of liquidity of the public debt market led to inflated rates for short-term money and the lack of a monetary arm to refinance the state debt. Despite its initial success, the bank's days were numbered due to the weakness of its capital, the incessant request for cash from its parent, and an inconsistent monetary policy. By 1445, the bank suspended banking activity and only delivered services to the Genoese state, the shareholders, tax collectors and suppliers. It re-opened for business to the general public in 1530 and finally closed in 1805. The *Banco* handled commercial banking operations and paid into the shareholders account the interest on *luoghi*. The latter was used as an income to settle transactions, and to fund overdrafts of other commercial banking operations. Deposit accounts were used by customers to settle payments. The "giro" system which enabled the fiduciary transfer of cash from one account to another without the need of physically transferring cash or writing a check, reduced the use of scarce resources and raised the velocity of narrowly defined money.

On par with the Florence bankers in the 13th century, the bankers from the Piazza De Ferrari in the 16th century Genoa were seen as one of the few people in Europe capable of mastering the best finance techniques and issuing large amounts of public debt at relatively low cost for the issuer.

These facilities were made available in conjunction with innovations in financial and monetary instruments including: the perpetual debt instrument, the marketability of debt instrument, the money market and the interaction between credit and money markets. Risk had always been an important factor, in the initiatives of the financiers of the St. Georges Bank. Because of the danger of the Barbary coast attacks, a network of several hundred watchtowers situated on headlands on the coast side, was built during the 15th and 16th centuries as an early warning system on possible intrusions. The first identifiable class of insurance as a business was marine insurance. Although it is thought that the first insurance policies originated 5,000 years ago from Chinese merchants tired of losing cargos in the stormy South China sea, the insurance mechanism was perfected by Babylonians around 1790 A.D. King Hammurabi, proposed the concept of bottomry, which allowed merchants to finance their shipping through loans from lenders. These loans were paid back, with interest, only after the safe arrival of the goods. But if the merchandise was lost in transit, they didn't have to pay a dime. Early forms of modern marine policies were built from these very ancient practices and have been traced to the Italian city states of Genoa and Palermo in the 14th century. The very first modern insurance contract was probably written and signed in Genoa in 1343. Its principles were very similar to ancient Babylonian ones: Merchants could take out loans guaranteeing safe arrival of shipments. By1500, marine insurance was available in all seaports of significance in France, Spain, Italy, Flanders and in England where early forms of marine policies are found in the records of the High Court of the Admiralty of England.

The capacity of the Genoese bankers to master international money transfers was a strong competitive advantage to serve the merchants attending the large European fairs. A strong institutional regime and a vibrant capital market put Genoa in a position of leadership again. The Spanish connection with Genoa reinforced the condottiere, admiral and statesman Andrea Doria's astute foundation of a Republic associating aristocratic and non-aristocratic families. He simultaneously managed to end the power of the two factional doge families, established a new constitution in 1528 and made the city state a satellite of the Spanish Empire of Charles V, Holy Roman Emperor, with ambitions to take over the reputation of Florence for financial innovation. It created a political regimen forcing property rights and contracts, capable of incubating naturally a stable financial system fuelling capital allocation and innovation. Genoa was regarded as the more innovative of the Italian state cities in financial instruments and markets. In 1535, Genoese merchant bankers established exchange fairs in which only bills were traded, acting as clearing centres for merchants all over Europe. The fairs became known first in Besançon, then Piacenza, Novi and Sestri Levante. The fairs became progressively specialised until trade in goods and money neatly separated into fairs of goods, such as the well-known ones of Champagne, and fairs of (money) exchange. The exchange fairs lasted eight days and were held four times a year at regular intervals in accordance with rules established by the Genoese senate, based on the Church calendar. The fairs utilised their own monetary system based on the gold "Scudo", their own unit of account. Compliance with the fair regulations was entrusted to a specific jurisdiction made up by of a consul and two councillors which acted as a Court of first instance. The primary players were bankers, merchants or other intermediaries willing to settle their firms' bills and as the case may be those of others. The fairs attracted merchants from all over Europe, settled their bills with a multiple clearing system that was a precursor of today's clearing houses, and issued new bills for use on individual trading markets or later exchange fairs. The success of these exchange fairs led to significant growth for more than half a century, during which time the Genoese became Europe's major financiers. Turnover started to increase in around 1550, accelerated after 1580, and peaked in the years 1596–1610, when the volume of bills traded per fair amounted to about 10 million gold scudos, four times a year, a figure equivalent to the annual revenues of Spain, France, England and Italy. From 1568, precious metals (especially the inflow of silver then gold) coming from the New World (South America) were shipped by the Spanish to Genoa, skipping Flanders. Genoa was then acting as the distribution centre of Spanish and Portuguese precious metals for all Europe.

As far as the operation of this complex credit market is concerned, exchange fairs were a credit market through which a considerable amount of money was moved from one marketplace to another. The exchange fair concentrated a large amount of paper money in few days time and in a single convenient place and to put it at once at the disposal of the circuit of credit in forms of loans that would be refunded after three months at the forthcoming fair. These fairs worked as a clearing house and a well-established "rendez-vous" that rhythmically and cyclically marked the time of the European financial calendar. The decline of the glory days of the Genoese exchange fairs started in 1620–1625, it was principally due to the suspension of Genoese funding to Spain, whose public finances were close to default due to wars, and the development in competing European centres of bills of exchanges that allowed endorsement, thereby enabling the payee to transfer the bill to a third party and collect the proceeds in his place of residence. The Genoese had a global understanding on how the financial system should be better serviced. However, as international commerce was growing, the merchants could no longer afford to be dependent on an institution such as a fair, where currency-prices fixing occurred every three months while in Amsterdam it was a daily process on which a very modern credit market was based.

The word "lottery" is believed to come from the Italian word "*lotto*", meaning destiny or fate. In the 16th century in Genoa, at the election of the Great Council, five positions were regularly filled from among ninety senators by means of a lottery. The public started betting on the possible outcome of these lotteries, and this is likely the origin of Lotto. Soon, the names of the senators were replaced by the numbers 1 through 90, and the game was operated by bankers. Subsequently taken over by the state, the idea to choose 5 numbers without replacement out of 90 spread throughout Italy and became the most popular form of lottery all over the world. The game, said to have been invented by Benedetto Gentille in 1610, was banned by Pope Benedict XIII in (1724–1730).[7] However, the first city of Italy in which lottery tickets were purchased for money is often said to have been Florence in 1530. There are early records of a lottery being organised in Venice but on 28 February 1522, a prohibition on all private lotteries was decreed. The official reason for the ban was to avoid fraud, and discourage vice, but it is more likely that the Venetian state had recognised a valuable source of revenues and shut down competition. Prizes were at first money and valuables but soon privileges and offices of the Republic were offered, including rights to collect customs and excise duty at certain points on certain products (e.g., tolls on Canale di S. Zulian,

---

[7] His successor Clement XII revisited the issue and set up a lottery in Rome.

or excise duty on wine). The game was so popular that some merchants tried to corner the market, buying as many tickets as possible in advance and selling the undrawn tickets with a fat premium when valuable prizes were involved.

The financial instruments previously used such as debt, equity, insurance or even entertainment as standard and liquid products moved towards more liquid secondary markets to better trade risk, under the rule of law. The former CEO of the iconic London based investment bank S.G. Warburg, David Scholey, remarked about Genoese financial markets in 16–17th century: "This Genoese system of international finance stands alone in history up until the present day as an example of an IFC [international financial centre] built not so much on locally based trade or primarily on a local surplus (although both elements were present), but rather on an efficient and sophisticated system for gathering the monetary surpluses of other parties, in part through a process of — to use a familiar phrase — securitisation, or the extension of paper credit. Although Amsterdam in the 18th century and London in the 19th century also based many of their financial activities on the issuance and discounting of securities, these were backed primarily by increasing volumes of trade and of surplus capital which were centered locally."

The Orange Revolution: The Opportunistic Rise of Amsterdam

When adventurers came down the river Amstel around 1100 in hollowed-out logs and settled in the wetlands and unwelcoming swamps surrounding the Amstel River, a shambles of shifting mudflats in which handfuls of fishermen and reed cutters slithered around were not viewed as a high prize. This was a low-lying landscape of constant change with the boundary between land and sea cyclically shifting. As locals joined forces to improve their lot, developing ever more elaborate systems to control the water that so often engulfed their rather unpleasant thatched homes, solutions were found by this vibrant and entrepreneurial community. In 1200, a dam was built across the Amstel river, giving the settlement its final name and marking the centre of what became through luck, ruthlessness and ingenuity a great city. This unique combination of seigneurial indifference to the area and enforced co-operation gave the region from its very beginning a unique social as well as geographical flatness, as well as the ambition to move beyond natural limitations.

The earliest recorded use of the name "Amsterdam" is from a certificate dated 27 October 1275, when the "hominess manentes apud Amestelledamme" (people living near Amestelledamme) were exempted from paying the bridge toll. The canny *"Aemstelledammers"* had a sharp business sense and began exacting toll money from the passing beer and herring traders of the roaring Eastern Sea Trade of the Baltics. They quickly became expert ship builders and beer brewers, attracting more interest in the emerging city. By the 13th century, the number of people engaged in some aspect of the textile industry in the Southern Netherlands had become more than the total engaged in all other crafts. In 1275, Count Floris V of Holland granted permission to the people living near the dam in river *Amstel* to levy tolls. But it wasn't until the year 1300 or 1306 that Amsterdam was fully acknowledged as a city. The right to free passage proved to be crucial for the economic development of Amsterdam. This concept would remain a founding idea of the Dutch economy and was later extended to the New World. Free passage meant that traders could operate cheaply and in safety. In particular, beer and herring proved popular and lucrative commodities to trade. For example, in 1323, Amsterdam owned the exclusive right to import beer from Hamburg. And the herring trade grew rapidly after the invention of herring curing.[8] This technique opened the way for the development of a real fishing industry as fishermen could catch more fish and thus make more profit. But still the city was missing a direct connection to the sea. This problem would be solved later by the construction of a direct canal to the sea. By the end of the 15th century, the city developed rapidly. After the Spaniards conquered Antwerp, many wealthy Jews fled to Amsterdam. The money they brought with them was used to organise trips to India, which proved a huge commercial success. As a consequence of the raising education level, the industrial base (textile, shipping), and the trade that went with it, Amsterdam, was the city of choice after Genoa. The city put a strong

---

[8] A technique that involved removing the fish's intestines directly after they were caught in order to keep them fresh longer.

and specific emphasis on warehousing and managed to excel in this area. When the Venetian patrician families transferred many of their talents and assets to northern Europe, the Venetian *fondi* provided the nucleus of the Bank of Amsterdam, which dominated Europe during the 17th century, and later of the Bank of England, which became the leading bank of the 18th century. The Dutch financial revolution was also coincidently triggered by the willingness of Charles V of Spain, the Holy Roman Emperor, to find an alternative source of funding to the Fuggers and other loan sharks of the time. He spurred the provincial governments of the United Provinces to pledge taxes to service the debt of the Habsburg state. The control of the tax proceeds was relinquished to the same one who had made heavy investments in sovereign debts. The Habsburg monarch supported the transferability of bills of exchange to third persons prior to the maturity date of the underlying commodity and recognised their negotiability. He also accepted the development of a contract market where trading of contracts for future delivery was a source of speculative profit, and which would come under the scrutiny and criticism of the Church. In 1555, Charles V granted the Netherlands to his son, Philip II, king of Spain. As Philip II was a Catholic and part of the Netherlands was Calvinist protestant, the Dutch resisted not only the new taxation, but also the intolerance and oppressive methods of administration of the Spanish king and his governor Prince Alba. In 1581, the Union of Utrecht proclaimed independence from Spain. In the late 1580, English raids against Spanish commerce and support of the Dutch rebels in the Spanish Low Countries prompted Philip II of Spain to plan to invade and conquer England. A giant invasion fleet was built by 1587, with the blessing of Pope Sixtus V, and readied for raiding England.

On 19 May 1588, the Invincible Armada set sail from Lisbon on a mission to control the Channel and prepare for the invasion of England. In 1588 off the coast of Gravelines near Calais, France, Sir Francis Drake, vice-admiral of the British Navy, defeated the Spanish Invincible Armada on behalf of Queen Elizabeth I and paved the way for English and Dutch sea dominance. The Spanish defeat consolidated the earlier and still fragile foundation of the Dutch Republic(1581), officially known as the Republic of the Seven United Netherlands, which had been taking place after a Calvinist rebellion against the Spanish led Holy Roman Empire.

The ghastly fate of Antwerp, its sister city, once the biggest importer in the world — its people slaughtered, the survivors violently catholicised or expelled and its access to the sea blocked for two centuries — could easily have been shared by Amsterdam.

The ambition of the Dutch merchants was to break the monopoly held by Spain and Portugal over the spice trade, and in particular to break into their lucrative route via the Cape of Good Hope. In 1595, the design of the Dutch flyboat "fluit" at Hoorn, gave a decisive advantage to the Dutch navy: this new vessel was a versatile heavy duty long distance sea-going barge, rather cheap to build and sail. The ship was capable of running any potential rivals out of the market. The population explosion of the 16th century, created a strong demand for corn as food surpluses diminished. The Dutch took this opportunity to trade grain and establish their dominance in the north and south of Europe. On the military front, Francis Drake would be instrumental in attacking the Portuguese vessels turning the Cape, and this would result in serious losses for both the Portuguese and the Spanish fleet. Typically the Iberians would lose 11–15% of their cargo while the Dutch would only lose 4%. Both Holland and England shaped their national identity through trade in opposition to Iberian dominance. The rise of the Amsterdam seaport as a financial centre coincides with its leadership on long distance trade to the East and West Indies. In addition, Amsterdam also mastered credit instruments to support trade, just like the Italian city states decades before. The successful launch of new ventures such as the deliberate promotion of trade with the East Indies, broke into what had been a Portuguese trading monopoly since 1590.

In 1602, Johan van Oldenbarnevelt, acting as the virtual Prime Minister of the young Dutch Republic, took the initiative to establish the Dutch East India Company. The Amsterdam office of the Dutch East India Company became the world's first stock exchange by trading in its own shares, and the largest commercial enterprise in the world with a fleet of more than a 100 ships, thousands of employees, dozens of offices in Asia, and six establishments in the Netherlands. The capital of the company was formed for 21 years, and the subscription to the capital was open to every resident of the United Provinces, responsibility was limited to the capital contributed and there was no guaranteed return. The trading business of the VOC, the Dutch East India Company, did not start as a great success and most of the company proceeds were derived from piracy and in particular the capture of Iberian vessels. In 1608, Isaac le Maire, a founding member of the Dutch East India Company, and one of the wealthier entrepreneurs of the country, organised a large short-selling syndicate on the VOC shares with the objective to launch the first recorded bear attack on the listed shares of an underperforming firm. The syndicate managed to borrow shares and then sold them, pushing the share price down but ultimately failing to break the upward trend of the Dutch East India Company share price. Several other traders who also joined the VOC hit squad to speculate on their own account went bankrupt as they had to buy shares at prices much higher than the ones they negotiated for future delivery. One of the consequences of the attack was the ban[9] on short selling in 1610 by Frederick Henry, the Prince of Orange who ruled the Netherlands, but the practice remained rampant. This good intention created the possibility of defaulting through appealing to the Prince. Too smart to fail, would find its first credentials in Amsterdam.

Free coinage was granted to the Wisselbank of Amsterdam (Bank of exchange) which began operations on 31 January 1609. It was founded after a period of great monetary chaos and fraudulent private banking. The bank operated upon the principle of maintaining at all times a 100% reserve ratio with respect to "demand" deposits. For a very long time, over one hundred and fifty years, the Bank of Amsterdam scrupulously fulfilled the commitment upon which it was founded. From a financial perspective; the bank offered everyday the services that the fairs would only provide from time to time, it was designed to meet two urgent requirements of the Dutch merchant bankers: the need for a bank of deposit and change, but above all for a trusted "guarantor" of foreign trade and international payments. The bank sovereign mission was to preserve the metal integrity of the coins circulating within the United Province, so that the florin's intrinsic value would not diverge too much from the official foreign exchange value. The reserve bank, whose institution had been strongly supported by the merchants, became the bullion warehouse of Europe modeled on the Venitian Banco di Rialto of 1587. The heightened trade and commerce in

---

[9]Buyers were allowed to "appeal to Frederick", meaning to repudiate such contracts on appealing to the Prince.

Holland served to attract coin and bullion from throughout the world. It was established within the European credit market to coincide with the development of the Genoese fairs. Shortly after its creation, the Wisselbank did not grant any sort of credits, but simply safely held the deposited coins in its vault. Its primary mission would be monetary stability through the enforcement of the minting ordinances to fight debasement[10] which was responsible for inflation and monetary chaos. It received the monopoly on money changing, on issuing bills of exchange valued in excess of 600 guilders and on bullion transactions. This would represent a colossal privilege over the financial sphere, in the middle of a shipping hub and a trading centre connected to a large empire. The city of Amsterdam had a majority share in the organisation, which was to become the first modern multinational company of the world. The result was a period of unprecedented prosperity, causing the 17th century to become known as the Golden Age. Later the great increase in the deposits of the Bank of Amsterdam stemmed from its role as a safe harbour for capital fleeing the speculation that the system of John Law produced in France in the 1720s. The Bank of Amsterdam was the last bank in history to maintain a 100% reserve ratio. Adam Smith pointed out that even in 1672, when Holland was in danger of being invaded by the King of France, the Bank of Amsterdam satisfied every last request for repayment of demand deposits; this acted as an even more impressive reinforcement of the public's confidence in the solvency of the bank. Unfortunately, in the 1780s, the Wisselbank started to deviate from its founding principles. From the time of the fourth Anglo-Dutch war, the reserve ratio had decreased drastically, after the city of Amsterdam demanded the bank loan it a large portion of its deposits to cover growing public expenditures.

Some merchants were only reluctant to deposit their heavy coins in the bank, as they needed sufficient funds in their Wisselbank account to settle the financial obligations related to their trade and purchased for cash these funds from other Wisselbank depositors having an excess amount of money

---

[10] Debasement meant reducing the precious metal content of a coin; either *by weight* (smaller coin) or *by fineness* (by adding more copper in the alloy); or *by raising the face value*, the official value of the coin.

in their Wisselbank account. An open market in Wisselbank funds solved the problem, and a second unit of account, the "banco florin," was born. In order to provide an incentive to depositors with excess cash, buyers had to offer a premium or "agio", which could be rather unstable but was later stabilised by open-market operations based on short-term certificates of deposit of *bonafide* heavy currencies or bullions. The "banco florin" applied to funds held at the Wisselbank, and to bills payable in Wisselbank funds. By the mid-17th century, the Dutch monetary system had dual units of account (the original unit of account, the current florin and the banco florin), foreign and domestic coins, inside money, and funds held at the Wisselbank.

1602 was the year when the States-General of Netherlands gave the Dutch East India Company[11] a monopoly over Asian trade. It consolidated all the six preexisting trading companies competing with each other into a single one governed by the "Heeren Seventien" (the XVII Lords). The lords were the representatives of the six Dutch East India Company chambers of Amsterdam, Delft, Enkhuizen, Hoorn, Middelburg and Rotterdam. The firm became an "independent power, a state within the state"[12] with incredible economic strength. The Dutch East India Company was empowered to build strongholds, wage war and enter into agreements in the name of the States-General. The company was formed on a capital base of 6.4 million guilders divided in six fixed portions between six different Dutch cities. The investment was not liquid, the management was not appointed by shareholders and the funds were to be returned to shareholders only in 10 years. In between, the secondary market would only provide liquidity on the investment. This was an incredible incursion on modern finance, and very comparable to what we still see today. The firm did not pay dividends until 1610, much to the disappointment of its shareholders. It was to be considered only as a pure growth equity play, provided that the secondary market worked. An interesting incidental episode in the emergence of new international financial centres and of their interconnection is certainly the establishment in 1609 of an urban settlement called

---

[11] Vereenigde Oost Indische Companie, the powerful United Netherlands Chartered East India Company also named VOC.
[12] Fernand Braudel (1992).

New Amsterdam on an island full of wolves and bears wandering through fields of strawberries, called today Manhattan, by an English explorer Henry Hudson, then in the service of the Dutch East India Company.

On 1595, Christmas day, five VOC, Dutch East India Company, ships reach Bantam in Java, Indonesia, and encounter an impressive blockading fleet of Portuguese vessels totalling 8 galleons and 22 galleys. They engaged this fleet in intermittent battle until driving them away on New Year's day. The improbable result of the confrontation led to the final loss of the undisputed dominance of the Iberians (Portuguese and Spanish) in the spice trade to Europe. Between 1595 and 1795 around 4,800 sea journeys to the Far East were made with less than 4% of the vessels being lost. The firm provided its captains with detailed information on sea routes, prevailing winds, sea currents, shallows and orientation points. The VOC made its own sea charts, and created various navigation instruments in their own workshops to build their advantage. The Dutch East India Company was operating a phenomenal fleet of 5,000 ships and managed to send almost a million people to Asia, more than the rest of Europe combined.

The flourishing economy of the city and the free spirit of the Republic also attracted talented immigrants, especially those being persecuted for their religion. The city soon had difficulties to accommodating the influx of population. In 1610, the Amsterdam patricians approved the Plan of the Three Canals, one of Europe's more ambitious urban planning projects of the time. It was set to dramatically expand the size of the city from 450 to 1,800 acres. Three major canals were built around the old city, one after the other. This was how Amsterdam's famous ring of canals was formed and how the city acquired its familiar half-moon shape. The city's population in 1567 was 25,000; in 1620: 100,000; and in 1660: 200,000. Just like its great Italian predecessor cities, Amsterdam also provided a context for a great cultural flourishing, one that is associated with the name of Rembrandt, not to mention all the other fine Dutch artist of the 17th century.

From 1621, the decline of Genoa and the Mediterranean region was confirmed, after the New World gold shipments declined in the Mediterranean. In the 17th century, the European economy was still very agrarian but quickly transitioning through the diffusion of craftsmanship and small urban merchants. Amsterdam obtained control of trade in northern goods together with the trade in spices from Eastern Mediterranean to Indonesia. A large armed fleet was sent out, and it seized areas in which the Dutch wished to trade, including Cape Town, parts of India, Batavia on Java, the Moluccas, and Nagasaki in Japan. After the Dutch West India Company was founded in 1621 to monopolise trade with the New World, Holland captured the entire Spanish treasure fleet in Cuba (1628). In 1670, about 10% of Dutch adult males were sailors, and the Dutch fleet was scouting the seas with more vessels than the rest of Europe, that is more than England, Scotland, France, Germany, Portugal and Spain combined. The VOC, Dutch East India Company, was then the richest corporation in the world, paying its shareholders an annual dividend of 40% on their investment despite financing 50,000 employees, 30,000 fighting men and 200 ships, many of them armed. The secret of this success was simple. They had no scruples and no mercy whatsoever: "the Dutch committed all the crimes secret and public, to steal from other trading nations the culture of spices".[13] The VOC's first conquest was the Banda archipelago, formed of 10 small volcanic islands in today's Indonesia, as its fiercely independent Islamic merchants never allowed Spain or Portugal to build forts on their islands: they insisted on their freedom to trade their precious nutmeg and mace with all nations. Great Banda also served as a redistribution centre for cloves and exotic aromatic precious woods. The price of nutmeg in Goa was 30 times what it cost in Banda, this would not be unnoticed. The Dutch East India Company's most successful head, Jan Pieterszoon Coen, managed to convince the Bandanese merchants of his firm's God-given right to monopolise the nutmeg trade in the VOC's typical style: he ordered every single male adult butchered. To better assert its new leadership, Coen also brought in Japanese mercenaries to torture, slice and decapitate village leaders, displaying their heads on long poles. This was certainly convincing enough for the population who finally resorted to grant the nutmeg exploitation privileges to the VOC. Early in the 1770s, French adventurers smuggled spice cuttings to the island of Mauritius in the Indian Ocean, but it took thirty more years before the young plantations yielded enough cloves to break the monopoly.

---

[13] Abbé Raynal, *Philosophical and historical history of European settling in the two Indies*, T.6., Elibon Classics Series (1773).

Long-distance shipping was in the hands of Europeans, mostly from Dutch and British origin. The merchants and the vessels from the north of Europe relentlessly put pressure, including by piracy, on the Mediterranean region. In the 18th century, the honest Abbé Raynal explains the whole matter in a few words: whilst the Portuguese robbed the Indians, the Dutch robbed the Portuguese. At the same time (1570), the Mediterranean and beyond was overwhelmed by cheap, bad quality cloth from the Low Countries which greatly harmed the expensive Italian clothing industry. The dissemination of counterfeited, bad quality Venetian cloth finally managed to ruin the high end reputation of fine Italian cloth. The shift of European trade from the Mediterranean market to the North Atlantic overthrew a century old pattern of international trade and established the basis of the preeminence of Northern Europe at the dawn of the industrial revolution.

As early as the 17th century, a large scale option market developed in Amsterdam. The option concept, already experimented in Flanders, was nothing new as it was detailed a thousand years ago, in the book of Genesis. Jacob contracted with Laban to carry out seven years of labor to marry Rachel. Later, the principle of options was precisely sketched by Aristotle in Politics, when he quoted mathematician Thales who was able to predict in a probabilistic way the olive harvest and subsequently book the olive presses at a cheap price, to sell at a higher price the rights to press. In addition, pledging of shares of widely held corporations such as the Dutch East India Company as collateral for private loans occurred almost immediately in the Netherlands at the beginning of the 17th century and opened new avenues for business: with collaterals as a guarantee, merchants got credit more easily in Amsterdam and at a cheaper rate.

One of the first large scale financial bubbles originated from there in 1636–1637 with the exuberant Tulip mania. We still have a very poor understanding of the forces driving such speculative bubbles which can be considered a form of psycho economic illness or an institutionalised gambling desperation to get wealthy, although we do know that the availability of too much "other people's money"[14] is a triggering factor. A speculative bubble is a "peculiar kind of fad or social epidemic that is regularly seen

---

[14]This expression was first used by Adam Smith in the *Wealth of Nations*, Book V, Chapter 1, §107 (1776).

in speculative markets; not a wild orgy of delusions but a natural consequence of the principles of social psychology coupled with imperfect
news media and information channels."[15] The tulip bulb forward and
option market provided all the necessary background for building one of
the most important financial bubbles as traders realised that buying call
options could be even more lucrative than buying the underlying (i.e., tulip
bulbs): tulip traders were found conducting their business in hundreds of
Dutch taverns, with some bulbs changing hands ten times a day. A good
trader could earn up to 60,000 florins in a month — approximately USD
61,710 adjusted to current U.S. dollars. Weavers and farmers would mortgage whatever they could to start trading in the tulip market. As expected,
the bubble fed on itself, and was supported by implausible projections of
potential demand. Taxonomists believe that the flowers had travelled
originally from the slopes of the Pamirs and the valleys of Tian Shan
mountain that run along China Western border to Constantinople, where
it was regarded as the flower of God and finally to Europe, presumably in
1593, by a botanist and honorary professor at University of Leiden, named
Carolus Clusius who was curious to study it for medicinal purposes. The
flowers were definitely very different from every other flower known to
horticulturists in the 17th century. Their colours were more intense than
those of ordinary plants. Rare bulbs commanded a large price premium
and could be worth more than a hundred times their weight in gold, but
ordinary tulips were sold by the pound. Around 1630, as a new type of
fancier tulip appeared, professional tulip traders, sought out flower lovers
and speculators alike. From the 1630s, the demand for the flowers grew
quickly, but the supply of exclusive bulbs did not as it took about seven
years to grow one from seed. And while bulbs can produce two or three
"offsets," annually, the mother bulb only lasts a few years. The highest
recorded price paid for a tulip bulb in 1637 reached 5,200 guilders, about
twenty one times the annual income of an honest craftsman. The bubble
was blown with easy credit, as usual, and forward market and popped by
calling in loans. It all began in Haarlem, at a routine bulb auction when,
for the first time, the lead auctioneer refused to show up and ran. Within
days, the panic on the tulip market had spread across the country, demand
evaporated and prices crashed. It is remarkable that the memory of the

---

[15] Robert J. Shiller, *Speculative Asset Prices*. Nobel Prize lecture (2013).

disastrous Dutch tulip bubbles continued to strike the imagination of economists and haunt Western economies for centuries. However, the mania would not have any immediate consequence for Amsterdam. This bubble differed in one crucial aspect from the contemporary subprime crisis in that even at its height, the Amsterdam Stock Exchange, well-established in 1630, would not touch the tulip market and the financial products packaged on tulips, and international markets would not interconnect on trading speculative bulbs. Therefore, even if the burst made some noise, the speculation in tulip bulbs was developed over-the-counter at the margins of Dutch economic life and it had finally a negligible impact on the real economy.Amsterdam as the financial centre of Europe stabilised for two centuries as a city state until the slow emergence of London. At this time, Amsterdam was almost self-ruled as a free city and very lightly ruled by the United Provinces (what became Netherlands). It seems as if the wave of financial crisis of the 17th century only strengthened Amsterdam as an IFC.

Amsterdam's influence as an international financial centre peaked in 1648, when the peace of Westphalia ended both the 80 Years' War of independence from Spain and the 30 Years' War in Germany. By 1650, Amsterdam was still the centre of the world. Problems started to accumulate when Oliver Cromwell landed a blow on Dutch naval supremacy with the Acts of Navigation passed by the Rump Parliament in 1651 in the wake of an unsuccessful negotiation between the English Commonwealth and the United Provinces. Although, it did not mention explicitly any nation, the Act was aimed at the Lower Provinces as it stipulated that goods could be only imported on the territory of the English Commonwealth by English ships, or by ships originating from the nations where the goods were originally produced. This piece of legislation was an attempt by the English government to closely supervise freight trade and curb the Dutch dominant position at sea. This was an illustration of Mercantilist protectionist theories which emphasized the need for a nation to control its trade, outsmart rivals, minimise the exit of precious metals (gold and silver) and develop a positive balance of trade. It led directly to the first Anglo-Dutch war of 1652–1654 which culminated in the defeat of the Dutch fleet in 1653. The Acts formed the basis of English overseas trade philosophy for 200 years as further Navigation Acts imposing various trade limitations were subsequently passed. Following the war, Cromwell who was a Calvinist puritan extensively negotiated with the Jews of Amsterdam about resettlement[16] until it became a reality in 1655 with their promise to make London a better Amsterdam. Another set of three naval wars fought between England and the Lower Provinces until the American Revolution reflected the complicated relationships between the English throne and the house of Orange on the one hand and the bitter economic and military rivalry between these two prominent trading countries on the other end.

In the 1690s, a Scottish murderer, compulsive gambler and deviant financial genius sentenced to death for dueling narrowly escaped London justice. He seeked refuge in Amsterdam which had become the European free city of financial innovation, this was before he became responsible for the Finances of France. Born in Scotland in 1671, John Law was the son of a goldsmith, who settled in London in 1692 and became involved in a number of disastrous ventures and gambling adventures before finding a safe haven in Amsterdam. Within a stone's throw from Piazza San Marco, was an old church of the 8th century, Chiesa di San Moise, later restored with a baroque facade finish in 1668, and was once notably named the most ungainely church in Venice.[17] The central nave holds a small tired pink marble forgotten tombstone of the one who fled France to Venice to finish his life after the bankruptcy of the Banque Royale, with this epitaph "Honori et memorial Joannis Law Edinburgenses Regii Galliarum Aerarii Prefecti Clarissima," "To the memory of John Law, Distinguished Controller of Treasury of the Kings of the French." Another interpretation could be "Here rests the man who managed to sink the already disastrous finances of France, and possibly triggered the French revolution."

Gradually, the scale of English merchant shipping overtook the Dutch in the first half of the 18th century. It reached 421,000 tons in 1751 and just went on growing into the 20th century. The northern Netherlands also ceased to be the most industrialised and technologically advanced area of

---

[16] In 1290 all the Jews, who had a reputation as extortionate moneylenders, were expelled from England by King Edward I who diligently seized their assets. The expulsion edict remained in force for the rest of the Middle Ages.

[17] The 19th century English art critic and writer John Ruskin, W.D. Howells, American ambassador in Venice in the 19th century described it as "in every ways detestable".

Europe. Dutch trade, industry and technology were stagnating; by 1735, dwindling spice income had been overtaken by textiles. But Amsterdam still remained the financial centre of Europe right through the 18th century. The actual buying and selling of bills of exchange was centered on Amsterdam and it became more and more the capital market for all of Europe. It was still the ideal place from which enterprising owners of capital could invest abroad. This development had collateral consequences for ancient routes. In the Middle East for example, the decline of Aleppo (Syria) in the 1700s, a traditional caravan centre was clearly related to the opening of the new sea routes by Europeans.

The degradation of relationships between England and the Dutch Republic became more palpable in 1777 when the British authorities audited the extent of Dutch investments in British national funds, Dutch investors realised that they were now unwelcomed in England and felt the pressure to either withdraw or conceal their holdings. The crisis reached its peak when Dutch investors continued financial support of American colonial aspirations throughout the American Revolutionary War which provoked British retaliation attack on Amsterdam in 1784. This was followed by much higher volatility on the London stock market. At the end the 18th century, Dutch banking had become extremely vulnerable. Amsterdam's bankers, despite the city's preeminence as an international financial centre, had suffered severe loses following the crises of the 1760s and 1770s. When the bankers Hope (1794) and Baring (1795) moved to London it was a sure sign that the time had come for Amsterdam to leave the way to London. The population of Amsterdam stagnated, barely rising from 200,000 with that of London continuing to rise: from 575,000 in 1700 to 865,000 in 1800.

Shortly afterward in 1795, the Dutch Republic collapsed before the French armies. In 1799, 178 years after its foundation, the year Napoleon overthrew the French Government, the Dutch East India Company finally went bankrupt only to be remembered as one of the most successful but ruthless sea trading companies in the world. Until 1806, the Batavian Republic, as the Netherlands was then known, remained officially independent of France but little took place without the approval of the French. Although Napoleon was a military genius, he did not understand the potential of rallying Dutch financiers, as finance was clearly out of his scope of personal expertise. His Continental blockage only succeeded in displacing the European IFC from Amsterdam to London as Paris was not a likely successor to the Dutch Republic in this field. London had become a safe harbour as a result of Napoleon's forced expropriation of European nobility properties and wealth. This conveyed the emergence of a new breed of investment bankers in London.

Secondary Places, including the Much Specific Case of France

A number of other European cities definitely had the potential to become leading international financial hubs, but never really made it. Conversely, a country like Italy managed to produce several IFCs or key financial cities (Venice, Genoa, Florence), some cities managed to become IFCs in Northern Europe (Bruges, Antwerp, Amsterdam and later London), some others would never go beyond becoming regional hubs, in spite of very significant strengths and influence (France, Spain, Portugal, Germany). The reasons behind the emergence of the stronger hubs, and understanding why a number of gifted others would never go beyond regional leadership sheds a useful light on international financial leadership in general. The list is impressive: Nantes (France), Saint-Malo (France), Bordeaux (France), Cadiz (Spain), Seville (Spain), Lisbon (Portugal), Porto (Portugal), Hamburg or Lübeck (Germany). Each city's internal dynamics must have been very different, just like the ambition to lead trade on a global basis must have been a defining condition.

The definition of "unimportant seaports" includes: "those with a poor or backward hinterland and few external connections; with a small or no share of national imports or exports, and contrary to expectations, a small share of coastal trade, which was also dominated by major ports; with exceptions they owned and built a few ships; they had inadequate facilities for larger ships; few warehouses and logistics, no comprehensive mercantile community or direct foreign linkage; few industries and small population; in sum they had no opportunity for self-generated trade." This definition related to sea trade can be extended to finance as the next stage of seaport dominance. Clearly those with no proactive and asserted international ambition, and in particular no navy and poor infrastructure, had no chance to emerge. The lesson will not be forgotten a few centuries later by another aspiring power to international trade domination — America.

In France from Philip the Fair, centralisation has been a prime and decisive feature of French political life, even if the real economic centre of France was Lyon especially since the success of its fairs in 1461. Lyon was a very cosmopolitan and vibrant business city with open access to Italy, and Switzerland. The King of France, Francis I was regularly taking up residence near the Saone river, and he granted the city an exemption for lending money.[18] It is quite puzzling that after 1450, as the international merchant community was mostly dealing with Lyon and Antwerp, Jacques Coeur, a savvy businessman and "Grand Argentier du royaume de France"[19] probably reflecting on the power of the Medicis, put all his energy in establishing the dominance of the French galleys in the Mediterranean and was ennobled. He was late by more than a century; the market was gone already. At the same time, in Austria, the Fuggers were opening meaningful opportunities in the East, while the Genoese were sailing to Africa and thought of India and Asia.

The restructuring of the French public finances initiated by Colbert in the first years of the reign of Louis XIV, created a deep financial anxiety in Paris. In 1663, the King decided to redeem the annuities ("rentes") issued by the French crown, creating a strong emotional response as it was a significant source of income for those among the Parisian population who were fortunate enough to save some money. The proceeds of the first new perpetual bonds issued by Colbert in Paris in 1673 and 1674 were disappointing, emphasizing that the city, poorly connected to the rest of the kingdom by uneven roads, was not yet the pivotal financial centre of France. The use of heavily loaded waggons and carts became more common, and as prosperity increased, so did the traffic and the need for wider roads. But the dust surface of the new roads only became mud and pain in the cold and rainy season. Waterways were under such circumstances the preferred choice for valuable cargo. It is no surprise that Lyon was already firmly established as an international trading and financial centre

---

[18] This was also much needed to finance the King's war against Italy.

[19] Jacques Coeur, a merchant and businessman, was appointed by King Charles VII, Steward of the Royal Expenditure of France in 1438. He struggled to reorganise the royal finances which were close to bankruptcy due to the war with England in particular.

as it easily connected through the Saône to the Rhône River a key European waterway of 330 km to the Mediterranean. A connection with the Rhine was originally planned from 1784 onwards but finally opened in 1834 but was disrupted by technical hurdles and wars. Paris only took over after the sensational bankruptcy of Samuel-Jacques Bernard, a Jewish banker and accredited money lender to Louis XIV, over payments due in 1709. Bernard had the desire to set up in Lyon a high profile bank which under his supervision would lend money to the King through interest bearing bills in exchange for royal bank notes. The plan was probably to establish in France a Royal Bank comparable to the Bank of England, but he met some formidable opposition as the market was seen to be in the hands of too narrow a circle of bankers. Trudaine[20] wrote that "This Bernard business has upset the Lyon market beyond repair; things are getting worse everyday." This was indeed to show that the financial crisis was serious, with consequences as far as Geneva and Germany. Following the crisis, reports were made that the once famous Beaucaire fairs ("Foire de la Madeleine") held in July which took place in a convenient river port on an ancient roman crossroad, 250 km south of Lyon, were deserted. Eventually, the failure of the Bernard attempt led to the creation of the Banque Royale in Paris (1716)[21], under the direction of John Law, a Scottish adventurer. The resulting scandal of the rue Quincampoix experience would lead to a financial crisis of another magnitude. France was split between an economy open to overseas trade on the coastline and an agrarian society in the interior not very interested in such far-flung adventures. The main French maritime cities involved in overseas navigation and trade during the sixteenth and seventeenth centuries were backed by local merchant and maritime communities, rather than by the central power of Versailles or Paris, and depended more on piracy (in the ports of Normandy and Bretagne: Saint-Malo, Brest) and smuggling, (in Nantes or Bordeaux), than on official trade and economic policy led by the French state, even during Richelieu's or Colbert's regencies. It is very likely that France could have

---

[20]Charles Daniel Trudaine (1703–1769) fulfilled the role of counsel, Councillor of State and general intendant for Riom, he was chosen in 1743 to head the bridges and roads department as intendant of finances of France.

[21]The bank was initially called Banque Générale, and became Banque Royale in 1719.

been a powerful international financial centre if its political capital had been located on, or much closer to, one of the powerful Atlantic seaport rather than in the middle of France, but this was seen as too risky a gamble to the unity of the kingdom. It would have been even more likely if such city was a free city where merchant entrepreneurial spirit was well aligned with internal politics. But most of the French coastal cities had difficult relationships with the central royal power. Brittany, a fragmented province on the Atlantic coast, ruled by several Breton lords remotely allied with the French Kingdom, and in Bordeaux the English had made their home since the accession to power in 1154 of Henri Plantagenêt, spouse of Aliénor d'Aquitaine. The English who had settled in Bordeaux were often busy shipping claret, "Graves", to London until the export of wine was interrupted by the outbreak of the Hundred Year's War between France and England. The war disrupted French political life for decades and damaged the economy by inflating long-distance overland transportation costs. The resulting crisis encouraged a radical shift in the structure of long distance international trade in favour of Northwestern Europe. In the 15th century, thanks to the Italian merchant-bankers, Lyon became a vibrant economic centre: silk, wool, spices and other precious goods were traded along the Rhône. The rapid growth of these fairs has frequently been ascribed to French public finance related matters, but a drastic monetary policy had in those years weakened the institution of the fair. As French merchants and their Italian colleagues alike were clearly boycotting the Ligurian financial operators, the Genoese bankers set up other fair locations, and chose Besançon, leading to the rapid decline of Lyon.

Despite Paris becoming a place to meet and be seen, where Lombards were already well established and the leading fortunes since 1300, this may not be genuinely considered as the most salient contemporary explanation of France secondary financial ranking as an IFC compared to its overall geo-economic position. In the Parisian riots of 1382 and 1413–1418, the Lombards were chased by a furious crowd in the streets of Paris, and their properties looted; such a rapid accumulated wealth could not be honest, especially when the people were hungry. And if the Jews did not share the fate of the Lombards in the latest riots of the 15th century, it was because they had been already expelled from the kingdom in 1394. Despite these sporadic reactions, the integration of Florentines, Luccans and other Italian merchants was generally smooth, especially when patronyms from obvious foreign origin were adapted to disappear in the *lingua franca* of the host country.

Another more plausible reason may be that the very first international financial crises, the one that was the big bang of financial capitalism, occurred in France in 1719[22] under the stewardship of the already mentioned genius Scottish gambler and economist,[23] obsessed by the idea to create paper money and clever financial schemes. John Law de Lauriston is said to have mentioned to Victor Amadeus II, Duke of Savoy that he had discovered the secret of the philosopher's stone, which was to turn paper into gold, what he called the "System". But it was reported that the wise Duke, skeptical, uttered that 'he was not rich enough to ruin himself'. Law arrived in France in 1712 or 1713 with proposals to improve the government's credit but was turned down by Louis XIV. After the King's death in 1715, he was finally allowed to open in 1716, the Banque Générale, a privately owned bank issuing notes payable to the bearer on demand into a species of a particular type. Once the bank had earned people's trust, it began to issue notes far exceeding deposits and to extend loans against deposits. The quantity of bills in circulation increased very rapidly, and again a significant artificial economic boom resulted, comparable to some extend to the tulip mania in Holland eighty years before. In this context, risky ventures were always tremendously tempting, because when they went reasonably well they yielded enormous profits. His Mississippi innovative investment scheme was designed to exploit through the Compagnie d'Occident the untapped potential of the Mississippi river drainage claimed by France in Louisiana and subsequently to rescue the French royal finances. Many countries had created central banks but France had not. John Law convinced the French regent Philippe d'Orléans, that he could liquidate the government debt[24] which was plaguing the French finances by a system of credit based on paper money. Although the

---

[22] Larry Neal, *I am not a Master of Event. The speculations of John Law and Lord Londonderry in the Mississippi and SouthSea bubbles*, Yale University Press (2012).

[23] He exposed his monetary theory in "*Money and Trade Considered, with a Proposal for Supplying the Nation with Money*" published in Edinburg, Scotland (1705).

[24] French public debt at the time represented about 10 years of tax revenues.

French government, knew that Law was potentially a dangerous individual, a gambler and possibly a British spy, France's financial problem let the government gamble on the arrival of a providential man. The government thought it had little to lose, as the French finances were getting close to their third bankruptcy in less than a century. The Compagnie de l'Occident was granted the control of trade between France and its Louisiana and Canadian colonies for 25 years. In Canada, the French would trade in beaver skins. In the Louisiana colony they would trade in precious metals. This Colony included the Natchez district and the area along the Mississippi Gulf Coast in present-day Mississippi. Many had heard the rumour that this land was rich in silver and gold, the basis of the world's strongest currencies. The French monetary system consisted of two distinct parts. One was coins minted with gold and silver bearing the king's effigy but with no indication of value.[25] The other part was the unit of account, the livre (or franc) required for all contracts and debts, including bills of foreign exchange. The relation between the coins and the unit of account was discretionary and set by the King of France with immediate effect and with no control or registration in any court.

One of the earliest and greatest public road shows on the over exaggerated promises of the wealth of the Mississippi River managed to turn into a goldrush and the price of the listed shares of the Mississippi company sky-rocketed in feverish speculation. The price of shares of the Compagnie des Indes rose about 20-fold, whereas the shares of the South Sea Company rose only about six to seven-fold. However the mismanagement of the colony was a huge issue, highlighted by the soft speaking Abbé Raynal who mentioned that the Mississipi region was the "terror of free men" and so poorly managed from Paris, possibly because the French could not use the equivalent competence of the Dutch East India Company or the British Honourable East India Company. He regretted that: "this State [France] buying overseas every single year 17 million pounds of tobacco, could have easily produced it to its satisfaction in Louisiana."[26] Few people realise how huge the Colony was at the time, it stretched for

---

[25] The specifics of the coins, size, weight, imprint, were set by edicts of the King.

[26] Philosophical and historical history of European settling in the two Indies, Abbé Raynal, T.6. 1773, Elibon Classics series.

3,000 miles from the mouth of the Mississippi River to parts of Canada. It included the present-day states that hug the river: Louisiana, Mississippi, Arkansas, Missouri, Illinois, Iowa, Wisconsin and Minnesota. The colony of Louisiana's connection to the Mississippi River gave rise to the company's more popular name, The Mississippi Company. Law's company next purchased the right to mint new coins for France, and by October it had purchased the right to collect most French taxes. The rise and fall of the Mississippi Company became known as the Mississippi Bubble. The whole financial scheme was probably related to Law's distorted gambling perception of financial markets despite some great economic intuitions and his early fascination of the relationships between the Amsterdam Exchange Bank, the Amsterdam stock exchange and the Dutch East India Company. It may also be a consequence of the poor execution of a number of bright ideas which became corrupted due to the technical limitations of the time.

The Mississippi bubble resulted from a series of brilliant innovations and clever gambling which first started to bear results to rescue the troubled royal finance of France.[27] It started to be so successful that England imitated the French financiers in creating the South Sea Company. The French elite was not only buying Mississippi, it was pawning properties and jewels to be involved and grateful to be treated with contempt at Law's offices rue Quincampoix, Paris, a sure sign that the scheme was smelling a rat. However, the success was such that it sparked the need for more paper bank notes freely issued by the Banque Royale[28] also controlled by Law. The financial district in Paris became so agitated at times with investors that soldiers would be sent in at night to maintain order. The company's stock shares could initially be bought with only a 10% down payment. With these favourable terms, fortunes were made overnight. The new issue of bank notes, fully convertible to cash, continued until it became obvious that the bank had issued much more paper notes

---

[27] France had a debt of 2.8 billion pounds, about 10 years of fiscal income in France following Louis XIV's military campaigns.
[28] Formerly Banque Générale Privée created in 1716 by John Law who later convinced the French government to develop the use of paper money which was new for them. It absorbed the Compagnie Perpétuelle des Indes and was transformed into Banque Royale in 1719.

than its cash or metal deposits. The increase of money supply started to translate into inflation and the wisest investors, such as the Prince de Conti or the Duc de Bourbon, publicly converted back their bank notes into gold and silver; leading to investor panic.[29] The scheme resulted not only in one massive run but in a severe double financial crash in France and England. At the heart of this crisis was a political scandal: on the one hand, John Law de Lauriston as the now wealthy Controller General and Superintendent General of Finance, controlling all of France's finance and money creation and mastermind of the Mississippi scheme and on the other hand Thomas Pitt Jr., 1st Earl of Londonderry, Governor of the Leeward Islands, Colonel in the Princess of Wales own Regiment of Horse. Pitt, the son of one of the wealthiest merchants of the time, connected with Law as a wild speculator on the London, Paris and Amsterdam stock market so as to become his main partner in England. As he also sat as an influential Member of Parliament, Pitt was considered untouchable in England. On the French, side the lasting consequence on investors may be found later in October 1720 in the catastrophic management of the Law crisis which did not elicit any policy response when, John Law's creation "Banque Royale" collapsed after a bank run. Law dubbed "Messire Quincampoix" fled to Brussels and Venice spending his final years as an impoverished gambler before passing away in 1729.

The Paris Brothers, bankers exiled by Law, were promptly recalled and mandated to clean up the mess and liquidate the Law system. The Paris plan relied on committing the government to the level of debt service that prevailed in 1718, and treat the claimants as fairly as possible. A private individual who had been forced to accept Law's paper money as legal tender in repayment or a debt bondholder who had been led into the debt conversion scheme, should be treated differently from a speculator. In order to achieve that, the Paris Brothers engineered an incredibly sophisticated scheme called the "Visa" leading to the individual review and subsequent rating of each of the 510,000 claims filed. Each claim was verified with the assistance of notaries and rated with a coefficient ranging from 5% for undocumented claims to 100% for the one being forced to accept Law's paper money. This process lasted from January 1721 to September 1721 and mobilised and trained a huge staff of clerks,

---

[29] 17 casualties are found dead as a result of the riots near Law's offices Rue Quincampoix, Paris.

including some from the Netherlands, Spain and Italy as it was sometimes difficult to find competent people. The result is that each claimant received a certificate for a government bond, life annuities and perpetual annuities, valued at the level of each claim multiplied by the rating coefficient. This unprecedented effort remains a powerful testimonial of the French government desire to treat the debtors of the Law system as best it could. The dismissal of Duc de Bourbon in 1726 in favour of the young King's[30] tutor, Cardinal de Fleury, Bishop of Fréjus, unfortunately led to the disgrace of the Paris Brothers. The new government led by Fleury cut corners and simply eliminated the small perpetual and life annuities of less than 20 livres per year, annuities held by the small holders which the Paris brothers had carefully taken care to protect during the Visa. Furthermore, the life annuities created since 1720 were reduced by a factor ranging from one sixth to two thirds.

Law's bankruptcy, aggravated by Richard Cantillon's manipulations,[31] was left to fester mistrust for a long time in the French monetary and financial system. The losses were so heavy and the suffering so immense that for over a hundred years it was even considered a "faux pas" in France to utter the word "bank," a term which for a time was synonymous with "fraud."[32] The consequences in France were serious in the French psyche. It resulted in a weaker interest in finance and financial markets, a stronger

---

[30] Louis XV would inherit the French crown in 1715 from his grandfather Louis XIV at the age of 5. During his almost 59 years reign, he was considered mildly interested in the government of France.

[31] The Cantillon bank loaned money to its customers to buy shares in Law's Mississippi Trading Company, and requested them to keep the block shares as collateral. The Irish banker Richard Cantillon, who was an unscrupulous trader, misappropriated the deposited securities, sold them at their peak and kept the proceeds from the sale. Once the shares had crashed, Cantillon bought them back for a fraction of their peak price and restored the client deposits. After pocketing the difference, he turned to his clients and demanded repayment of the loans he had initially made to his clients ruined by the crash. Most were unable to return the money, since the collateral they had at the bank was worth close to nothing. These fraudulent operations led to multiple criminal charges and civil suits against him. He fled in a hurry to England where finance practices were more lax. He was murdered, or staged his disappearance, at his London home in 1734, after 12 years of litigation, two arrests and the constant threat of imprisonment.

[32] Jesus Huerta de Soto, Bank, *Credit And Economic Cycle*, p. 100, Ludwig von Mises Institute, (2002).

appetite for gold and property conservation and a delayed financial deepening. Another major crisis, fiscal this time, probably aggravated the people's perception that the government was finally incompetent, and led to the final days of the French monarchy in 1789. Emile Pereire sadly noted in 1834 that there were no banks outside of Paris, in contrast with England, which had five or six hundred. London emerged as the undisputed leader in international finance after 1873, especially outside the Continent, but Paris was by no means cast completely in the shadows.[33]

Lisbon in Portugal, was undoubtedly one of the leading coastal cities of Europe, in the 16th and 17th centuries but never really managed to become a truly international finance hub, very likely due to its internal dynamic and lack of capacity to mobilise sufficient human resources for this purpose. As early as the 15th century, Lisbon was a busy commercial centre, at the western most edge of the known world, were traders, seafarers, astronomers, geographers and scientists, were all keenly debating the possibility of the existence and discovery of a "new world", or of reaching the East by sailing west. In 1476, a young Genoese sailor fighting against the Portuguese off Cape St. Vincent (Sagres, Lagos), had to swim to the shore of Portugal with the help of a wooden oar after his ship was attacked by French privateers off the coast of Portugal and burned. The young man then moved on to Lisbon which had a considerable community of active and entrepreneurial Genoese. Christopher took an active part in the sailing debates of the time and began to seek a patron for his intended expedition to find a new route for the Indies. His expedition was patronised by King Ferdinand and Queen Isabella of Castile in April 1492 getting Genoese Bank of St. George's financial backing for part of the expenses. On Friday 3 August, the Genoese navigator Christopher Columbus set sail from the Spanish port of Palos in command of the carrack Santa María and attended by two little caravels, the Pinta and the Niña. His objective was to sail west until he reached Asia (the Indies). San Salvador in the Bahamas was sighted by Rodrigo de Triana, one of the Pinta crew members on Thursday 11 October 1492, and they landed the following day, the vessels continued their journey to Cuba and then *La Spañola* (Hispaniola, now the

---

[33] Kindleberger, Charles Poor, *The Formation of Financial Centers*, Princeton University, Princeton studies in international finance n°36, (1974).

Dominican Republic) before sailing back to Spain. In fact, Columbus never set foot in the land that would become the United States of America and never even saw it. He was convinced that he had found a new route to China, Japan, and discovered the region of King Solomon's fabled gold mines and the pagodas with golden roofs described by Marco Polo — which were most probably situated in Burma. Amidst this geographical mistake, power and greed soon took over, the search for the mythical gold led to an unspeakable genocide. Armed with the latest weaponry and armoured mastiffs trained to rip people apart, the Spanish tortured, maimed, raped, slaughtered and burned the Hispaniola inhabitants in search of precious metals, the island became the shadow of what it was before the arrival of the Spaniards. The discovery had fundamental consequences in the development of international trade and world finance. It certainly led to the opening of a broader trading space and the Mediterranean which had been the cradle of modern finance became a space of secondary importance.

A significant Italian community was present in Lisbon and involved in trade, its members also participated to the voyage of exploration and discovery of the New World. Foreign commercial agents were mobile in Europe and capable of settling from one city to another as necessary. But in spite of its immense wealth related to the trade with the New World, Lisbon could not organise innovative business models as those sponsored by the Dutch East India Company or the English East India Company. The first reason was probably the lack of political strength which resulted in a poor long term development vision reflected by i) Lisbon's inconvenient agricultural hinterland and terrestrial communications at the exception of good connection with neighbouring Rabatejo and Alentejo and later by ii) the annexation in 1580 of the country by Philip II of Spain as a result of the weakening of royal power in Portugal. Another explanation connected to the first one is that the Portuguese strategy for dominance was in need of a stronger navy to fight against the Dutch and the English at sea and better control strategic seaports and commercial choke points such as Aden on the Red Sea. Building a stronger seafaring network would certainly have helped to further consolidate their trade dominance.

In Spain, only Seville with its influence limited down to the Guadalquivir River Valley, first, and then Cadiz, and ending well before

Jerez de la Frontera, emerged as a main seaport. One of the key innovations for the development of international financial centres originated in Barcelona in 1401: the *Taula de canvi*, was the first prototype of a public bank, founded as a treasury entity for the city of Barcelona and Catalonia, and administered as a department of municipal government. As prescribed in its by-laws, it accepted private deposits, reimbursed them or transferred them to others; it could grant credit solely to the municipality in order for it to repay its debts, but its first motivation was fiscal. It was not properly managed as the city could not resist the temptation of easy credit to fund food purchases or war. Only the Genoese better leveraged this defining innovation through the Casa di San Georgio and its related banks. Spanish cities' financial expertise could not compare to Genoa's position which was already a Spanish satellite under the protection of Charles V of Spain. The Holy Roman Emperor, heir of three of Europe's leading dynasties: the Houses of Habsburg, Valois-Burgundy and Trastámara was ambitious to leverage his relationship with Andrea Doria in Genoa to take over the reputation of Florence for financial innovation. Public banks introduced a breakthrough in the development of finance that was to lead eventually to the creation of issuing banks and the beginnings of the credit economy. The massive influx of precious metals from the Americas shifted momentarily the economic focus from the Northern Italian trading cities to Spain; specifically, Seville and the other Spanish business centres. However, without being political capitals, Barcelona, Seville or Lisbon were seen as only minor instruments of the kingdom's policy. Charles V was unable to keep the royal treasury from going bankrupt, which had very negative effects on the Spanish economy and subsequently on the bankers who had financed his projects. A catastrophic economic situation prompted Charles V to disregard the most basic ethical principles and seize funds where he could find them, in particular those deposited in the vaults of Seville's bankers. In an attempt to catch up on the New World race, Spain swallowed Portugal in 1580 following the death of its King Sebastian I and the resulting crisis of succession in Lisbon. Philip II of Spain united the two countries under the Iberian Union for 60 years, and let the Portuguese empire decline. For about 300 years, Iberian seaports would be trading on the basis of monopoly rights: As a result, most ports of the Iberian costs were forbidden to trade with the colonies. Crown monopolies would favour entrenchment, complacency and would not emulate competition between the Spanish Atlantic cities. Relationships with the other great neighbouring power of the time, Portugal, had always been difficult and contributed to dissipate a precious amount of energy which could have been better invested in a joint effort. Especially when the Atlantic seaways to the New World opened, there was a missed opportunity to shift together the economic focus of Merchant bankers out of the Mediterranean world. The wars in Flanders in the hands of a mediocre leadership were exhausting the Spanish crown's finance and military might. It cost two or three Armadas, the surprise destruction of the Spanish fleet by Admiral Heemskerck at Gibraltar (1607) and damages by the Anglo-Dutch naval raids in Cadiz and Portugal (1596). This led to wild inflation, cash strapped public finance, soaring levels of public debt and crushing taxation, resulting in the loss of morale and capacity for Spain to remain a leading financial and trading power.

In Germany, Lübeck and Hamburg, for instance, were nodal Hanseatic seaports by European standards, extremely active in the Baltic and beyond, but neither ranked as an imperial colonial capital, nor as a primary reception centre for overseas products. Lübeck was a hub for foreign agents, capital and merchandise and played the role of an operational and logistic transhipping centre that provided men, ships, capital and flag to those who, being at war, could not pursue traditional trade connections. No document designated Lübeck as head of the Hansa, although it was nearly so all of the time. The port of Hamburg was, simultaneously, an economic and financial centre, and its vitality and wealth depended over time on foreign capital and economic agents, even if its domestic dynamics were also quite significant as a transfer point from the Baltic to the North Sea. All around Amsterdam, the German and Scandinavian sea ports of the Baltic provided an influx of willing crews and sailors much needed for the development of Dutch naval supremacy. Just like the Florentine bankers in the 14th century, competences moved across Europe to the most appealing city to develop business and feed through its development.

Ports of secondary importance, just like financial centres of secondary importance, were needed feeders to the international ones. International financial centres could certainly never flourish alone without a rich network of alliances and satellite hubs. Meanwhile, the development of both primary and secondary hubs for transnational trading in Europe would announce the beginning of Europe's great age of imperial power.

The case of Russia is complicated, and it may hardly be summarised in a few lines. In early 1914, most financial observers would have given Russia a solid credit rating and strong chances to become a leading finance centre. The ruble was trustworthy and fully backed by gold, and the country's highly accomplished economists and bankers guided its financial management. Unfortunately, the cost of the First World War for Russia through the summer of 1917 reached between 38 and 50 billion ruble, which was an extraordinary drag for its emerging economy. To cover its expenses, Russia relied on a combination of foreign and domestic loans, unused funds from the pre-war budget, and currency emissions. Russia's budget was in deficit during the war to about the same degree as Germany and the UK. But Russia was forced to rely more extensively on quantitative easing than the other powers to compensate for the loss of lucrative markets and not so effective capital markets at the end of war. This was going to bear serious consequences, as it laid the ground for a radical opposition to the tsarist regime. Communism which negated the market economy was invented by a group of philosophers led by a state-less British resident "bourgeois" philosopher born in Germany, from Jewish origin baptised in the Lutheran church then proclaimed atheist who as a young boy scandalised his classmates by getting drunk, laughing in church, and galloping through the streets taking drunken donkey rides which occasionally turned into hooliganism. But this is more for the anecdote, and likely reflected an hyperactive personality. As a philosopher and economist, Marx who was an implacable critic of his time finally settled down and married in the Kreuznach church of St. Paul with Jenny von Westphalen with whom he had seven children. He did not mind working with a French anarchist, Pierre-Joseph Proudhon, who famously declared that "property is theft" but nevertheless wrote essays on how to make money on the stock market.[34] Contradictions may have been from time to time the evolution engine of history. As he was living in Paris, he met and discussed with Hegel the final communist revolution in history to

---

[34]Pierre-Joseph Proudhon, Manuel du spéculateur à la bourse, Paris Garnier Frères, Libraires éditeurs, (1855).

"understand the inner workings of capitalism" until he passed away in London in 1883. Marx saw historical process as proceeding through a necessary series of modes of production, characterised by class struggle, culminating in communism.[35] His writings were endorsed by the socialist anarchist opponents to the declining Russian monarchy which lead to the Russian revolution of 1917, and later by Mao ZeDong, who finally distanced himself from the Russian experience after 1949. On 29 December 1917, Vladimir Ilyich Ulyanov — Lenin and his Bolchevik Comrades declared the debt on the czarist bonds null and void, and thus worthless. This ruthless debt repudiation following the strong encouragement to invest from the French media "Lending to Russia is like lending to France" and Government, created an immense nationwide trauma as many European families, especially the French ones who subscribed about half of the 1906 bond issue, were not only fooled but ruined. The Russian bonds were especially popular in Paris around 1900, as nearly one and a half million individuals ranging from wealthy families to modest workers had bought them as a trusted security for retirement and cushion against inflation as the Russian rubble was pegged to gold. The Raffalovitch scandal of the 1920s showed that both the French conservative and the socialist press and many banking intermediaries received unethical commissions and bribes from Russia to oversell the bond issue. France which had hardly recovered from the John Law disaster was caught by another one of equally underestimated systemic importance for the country's savers. This episode was again surely detrimental to the development of a trustable international finance hub in Paris. For nearly eight decades following the October revolution, Russia's Imperial Bonds decorated bathrooms as wallpaper and piled up in attics.[36] Conversely, Russia could not access the Eurobond market. The Russian communist epoch culminated in the Cold war and terminated with the fall of the wall separating Eastern and Western Germany on 10 November 1989. After the disintegration of the

---

[35] Stanford Encyclopedia of Philosophy.

[36] It was not before November 1996 that Russian President Boris Yeltsin agreed to repay a nominal value of USD 80–100 for each of the estimated 4 million surviving czarist bonds in circulation in France. The French bond holder association were outraged, and claimed that the current value of their certificates was closer to USD 31 billion, including interest.

Soviet communist empire, Russia certainly had some ambition to become a respectable finance centre of international significance, and President Yelsin's 1996 initiative to clean-up the Russia European bond trauma was certainly part of the move. But aside from the difficulty in finding a suitable solution, a series of defaults complicated the plan. In 1998, a massive default on Russia's USD 160 billion debt rattled the entire global Russian economy. The trouble started when payments were missed on local Treasury obligations, and later extended to include foreign currency obligations and Minfin III foreign currency bonds. Russia's debts were eventually restructured in later years. During the 2008–2009 crisis, Russia was badly shaken again as the cost of insuring Russian bonds against bankruptcy rocketed to extreme levels, highlighting some fragility in its economy. Russia later linked with China in the hope of doing from the Eastern Asian side of the country what could not achieved from the Western side, but it is unlikely that Vladivostok, the ancient Manchu city of eternal light, can stand as a leading financial centre in the vicinity of already declared and strongly established Asian front runners. Russia has endured 100 years of intense trauma including two major revolutions, two world wars, a civil war and other military conflicts, years of famine and 70 years of Soviet repression that imprisoned and killed millions of its citizens. The way out of the disastrous 14th century in Europe is a resounding lesson which has shown that in spite of extraordinary pain, redemption was achieved. The emergence of the Enlightenment has demonstrated that its most powerful engine was both a truly shared multicultural humanist philosophy to foster the common good and an unquenchable thirst to explore beyond the "known world".

Chapter 4

THE TRANSATLANTIC
NEW FINANCIAL ORDER
IN THE 18th CENTURY

The Steady Emergence of London as Europe's Finance Centrepoint

The bankless "Londinium"

London lies on the River Thames, about 50 km from the North Sea. The river has influenced London's economy for many centuries. Rising tides especially during storm surges have led the Thames to flood the city more than once, and falling winter temperatures have led it to freeze during the Little Ice Age. In the 1st century A.D., the Romans came to Great Britain and built a settlement conveniently located near the mouth of the River Thames. The Romans chose the point where the Thames was narrow enough to build a bridge, but deep enough to handle seagoing vessels. The place was sacked by the Celts, rebuilt and soon became busy with vessels and home of the Roman Procurator, and was then named Londinium.[1]

---

[1] First mentioned in the Tacitus' Annals, a Roman historian and senator who wrote a history of the Roman Empire from the reign of Tiberius to that of Nero, in the years AD 14–68.

After the Roman Empire collapsed, the city fell into oblivion. About 400 years later, the Saxons, a confederation of Germanic tribes from the North German plains, found the area convenient for trading and settled. In the centuries that followed, the place was put under constant pressure by the Danish Viking raiders plaguing the North Sea since the end of the 8th century. When William the Conqueror invaded Britain in 1066, Lunduntown had already become the biggest town on the island. William made London his capital city and crowned himself King in Westminster Abbey on Christmas Day.

London has a rather simple 2000 year old history and has always been the main political and economic centre of England. Contrary to Venice or Amsterdam, London has never been a city-state. As the capital of an island, London has been spared by the Napoleonic wars and invasion since William the Conqueror, Duke of Normandy, in 1066, and the landing in Devon of the Dutch William III of Orange-Nassau, with the support of his own country.

The emancipation of London can be dated to 1597 with the closure by Queen Elizabeth I of the Stalhof after it faced violent attacks against privileges of position by the English merchants. This was the time when London withdrew from the Hanseatic alliance and terminated the Hansa members' trade privileges. The Steelyard ("Stalhof"), located on the north bank of the Thames by the outflow of the Walbrook,[2] near today's Cannon Street, was the main trading base of the Hanseatic League in London and enjoyed tax and customs concessions given by Edward I in 1303. The Steelyard was later reopened by King James I, but never regained its previous influence. King William III was born in the Hague, and was invited by Protestant English members of Parliament to oust and replace his father-in-law the ruling Stuart Catholic King James II of England in 1688.[3] King James fled by the Thames, was captured, fled again and landed in Ireland where, with French support, he raised an army but was defeated by William at the Battle of the Boyne in July 1690. James died

---

[2] Now a subterranean river in the City of London, used for shipping during ancient Roman times.

[3] This episode is remembered in England as the "Glorious revolution". William III was married to Mary, daughter of King James II of England.

in exile in Saint-Germain in France on 16 September 1701. Following this episode, William managed to transform England into a powerful and modern country. A sustained period of strong economic growth, the Great Divergence, started from 1750 for about a century in Northwestern Europe, resulting in overall better material living conditions in Europe and a significant increase in life expectancy, but still leaving behind a profound divide between wealth and health among human societies.

In the 17th century, Britain had already built up one of the world's largest overseas colonial empire. The North American colonies were lost after the War of Independence of 1776–1783. On the other hand, after the Seven Years War of 1756–1763, Britain captured Canada and India. Britain also took control of Dominica, Grenada, St. Vincent and Tobago in the West Indies. In 1707, the Act of Union was passed. Scotland was united with England and Wales, England became part of Great Britain. The foundation of the British Honourable East India Company (EIC) for spice trade[4] in 1601, a year before its arch competitor, the Dutch East India Company, led to the creation of a secondary equity market by the middle of the century. Contrary to the Dutch VOC model, the EIC shareholders were given real rights in the management of the company. The equity of joint-stock companies became listed and London developed a secondary equity market and a market for newly issued shares. Brokerage subsequently developed, providing London with a level of unparalleled expertise in the financial management of corporate equity. Stockjobbers, who acted as market makers, became a symbol of the new importance of the London stock market, not only for trading equity but also for dealing in the large increases in sovereign debt. In particular, Dutch stock jobbing in the British annuities became essential and necessary for the British government because it borrowed increasingly large sums. One should never forget the early symbiotic relationship between London and Amsterdam to explain the rise of Northern European finance as the dominant centre for money dealings. The long Anglo-Dutch relationship got later strained with the Fourth Anglo-Dutch War (1880–4), the Batavian

---

[4] As the Dutch managed to monopolise the spice trade (clover, mace and nutmeg) from the Moluccas, now Indonesia, the firm mostly traded products from India such as silk and colourful fabrics before it was liquidated on 1st January (1874).

Republic created under French revolutionary pressure in 1895 and finally with the incorporation of the Kingdom of Holland into the French empire by Napoleon Bonaparte in 1810.

The 17th century was also a century of hardship for London as it was struck twice by another final replica of the Great Plague in 1665, which killed an estimated 20% of its population at a disrupting rate of 7,000 people per week and by the Great fire a year later (1666) which destroyed 30,000 homes and most of the old city made of wooden buildings. Meanwhile, these tragic events did not prevent London from continuing to gradually assert its financial leadership over Northern Europe. The insurance business developed after Nicholas Barbon, an economist and physician who took an active part in the rebuilding of London after the Great Fire, started a building insurance business, selling fire insurance policies. The financial emergence of the city took some time and required fixing some key issues, such as the absence of public banking. But London managed to keep a very international profile: Lombard Street was named after immigrant bankers from Milan and its surrounding area. Compared to Amsterdam, the joint kingdoms of England and Wales and Scotland had no public bank, or wealthy merchants, or sophisticated bankers, much less a stock of metallic monies stored in a central secure place: Foreign bills of exchange in Britain were negotiated by "remitters", who were largely Italians and Dutch. The foreign bills were usually transferable by endorsement and virtually indistinguishable from inland bills of exchange. So those willing to receive immediate cash would go to the nearest commodity market and try to sell manually inland bills of exchange on London. No bank would be available to clear the bills between merchants. Sellers, especially cattle drovers after disposing of their herds for cash, would want to buy inland bills of exchange, rather than take the risk of carrying large amount of money back home. This "bankless economy" was in sharp contrast with Amsterdam sophistication and its Venetian model: In Holland, the Wisselbank was granted a state monopoly to swiftly clear in guilder in its books wholesale buyers and sellers, saving the hurdles to negotiate the bills on side markets. For smaller businesses, independent intermediaries would aggregate small accounts and deal with the bank on a wholesale basis. An early form of banking developed in London with the goldsmiths[5] who united into one business activity functions such as: maintaining safe storage of gold, silver and deposits of money; loaning out deposits of money (as well as their own money); transferring money holdings from town to town or person to person; trading in foreign exchange and bullion; and discounting bills of exchange. Before the goldsmith bankers, these activities were scattered, often as sidelines or by-products of other trading activities. Around 1633, goldsmith banking arose as an indigenous form of banking in England. Before the goldsmiths started to perform these duties in London, these essential services to the development of trade were rendered by Italians, Germans and particularly the Dutch.

Things started to change when the British sovereign debt market was created after the "Glorious Revolution" of 1688,[6] and was probably more efficient in many ways than the original Dutch innovation on the Dutch East India Company. The arrival of the house of Orange-Nassau on the throne of England ended wars between England and the Low Countries and sealed a quiet but privileged relationship between the two countries. Trade supremacy had shifted to England, with lower London becoming increasingly important as a centre of trade. War finance definitely dominated the political agenda in the 17th century, especially for the Low Countries surrounded by powerful and potentially hostile countries: France, England and Spain. In England, King William III, who came from the Low Countries, relied upon his financial Dutch advisors to introduce new financial techniques to England and fix the development of English finance, based on Dutch techniques, imported and later improved. The Bank of England modelled on the Amsterdamse Wisselbank was created in 1694 as a private joint stock company comparable to the East India Company or Hudson's Bay Company and its capital was formed based on

---

[5] Goldsmith banking can be traced back to Mesopotamia (first millennium A.D.), it existed in ancient Greece (Delphi, Didyma, Olympia) a least at the 7th century A.D., and by the 6th century it was well developed in Athens.

[6] The overthrow of King James II of England was organised by a coalition of Protestant English members of parliament and his son-in-law the Dutch stadtholder William III of Orange-Nassau to prevent an Anglo-French Catholic alliance gaining power in England.

a large domestic and international subscription of 1.2 million pounds to finance a loan to government of an equal amount at an 8% rate of interest. And there are indeed similarities between the Genoese *Casa delle compere e dei banchi di San Giorgio* and the Bank of England. It is said to have been started during the Nine Years' War by wine merchants who found themselves with liquid capital as they sold their stocks and had no opportunity to replace them. It was equally encouraged by William III to fund with long term loans his war against Louis XIV, King of France. But as a safeguard, the Bank was restrained from lending to the Crown unless explicitly authorised by Parliament. Subscriptions of capital came from a wide variety of persons: goldsmith-bankers, a larger number of small merchants and artisans, and a number of Dutch individuals, both naturalised and foreign. The bank executive committee, made up of a court of directors, was elected, and each shareholder with 500 pounds capital was entitled to vote for the Directors. The Bank of England's corporate structure, therefore, made it far more responsive to the economic and financial demands of its customers and especially its shareholders. In contrast, the decisions of the Bank of Amsterdam, were always subject to the opinion of the Amsterdam city authorities, or the Dutch East India Company, which had to deal with the provincial authorities that made up its senior management ("the Heeren XVII").

Compared to the services delivered by the Amsterdamse Wisselbank, the Bank of England enabled multilateral clearing of international payments among European merchants to occur thereafter. The Bank of England then quickly outstripped the Bank of Amsterdam as a focal point for the international payments system of Europe. The English market was based on the long-term sovereign debt owed to a government-chartered and supported joint-stock company: primarily the Bank of England or alternatively the New East India Company. The Dutch market was only based on a variety of debt instruments issued by the individual cities and provinces in the Netherlands. Even Dutch investors recognised the financial advantages for them that were created by the rapidly growing amount of British government debt available. They were meticulous observers of all the financial innovations developed in London and prompt to introduce them in Amsterdam where they would blend the best of Italian and English financial innovation.

The South Sea bubble initially drew many new Dutch investors into the London market as the price of South Sea stock was rising. The gold and silver mines of Peru and Mexico were the legendary Eldorado and, as Charles Mackay noted, "everyone believed them to be inexhaustible". When it collapsed, many of the Dutch investors were caught by the debacle on the new subscriptions and eventually in the new perpetual annuities generously distributed to the existing stockholders of the company. The South Sea Company was formed in 1711, with a very large, over 9 million pounds, purchase of short-term government debt. It was promised a monopoly of all trade to the Spanish colonies in South America, in exchange for taking and consolidating the national debt raised by the war of Spanish succession, whose value was intrinsically connected to the outcome of the war. In January 1720, the shares of the company were trading at 123 pounds. The directors of the company shamelessly ran a series of roadshows filled with false statements and overoptimistic claims which drove the share price to 175 pounds and finally to 330 pounds after the company was selected over the Bank of England to consolidate the British war debt into South Sea equity. The same year, a law was passed whereby all of the British national debt, with the exception of what was already held by the Bank of England and the East India Company, would be sold to the South Sea Company; resulting in the almost complete takeover of English public borrowing. This decision was certainly inspired by the French example of Law's Mississippi Company taking over the French sovereign debt in 1719 which was justified by the gains expected from the conversion of a rather illiquid sovereign debt into fractional shares easy to trade on the stock market. There were indeed business connections between John Law, responsible for the Mississippi Company debacle, and Thomas Pitt Jr., Earl of Londonderry, who was behind the South Sea scandal. The South Sea Company was not an isolated case in 1720, many other companies of lesser importance also tried to attract investors with dubious promises, each creating their own bubbles as the speculative frenzy mounted. However, the Mississippi Company and South Sea Company bubbles became textbook case of the most noticeable example of international criminal cooperation at the highest level of the State for the manipulation of financial markets. As the English authorities were getting concerned with the market situation, a Bubble act was passed requesting all joint-stock listed company to receive a royal charter. The South Sea Company got it and the general speculation pushed the South Sea Company stock price to 1,200 pounds. At such unreasonable valuation levels, investor confidence began to wane and the market crashed. The 1721 scandal highlighted the close interaction between the leading stock-jobbers in London and the leading merchant bankers in Amsterdam managing private portfolios in search of high and secure returns. The company was restructured with government intervention with one-half of the South Sea stock in perpetual annuities offering 5% interest for five years. Subsequent investigations revealed a web of deceit and corruption involving business leaders and government officials. In the House of Lords, Lord Molesworth suggested that the directors be sewn "in sacks, and thrown into the Thames". The crisis strengthened the role of the Bank of England which absorbed, through engraftment, the South Sea Company and launched, in 1726, its first irredeemable perpetual Three Per Cent Annuities. This decisive intervention managed to rebuild confidence and England came out of the crisis with a well-delineated financial system. London impressed foreign investors in its dealing with the South Sea crisis and this was overall beneficial to the reputation and fame of the market. But other shocks were recorded: In June 1772, the failure of a "rascally and extravagant"[7] banker Alexander Fordyce following unreasonable speculation, triggered general consternation and so did the failure of numerous institutions including the Ayr Bank in Scotland. The intervention of the Bank of England was again needed to avoid a deeper crisis, but aftershocks were felt as far as Amsterdam and the British American colonies. Later Adam Smith would use this example in outlining a set of regulations under which the monetary and banking systems would safely cooperate.

England's joker in the deck was probably game changing technological innovation and its capacity to integrate it with an exceptional economic drive. From 1712, a blacksmith from noble descent from Dartmouth named Thomas Newcomen made in the Midlands an early atmospheric steam engine for pumping water from mines. Newcomen's engine was a clever combination of familiar elements: piston and cylinder, pumps,

---

[7] Horace Walpole, a gothic author and politician (22 June 1722).

levers, valves and the process of producing low pressure by the condensation of steam in a vessel. Newcomen's invention followed Thomas Savery's in 1698 which he protected with a broad patent that covered all "vessels or engines for raising water or occasioning motion to any sort of millworks by the impellent force of fire." The broad scope of Savery's patent, later prevented Newcomen from patenting his own engine. Although his work was entirely independent of Savery's, Newcomen was required to build his engines under license from Savery. At the age of 18, having decided to follow the career of scientific instrument maker, James Watt left his hometown in Scotland for Glasgow and London. In 1769, he patented a more efficient steam engine through his invention of the separate condenser (1765), which avoided the necessity of alternately heating and cooling the cylinder. In 1785, his engine was adapted to driving machinery in a cotton factory. The use of steam engines to drive machines slowly transformed industry. The steam engine and the industrial revolution had started to transform business life in Britain changing forever long haul navigation and international trade. This technical revolution supported another revolution in risk appraisal and hedging against the risk of a contingent loss. The insurance of steam boilers' owners against loss of life or damage caused by boiler explosion, became a popular class of accident insurance. It again originated in England in the 1850s which contained the largest concentration of steam boilers in the world. The Steam Boiler Assurance Company, established in 1858, pioneered this class of insurance, followed by the Midland Steam Boiler Inspection and Assurance Company in 1862. This was somewhat related to fire insurance and although municipal or state-funded fire insurance originated in Prussia in 1623, with the establishment of the Great Werder Fire Fund, the first fire insurance companies were established in England. An earlier form of insurance was the corporate marine insurers in Europe, distinct from the individual marine underwriters, appear to be the Royal Exchange Assurance and the London Assurance, both established in London in 1720. From this date, until 1824 no other English corporate bodies were permitted to write marine insurance. This fostered the growth in London of individual underwriters who, by 1712, had adopted the name of Lloyds as a business address from the coffee house of Edward Lloyd, where such marine information was exchanged. Trade in the age of sail was a dangerous and uncertain business: a sudden sea swell or an unfortunate encounter could result in a merchant suffering a frightening business loss. The Lloyd's market opened in London around 1688 on London Tower Street, to a club of savvy underwriters, who established the Society of Lloyd's in 1787. The first informal gatherings of shippers and investors around 1688 were not intended to produce the first insurance mechanism, the Lloyd's coffee shop witnessed the first days of what was to become the world's best known insurance underwriting company in the world. Lloyd's coffee house was a popular gathering place for ship captains, ship owners and merchants, and became the go-to place for information about shipping and, eventually, marine insurance. There were more than 80 coffee houses within the City of London's walls; each one was a centre for entrepreneurs and merchants, and each had a specialist interest to offer. Lloyd made sure his coffee house became an intelligence centre second to none on the shipping market, and soon even the richly laden Spanish treasure fleets were insured in London. Most of the procedures established in 17th century are still in use today. The American Revolution of the 1770s, followed by the Napoleonic Wars in the early 1800s, showed how vital marine insurance could be to the development of the London financial centre. It brought large profits to those who could provide it — but it also brought huge losses, when the Lutine bell[8] would only ring one time. The London Company Market, as a prime insurance market, started to formalise in 1824 after a Bill was passed to abolish restrictions on insurance which had favoured Lloyd's. Over time, Lloyd's and the Company Market started to write a larger variety of risks, including complex risks with a high severity and low frequency such as natural catastrophe. The London Market then became a leading market for those that needed (re)insurance coverage for large, complex or bespoke risks. Clearly, the London market benefited from its set-up as a subscription market, where more than one investor shares a piece of the same risk, diversifying risks and giving companies access to a deeper pool of international capital.

---

[8]The Lutine bell was salvaged from HMS Lutine wreck and hung from the rostrum of Lloyd's Underwriting Room. The ship was ordered to deliver a vast sum of gold and silver, collected by City of London merchants to Hamburg but sank in bad weather with its cargo in 1799. Eventually, the bell would be struck when news of an overdue ship arrived — once for its loss, and twice for its safe return.

City dominance in modern times

London's development as an international financial centre (IFC) matured for much of the 1700s and was fully complete by the end of the century, in the 1780s, after the English defeated the Dutch in a series of four Baltic naval wars. At the time it took preeminence at the end of the 18th century, Great Britain had already achieved its union (Wales 1536, Scotland 1707, Ireland 1801) under a single state and had managed to build not only a significant transport infrastructure but also a powerful internal market. The strength of the British market heavily contrasted with the United Provinces (Netherlands) market dedicated to offshore trading, still incapable of feeding its population. In the 18th century, the EIC gradually prevailed over its Dutch arch rival in a competition to satisfy Europe's growing appetite for silk, cotton and also tea. Precious goods from Asia and the Middle East had already reached Europe in the early Middle Age but only to be enjoyed by a few. The trade was known by a limited number of merchants and the economic impact on the exporting countries was negligible compared to their development needs. However, much of the activity of the British banks was remittance, especially those which had quickly developed in the countryside. Landlords living in London received their rent twice a year in May and November, so that the banks were called upon at these times for London bills: Monies from agricultural counties such as Somersetshire and Hampshire was invested in the discount of bills from manufacturing counties such as Yorkshire and Lancashire. The role of the City in fostering the transformation of the United Kingdom from an agrarian towards an industrial economy cannot be better highlighted.

Prominent bankers and merchants had fled or relocated to London sometimes with the assistance of Dutch merchant-banks where they managed to emulate a large, deep and liquid market. Nathan Rothschild moved from Manchester to London in 1809, Antony Gibbs re-located from Portugal to London in the 1840s, Charles Jocelyn Hambros was a Danish banker from Copenhagen, in 1839, Henry Schroder, a Russian merchant banker established himself in the City in 1804, and Lazard Brothers & Co. moved to London from France in 1877. The Pax Britannica was a very auspicious period for the development of England's economic supremacy as it lasted roughly 100 years (1815–1914) — from the final defeat of Napoleon to the beginning of World War I. British strategy rested primarily with its Navy, which maintained an undisputed and much feared maritime superiority not only for the protection of shipping and communications with the overseas commercial interests and colonial empire but also for homeland defence.

Mostly from Jewish origin, the new London based financial elite was the one capable of mastering the most sophisticated and specialised credit and financial instruments and was in the best position to help find credit for the reconstruction of Europe after the fall of the French Empire. In addition, London happened to be a convenient place to attract and retain a large pool of skilled labour. The House of Rothschild epitomised the importance and the power of merchant banks in financing foreign governments. The major innovation of the Rothschilds was to create a true international bond market for sovereign loans. The first London international issue was arranged in 1817. It was a French Franc denominated loan to finance French war reparations. In 1818, Rothschilds arranged the first foreign loan denominated in sterling for Prussia with interest payable in London. This would be the first known Eurobond issue. A large concentration of dynamic deposit bankers, goldsmith bankers and other deposit bankers, discount bankers, insurers, jobbers, stockbrokers, asset managers, chartered accountants and lawyers provided a dense concentration of highly capable finance specialists that fed the growing markets for securities, commodities, ship chartering and insurance.

The first great age of economic globalisation is generally considered to have begun with the repeal of the Corn Laws in Britain in 1846, at the height of the industrial revolution. Trade tied the entire British Empire together, most often flowing through the network of strategically positioned free ports of the Empire: Gibraltar, Aden, Suez, the Cape of Good Hope, Singapore and Hong Kong. Between 1817 and 1848, the number of warships on foreign stations more than doubled (from 63 to 129). The Royal Navy acted as a serious deterrent to potential economic adversaries. The British also invented submarine cable and laid it between all of the significant points of their Empire, greatly improving connectivity and their capacity to follow the strengths, challenges and opportunities of their trade. In 1820, British trade was worth 80 million pounds, by 1897 it had increased almost tenfold to 745 million pounds and after the railroad was built in 1830, London was accessible from all parts of the country. Additionally, overseas investments were a significant source of British wealth. By the end of the century, Britain was the wealthiest of all nations, with over 1,700 million pounds invested overseas earning 100 million pounds of interest each year.

At the beginning of the 20th century, following the 1907 financial panic originating from America, the British Admiralty started to sketch the broad outlines of a plan for economic warfare that could wreck the financial system of Germany, its major trading rival of the time and cripple their fighting capacity.[9] Britain used its extensive networks to gather and leverage information about its opponents. London banks financed most of the world trade, and Lloyds provided insurance for international shipping. The premium was sensitive to distance, route, season and type of ship, as well as to news about hostilities or piracy. This web of constantly updated and reliable information provided an accurate and dynamic map of sensitive economic data and exposed the strategic vulnerabilities of opposing alliances. By 1913, London finance was already a close knitted community: 84.3% of the international financial services firms were located within the outer box (0.16 sq. m), with 69% within the inner box (0.06 sq. m). This high degree of concentration also suggests that there were significant benefits derived from co-locating close to each other to establish business relationships, just like the early Venetian or Florentine bankers near Rialto. Like in Venice, the City also lived as a reputation builder and spreader: shared knowledge and trust was key to the aggregation of discriminating competition[10] and linking input and output between the specialised financial firms in the Square Mile. The First World War was almost fatal for England financial dominance as the employment of unrestricted submarine warfare by the Germans in World War I almost brought Britain to the brink of starvation in 1916. Only the entry of the United States into the war and the reinstitution of the old convoying system repackaged to combat the German submarine threat saved the day. After the war, the Washington Naval Treaty (1922) limited

---

[9] Nicholas Lambert, *Planning Armageddon; British Economic Warfare and the First World War*. Cambridge, MA: Harvard University Press (2012).

[10] This is a reference to the work of both Joseph Schumpeter (Wien School) and Edward Hastings Chamberlin (Harvard University).

the construction of the traditional surface battleships among the major powers and, for the first time, put the United States at naval parity with England, historically the leading maritime power. This happened to be a major shift in the dominance of the world major sea-trading routes.

The shift in the world order after the First World War

By undermining financial stability, free trade policies, investment patterns and migration systems upon which international economic ties had developed, the First World War destroyed much of the foundations of the late 19th century globalisation, including the sterling pound status of international standard and reserve currency. The British Gold Standard Act reintroduced the gold bullion standard, as a peg to the pound in 1925 under Winston Churchill, which led to relative stability. But this was followed by deflation and the gold standard did not survive the Great Depression. It was abandoned in 1931 after Ernest Harvey, the Bank of England's deputy governor at the time, wrote to Ramsay MacDonald, the prime minister, and Philip Snowden, the chancellor, on 19 September 1931, saying that gold reserves worth about 100 million pounds were close to running out. This would lay the ground for the dollar-key-currency system. Aside from direct damages from the conflict, the War profoundly re-shaped the economic relationships between Europe and non-European southern countries that were European colonies in Africa and Asia. It also fostered the development of the U.S. economy as a leading provider of war supplies, and later as a participant in the war and victory. The First World War and its aftermath shrank foreign investment from nearly 20% of world GDP before the war to 8% by 1930, and 5% by 1945. The War requested a huge funding effort through the issuance of patriotic bonds. It stimulated a large number of game changing innovations — electricity, radio-communication, the burning of oil instead of coal, consumer goods: the watch, zips, and also airplanes, cars and trucks. Following the Great Depression, the financial centre of the world shifted from London to New York.[11] The decline of Europe's brightest financial lights closed, for now,

---

[11] F. Braudel, Afterthoughts on Material Civilisation and Capitalism, Chapter 3, Section I, in *The John Hopkins Symposia in Comparative History*. John Hopkins University Press: United States, March (1979).

a chapter in the European cities history of domination on the world economy. The dark years preceding the beginning of the Second World War only amplified this trend. As if history was repeating itself, much like Dutch shipping in the 18th century, London still remained the world centre for shipping finance, both ship-broking and marine insurance. Once again in the absence of a major external shock (especially war, or pandemy), a financial centre had proven to be capable of remaining resilient after it had ceased to be at the leading edge in trade and industry. The prevalence of the English language also played its part and so has its geographical position between the USA and Asian time zones.

The turnaround of London's financial centre in the 60's is remarkable and London's command of an international payments network (i.e., the market key infrastructure), through which world financial transactions could be channeled may have been instrumental in the resilience of City. Ten thousand kilometers east of London, both Hong Kong and Singapore, possibly stimulated by their priviledged connection with the City, worked very hard for years to capture number two position. Their strategic location in the middle of Asia, together with their economic achievements may revive the past paradigm of the city state IFC from the Middle Ages. The continuous dominance of London as a leading financial centre despite the self-exclusion of the UK from the Eurozone, as Britain's merchant fleet declined to less than 1% of the world's shipping and as it is facing German economic power, or the ambitions of the French, show the exceptional resilience of London's competitive advantages and its capacity to keep a sharp edge in tandem with New York. Back in 1999 Sir Willie Purves, former Chairman of HSBC, purposefully questioned whether "the UK is to Europe more as Manhattan is to the USA, or more as Hong Kong is to China?"

The Big Bang of 1986 was a forward move to lift barriers to competition and helped the City to better use the full potential of its banking system. That revolution was called "Big Bang" because new ways of trading shares came into effect on one day, 27 October 1986. During the Big Bang, the barriers of foreign ownership in local institutions were removed, resulting in numerous foreign takeovers of British banks. Foreign banks with more capital entered the market. Numerous former building societies became commercial banks. The City had burst from its former boundaries around the old "square mile" of the Lord Mayor's domain. Canary Wharf, formerly a wasteland in East London's dockland sprouts skyscrapers for global banks and in the West the City has also expanded in the choicer parts of the West End, like Mayfair, and between Blackfriars and St. Paul, while the skyline of the City square mile has been remodelled by new towers. The Big Bang contributed to rejuvenate the financial place and enhanced London's international standing and attractiveness for foreign entrants. A large community of business leaders perceived the UK's single, principles — based financial sector regulator — the Financial Services Authority (FSA) — as superior to what they saw elsewhere as a less responsive, complex construction of multiple holding company and industry segment regulators. Regulatory enforcement style and institutions mattered, with the United Kingdom's measured approach to enforcement seen as more results oriented and effective rather than the slow and unpredictable approaches in some jurisdictions or the punitive and overly public approaches in others. London was certainly helped for a period around the turn of the millennium by "light touch" regulation.

Many tended to focus on performance of the equity markets but the most liquid markets today are foreign exchange, interest rate derivatives, insurance and bond markets. These markets dwarf the equity market by orders of magnitude. Even by conservative estimates, London dominates all of these markets by sheer magnitude of transaction volume. London has transformed into an increasingly sizeable and attractive talent hub for qualified professionals with the kind of structuring and pricing skills that used to be available only in New York, thereby reducing New York's competitive advantage and further increasing the likelihood that even more financial innovations will occur in London and consolidate its position as a key hub.

The Takeover of the First Place by New York

Following a series of regulation on capital control from the beginning of World War I onwards, it seemed obvious to many at the end of World War II that London had lost its world leading position to New York as the world's leading financial centre. Even then, the eclipse was not final and London managed to fight back and edged out New York regaining the title several years ago.

In the early days of the United States, Boston, MA, not New York was the major shipping centre and the national centre of commerce, with commodities and bonds financing the growth of the youthful economy. The city was founded in 1630 by a small fleet of English Puritans who sailed from England to flee religious persecution and landed in Massachusetts. Boston developed as the capital of New England, and its State Street area became a leading financial centre in the 19th century[12] which financed the development of American railways. But the city never managed to build a concentration of financial activities, which could finally rival New York's, possibly because it preferred to retain and capitalise on its pre-eminence as an intellectual centre. In the 19th century, Philadelphia was initially better positioned to become a leading financial hub: it commanded central banking in the United States through the Second Bank of the United States, was the location for the nation's first merchant banker, and was the first entry point of European capital into the United States. After the Philadelphia blaze of 1730 which was the most disastrous fire in the city, Benjamin Franklin noted in his Gazette that "an Ounce of Prevention is worth a Pound of Cure" and later founded America's oldest insurance company in 1752 as the Philadelphia Contributor for the Insurance of Houses from Loss by Fire. Franklin's company was the first to make contributions toward fire prevention and advised against certain fire hazards, refusing to insure certain buildings where the risk of fire was too great.

New York only managed to win financial pre-eminence after it successfully floated the bonds financing a strategic and widely visible new project: The Erie Canal linking the Great lakes to the Hudson River and the Atlantic Ocean. The project led to the construction in 1825 of the most important waterway in American history connecting Canada to the New York natural harbour. Baltimore also competing with New York for financial dominance was slow in building the Chesapeake and Ohio Canal. New York financiers cleverly rallied President Andrew Jackson, at loggerheads with the leadership of the Second Bank of the United States which was eventually privatised in 1836, before going bankrupt. This was excellent news for Wall Street who got rid of one of its arch competitors,

---

[12] By 1842, over 40 banks and insurance companies were located in Boston, a very significant number for the time.

but bad news for financial stability as the overloaded credit structure began to totter in 1837. New York banks were hit tremendously by defaults, and many States subsequently defaulted as the sources of European capital dried up. The crisis spurred a shift toward mutualisation for life insurance companies. Between 1838 and 1849, only one life insurance firm raised capital on a stock basis. During the same period, 17 mutuals, requiring little initial capital, were chartered. The reputation of the place was badly shattered. Joint stock companies were led by the famous names of American financial history — JP Morgan, Drexel, Cook and others raised fresh capital and took over the charge of financing the much needed infrastructure. By 1849, New York's reputation as a financial centre what not only saved but confirmed by a spectacular turnaround. European investors were back, eager to invest in a trustworthy innovative and competitive place capable of delivering handsome financial returns.

New York was founded in the early 17th century, by Dutch adventurers, fishers and fur traders. Located at the mouth of a river and first mapped by Henry Hudson, the place was named New Netherlands after the interests of those who had funded and prepared to colonise it. Unlike most New World colonies including Boston, New Netherlands was not an escape from religious persecution or a state sanctioned colonial expedition. Rather, the founding of New Netherlands was funded by private merchants, for commercial purposes, to cut into French fur trading in the New World. Thus was founded the fortified city of New Amsterdam, the most important Dutch outpost of the New World. In 1664, the English, who controlled New England in the North and Virginia in the South, took over the New Amsterdam area and forced the Dutch to surrender the city. New Amsterdam was promptly rechristened New York. The city, founded on the basis of profit, was to become one of the most important seaports and trading centres of the American colonies. However, financial activity was limited and mostly oriented towards London until the Revolutionary war. No doubt that history heavily contributed to giving to New York its specific mercantile DNA. From the 1792, Buttonwood Agreement[13] to the

---

[13] In March 1792, 24 of the leading New York merchants met secretly at the Corre Hotel to find ways to bring order to the emerging securities business. On 17 May, these men signed a document called the Buttonwood Agreement, named after their traditional meeting place

1929 Crash, Wall Street took 137 years to become an IFC. A century of wars in Europe from Napoleon to Bismark followed by World War II left the European economies agonizing. The early 1900s saw the rise of huge fortunes made on Wall Street, but fallout from the Great Depression devastated the country. It led to a long-time economic collapse and depression that was to continue until the start of World War II. The rise of New York as the financial centre of the United States, then as a world financial centre, winning out initially over Boston, Philadelphia and Baltimore in the first quarter of the 19th century which all had strong hinterlands, and beating back, so to speak, later challenges from Chicago and St. Louis, speaks loudly for the determination of the financial elite of New York.

After 1815, New York gradually took the lead on the East coast in championing superior conditions for business as British supplies accumulated during the war were dumped there. The city enacted an auction law that made all sales final and forbade withdrawing goods once offered for sale, while jobbers, wholesalers and country merchants flocked to the port. In 1818, a New York merchant started the first liner service with Liverpool. New York bankers backed the shipping services industry to ensure that cotton bound for Liverpool from New Orleans, Mobile, Savannah or Charleston would be shipped coastwise to New York. New York had this incredible capacity to attract people, money and business. The financial centre was a port, but the connection of finance to seaports had over time diminished, and New York still remained a strong IFC being neither an administrative capital nor a central location. In 1865, from the ashes of the American Civil War, which had started four years before, sprung an economic powerhouse. The development of the corporate bond market, mostly a railroad bond market in its early years, an American financial innovation that later spread to the rest of the world, is a reflection of the construction of U.S. financial dominance. The rise of New York as

---

under a Buttonwood tree. They committed to trade only securities between themselves, would adhere to a set of commissions and would not participate in auctions. By 1793, there were too many brokers to meet under a simple tree, so they took space in a building on the corner of Wall and Water streets, called the Tontine Coffee House. This new venture was to become the New York Stock and Exchange Board in 1817 to compete with Philadelphia's relatively advanced stock exchange.

Finance Masters

a financial powerhouse was supported by a strong stream of financial information innovation led by a pool of successful entrepreneurs. From the dawn of printing by movable type in Europe (1445) to its mechanisation and the spread of electrical telegraph, market structuring products emerged in the New World such as the market index (Dow, Jones), the rating industry (Poor, Moody, Fitch), the introduction of reference publications on strategic commodities such as oil (Platts), and the first market stock ticker which allowed much faster financial information circulation. The advent of the ticker in 1867 revolutionised the markets by making up-to-the-minute equity prices available to investors around the country. The ticker was the brainchild of Edward Calahan, who configured a telegraph machine to print stock quotes on streams of paper tape. His purpose was to replace the messengers who relayed stock, bond and commodity prices to brokers and investors with a faster and more efficient device. In 1869, Thomas Edison designed the mechanism that synchronised all the ticker machines on one line and patented a perfected, easier-to-use version of Calahan's ticker which was his first lucrative invention. All these innovations were pointing to America as the very place where a new world was being invented. In New York, just like in Florence, Venice or Genoa in the Middle Ages, innovation clusters again were the metrics where the emergence of a financial centre could be measured, because they establish economic young shoots around which self-reinforcing agglomerations grow.

The National Banking Acts of 1863 and 1864 laid the framework of the banking system beyond the Gilded Age[14] in the U.S. monopolising the printing of bank notes and defining how banks could acquire national charters. Bank runs were common before the Civil War and then occurred in 1873, 1884, 1890, 1893, 1896 and 1907. Insurers also paid a significant price during the depression years of 1871–1874: 46 life insurance companies ceased operations, with 32 failing outright. This resulted in USD 35 million losses for policyholders.[15] The experience of U.S. financial crises

---

[14] A term coined by Mark Twain in "The gilded age: A tale of today", a novel depicting the 1870s to about 1900, an era of post-civil war economic growth and serious social problems in the U.S.

[15] Corey Dahl, 9 September 2013 in *A brief history of Life Insurance*, LifeHealthpro. http://www.lifehealthpro.com/2013/09/09/a-brief-history-of-life-insurance?t=life-products.

in 1893 and 1907, where there was a dependence on gold shipments from Europe symptomatic of a deep structural weakness. The 1907 financial panic emanated from America but affected the rest of the world. It showed the necessity of mobilising financial power in a more effective way. This panic, however, did not trigger a broad financial collapse. Yet the simultaneous occurrence of general prosperity with a crisis in the nation's financial centres persuaded many Americans that their banking structure was sadly out of date and in need of major reform.[16] One of the weaknesses of the American trade system was the absence of an endorsement option on domestic bill of exchange by a lender of last resort capable of providing cash to the merchant banks, especially in the case of a crisis. The resulting liquidity crunch would likely choke the whole economy and only deepen the crisis.

The United States realised that a Central Bank modelled on the Bank of England or the Imperial German Reichsbank[17] could be a defining step to rely on its own financial trading system and handle bills of exchange exactly as the London market. Paul Warburg, the American immigrant younger brother of the great Hamburg investment banker Max Warburg, personal advisor to Kaiser Wilhelm II played an instrumental role in this construction. "The U.S. is in fact at about the same point that had been reached by Europe at the time of the Medicis, and by Asia, in all likelihood, at the time of Hamurabi" explained Warburg.[18] He advocated for the creation of a state bank that would follow on the early controversial Alexander Hamilton experiment[19] who wanted a state-of-the-art financial set-up, like that of Britain or Holland. On 23 December 1913, the Federal Reserve Bank was created on the basis that it was considered strategic for

---

[16] Federal Reserve Board of New York, the founding of the Fed. http://www.newyorkfed. org/aboutthefed/history_article.html.

[17] The Reichsbank was modelled on the Bank of England but included an innovative feature, the right to issue notes beyond those backed by gold.

[18] Paul M. Warburg, *Defects and Needs of our Banking System*. New York Times, 6 January (1907).

[19] The First Bank of the United States was established in 1791, but the Bank's influence was frightening to many people and an 1811 proposal to renew its charter failed. In 1816, a bill to charter a Second Bank of the United States was introduced in Congress, with the same faith. Twenty years later, its charter was not renewed as the Bank was considered a threat to democracy.

the development of the American economy with a clear reference to military or naval reserves. "The stronger the Federal Reserve Banks become, the stronger will be the country and the greater will be its chances to fulfil with safety and efficiency the function of a world banker. The basis of this development must be confidence."[20] Based on the fear that a single bank would dwarf any other financial institution in the country, the Reserve Bank Organization Committee announced on 2 April 1914, its decision, to establish 12 Federal Reserve Banks to cover various districts throughout the country. But the creation of the Feds was still not enough to avert bank runs and sharp contractions in the financial markets in the 1920s and 1930s. It is only recently in contemporary history that crises have become scarcer. Nevertheless, the rarity of full-blown crises does not mean that there have not been episodes of acute financial stress.

When First World War started, the North American economy was in recession. A four year economic boom ensued during First World War, first as European allies began purchasing war supplies and then as the United States joined the battle in 1917 unleashing massive Federal spending. When the war began, the United States was a net debtor in international capital markets, but following the war, the United States began investing large amounts internationally, particularly in Latin America, thus "taking on the role traditionally played by Britain and other European capital exporters." With Britain weakened after the First World War, New York emerged "as London's equal if not her superior in the contest to be the world's leading financial centre."[21] This positive impact probably changed the American all liberal economic perception that a more significant involvement of the State especially during crisis would be necessary, and inspire a new generation of reformers. However, the United States could not immediately play the role that United Kingdom had performed in the world economy before First World War, or even later in the interwar

---

[20] Address of Hon. Paul M. Warburg of the Federal Reserve Board before the Twin City Banker's Club of St. Paul and Minneapolis at the Minnesota Club, St. Paul, 22 October 1915.

[21] Carlos Lozada, the National Bureau of Economic Research Commenting on NBER Research Associate Hugh Rockoff Study: Until It's Over, Over There: The U.S. Economy in World War I (NBER Working Paper No. 10580). http://www.nber.org/digest/jan05/w10580.html

period, simply because the U.S. was never as involved in the world economy as Britain had been. In 1775, the first American Navy, Rhode Island Navy, was commissioned by the Rhode Island assembly. The armed ships were among the first to actively fight back against the British. Understanding the need for ships to fight British sea power, the Continental Congress established the Continental Navy. On 21 July 1916, Congress passed "the big Navy Act" — the U.S. Naval Act of 1916, an ambitious plan to make the U.S. Navy larger than the British Royal Navy. America realised that its emergence as a leading economic power and financial centre needed to be supported by a strong U.S. navy. Because naval forces have always been expensive to build, they remained quite scarce but were always feared because of their ability to control sea trading routes. Whosoever commands the sea commands the trade; whosoever commands the trade of the world commands the riches of the world and consequently the world itself.[22]

On 4 December 1928, President Coolidge sent his last message on the state of Union noting "No Congress of the United States ever assembled, on surveying the state of the Union, has met with a more pleasing prospect than that which appears at the present time. In the domestic field there is tranquility and contentment ... and the highest record of years of prosperity." As usual, who could have seriously predicted that this was too good to last. Ten months later, the world had changed: the Great depression, vividly illustrated by the bursting of the stock market bubble of 27 October 1929, rocked the basis of the American society as it sent Wall Street into panic ruining so many investors. Hot money[23] started to evaporate, and a record 12.9[24] million shares were traded on "Black Thursday." On "Black Tuesday", the most infamous day in Wall Street's history, some 16.4 million shares were traded after another wave of panic

---

[22] Sir Walter Raleigh, A Discourse of the Invention of Ships, Anchors, Compass, & c., *The Works of Sir Walter Ralegh, Kt.,* vol. 8, p. 325, (1829, reprinted 1965).

[23] The real estate boom in Florida triggered a classic financial bubble which was a clear signal that hot and easy money would lead to a collapse of the system on its own weight. The analysis of the recent 2008 subprime crisis shows how difficult it is to defuse and stop this irrational exuberance.

[24] To put that into perspective, a total of 3,875,910 shares were traded on 12 March 1928 which was considered a record set for trading at Wall Street.

swept investors and sent the world financial markets into a tailspin with disastrous effect. This time, the panic of selling made sure, once and for all, that there was to be no quick fix, that the recovery would be slow and painful. There was nothing in sight comparable to the recovery of gains seen on the Thursday. The Dow Jones closed at 230 — down 23% from the opening of 299. The market had crashed. Millions of shares ended up worthless, income contracted, private investment collapsed, production slowed down in numerous industries and unemployment soared upwards of 13 million. In 1932, President Hoover told his friends, "we are at the end of our string ... there is nothing more we can do". The country was in the grip of the Great Depression. American GDP continued to contract from USD 790.9 billion in 1929 to USD 577.3 billion at the end of 1933. Bank runs swept the United States again in the spring and fall of 1931 and the fall of 1932, and by March 1933, over 4,000 banks had failed during the previous two months. Bread lines stretched all over the streets of the largest American cities. As the new President of the United States Franklin Delano Roosevelt delivered his first inaugural address to the American people observing that "So, first of all, let me assert my firm belief that the only thing we have to fear is fear itself — nameless, unreasoning, unjustified terror which paralyses needed efforts to convert retreat into advance." The markets were waiting for a leader to change course. After showing early signs of recovery in spring of 1933, the economy continued to improve throughout the next three years, during which real GDP (adjusted for inflation) grew at an average rate of 9% per year. On June 1933, the Glass–Steagall Act, or "Banking Act" established a deposit insurance mechanism under the FDIC and strictly limited commercial banks' participation in the securities markets, in part to end the practices of the 1920s, when banks sold highly speculative securities to depositors. Seventy years later, FDIC regulated banks would argue that their problems stemmed from the Glass Steagall Act. Beginning in 1987, the Federal Reserve accommodated a series of requests from the banks to undertake activities forbidden under Glass–Steagall and its modifications.

A sharp recession hit in 1937, caused in part by the Federal Reserve's move to increase its requirements for money in reserve. With Roosevelt's decision to support Britain and France in the struggle against the Third German Reich and the other Axis Powers, defence manufacturing geared up, producing more and more private sector jobs. The Japanese surprise attack on Pearl Harbour (Oahu Island, Hawaii) on 7 December 1941, led to the American declaration of war, and the nation's factories went back into full production mode, pushing demand for goods and services. In spite of the extreme severity of the financial crisis, Wall Street was back on its feet as the world leading finance centre with the only world reserve currency on hand. East of the Atlantic, Europe was on fire since 1939, and on the other side of the Pacific, Japan was trying to build a colonial empire equivalent to its German allies, with Italy nostalgic for its Roman Empire and former financial dominance.

America managed to resist and step aside from the massive destructions of World War II, losing 500,000 soldiers in a conflict that killed 50 million and left Europe in chaos. However, it played a pivotal role in the resolution of this world crisis, contributing its own forces to the conflict after the Japanese surprise attack on Pearl Harbor, Hawaii, on 7 December 1941. As one of the winners, it presented the only viable economic solution for rebuilding a free Western Europe in the form of a massive economic assistance in U.S. dollars (Marshall Plan). From 1st July to 22nd July 1944, the Bretton Woods conference established a new financial order based on the U.S. dollar, which stood as the cornerstone of the development of American economic and financial supremacy. New York was definitely established as the inevitable international financial hub for the reconstruction of the "free world". The reconstruction was coupled with a significant effort to contain the Soviet threat: the strategic nuclear deterrence programme was accelerated and the U.S. Navy continued to espouse the importance of sea control as an integral part of sea power and as its unique contribution to the Cold War. The parallel between today's role of the U.S. and England and the Pax Britannica, while not perfect, is certainly striking. As an effort to build up the power of the U.S. Navy, it became publicly known that an electronic computer, with the acrostic ENIAC was being used to compute ballistic tables. By the end of the war, computation for the Navy was almost complete, and the ENIAC team was looking for new work. Initial trials showed that for finance or econometric calculations, the computer would save an incredible amount of time but unfortunately it was down 80% of the time. It took another decade to make sure that the machine availability would not be an issue any more.

Even after the Second World War victory and the beginning of the second age of globalisation, New York only slowly became a true financial centre, especially for international investment flows. Foreign issues amounted to only USD 4.2 billion between 1955 and 1962 as opposed to USD 126.5 billion in national U.S. issues. In London, still the second largest financial centre and more internationally-oriented than New York, foreign loans between 1950 and 1958 averaged only 61 million pounds annually; before the First World War, they had averaged almost 200 million annually. However, the New York City that emerged from World War II was a dramatically different place than the city that had entered it four years before. It had grown into the nation's largest wholesaling centre, accounting for a fifth of all wholesale transaction in America, the world's biggest port, handling 40% of the nation's waterborne freight, and it was the world's financial capital. The last great sea battle occurred in 1944. Since then the world's ocean has been open to free trade and navigation by all nations as a matter of American policy. The ability to enforce this policy and the absence of serious challenges to it can be considered as a product of the superiority of the U.S. Navy. This ability to control the flows of trade matters as 90% of the world trade in volume moves by water mostly in containers, equivalent to 65% of trade in value terms, the rest being air cargo and truck freight.

The double capitulation of Germany on 8 May 1945 and Japan on 2 September 1945 following the explosion of two American nuclear bombs in Hiroshima and Nagasaki started an even more dangerous episode in the history of international relationships. The Allied forces were celebrating their victory over the Third German Reich only to realise that the antagonism between the Soviet bloc and the free World was leading to another war, supposedly cold this time, punctuated with the development of the largest and most destructive military arsenal in the annals of human history. Leading naval forces had always been expensive to build, relatively scarce but extremely valuable from an economic standpoint. The command of the oceans achieved by the United States at the end of the Second World War put it in a military and economic position of leadership and advantage that could not be matched by the Soviet Union in the nuclear age — short of risking a nuclear reprisal. America mobilised its enormous industrial, military and financial resources to lead the competition against the communist world during the Great Moderation an epoch of calm for the banking system (1945–1975), with few banking failures. Communism as a political system was terminally hit in 1991 by the disintegration of USSR. Communism's second death followed Mao Zedong's passing away in 1977 and Chinese Leader Deng Xiaoping's decision in 1978 to abandon many communist doctrines and incorporate elements of the free-enterprise system into the Chinese economy.

Following the two consecutive bloodsheds of First World War and Second World War in Europe, the American financial preeminence strengthened, heavily supported by the new international status of its currency. The U.S. dollar had started dominating world transactions and was considered the reference currency whether it was related to gold or not. SWIFT[25] as a global conduit for international transactions became a very reliable instrument for measuring monetary dominance, and provided useful statistics showing that the U.S. dollar represented an overwhelming 87% of the SWIFT transactions, followed by the Euro (6.6%), Sterling and Yen, with Chinese Yuan arriving in fifth position. On the other side of the Atlantic busily trying to reconstruct a devastated continent with the financial assistance of the United States, a relatively innocuous event took place which was the creation of the European Coal and Steel Community chaired by Jean Monnet in 1952. It was followed by its merger with Euratom in 1967, which resulted in the creation of the European Community. Both side of the Atlantic were then busy dealing with the double hurdles of oil-shocks triggering high levels of inflation (1973–1974 and 1978–1979) and the Cold war arms race until the crash of the Latin American economies in August 1982 which was almost coincidental with the death of the Communist old guard Soviet leader Leonid Brezhnev in November. His successors had to admit the need to put an end to the arm race and adjust the past Soviet doctrine.

The 1987[26] stock market crash occurred on "Black Monday", 19 October. The Dow Jones Industrial Average fell from 2246 to 1738, losing 22.6% of its total value. This crash marked the end of a five-year

---

[25] See Chapter V, the importance of being networked.
[26] While the 1987 crash was attributed to computer selling programmes, it is still inconclusive that computer trading and derivative securities were the major causes of the crash.

"bull" market that had seen the Dow average rise from 776.92 points in August 1982 to a high of 2,722.42 points in August 1987. After the 1987 crisis, many predicted that Tokyo was going to overtake New York as the leading financial centre. However, the American market soon recovered after the crash. Differential growth in the United States and Japan relegated Tokyo as a secondary regional IFC. The 1998 failure of Long-Term Capital Management is said to have nearly destabilised the world's financial system. Members of the LTCM's board of directors included the distinguished Myron S. Scholes and Robert C. Merton who shared the 1997 Economy Nobel Prize, for a "new method to determine the value of derivatives". The investment fund strategy focused on "convergence-arbitrage" trades, trying to take advantage of small differences in prices among near-identical bonds. The investment model was set for a commercial bank but underestimated the amount of capital needed to cover potential market risks. Initially successful with annualised return of over 21% in its first year, 43% in the second year and 41% in the third year, it lost USD 4.6 billion in less than four months following the 1997 Asian financial crisis and the 1998 Russian default on its sovereign debt. The LTCM bankruptcy impact was such that it required the intervention of the New York Federal Reserve to bail it out and avoid catastrophic financial contagion. Fresh funds came just in time to avoid the meltdown, and the management of the crisis showed the capacity of the regulatory authorities. However, this was possibly a flagrant exhibition of "the too smart to fail" paradigm, and it was not going to be forgotten, as more than 17,000 banks had gone under in the U.S. since 1865, an average of 115 every year. With the exception of a few "accidents" including LTCM, the thirty year period from the mid-1980s to 2007 was a period of calm after the volatility created by the years of inflation of the 70s. The Great Moderation was certainly the result of a better understanding of financial policies which could be used as "fire extinguisher in the kitchen, preventing larger disasters"[27] and their impact on economic stability. At the same time, the economy was transitioning again from a post oil-crisis model, while innovation in the IT sector had a transformational role in economic structure and accelerating international trade.

---

[27] This analogy was developed by Nobel Laureate Christopher Sims in 2012.

To date, New York has managed to withstand an impressive number of economic storms of historical severity including the Saving & Loans debacle of the 1980s, the September 2001 terror attacks and lately the 2008–2009 subprime crisis recession which actually started in the last quarter of 2007,[28] the worst in seven decades. New York still remains the undisputed leading global financial centre, and such resilience cannot come only as a coincidence. In the face of history, it seems that the three biggest risks for New York do not include the capacity of the financial centre to withstand economic crisis but most probably are i) the risk of complacency, triggered by arrogance, ii) the risk of unethical behaviour and insufficient competition and iii) the risk of overruling capable to stultify innovation and dynamism in Wall Street. There will be ups and downs, as usual in history, but provided world investors are persuaded that there is no better place to manage wealth, incumbent financial centres will keep a decisive advantage. This is possibly one of the most obvious explanations of their resilience despite the shocks that rock the markets from time to time.

A very striking fact is that if the total amount of subprime mortgages in the United States were considered worthless, the total losses to the financial system would have been about the size of one bad day at the stock market, since they just were not that big. As is well known, the financial crisis in the United States was preceded by a major financial boom. Credit eased and real estate prices surged for several years against the backdrop of strong financial innovation and an accommodative monetary policy. The interconnectivity of the finance hubs led to European global banks sustaining the shadow banking system in the United States by drawing on dollar funding in the wholesale market to lend to U.S. residents through the purchase of securitised claims on U.S. borrowers. The resulting problem was that subsequent losses were distributed and repackaged throughout different securities and different places and nobody really knew where they were and who was going to bear the losses ultimately.[29]

---

[28] According to the U.S. National Bureau of Economic Research.

[29] Chairman Bernanke, The Federal Reserve and the Financial Crisis The Federal Reserves Response to the Financial Crisis, Lecture 3, George Washington University School of Business, 27 March (2012).

The financial crisis highlighted the pivotal role of international financial linkages between banks in the global economy. The Lehman Brothers failure stressed global interbank and foreign exchange markets because it led to a run on money market funds, the largest suppliers of dollar funding to non-U.S. banks, which in turn strained the banks' funding. "Whenever there was a doubt about a firm, just like in a standard bank run, the investors, the lenders, the counterparties would pull back their money quickly because of the same reason that depositors would pull their money out of a bank that was thought to be having trouble. So there was a whole series of runs which generated huge pressures on key financial firms as they lost their funding and were forced to sell their assets quickly and many important financial markets were badly disrupted". The 2008–2009 crisis, whose main ingredients can be found in academic journals before it started, where global and the financial services industry were at its heart, revealing inadequacies including regulatory gaps, ineffective supervision, too limited participation of independent economists to policy, opaque markets and overly-complex products. It resulted in the top American and European biggest, largest, most complex international financial institutions being at the brink of failure. This was quite a change compared to the 1929 crisis where only small banks were affected. The crisis was contagious and created a global slowdown: fears of another Great Depression, a second 1930s depression, were very real, which would be much worse than the 2008 recession. When the crisis struck, it created a major shock to the financial system, with sharp increases in credit spreads and large losses to financial institutions. There was an urgent need for action — and the actions wanted were to the question, "What must be done?", not "How did we get here?", this part came later in order to clean-up and rebuild confidence in the financial system. Our failure to foresee or prevent the financial crisis, is a sore reminder of the dangers of hubris.[30] However, modern economics, unlike 1929 economics, was able to answer the question more clearly about what to do: it told to quickly boost demand with quantitative easing. The view is increasingly gaining acceptance that without the forceful policy response that stabilised the financial system

---

[30] Economist Jean Tirole's speech at the Nobel Banquet in the Stockholm City Hall, 10 December (2014).

between March 2008[31] and early 2009, a catastrophic outcome in the economy could certainly have been expected.

In 2008, The Federal Reserve Board, the Treasury, other institutions (such as FDIC) and U.S. lawmakers worked to rebuild a web of financial regulations and raised taxes. This was after the credit crisis and recession destroyed trillions of dollars in household wealth, over 8.5 million jobs with unemployment rising to 10%, created hardship for the families who were forced to leave their homes and disrupted communities. U.S. Treasury Secretary and New York Mayor purposefully warned at the time that excessive U.S. regulation would desert Wall Street and drive investment firms to London again. The Senators investigation found that the crisis was not a natural disaster, but the result of high risk, highly complex financial products; undisclosed conflicts of interests; and failure of the regulators, the credit rating agencies, and the market itself to reign the excess of Wall Street.[32] "The goals of this investigation were to construct a public record of the facts in order to deepen the understanding of what happened; identify some of the root causes of the crisis; and provide a factual foundation for the ongoing effort to the country against the recurrence of a similar crisis in the future."

This statement shows that understanding and preventing the recurrence of what happened is taken seriously, together with protecting the international position of New York as the world leading financial hub. It came out with a clear set of conclusions: i) review structured finance transactions, ii) narrow proprietary trading exceptions, iii) design strong conflict of interest prohibitions and iv) study bank use of structured finance. The failure of the Office of Thrift Supervision (OTS) to stop unsafe and unsound practices that led to the demise of Washington Mutual, one of the nation's largest banks is quite appalling. Over a five year period from 2004 to 2008, the OTS was diligent and identified over 500 serious deficiencies at Washington Mutual, yet failed to take action to force the banks to improve their lending operations and possibly impeded

---

[31] The failure and bail out of Bear Stearns was viewed by some as the official start of the financial crisis.

[32] Permanent sub-committee on investigations — United States Senate, Wall Street and the financial crisis, Anatomy of a financial collapse, 13 April (2011).

oversight by the bank's backup regulator, the FDIC. The U.S. Senat recommendations can be put as a parallel to the John Law's Mississippi scheme of 1720, which managed to ruin many French private investors. One of the reasons for these analogies is to show that although we have made incredible progress in the processing of complex information quite similar ethical causes, and benign neglect, are still creating the same consequences almost 300 years later. This is precisely what the United States Senators pointed out and wanted to address in their report. Bernard "Bernie" Madoff, the most extraordinary swindler of the heady pre-recession years, was arrested on 11 December 2008, following his 65 billion-dollar old boys Ponzi scheme over the course of two decades. Yet, he was a highly respected and established financial expert and would earn his investors' trust because whenever they requested a withdrawal, Madoff's investment company got their money to them promptly. He pleaded guilty to 11 federal felonies in March 2009 and is serving a 150-year sentence, but the distrust that his dealings directed toward the financial system is indelible. Some would object that if Ponzi schemes are such a bad thing, then why have they been allowed to proliferate so that all top American banks were dealing in credit default swaps and other make-believe rackets, and why are not all the people responsible for this crisis in the cell block in Lower Manhattan where Bernie Madoff now resides.[33] Part of the answer may be a non-visible "termite effect" resulting in so many mortgage specialists being ignorant of the extent of the damage they were inflicting on the economy as a whole, although they were very much concerned with keeping their position and bonuses. In this context, it is also remarkable that all the leading financial centres rested on the foundation of a distinctive common law system, considered to be of the most efficient and equitable frameworks ever devised to ensure the smooth running of free market capitalism. This Anglo-American common law approach differs fundamentally from other legal systems in Europe and in most of Asia in its flexibility and reliability.

---

[33] Comment from director Michael Moore quoted in "Where are Bernie Madoff and his inner circle now", Time Magazine, Sam Frizell, 11 December (2014).

The 2008–2009 crisis put shadow banking[34] under the limelight, a fast developing "system of credit intermediation", fuelled with commercial paper and repurchase agreements (repos) providing cheaper financing, and money market funds and also providing better returns for consumers and institutional investors. Shadow banking involved entities and activities either outside the regular banking system or which had developed out of prudential regulation and supervision. It performed important functions in the financial system such as creating additional sources of funding and offered investors alternatives to bank deposits. But because they are not subject to traditional bank regulation, they cannot, just as commercial banks can, borrow in an emergency from the Federal Reserve and do not have traditional depositors whose funds are covered by insurance. They, therefore, pose potential threats to long-term financial stability. Typically, shadow banks would include broker-dealers that fund their assets using repos, finance companies and money market mutual funds that pool investors' funds to purchase commercial paper or mortgage-backed securities. The problem was complicated by commercial banks owning or controlling shadow banks. The opacity of the governance and ownership structures between banks and shadow banks, characterised by a lack of disclosure of information about the value and the location of their assets was coupled with little regulatory or supervisory oversight of the type associated with traditional banks. It made the whole system intrinsically unstable. An investor crisis of confidence fuelled by growing doubts on the value of shadow banks' assets would likely result in fire sales at a discount and finally a bank run. And this is what happened. The size of the global shadow banking system was estimated at around Euro 46 trillion in 2010, having grown from Euro 21 trillion in 2002, representing 25–30%[35] of the total financial system and half the size of bank assets. Shadow banking showed its capacity to create risks of a systemic nature, in

---

[34] The term "shadow bank" was coined by economist Paul McCulley in a 2007 speech at the annual financial symposium hosted by the Kansas City Federal Reserve Bank in Jackson Hole, Wyoming.

[35] In the United States, this proportion is even more significant, with an estimated share of 35–40%.

particular due to the complexity of shadow banking entities and activities; their cross-jurisdictional reach and the inherent mobility of securities and fund markets; and, the interconnectedness of shadow banking entities and activities with the regular banking system.

On the stock market side, it was reported that the stock market was "rigged" by traders and more and more sentient trolling algorithms which may front run orders placed by investors. Front-running is the practice of buying a security before a competitor does and then selling it for more than it would have cost if it had not been purchased early. High Frequency Trading made this practice easier because it takes advantage of sophisticated tools and computer algorithms to buy and sell securities in microseconds or less. Since almost 2007, the traditional picture of what is a stock market has disintegrated. The thick necked guys on steroids with coded colour jackets shouting in the trading pits have disappeared, and if some remain, they are mostly a memory from the past. IT infrastructures have swallowed the market and buried it into highly secured refrigerated and dark vaults. Given how critical financial operations are to economy and security, one might expect this infrastructure to be on par or more securely protected than most other agencies. Over the last two decades, financial markets have become increasingly reliant on technology to handle the expanding volume of their business. Today, exchanges like the NYSE process millions of trades a day electronically. An investigation led to identified that even team members transmitted sensitive non-public information about major financial institutions using their personal e-mail accounts. They used unencrypted laptops to store sensitive information, in violation of administrative policy. Their laptops also lacked antivirus software. In the worse cases, the laptops contained "vulnerability assessments maps and networking diagrams of how to hack into the exchanges".

The evidence suggests that both New York and London, not to mention Hong Kong and Singapore are beacons of the world's best and brightest talents. Compared to the other world class financial centres, U.S. immigration policies made it harder for non-U.S. citizens to move to New York for education and employment, which works directly against New York's competitive advantage. By contrast, the ease for talented professionals to move within the European Union, Hong Kong or even Singapore is a significant factor why the best people concentrate in other leading financial centres where immigration practices are more accommodating. In spite of its financial muscle, New York needs to improve its game as it is just recovering from a time when it was encumbered with excessive multi-layered and overlapping regulatory agencies, a prohibitive litigious culture due to the ease with which litigants can sue American companies in the courts for all kinds of trivial reasons and restrictive regulatory reforms designed to prevent another Enron scandal. Congress passed the Sarbanes–Oxley Act (SOX) in 2002 in direct response to significant cases of corporate malfeasance, which occurred despite the legal and market requirements for corporate governance oversight in place at that time. The flawed implementation of the 2002 SOX and especially Section 404, produced far heavier costs than expected, aggravated the situation, as has the continued requirement that foreign companies conform to U.S. general accounting standard practices rather than the widely accepted — many would say superior — international standards (IFRS).[36] All this may have started at some point to undermine America's entrepreneurial culture and damaged Wall Street's innovation capacity.

It is estimated that the capital-markets' businesses of banks will be materially affected by regulatory reforms in Europe and the United States.[37] Using 2010 data as the baseline, it is probable that the post-crisis average return on equity (ROE) of about 20% across the top 13 global financial firms will be reduced to about 7%, before any mitigation actions. Those actions are likely to push ROE up to about 11–12%. Some expected changes in pricing and business models will likely boost ROE further, to about 12–14%, well below recent levels.[38] Some more change will be needed in the structure of the financial system: improving trade pricing to account for funding costs, counterparty risks and collateral effects, and by creating an automated centralised collateral inventory that minimises the costs associated with margin calls: Those adopters are

---

[36] City of New York and United States Senate "Sustaining New York's and the U.S.' Global Financial Services Leadership," prepared by McKinsey & Company and New York City Economic Development Corporation (New York: Office of the Mayor), (2006).

[37] The regulations considered include Basel II.5, Basel III, the Dodd-Frank Act, EMIR, CRD2 and other regional regulations.

[38] McKinsey, Day of reckoning? New regulation and its impact on capital-markets businesses, Working papers on risk n°29, October (2011).

likely to significantly mitigate the negative impact of the regulatory changes on their profitability. The analytics needed to draw insights from this data is enormous. The benefit of developing a centralised collateral inventory, or a consolidated view across silos, is improved and so is time-to-market decision making. A complete view of the pool of assets to choose from can support the use of complex optimisation algorithms capable to reduce funding costs, and take into account operational and trading objectives. This change has triggered another wave of unprecedented IT investments creating an even higher barrier to entry for aspiring IFCs.

The Need of an Asian World Class Financial Centre, after the Second World War

Time zone specialisation enables each financial market to process transactions in stocks, commodity futures, gold and other financial products in a timely manner. Views on whom should get pre-eminence as a third global financial centre are split, but the current situation is that Asia is home of three centres of international significance: Tokyo, Hong Kong and Singapore. The contours of a new financial landscape are emerging since the 2008–2009 financial crisis: its formation is still in progress and Asia is one of the driving forces. Some consensus has emerged that if another new global financial centre develops, the chances are that it could be located in Mainland China. Shanghai, another seaport city located at the juncture of Huangpu and Yangtze River, right before the latter joins the Pacific Ocean was previously the major Asian financial centre from 1905[39] until 1940 before being devastated by the Sino-Japanese War. The Communist foundation of the People's Republic of China in 1949 brought an end to this ambition. After 1947, Shanghai fell out of the top ten financial centres and never has re-entered that group. Since then, Shanghai has managed to develop a significant pool of financial activities in the new Pudong area of Lujiazui on the other side of the Huangpu River. The government of the People's Republic of China has set a goal of turning Shanghai into a true global financial centre by 2020, a target with which the municipal government of Shanghai is in enthusiastic agreement. The

---

[39] Shanghai was then considered among the top ten financial centres of world significance, but still behind Hong Kong on average.

municipality is consequently making great efforts to promote the Shanghai financial hub but the city is still far from becoming a financial centre of truly international significance, despite a world class financial infrastructure, a strong domestic pool of talents and notable efforts to attract international experts. In this perspective, China is carefully pushing the development of an overseas offshore Renmenbi (RMB) centre for Asia, with a particular focus on Hong Kong, and beyond. So far this has generated more volume than the incremental value-added needed to strengthen the development of an indigenous IFC. Its Pudong new free-trade is one of the clearest sign of the city's ambition to become the largest Asian financial centre, eventually capable of rivalling London and New York. This first cut assertion must be revisited in the light of the return of Hong Kong to Chinese sovereignty in 1997, making the triangular Asian game between Hong Kong, Singapore and Tokyo a little bit more subtle, in the context of a possible Hong Kong — Shanghai joint bid for supremacy.[40]

Financial markets in Asia are still behind their potential and are fragmented. The region remains heavily reliant on bank lending, and capital markets are not deep enough to recycle Asia's large and diverse pool of savings. Size matters, but, as seen before, it is far from being a sufficient factor to become a dominant financial place. Other factors, such as leadership, cultural freedom, functioning institutions, innovation and ethics, can make or derail the ambitions of powerful and well established candidates.

Medieval Japan: A Secluded Archipelago Split in Internal Feuds

The Japanese archipelago is an island cluster of 145,000 sq. km, quite similar in size to the British Isles, both at a comparable distance from Eurasia, and sharing quite similar climatic features. Japan is situated in the North Eastern tip of Asia and its insularity naturally limits interactions with other countries: there was a Chinese Japan since the 6th century and the emergence of a Westernized Japan afterwards. By the 12th century, the imperial power of the Kyoto based Mikado was in the hands of the

---

[40] Shanghai-Hong Kong Stock Connect is a pilot programme that links the stock market in Hong Kong and Shanghai. Investor can trade and settle shares listed on the other market via the exchange and clearing the house in their home market.

Fujiwara, a warrior clan, which had been dominating Japanese politics in the Hean period since 794. Aristocrats preferred the life at the court rather than the administration of their estates which resulted in great disorder in the provinces with warrior gangs constantly fighting each other. The Japanese Western era started in 1868, marking the end of the nearly 700 years shogunate. From the mid-12th century through the Kamakura (1185–1333) and Muromachi (1336–1573) to the mid-16th century, this epoch is often described as Japan's medieval age, chûsei. This period is included in the endless 700 years shogun era from the first Kamakura shogunate in 1192 to the Imperial restoration in 1868. Although the imperial court in Heian continued to claim authority, the warrior government known as the Kamakura bakufu[41] located in Edo[42] dominated political life. The improvement in agricultural technology and in particular the more extensive use of iron tools and double cropping contributed to higher yields and the formation of surplus of food. As a result, local markets become more frequent but never reached the size of European fairs. The trade with nearby China led to the development of financial transactions and money lending became more frequent. It led to financial strains, and interest rates soared: Many warriors became so indebted or insolvent that the bakufu issued a debt moratorium edict (tokusei) in 1297. In China, Khubilei Khan, the grandson of Gengis Khan, founded the Yuan (Mongol) dynasty establishing the Mongol power in Dadu (Beijing). When his attention turned to the Japanese Archipelago in 1268, he sent a missive to the "King of Japan" asking that the Japanese pay tribute to China. The request and subsequent ones were ignored, therefore Khan prepared for the invasion of Japan in 1274 and 1281.[43] The preparation for war with China and the subsequent retribution of meritorious warriors resulted in significant economic hardship. The following Muromachi bakufu was an unstable warrior government, described as a coalition of shogun and

---

[41] *bafuku* means in Japanese military language "general headquarters", or tent government. The word was used historically as a national government headed by a shogun ("Japan most powerful general", but nothing more until 1603 when he obtained the title of Japan secular ruler from the emperor) and the *han*, related estates of provincial lords known as *daimyo*.
[42] Currently Tokyo. The Tokuwaga military government was headquartered in Edo in 1615.
[43] The Chinese invasion fleet was sunk and repelled twice by violent storms to be known as "divine winds" (*kamikaze*). Japanese relations with China were not reinstated until the 14th century.

shugo.[44] This led to extreme fragmentation of the country but managed to stimulate the economy and commercial growth. The erosion of estate holdings (shôen) and old guilds led to further progress in farming and markets became better supplied. By the 1500s, a class of 250 territorial military lords, daimyo, emerged. They established and maintained their agricultural estates (called "han"), built castles, and established competing cities around their castles.

The abundance of goods stimulated somewhat the development of merchants, peddlers and transport agents: products from distant provinces found their way to the Kyoto and Kamakura markets. Trade developed with Ming China: Silk, medicines and art objects were prized in Japan. More importantly, copper coins were imported from Song and Ming China, and although coinage was not done in Japan,[45] the use of money, bills of exchange and pledges were all accepted. An informal network of freebooters was sailing out of small ports of Honshû and Kyushu. Japanese pirates established contact with the outside world, possibly with Portuguese and Spanish merchant ships. In 1543, the first contact with Europe took place on sea as two or three Portuguese traders were ship-wrecked on a Chinese junk off the coast of Tanegashima (Kyushu) and carried to Japan in the backwash of the tide. They were soon followed by the Jesuit missionaries[46] led by Francis Xavier who arrived in Japan in 1549. Following the slow development of the Japanese merchant economy and the extension of maritime networks along the coastline of Japan, the Nobunaga and Hideyoshi acting shoguns[47] were leading a much wealthier country compared to the Ashikaga era. From 1540, Japan found itself connected to and drawn into a commercial network of sea faring merchants that had links with Western Europe. At the end of the Tokugawa Bafuku's first century (1697), the farming production of the shogun estate represented 17% of the country's total. Additional income was coming from

---

[44] Powerful branch family members and vassals of the Ashikaga, a warrior family from eastern Japan, with military authority over provinces.

[45] Aside from imported coins, Japanese coins were minted in imitation of Chinese and the coins of other countries, namely the mochu-sen (模鋳銭) were also in circulation.

[46] The order was established in 1540.

[47] Both refused to endorse the discredited title of shogun, and prefer to base their authority on their own force of arms and court titles.

copper, silver and gold mines and the administration and taxation of Japan's important cities, and in particular: Edo, Japan's capital city, Kyoto, the ancient imperial city and a great manufacturing centre for silk and high quality goods, Osaka, Japan's busiest harbour, and Nagasaki, the nation's only harbour open to foreigners.

Japan's Tokugawa Shogunate, marked the beginning of the early modern Japan (Edo Period) starting with its unification in 1590 and the emphasis on the reestablishment of order — in social, political, and international relations — following a century of civil war. The Shogunate issued in 1615 a 17 article set of "Regulations for the Imperial Palace and Aristocracy, *daimyo*" revised in 1635 to further instruct the *daimyo* to keep the transportation infrastructure in good condition. Great names, *daimyo*, were prohibited from instituting toll stations or imposing embargoes. This was to facilitate free trade and communication across the country. The 300 year transition between a Japanese embattled feudal culture to a unified, peaceable Japan capable of becoming a world class hub for business and finance was very short compared to European standards. By the latter half of the early modern period, wealth increasingly resided with the merchant class, formally the lowest on the social hierarchy. Itinerant merchants travelled from estate to estate setting up markets and trading centres once or twice a month. These occasional markets evolved into permanent market sites as the ongoing demand for goods increased steadily. Artisans also aggregated and settled in such locations to sell the goods they produced. The development of market towns was a direct result of this commercial activity. A unique form of money known as gold and silver wraps, which were paper-packed gold and silver coins, started to circulate for the settlement of large transactions.[48] The coins were packed in traditional Japanese rice paper and sealed. On the obverse side, the name of the preparer, the amount included, and the date of wrapping were written with a brush to certify their value. Wraps circulated as money at face value and no one tried to break seals nor to check the amount included, relying on the high credibility of sealers such as the Gold Mint, the Silver Mint and prestigious money changers. Gold and silver wraps were first prepared by the Gold Mint and the Silver Mint by the order of

---

[48] And in smaller denominations for offerings.

the Tokugawa Shogunate government but prestigious ryogaesho (money changers) also started to prepare the wraps backed by their high credibility since the late 17th century with the growing demand for a large denomination currency to settle many large transactions. Thus, the use of wraps was mainly limited to the Shogunate government, feudal lords and large merchants. The Mitsui family, who occupied a leading position among the ryogaesho (money changers) in Edo in preparing wraps, requested the Shogunate to enhance their business of wrapping and sealing money to include the monetary tributes of feudal lords to the Shogunate government. This can be considered a significant attempt to start managing the sovereign debt, but it was not accepted. Another illustrious family, the Konoike, who descended from samurai, began in sake-brewing and the shipping business in 1656 and moved into financial lending, primarily to the powerful land-owning *daimyo* class in the Osaka region. In 1670, the money exchange was among the Big Ten organisations chartered by the Shogunate to provide financial services to the Japanese government. For about forty years from the end of the 17th century to the first half of the 18th century, a series of recoinages was carried out. They greatly contributed to an increase in the profitability of money changers operations and strengthened their financial position. Money changing banks mainly in Osaka and Edo, were primarily engaged in the trade of coins. Banks in Osaka developed a highly advanced system of settlement using various kinds of bills drawn on deposits, but did not make transformation i.e., use these deposits for lending, but employed only their own capital.

Around 1700, the military lords taxed their subjects in rice, then auctioned the lots in large cities, in particular Osaka which emerged as the major trading centre for rice in Japan. Only authorised wholesalers were allowed to participate: the winner would receive a rice voucher that would be settled shortly thereafter for cash. The vouchers, represented real money and eventually became transferable; and subsequently a new market in the buying and selling of rice vouchers developed among the merchants. Osaka merchants increasingly engaged in "prepayment bills" trading, which led to a frantic speculation on the price of rice, before it was banned. The Dojima Rice Exchange was officially authorised in 1715 by the Shogunate and traded on two compartments; the shomai and choaimai. The shomai market, was a forward market, while choaimai was trading on rice bill futures. In this context, sayatori was arbitrage between forward and futures contracts. The choaimai trade was kept on books and no cash or cash equivalent (vouchers) was exchanged; all information regarding the trade was notarised at a clearinghouse financially responsible for the transaction completion, where traders had deposited accounts. It was mandatory that all contracts be settled no later than four months prior to the closing of the contract period. Settlement had to be done with cash or with an opposing contract position. With a few interruptions and several interventions from the Shogunate to regulate the market, the Japanese rice exchanges, the ancestor of all futures exchanges, would operate until 1937.[49]

The evolution of the Japanese economy helped domesticate samurai warlords. They lost their medieval ferocity, their right to wear arms and became more active in bureaucracy. One official, the Great Elder, tairô, had a remarkable status alongside the shogun and stood above all bakufu councils. In 1858, the tairô, responsible to the shogun alone, signed treaties of Amity and Commerce with the United States, and later with England, France, the Netherlands and Russia, in spite of the unsuccessful attempt of the shogun to secure the seal of approval of the emperor in Kyoto. This opening to foreigners was seen as a great embarrassment which resulted in the assassination of the Great Elder and subsequent strained relationships with Western nations. A "Statement on the Expulsion of the Padres" issued in early 1614 was issued by the Shogunate. The "Act of Seclusion" (1636) was promulgated, Japan closed for 200 years to Western Europe, but not to commercial relations with East Asian nations, in particular Korea and China. An office for the complete eradication of Christianity in Japan was opened in 1640. This regulation was going to hit hard Portuguese traders who had the monopoly of carrying freight between China and the harbour of Nagasaki. The arrival of the Dutch in 1609, and their establishment in Hirado was a clear alternative to the privileged relationship with the Portuguese who quietly continued to help the development of Christianity in Japan. In autumn 1637, a massive peasant upsurge broke out in Amakusa and Shimabara, the Shogunate blamed the pernicious influence of Catholicism, but it was in reality a revolt against

---

[49] It was dismantled and replaced in 1939 by the Rice Government Agency.

misery and outrageous taxes. The Dutch tactically assisted in breaking the revolt, and many Japanese Christians were executed, possibly up to 37,000. A decree was promulgated in 1639 pointing at "the sectarian rabble who plotted evil and were accordingly executed". The Shogunate told the Portuguese to never cross again the sea to Japan in their ships. The Dutch were permitted to retain a small outpost in the artificial island of Deshima, originally built to confine their Catholic rivals in the Nagasaki harbour. Japan continued to live a segregated life until 8 July 1853, when Commodore Matthew Perry of the U.S. Navy, commanding a squadron of two steamers and two sailing vessels, sailed into Tokyo harbor. Perry, on behalf of the U.S. government, demanded a treaty permitting trade and the opening of all Japanese ports to U.S. merchant ships, the absence of Japan naval forces highlighted the Shogunate incapacity to deal with the situation. The 13 November 1852 letter from American President Millard Fillmore to the Emperor of Japan, mentioned: "I have no other object in sending him [Perry] to Japan but to propose to your imperial majesty that the United States and Japan should live in friendship and have commercial intercourse with each other." Demands for reform became louder: the last Tokugawa Yoshinobu shogun resigned in 1867. When the Mutsuhito emperor, his pro-imperial factions and the anti-Tokugawa brought down the old medieval order, few were to regret the defunct Shogunate. From the Meiji Restoration of 1868 emerged a bustling urban culture, nurtured by the newfound wealth and sophisticated tastes of merchant city dwellers. The defunct powerful city of the Shogunate Edo was renamed Tokyo, the young emperor take up residence in the city at the Tokugawa castle. Tokyo then became the official capital of Japan.

From 1868, the new masters of Japan worked hard to improve their country status, they faced a classic expansion dilemma: building a new economic superpower based on industry, trade and finance or creating an Asian military empire inspired by Bismarck's model in Prussia. Japan was a late-comer in the 19th century industrialisation race, Japanese historian shared the German school view[50] of the nation-specific nature of development, implying that their stage theories were more or less nation-specific

---

[50] Many German historians from Leopold von Ranke to Friedrich Meinecke thought that Germany had little to learn from Britain or France.

and culture-bound. Between the Meiji restoration and the end of the Second World War, under the pressure of the agrarian nobility and the military, Japan chose to embark on a doomed dream of building an empire stretching from Alaska to Singapore, in imitation of the other Western colonial powers and in fear for the security of their home country. The great northern island of Hokkaido and the Ryukyu Islands in the south became part of the empire. For a while after the Meiji Restoration, most of money issued in the Edo Period continued to circulate. Money changers were still actively wrapping and sealing gold and silver coins actively. Yasuda Zenjiro, a founder of Yasuda Bank, began wrapping and sealing gold and silver coins in addition to conducting a profitable money exchange business in the Nihonbashi district of Edo in 1864. Yasuda's ability to appraise gold and silver coins was so good that the "Yasuda Zenjiro Wrap" enjoyed a high reputation. Gold and silver coins were wrapped to reduce the costs of appraising and weighing silver generated by each transaction. However, the wrapping and sealing of gold and silver coins collapsed with the issue of new gold and silver coins and the denomination of the "yen" after the New Currency Act of 1871. At the time of the Meiji Restoration in 1868, Japan had no modern banking system except for a few foreign banks doing business for foreign trade at authorized ports such as Yokohama and Kobe. This changed on 15 November 1872, when Japan established a national banking system modelled closely on that of the United States but still with a significant difference: Japan's banking system was much smaller and far less experienced[51] than their American counterparts at the time. One of the purposes for establishing the Bank of Japan in 1882 was to "facilitate finance" by promoting the nationwide integration of the regional financial markets, which until that point had been divided and functioned independently. Regional differences in interest rates contracted in the late 1890s and due to the Bank of Japan's network, and more specifically corresponding transactions, between the Bank of Japan and private-sector financial institutions and the local Bank of Japan offices, served to activate inter-regional movements of funds through the funds transfer services provided. Compared to the

---

[51] By 1863, the United States had over 80 years of experience and a well-established banking system with over 1,400 banks.

European medieval leading finance cities, Japan was just at the beginning of a deep transformation. Prior to 1935, Yokohama, a seaport in the South West of Tokyo Bay, was the leading IFC of Japan.

In 1942, an estimated 80% of the wealth was still concentrated in the hands of a few (15) families. A feature of the post-war Japanese economy was the delay of catch up during the 50s followed by rapid economic growth during the 60s and early 70s. The remarkable growth of the Japanese economy after the Second World War took place "under the protection of its unique financial system, which was extremely efficient, given the conditions that prevailed at that time."[52] Tokyo only became Asia's pre-eminent banking and finance centre in the early 1960s, and has been since then been the bedrock of Japanese banking, securities, insurance and professional services despite the emergence of two financial state cities: Singapore and Hong Kong. Tokyo, situated on the south east of the island of Honshu, is a busy harbour well positioned to take the lead in finance in Asia. The city sits conveniently in a time zone that makes it a natural time bridge between North America and Europe. However, the matter is still sensitive and it is not certain that Japan is fully prepared to endorse such a responsibility. The post-war trauma of the defeat including the destruction of the institutional framework of the economy, the Japanese language and a landlocked culture constituted a formidable barrier to internationalisation, especially compared to a more informal and casual atmosphere in the former British colonies of Singapore and Hong Kong.

It was only in the second half of the 1970s that the market started to deregulate and by the 1980's, the isolation of Tokyo's market had to come to an end because the rapid trend toward global interdependence made it unacceptable for a nation of Japan's economic standing and strength to maintain closed financial markets. The Japanese financial markets opened up slowly: the first internationalisation of financial markets occurred in 1984 and the Japanese Big Bang in 1998 led to a rapid growth in gross inward and outward investments. The Japanese government commenced the Financial System Reform, called the "Japanese Big Bang," in

---

[52]Yusuke Kashiwagi, Chairman of the Bank of Tokyo, in his Per Jacobson Lecture during the meetings of the International Monetary Fund in Washington, September (1986).

November 1996 under the three principles of "Free, Fair, and Global," aiming to rebuild the Japanese financial markets into an international market comparable to the New York and London markets. With Japan having endured a waterlogged economy for over a decade, many banks have found too little business in Tokyo to warrant their remaining there. Japan's new economic dynamic changed this, especially since China made no mystery of its ambitions to take the lead in finance. But the 1990s were a lost decade for the Japanese financial system and its problems reverberated on the whole Japanese economy. Between November 1997, when Yamaichi Securities and Hokkaido Takushoku Bank were closed and October 1998, when the Diet passed the bank recapitalisation legislation, Japan's banking system tanked and was on the brink of financial collapse. This came as a shock since no Japanese bank had reported an annual loss from the end of Second World War to 1995 — presumably because the low disclosures requirement permitted them to do so. This led to a perception that Japan was on the trend of a permanent decline, as the amount of accumulated "guaranteed" bad loans by the Japanese financial industry on riding the real estate Heisei bubble since the end of the 1980s was unprecedented in the history of an OECD country, possibly around 15% of GDP. It remained impossible to explain based on standard asset pricing models how in 1989, the few hundred acres of Tokyo land on which the Imperial Palace stands could have been worth all of the land in Canada or California.[53] To turn the ship around, the Bank of Japan gained its independence from direct Government control in April 1998 and the Obuchi government granted real power to the Financial Reconstruction Commission to lead the clean-up, with the ultimate threat of nationalisation. The turnaround was brutal, the banking sector consolidated and it showed that the days of the old slow-hand relationship based policy were over, especially since it collided with a profound mutation of the Japanese economy. Japan was willing to protect above all the reputation of its financial sector, but much work still remained to be done. Markets do not easily heal when there is a large inventory of assets overhanging them, waiting to be depreciated and sold at the real price.

---

[53] Allen, Franklin, and Douglas Gale, Bubbles and Crises. *Economic Journal*, 110(460): 236–255 (2000).

Aside from the change of policy, Tokyo's appreciation is certainly the result of the successful liberalisation and internationalisation of the Japanese financial markets. And a final reason is the accumulation of Japanese dollars, which is eventually destined to be recycled abroad. Less than two thousand kilometers west from Tokyo, Shanghai's financial community is repeatedly stating its ambition to rebuild a strong financial centre and leverage it as a world class financial centre, chiefly as a rival of Tokyo and Hong Kong. But it is still unclear whether China, "will develop an onshore Manhattan or need an offshore London." The role of Tokyo as the third IFC has been possibly overestimated. Japan's powerful economy has generated strong flows related to the trade of the large Japanese companies. However, few multinational companies from overseas and few international banks have chosen Tokyo as their regional command centre in Asia. For this reason, both Hong Kong and Singapore have established a strong international record taking respectively the third and fourth place in many leading rankings. Both are clearly raising their profile to become the financial hub of the Pacific region, attract Tokyo in their orbit and challenge London's position. At the scale of the Pacific Ocean of 156 million sq. km., these uncertainties compare with the struggle between Italian cities in the High Middle Ages in the Mediterranean Sea (2.5 million sq. km.).

After the 2008–2009 financial crisis, China decided to push its financial institutions abroad and actively built renminbi offshore trading platforms "in an orderly manner" with a clear objective to establish its currency internationally. China and Russia are leading joint initiatives to develop a new renminbi based financial system, rating agencies, and routing platforms as a competing parallel to the current dollar or euro denominated ones. A multipolar financial world is possibly emerging, and once again geopolitics is intruding into leading banking practices. Shanghai has started the development of a banking centre with the ambition to become an internationally leading one. Although politics are intimately linked to trade and can lead to commercial or financial collaboration or rivalry, to political conflicts and even warfare, history show that it does not provide the decisive argument for one place to become a better IFC than the other. Financial dominance in the Early Modern Age could be better explained based on political, military and economic contexts, rather than on specific internal dynamics or geomorphological constraints. Today, it seems that diversity and freedom for people to learn, share and trade in a trusted ecosystem would be much more decisive than muscles and constraints as decisive factors for dynamism.

Vertical and Horizontal Challenge: New Geographies and New Industries

Along with South Korea, and Taiwan, Hong Kong and Singapore were called the "Four Tigers" of Asian economic prosperity in the 70s. During and after the 1980s, Hong Kong and Singapore emerged as new Asian financial markets supplementing Tokyo, and possibly outpacing it at some stage as the largest Asian financial hub. Investors are establishing greater presences in Hong Kong, and Singapore as they try to get close to new investment opportunities. Both Singapore and Hong Kong have the distinctive feature of being former British possessions and both are seaports strategically situated along international sea trading routes. The ongoing competition between both city states can be traced back to the days of their entrepot status. Financial markets in Singapore and Hong Kong were set to meet the demand of transhipment in trade during the 1960s. In the 1970s, the development of the Euro-Dollar market and the influx of capital flow in Asia boosted the emerging financial activities in these two centres.

Singapore, a strategic outpost in South East Asia

Singapore Island was known to sailors as early as the 3rd century and originally was inhabited by fishermen and pirates. It served as a trading outpost with warehousing facilities for the Sumatran Empire of Srīvijaya. In Javanese inscriptions and Chinese records dating to the end of the 14th century, the more common name of the island is Tumasik, or Temasek meaning Sea Town, a rather infertile, pirate infested island nest where men and women tied their hair in knots and wore short jackets and sarongs sewn from blue materials. A 17th century Malay manuscript noted the 1299 founding of the city of Singapura ("lion city") after a strange, lion-like beast that had been sighted there. Portuguese explorers took the port of Malacca in 1511, forcing the reigning sultan to flee south to the Johore Sultanate, a move that incorporated Singapura. But after the Portuguese burned down the trading post at the mouth of the Temasek River in 1613, the Singapore Island was largely deserted. The arrival of Sir Thomas Stamford Bingley Raffles in 1819, lieutenant governor of the British enclave of Bencoolen in Sumatra and an agent of the British East India Company, changed the destiny of the place after he obtained permission from the local Malay official to establish a trading post. He called it Singapore,[54] after its ancient name, and opened the port to free trade and free immigration on the south coast of the island at the mouth of the Singapore River. At the time, Singapore thick with swamps and jungle had only a few hundred inhabitants, and was technically under the loose jurisdiction of the Sultan of Johore. The place was under tight Dutch scrutiny to avoid the establishment of a permanent British presence. Raffles who was a smart diplomat outmaneuvered the Dutch and signed a treaty with the new Sultan and the Temenggong.[55] He got permission to establish a trading post in exchange for the payment of an annual fee, leading the Dutch to protest that this acquisition was illegal. It was a bit late for them to complain but the matter was finally resolved peacefully in 1824 under the Anglo-Dutch treaty. This change attracted many merchants who had long lost money to the Dutch monopoly and were willing to take their revenge. The population increased steadily amid problems of giant rats, hungry crocodiles and ferocious tigers harassing the settlers. Among the goods traded at the port in the 1850s were silk and tea, from China, and ivory, ebony, antimony and spices from southeast Asia. Ships from India and Britain also brought opium and cloth. By 1860, three banks had been established. The founding of Hong Kong in 1841 prompted some worries about the development of trade with China but these fears proved to be unfounded. By the end of the century, Singapore was one of the major ports of the British Empire. The primary attraction of Singapore was its multicultural port and coaling station for the steamships sailing back to Europe, and it benefitted greatly from the opening of the Suez Canal (1869). By 1903, Singapore had become the world's seventh busiest harbour in terms of tonnage, and had managed to keep out of a disastrous

---

[54] An anglicized version of the word Singapura, a Sanskrit word that means the "Lion City".

[55] The territorial chief of the southern part of the Malay Peninsula, including Singapore.

involvement in the First World War. It celebrated a year after the armistice the centenary of its founding by Raffles. By 1947, Singapore entered the top ten IFCs, securing a position as Southeast Asia's financial hub of choice.

After Singapore broke away from the Federation of Malaysia and gained independence in 1965, the new ambition of Lee Kwan Yew, the city state's founding father, was to transform Singapore into an industrial centre as well as being a centre for other trading activities. Singapore's financial expertise was developed first to support the industrialisation and then as a key industry segment of its own together with fiscal competition from Hong Kong. Singapore started to develop an outward looking financial development strategy and focused on developing business with the nearby countries of Thailand, Indonesia, and Malaysia, or what became those nations. In just over four decades, Singapore established a thriving financial centre of international repute, serving not only its domestic economy, but also the wider Asia Pacific region. An Asian offshore interbank market started to develop after 1968 when Singapore launched the Asian Dollar Market (ADM) and introduced the Asian Currency Units (ACUs). The ADM was designed as an alternative to the Eurodollar market, so the ACU regime enabled mainly foreign banks to engage in international trade under a favourable tax and regulatory environment. The Singapore Stock Exchange was incorporated in 1973, after the split with the Malaysian Stock Exchange, and developed its own route to become a leading international exchange. However, this was certainly not a straight line development for the Merlion city: the 80s started with banking failures and ended with a market crash in 1987.

Again in 1997 the Asian financial crisis hit the region and South East Asian economies like Indonesia, the Philippines and Thailand were badly ravaged. Singapore and Hong Kong were not spared from the spillover effects of the crisis, but both managed to handle the blow. However, unlike Hong Kong, Singapore's role as an IFC in Asia does not stem from bilateral flows with Mainland China even if the relationships is good, particularly regarding Foreign Direct Investment (FDI) where the process of China's capital account gradual opening is more advanced than for other types of capital flows. Singapore has built on its intrinsic quality of service to non-resident third parties. In some ways Singapore resembles

London as it is not, like New York and Hong Kong, supported by a large domestic economy.

In the post 2008 global crisis landscape, Singapore's value proposition in this new landscape rests on four pillars: smart regulation; diverse ecosystem; pan-Asian focus; and a deep talent pool.[56] Since the global financial crisis, a higher premium has been placed on well-regulated financial centres. Singapore's strategy is to set high standards but it implements them in a way which is practical and makes business sense. Singapore's monetary authority (MAS) established in 1971 by the Monetary Authority of Singapore Act, ensures that banks meet high prudential standards, exceeding international norms in several areas. It functions as a *de facto* central bank for Singapore and hence serves as the banker-of-last-resort for the city state's banking system. During the global financial crisis, this ensured that adequate safeguards were in place and confidence sustained. Post-crisis, the Singapore's banks seem well-placed to meet the new global capital requirements and liquidity standards. Maintaining high standards is compatible with fostering a vibrant financial centre. The way Singapore works is interesting as the Monetary Authority of Singapore (MAS) consults the industry and other stakeholders when introducing significant new regulations, and the only exception being when the issue is market sensitive.

A recent crisis in metal-backed finance has shown how a market shift can quickly occur, on the basis of mistrust after the Chinese state-owned commodities house Citic Resources announced that more than half of its alumina stock held at Qingdao Port in the northeast of China was missing. Dezheng Resources, and its related companies allegedly used fake warehouse receipts for about 340,000 tonnes of copper, aluminium and alumina. The news intensified competition between offshore and onshore rivals in the multibillion dollar business of securely storing the world's commodities in China, the world's biggest producer and user of base metals. Metals collateral such as copper, zinc, nickel or aluminium ingots are often used to back financing deals in China. These metal-backed financing

---

[56] Ravi Menon, Managing Director of the Monetary Authority of Singapore, at the Investment Management Association of Singapore's (IMAS) 14th Annual Conference, Singapore, 13 March (2013).

trades became popular in recent years, following the sharp increase in the quantity of commodities imported to support China's fast growing economy. In a classic transaction, a trader importing metals can obtain a good standing documentary usance letter of credit from a reputable bank overseas, with the bank involved then paying the metal exporter for the shipment. Having taken delivery of the metal, the importing trader can then promptly sell it on to an end-consumer before having to repay the bank that had issued the letter of credit. The trader can use the funds from the sale to gain a higher return by buying investment products or by reinvesting it into more metals. However, following the Qingdao and Penglai scandals in Shandong province, which have extended to gold,[57] leading market participants are relocating their commodities storage in South East Asia, specifically to Singapore and nearby Johor in Malaysia and South Korea. The shift out of China of nickel and zinc has not stopped such deals, but it has made them much more complicated and more expensive to execute. The scandal has raised wider concerns over the security of other metal in warehouses in Northern China, and has shaken the confidence of major participants in the capacity of third parties local agents to oversee the depots, and has led many banks to cut their exposure. Faced with the prospect of large losses on Mainland based collateral, financing deals had become less easy logistically with the storage of metals to other remote Asian locations, specifically as end-consumers of the metals mostly remain in China. Suspicion of the metal exposure and practices of the China shadow banking sector has spread over associated sectors, including the scrap metal recycling sector which is also struggling to raise cash. The shift has been also accelerated by more competitive fees and more business oriented regulation of competitors. Nearly 80% of the London Metal Exchange's nickel inventories in Asia are now being stored in Singaporean–Malaysian and South Korean warehouses. Nevertheless, Shanghai has been spared and is emerging as a trustable storage area, thus consolidating its ambitions in the finance sector.

Singapore has a diverse financial ecosystem which is currently smoothly integrating. The various parts of the financial sector not only

---

[57] The National Audit Office's (NAO) uncovered tens of billions of renminbi (RMB) in loans obtained on the basis of false gold transactions.

serve important functions in their own right, but are mutually reinforcing. Singapore is already capable of providing a wide and diversified suite of financial services, as a funding centre, as an asset manager, as an insurance centre, as a bond market, as a foreign exchange trading centre (fourth largest forex market in the world) and as a derivative trading hub. The city state accounts for an estimated 4% of the global market for offshore financial services. As a follow-up of the 2008–2009 crisis and related worldwide deleveraging, Singapore is differentiating in building a significant debt capital market. This will consolidate the development of a large market for the financing of long term and cross border infrastructure projects, notably in South East Asia. Singapore's ambitions to address three new areas of opportunity: ASEAN connectivity such as collective offerings of cross border investment opportunities, OTC derivatives infrastructure such as mitigating clearing risk in OTC transactions (SGX AsiaClear), and offshore RMB business as RMB denominated trade and investment are expected to grow. One of the challenges for the city is to provide a differentiating and competitive answer to the possible emergence of a Hong Kong–Shanghai single financial hub. This is echoing in the Pacific region the stiff competition between Italian cities in the Mediterranean region for financial dominance in medieval Europe. In this context, history has shown that the outcome may be difficult to predict.

Hong Kong, the gateway to China

Hong Kong's history seems to have been primarily determined by its geographical position. The territory of Hong Kong is comprised of two main islands (Hong Kong Island and Lantau Island) and a mainland hinterland. It thus forms a convenient natural geographic port south of the Guangdong province. Britain started its occupation of the rock of Hong Kong on 25 January 1841, and used it as a military staging point. When China was defeated in the first Opium War in 1842, it had to cede Hong Kong by the Treaty of Nanjing. The British colony quickly became a regional centre for trading services based particularly around the Hong Kong and Shanghai Bank and merchant companies such as Jardine Matheson. In 1841 there were only 7,500 Chinese inhabitants in Hong Kong and a handful of foreigners. Then Hong Kong developed as the most important entrepot until the Sino-Japanese War, and Hong Kong's occupation in 1941. Hong Kong housed the most highly capitalised firms and the decision makers with the greatest expertise in finance and trade in Asia — including China, and their networks reached deep into most of the countries of the region. In 1860, at the end of the Second Opium War, Britain gained a perpetual lease over the Kowloon Peninsula, which is the mainland Chinese area just across the strait from Hong Kong Island. This agreement was part of the Convention of Peking that ended the conflict. In 1898, the British and Chinese governments signed the Second Convention of Peking, which included a 99-year lease agreement for the islands surrounding Hong Kong, called the "New Territories." The lease awarded control of more than 200 surrounding small islands to the British. In return, China got a promise that the islands would be returned after 99 years. On 19 December 1984, British Prime Minister Margaret Thatcher and Chinese Premier Zhao Ziyang signed the Sino-British Joint Declaration, in which Britain agreed to return not only the New Territories but also Kowloon and Hong Kong itself when the lease term expired. China promised to implement a "One Country, Two Systems" regime, under which for fifty years Hong Kong citizens could continue to practice capitalism and political freedoms forbidden on the mainland. On 1 July 1997, the lease ended and the government of Great Britain transferred control of Hong Kong and surrounding territories to the PRC.

From the second half of the 19th century and continuing into the first half of the 20th century, Hong Kong operated as the key command centre for the allocation of Asian financial capital in its broadest form. Hong Kong's stature as an IFC then gradually developed from the 1950s. The city continued to develop as a gateway to Mainland China and became a regional headquarter and regional office place for the world's largest firms. The growing need for an increased level of professional services also supported the sophistication of the place as a diversified finance hub. The Open Door Policy of the PRC in 1978, under the stewardship of Deng Xiaoping, following the death of Mao Zedong in 1976 marked a new era. With the Chinese economic take off, Hong Kong's integration with the mainland accelerated as it regained its traditional role as China's preferred supplier of high quality commercial and financial services. Hong Kong maintained a solid position within the top ten IFCs, albeit with fluctuations in rank. The banking system, with assets representing 7.5 times GDP, is highly capitalised, international, and liquid, and the securities markets are deep, liquid and efficient. Hong Kong is the place where a world class finance industry and the massive resources of China converge in one single seaport city. This unique convergence allows Hong Kong to be China's gateway to the world's financial markets — leading global investors to opportunities in China and giving them access to mainland China's increasing wealth pool. The direct connection between Hong Kong and Shanghai stock markets since November 2014, is a first step in the integration of financial markets in China. Shenzhen stock market will follow in order to offer a broader set of opportunities to investors. For the moment, the convergence is gradual, which is quite typical of the Chinese way to test the water: daily transactions are limited to RMB 23.5 billion and total volume is capped to RMB 500 billion. Overall Hong Kong has been a fertile ground for the experimentation of Chinese finance: not only the first RMB offshore market was created in Hong Kong, but also the first offshore RMB denominated bond market ("Dim Sum" market).

Hong Kong has retained its common law system and developed a judiciary system well rounded in hearing commercial cases. The rule of law, upheld by an independent judiciary, is one of the key success factors of Hong Kong's development as a leading commercial and financial centre, providing an efficient and secure environment for individuals and businesses. Hong Kong has stood the tests of numerous financial crises: the 1994 Mexican and Latin American "Tequila" crisis; the 1997 Asian financial "baht" crisis; the 1998 Russian default and Long-Term Capital Management crisis; the 2000 dotcom crash; and the 2008–2009 Great recession. Singapore could benefit from doubts cast over Hong Kong capacity to continue to handle a pivotal role if the neutrality of its judicial system is not safeguarded. The publication in Hong Kong in June 2014 of a white paper from Mainland China calling on judges to be "patriotic" actually fuelled concerns about the interpretation of such a recommendation.[58] Many global banks no longer need a full licensed

---

[58] Singapore jostle with Hong Kong for financial crown, Jeremy Grant, 16 October 2014, *Financial Times*.

bank in Hong Kong following the wave of concentration which took place among the world's largest banks. Thus, the remaining licensed players are huge global banks; virtually all of the world's top 50 banks already operated in Hong Kong as licensed banks. As a consequence, many of the traditional main street activities of banks have either stagnated or declined. The evolution of traditional banking coincides with the growing importance of professional services, and these businesses, as a net services exporter, point to the increased strength of Hong Kong as an IFC. This comes with the development of a deep back office hinterland in Mainland China, Guangdong province and specifically the Shenzhen metropolitan area. Reciprocally, the Shenzhen municipality institutionalised a program to explicitly lure back office jobs from Hong Kong. It compares well with the movement of back office financial jobs from financial hubs in North America or Europe to their surrounding suburbs or even farther out to satellite cities.

For example, Hong Kong dominates as the centre of private equity funds in Asia. Supply-side factors have played an important role in establishing Hong Kong as an IFC. The rapid growth of Hong Kong as an asset management platform and hedge fund centre in Asia rests on its high concentration of financial institutions, well-functioning legal and regulatory systems, and highly skilled and flexible labour force. In the mid-2000s, Japan had about the same amount of private equity funds under management, but almost 90% of its portfolio was invested in Japanese companies. In contrast, Hong Kong is the reverse image; about 90% are logically invested outside Hong Kong in Asia. The city accounts for an estimated 4% of the global market for offshore financial services, a level comparable to Singapore. As one of the leading financial services centre in the world, Hong Kong benefits from the positive clustering effect described above to a greater extent than any of its direct competitors.

Hong Kong has long served as the bridge between China and the world, conveying trade and investment flows both ways. The status of the city today is ambiguous: It is sealed off from the mainland but more and more closely connected to it; a special administrative region (SAR) that is fully integrated into the global economy but ultimately controlled by the Communist Party in Beijing. Hong Kong SAR has benefited from a first-mover advantage as the Mainland's financial system further integrates with the world, but now keeping this momentum within an international scope will be critical in the long run. The political fallout from the recent "Occupy Central" protests in 2015 have emphasised that keeping the *status quo* is not so simple, especially in the light of Shanghai publicly declared ambition to rival London and New York as a financial centre. The late-20th century witnessed an explosive growth of Hong Kong as an economic command centre, but the deviation from that trajectory beginning around the mid-1990s raises questions about its capacity to be ultimately Asia's leading financial hub if China centricity gains on the international dimension of the place. Hong Kong was always said to have a deeper and broader market structure than Singapore, but this is changing quickly. Half of Hong Kong's exports are directed to Mainland China; 20% of its bank assets are loans to Chinese customers; Mainland Chinese visits account for 10% of Hong Kong's GDP. Much of the economic activity in Hong Kong is difficult to interpret statistically and in an accurate manner, for example, the round tripping of capital often classified as FDI. A growing source of uncertainty has become mainland China's increasing presence in Hong Kong's banking sector raising fears of spillover of possible financial instability. Conversely, the Chinese economy's direct exposure to Hong Kong has become very small, so how much does Hong Kong really matter as a singularity for Mainland, should not be overestimated. The city may have reached a zenith as an IFC, but can still continue to be a valuable testing ground for Mainland China.

Dubai as a centre for Islamic finance

Established in 1971, the United Arab Emirates comprises seven Emirates, Abu Dhabi is the country's capital and Dubai its economic centre. This populated city enjoys a peculiar "insular" onshore situation deep behind the strait of Hormuz in the Persian Gulf. Since it opened in September 2004, the Dubai IFC has attracted leading international firms and set-up the NASDAQ Dubai which lists equities, derivatives, structured products, Islamic bonds (Sukuk) and other bonds. The Dubai model is an independent risk-based regulator with a legislative system consistent with English common law. The centre free zone positions as a U.S. dollar denominated environment tax heaven authorising 100% foreign ownership with a guarantee of a renewable tax free holiday on income and profits.

The origin of finance compliant with the Quran is as old as the religion itself. Islamic financial products work on the basis that the capital provider and the entrepreneur share the risk of investments on agreed terms. Although interest and gambling are not permitted, there is no Islamic law against wealth creation. Prophet Muhammad was a businessman, as were several of his companions and successors. His wife came from a wealthy family and was an investor. Mercantile trading practices represented the *modus operandi* of economic life in the early Islamic civilisation, much before the commercial revolution took place in Europe. Just like Christendom in the Middle Ages, making money with money was generally frowned upon. The record of early Muslim businessmen engaged in transactions based on Shariah,[59] and other Islamic principles are documented from the mid-7th century to the mid-13th century. During this era, the Arabs established land and sea trade routes stretching from the strait of Gibraltar to the South China Sea along which flowed trade based on the principles of Islamic commerce.

Dubai has also been standing out as a welcoming location for hawala transactions worldwide. There are over one hundred exchange houses operating in Dubai which has been known for decades for being one of the world centres of a widespread practice called "hawala",[60] generally meaning transfer in Arabic, sometimes trust. In the absence of, or parallel to, formal banking sector channels, it is one of the most popular informal funds transfer system based on trust that operates through hawaladar brokers, sometimes called "bankers", operating informally in travel agencies, laundries, bazaars or commodity stores. Hawala was primarily rooted in facilitating trade between distant regions at a time when conventional banking instruments were either absent or weak. The hawala system has existed since the 8th century between Arabic and Muslim traders alongside the Silk Road and beyond as a protection against theft. The system further developed in Dubai in the 1960s through gold smuggling in India

---

[59] Shariah according to the Grand Mufti of Egypt, Shawki Allam is not the Islamic divine law but an interpretation of Islamic norms at a certain epoch, made by lawyers.
[60] Hawalah has different terminology according to geography: underground banking, fei-ch'ien (China), hui kuan (Hong Kong), hundi (India), hawala (Middle East), padala (Philippines) and phei kwan (Thailand).

and Pakistan after the traders could not repatriate their money back to Dubai. At the same time, a large population of foreign workers had settled in Dubai and was willing to send money back to their families. The workers gave their remittances to gold traders and gold traders paid in return the monies to the workers families less a nominal fee. The system continued to prosper despite remitting countries generally having fairly liberal foreign exchange policies and strong financial sectors. The continued success of informal fund transfer systems raised concerns about the possible use of such anonymous networks in evading international sanctions, money laundering and terrorist financing as hawala has the power of "moving money without money moving at all", and without leaving traces or records.

Dubai stands as a champion in the renaissance of Islamic finance and wished to capitalise on the ancient Arabic tradition of trade at the junction of Asia and the Western world. The caravan trade between the Indian Ocean and the Mediterranean Sea has passed through the Arabian Peninsula ever since antiquity, although the contemporary Islamic population growth and the hydrocarbon resources availability are objective factors in Dubai's financial ambitions. As the 10th century approached, the centre of Islamic commerce gradually shifted from Iraq and the Persian Gulf to Egypt, the Red Sea and the harbours of the Arabian Peninsula. Cairo replaced Baghdad and the commercial links with Fatimid Egypt strengthened in the Mediterranean, particularly Sicily, Tunisia and Syria. Egypt holds a specific position in the history of Islamic finance as its recognised birthplace. In the 11th century, a group of merchants represented by the Egyptian Karimi family first emerged. Distinguished by their entrepreneurial skills, they soon attained great reputation, wealth and influence in all the important eastern markets and became known not only in financial activities but also in politics. From the 12th century, the Karimis and the Franks dominated commercial activities between East and West and displaced the Jewish and Christian merchants of the Byzantine, Ayyubid and Mamluk empires. The Karimi specialised trading centre, emerged on the main trade routes from the Indian Ocean to the Mediterranean. Places known as *funduqs* developed into virtual stock exchanges, entrepot and trading centres. Well known merchandise markets such as the *Suq al-Attarin* or *Al-Buhar* were the head office of the family business activities in Alexandria. Their capitalism rested primarily on commercial (textile, spices, slaves, furs, grain and mining products) and financial transactions. Karimi trade routes by sea led through the Red Sea and the Indian Ocean as far as China, and the land routes in times of peace went from Egypt through Syria, Iraq and Iran. As the Ottomans conquered parts of Asia Minor, the Karimi followed and expanded. They financed projects as one of their methods of acquiring capital, and operated a type of banking institution for loans and deposits. Their patrons were not only the Sultans and Emirs, but also the Frankish merchants whom they helped with credit — and also with soldiers and weapons as necessary. The golden age of Islam dwindled in the wake of the Mongol invasion led by Gengis Khan's grandson Hulagu, in the late 13th century. "The Mongols wreaked death and devastation wherever they rode from China to the plains of Hungary, but nowhere more so than in Persia, where most of the great cities were demolished and their inhabitants annihilated. The total population of this area may have dropped from 2,500,000 to 250,000 as a result of genocides and famine."[61] During the Ottoman Empire (1301–1922), global trade grew especially with Spain to start with, but the development of Islamic finance products remained limited. Trading ventures necessitated the evolution of financial capitalism. The practice of lending at interest, albeit surreptiously, with the development of financial capital, was apparently well known in the Meccan society in which Islam first appeared. It was quite customary for the creditor to calculate an interest as a proxy for the default risk and include it in the sum owed without stating it separately in the agreement. The Islamic contract Mudarabah is a partnership arrangement producing *in fine* a gain or a loss. It spread through Italian merchants in the high Middle Ages who called it "Commenda" a forerunner of the contemporary limited responsibility company. The use of this type of contract was not widespread in the Islamic world until the introduction of numerals which emerged with the mathematical innovations of Muhammad ibn Musa al-Khwarizmi, who introduced the Indian positional numerals with index values and zero for the purpose of making

---

[61] Ross E. Dunn, *The Adventures of Ibn Battuta: A Muslim Traveler of the 14th Century.* University of California Press, Berkeley (1989). http://ibnbattuta.berkeley.edu/3iraq.html.

rational calculations resolving the questions of business transactions. With this development, numbers and the numerical system became the framework for the capitalistic industrial economy.

The first Sukuk[62] was probably issued later in 1775 by the Ottoman Empire when it borrowed money against future income on tobacco customs levied to fund its budget deficit. The emergence of Sukuk has been the most significant development in Islamic capital markets in recent years. Sukuk instruments link sovereign and private issuers in the Middle East and Southeast Asia, with a wide pool of investors, many of whom are seeking to diversify their holdings beyond traditional asset classes. Funds raised through Sukuk are allocated to infrastructure initiatives and other deserving projects in the Islamic communities worldwide. The first Islamic bank was established in Egypt in 1963 under cover for fear of projecting an image of Islamic fundamentalism which was incompatible with President Nasser's views. This experiment took the form of a savings bank, the Mit Ghamr savings bank that combined the idea of German savings banks with Shariah principles based on profit-sharing in the Egyptian town of Mit Ghamr, a centre for aluminium production until 1967. Later, the Nasir Social Bank, established in Egypt in 1971, was declared an interest-free commercial bank. Although Egypt was a pioneer in Islamic finance, a disorderly early development of Islamic investment companies led to the emergence and bankruptcy of finance houses, most notably the El Rayan Company which set up a Ponzi scheme that later collapsed in the late 1980s. This resulted in a stained reputation, and led authorities to remain circumspect about its potential benefits. Gradually, authorities permitted the existence of the first Islamic financial provider, an Islamic window set up by the reputable Bank Misr, and the establishment of the first fully fledged Islamic bank, Faisal Islamic Bank in 1979. The first bank to be explicitly based on Shariah principles was created by the Organisation of Islamic countries in 1974, but the Islamic Development Bank was not open to the public. By the end of 1970, several Islamic

---

[62] Sukuk commonly refers to the Islamic equivalent of bonds. However, as opposed to conventional bonds, which merely confer ownership of a debt, Sukuk grants the investor a share of an asset, along with the commensurate cash flows and risk (*Source*: IDB, What is a Sukuk?).

banks had been established throughout the Muslim world, including the Dubai Islamic Bank (1975). Other centres of expertise including Singapore and Kuala Lumpur (Malaysia), the leading Sukuk issuer, are also willing to become pivotal players in Islamic finance. A Kuala-Lumpur–Singapore alliance for this purpose can prove a formidable obstacle to Dubai ambitions in the future. The emergence of new heavyweight investment vehicles may ultimately make a difference.

Although, this is still early days, a regional financial hub will probably emerge in Sub-Saharan Africa (SSA) in the next decade since this region has become the second-fastest-growing in the world. The banking sector in SSA has expanded steadily recently but still remains fragmented and fragile. The African banking landscape in recent years has seen the emergence and rapid expansion of pan-African banking groups. Innovative and successful experiences such as the mobile money service launched in Kenya to facilitate cheap and secure money transfers to rural areas and payments on microloans has nearly as many subscribers as Kenya has adults — 19 million people from a population of 43 million. This is likely the early days of a new form of business integration between telecommunication carriers and financial institutions for consumer banking services. Two major groups, originating from South Africa and Nigeria, have created significant cross-border networks and are gaining a significant presence in areas traditionally dominated by the European and U.S. banks. These two countries have expressed their ambition to develop their presence in the financial sector and emerged as possible financial SSA hubs. Location, stability and quality training of the young finance professionals and the capacity to implement world class international supervision standards in the industry will be decisive factors in this endeavour.

The rise of powerful asset managers

The development of finance hubs in new export driven economies have been further energised by the emergence of heavyweight private equity investment vehicles, which are recently born creatures in the capitalist zoo. The first private-equity firms are thought to be American Research and Development (AR&D) Corporation and J.H. Whitney & Co., both founded in 1946. AR&D was the brainchild of New England businessmen who believed that innovative businesses were failing due to a lack of capital and managerial experience. In 1957, AR&D logged a home run with its USD 70,000 investment for 70% of the capital of Digital Equipment Corp confirmed in 19 August 1966, after Robert Lehman happily agreed to take it public in leading a USD 8 million offering to sell 375,000 shares of stock in Digital Equipment. AR&D's share was worth USD 355 million, an annualised return on capital of 101%. Scandals scarcely made the headlines of the industry, and private-equity and venture-capital firms helped fund the technological revolution unleashed by the microprocessor which itself deeply transformed the way markets and financial hubs operate. As a whole, asset management has long lived in the shadows of the banking and insurance industries, but this has started to change and capital investment funds are currently asserting themselves as key constituents of leading financial hubs. Infrastructure investment needs estimated at USD 40 trillion by 2030[63] are likely to raise the profile of heavyweight funds, especially since banks will need to comply with more stringent regulations imposed in the wake of the Great Recession. The industry comes in many different flavours: angel investment and seed, venture tech capital, development funds, restructuring funds, quantitative funds, leveraged funds, diversified fund powerhouses — just to mention a few. It is not surprising that industry players have a fuzzy and mixed public image public being mostly identified as speculative hedge funds such as the Soros Fund Management or long term investors such as Berkshire Hathaway. George Soros is mostly known as "The Man Who Broke the Bank of England" after his short sale of USD 10 billion worth of pounds, giving him a profit of USD 1 billion during the 1992 Black Wednesday UK currency crisis, and Warren E. Buffett is well established as the superlative long term investor of Omaha, Nebraska. It is fairly consistent with the anticipated future position of asset management that some of its champions have already started to implement cutting edge decision making methodologies to systematically reduce mistakes, and rely on articulated buy–sell decision process to balance intuition and optimise asset allocation. Asset management is likely to become a strong branded force to be

---

[63] PWC, Asset management 2020, A Brave New World, Chapter 1, p. 20.

counted with in the future, with the likely desire to have a more transformational, visible and positive social impact than other finance industry players. The SWF acronym irrupted quietly in the finance arena at the beginning of this millennium. "Sovereign Wealth Funds (SWF)" stand for pools of assets managed in special-purpose investment funds owned directly or indirectly by a national or state government to achieve national objectives as effective custodians of national resources. SWF came under the limelight in 2006 with the controversy surrounding the attempted purchase by Dubai Ports World, a leading state-owned marine terminal manager of port management operations at six major U.S. seaport terminals. The proposed investment raised national security concerns in the United States and beyond that led to a wider debate about the characteristics of sovereign investors. SWF may be funded by a balance of payment surplus, official foreign currency operations, the sale of strategic assets (e.g., privatisation), or from resources such as oil or proceeds from general tax and other revenue. Most of the world's largest sovereign wealth funds are funded by the proceeds from hydrocarbon resources (Norway, the Middle East). These funds have been created to manage the proceeds from the sale of non-renewable resources, such as oil and gas, for future generations. Asian and American sovereign funds are primarily funded out of government revenues, foreign exchange reserves, or social contributions. This direct relationship to national and personal finances can produce different expectations regarding those funds operation and performance.

Many countries own multiple funds, e.g., Singapore has two, the People's Republic of China has five including one in Hong Kong, and the UAE has seven, including one in Dubai. France's "Caisse des Dépots et Consignations" one of the oldest funds, was created on 3 July 1816 by King Louis XVIII and can be considered a type of Sovereign Fund, or the closest thing to it. Another distinct type of state-controlled fund is related to the financing of social insurance and in particular pension. As early as 1425, the commune of Florence created the Monte delle Doti, a social insurance system set up as a Dowry fund. In the 14th and 15th centuries, dowries were the keystone of the matrimonial strategy, and it was the duty of every Florentine *capo famiglia* to marshal his family resources properly to endow his young nubile daughters. Today the largest world social insurance fund is the American Social Security Trust Funds with USD 2.8 trillion under management. As of June 2015, sovereign wealth funds excluding social security funds, managed an aggregated USD 7.2 trillion in assets (more than twice the level of 2008), with USD 4.3 trillion originating from oil and gas sovereign wealth funds[64] and USD 2.8 trillion originating from Asia. These figures, however, may double count some sovereign assets, by including central bank assets that are already captured in official reserves. Nevertheless, this stellar amount represents approximately the sum of Japan and Germany GDPs[65] in 2015, but only 9.5% of the USD 76 trillion of assets managed by the asset management industry.[66] Their investment decisions and portfolio allocation are linked to their stated investment objectives and governance structure. In particular, SWFs can help alleviate the impact of the "Dutch disease". This phenomenon was observed in the Netherlands in the 1960s following the discovery of Groningen's natural gas. The "Dutch disease" hypothesis posits that a boom in the natural resource sector shrinks the manufacturing sector through crowding out and an appreciation of the real exchange rate. The reinvestment of part of the hydrocarbon proceeds in foreign assets associated with changes in hydrocarbon exports is a rational strategy to hedge those risks.

The footprint of these funds has raised considerable concern not only about financial stability but also about corporate governance and possible political interference. As most sovereign wealth funds are guided by long-term investment objectives, their investment policies are more likely to be a stabilising rather than a destabilising factor on markets. Nevertheless, it is feared that the concentration of investments in narrow market segment can foster the development of asset bubbles and excessive concentration in certain class of assets can distort both markets and yields. Their size gives them the power to move, and potentially destabilise, financial markets with their investment decisions. In 2012, during the midst of the European debt crisis China Investment Corp.'s[67] chairman publicly declared it would no longer purchase European government bonds

---

[64] Source: Sovereign Wealth Fund Institute (SWFI), October 2015.

[65] Current prices.

[66] IMF, The asset management industry and financial stability, April 2015.

[67] CIC is the main People's Republic of China SWF with USD 747 billion under management (*source*: SWFI) with diversified overseas investments including stakes in Heathrow airport, Thames Water in the UK, Australia EastLink Highway and others.

because of concerns about the region's financial turmoil.[68] This decision and its public announcement, while justifiable by the fund's investment mandate, contributed to the instability that roiled European markets during that year.[69] Therefore, the ability to contribute to financial volatility through shifts in SWF asset holdings remains a real possibility, especially in the context of a more complex geopolitical environment.

Clear corporate governance, a reasonable degree of transparency and full accountability are especially important in the context of a better acceptance of sovereign funds, as their investment logic may obey different criteria than the value maximisation objectives of the main street asset management firms. This applies in particular when a country intends to boost home country "national champion" firms by helping them establish controlling positions in foreign markets, and when the reciprocity of investments is not permitted by the investor legislation. The possibility that SWFs may pursue national political objectives for their home country, and the risk that their investment policy may depend on country-specific circumstances rather than on standard value creation has generated a certain amount of anxiety. To defuse foreign and domestic concerns, leading SWFs have embraced the Santiago Principles. These principles establish a number of best practice guidelines for SWFs in terms of activities and disclosure. For now, the track record of the SWFs has shown that the fears of their possible interference in sovereign economies were misplaced as in 2007. SWFs were among the ones ready to move forward to rescue an ailing banking sector badly shaken by the subprime crisis. Sovereign investments of the magnitude of USD 50 billion were disclosed in 2008 in the U.S. financial industry, showing that a new type of financial stabilisation power could be used for the common good by using those investment vehicles.

The emergence of regional financial centres and global investment funds has possibly slightly complicated the financial picture, but looking back, regional challengers (such as Florence in the 13th century or Bruges

---

[68] Martinez Andres, "CIC Stops Buying Europe Government Debt on Crisis Concern" Bloomberg.com, 10 May 2012. accessed 9th October 2015 http://www.bloomberg.com/news/articles/2012-05-09/china-investment-stops-buying-europe-debt-on-crisis-concern-1-
[69] See references, Nicholas Borst, Federal Reserve Board of San Francisco.

in the 15th century) have always been competing for a global leadership, and they have been surrounded by and tactically allied with secondary financial centres with significant regional influence capable to act as flow concentrators for the leading centre. In the context of such competition, history has shown that major geopolitical disruptions were the prime responsible for profound shifts and capable to derail the most hardened ambitions.

Brexit and the City

On June 23rd, 2016, the United Kingdom European Union membership referendum, known as the Brexit referendum, resulted in a 51.89% vote in favor of Britain's leaving the EU. If Article 50 is triggered to start exit negotiations, this can mean much to the City losing or weakening its access to the single market, prompting major banks to consider relocating. As seen over the long history of financial centers, leading players making contingency plans to move their banking activities outside London in the event of the Brexit implementation, possibly to Dublin, is an indicator of a likely banking exodus and the possible decline of a world financial hub. Just like its illustrious predecessors, the dominance of London may have come to an end, this time democratically through the very will of the British citizens.[70]

---

[70] With the notable exception of Scotland, London and Northern Ireland where the vote was in favor of remaining in the EU.

Chapter 5
POOLS, BOTS AND TROLLS

The Importance of Being Networked

As aforementioned, international financial centres in the High Middle Ages were built with a political vision and financial expertise by merchants tightly organised in arts or guilds, and with a strong navy and a smart "hinterland". Business alliances were very much key to access the initially lucrative and critical sovereign debt market. The horizon expanded first over the Mediterranean, then over the limits of the known world in India, Asia and the Americas, finally after the Appolo 11 astronauts descended the nine-rung ladder of their Eagle Lunar Module on 21 July 1969 and returned. The Venetians managed to extract a strong position from their exceptional relationship with Byzantium, the Genoese dominated by Venice engineered their return with the Iberians, the Dutch and the British mutually emulating their domination of pre-industrial revolution finance, before going to war with each other. New York emerged from the ruins of Europe devastated by two consecutive World Wars, with London managing to keep a leading position on finance. As Asian tigers accelerated their growth after World War II and as China later shifted away from communist economy under Deng Xiaoping's stewardship, the competition for another leading financial centre got under way.

In feudal society, the relationship between ruling on the one hand and the production or merchant activities on the other hand was clearly split, except in city states when the ruling and merchant elite coalesced, and were arbitrated by the Church — itself split between the higher and lower clergy. The economic bridge between the two would be based on the provision of regalian services — such as justice, police, army, money issuing, the payment of taxes and fees and the recognition of an established order. However, a seat at the city council, or its equivalent assembly, in Venice or Bruges was the opportunity for a merchant to show that his business was respectable and wealthy, and more importantly to develop fruitful business relationships. And there was soon a son, a daughter or a nephew to marry. At a time when friends could also be your worst enemies, family and community alliances were of the utmost importance for the development and the consolidation of the court, and for the merchant banking industry. The prestige of a cardinal's galero or an episcopal throne could bring significant goodwill to the eponymous merchant banking business. Bartolo Bardi, became bishop of Spolete in 1320, Angelo Acciaiuoli bishop of Florence in 1383 and cardinal in 1384. The election of two Medici to the papacy, Leon X in 1513 and Clement VII in 1523, showed that between power and finance, power had become an essential ingredient of financial dominance. Son of a banker, and father and uncle of two Popes, Lorenzo the Magnificent de' Medici, vividly illustrates how one of the most successful merchant banker families managed to climb the ladder of power to facilitate the expansion of the scope of their business. But this was not to last forever, and thus is not the demonstration of an intangible principle. If a single word defines the functioning of financial hub since the Higher Middle Ages, it is complexity, as their organisation got larger, adopted complicated networked structures, becoming increasingly international, and dealing with more risk factors for key parts of their operations. Allies, partners and associates always formed the invisible background of those successful international ventures, and the strongest were always those built on a "nation", and a set of shared values or experiences. Over the last 900 years, leading financial hub participants have tried to build or improve their communication systems, from the Scarsella dei mercanti fiorentini de 1357 founded as a courier cooperative of 17 Florentine merchant companies to 21st century optic fibre networks connecting intranets or stock exchanges. Their common purpose has always been to know, before others do, in order to take advantage of the time difference to draw clearer conclusions and make better decisions, sometimes even crossing the red line; money especially since it becomes a game has always been addictive. The speed with which talented entrepreneurs have been promoted into leading bankers with solid business networks is directly related to how fast they were capable of making better decisions than their peers, because they were able i) to access quicker than others a range of appropriate and first hand commercially actionable information and ii) to flawlessly execute their trades. The lack of foreign market and internationalisation knowledge increases perceived market uncertainty and risk. When firms go international, their networks tend to change; when going international, firms establish formal and informal business relationships, both with domestic as well as international actors. But admittedly, learning from the experience of others is a discrete process. Critical factors such as the nature of the knowledge, relationship strength, absorptive capacity, learning orientation and organisational embeddedness do affect knowledge transfer. In an international context, the process can be expected to be further complicated by the fact that participants have different cultural references, ethics and political agendas. As a result, it takes more time to build trust and mutual understanding.

Technology has transformed the speed, efficiency and complexity of financial instruments and transactions. It has virtually eliminated barriers to the flow of capital, which now freely relocates to the most efficient markets, in all corners of the globe. As internet revolutionised numerous business models in the mid-90s, finance practitioners saw the opportunity to improve services by streamlining complicated decision and execution processes. Finance has come to see the whole world as its domain, and information technologies fused into powerful communication tools to facilitate decision making, so collaboration through networks is seen as a way to glean new insights, reach new markets, outwit competitors, reduce costs and raise revenues. Typically, a business network is represented by a growing collection of insider and outsider professionals, preferably in different geographies with a broad array of experience and knowledge, to which an individual is connected and with which he is in regular contact to have informal professional conversations, exchange views on matters of interest and request or provide some sort of assistance. A great deal of academic research have shown that asking for advice is a behaviour tied to professional success, possibly as it develops the idea of going beyond ones limitations. The most successful builders of financial hubs all feared that their efforts to build a networking relationship, especially when it came to governmental relationships, would be met with rejection. While this fear is grounded in human nature, the experience has shown that it is largely unfounded; "Begin, be bold, and venture to be wise."[1] As financial hubs developed, financial networks became even more powerful working as a two-way street.

Unlike a number of aspiring IFCs, and unlike New York where professional immigration has become more difficult,[2] London has a long history of openness and a tradition of welcoming foreign traders, although this perception has recently changed to London becoming a possibly less welcoming place for foreigners.[3] Informal networks provide fast, secure and restricted access to confidential or expert knowledge which gives participants the capacity to make better decisions than competitors. In all of their decision making process, the financial community share this knowledge through informal social networks. Among the most powerful of these social networks are those which exist in a financial hub because they permit the greatest amount of knowledge sharing in the most effective way. International financial centres are not only financial and geographical nodes, but also, and more importantly human and knowledge nodes directly connected to innovation and the delivery of high quality services.

The Bank of International Settlements highlighted the necessary relationship between financial centres and acknowledges that no international financial centres can operate isolated on its own. However, few finance businesses adequately articulate the value and need for trust, or share and make the effort to formalise and train their staff in the critical components

---

[1] Quintus Horatius Flaccus (December 8, 65 B.C–November 27, 8 B.C), known as Horace, was the leading Roman lyric poet during the time of Augustus.

[2] "An important and complex decision", according to The immigrant visa process, U.S. Department of State, Bureau of Consular Affairs http://travel.state.gov/content/visas/english/immigrate/immigrant-process.html

[3] The Global Financial Centres Index Survey, Zyen, (2014).

of trust. They have rather focused more generically on formal codes of corporate governance and ethics. Leading financial centres, and medieval fairs — their predecessors, never developed in isolation. Their participants were from the beginning closely connected based on mutual trust and shared interest as far as secondary feeding centres, specialised or regional which may even have had stronger positions than the principal centre in one specialised area. Liechtenstein which is only 160 sq. km with a population of 37,000 has its origins in a German Alemanni tribe which settled in the area in 500. A.D. and became a sovereign state in 1806 with the end of the Holy Roman Empire. From the end of the Second World War, it evolved from a modest agrarian economy to a modern and stable regional financial hub specialising in private banking. The Principality while part of the European Union is also closely linked to Switzerland by a customs and monetary union. On the financial side, the Vaduz financial centre connects naturally to the Zurich finance centre, which itself connects with London. The prime centre and back office centre "hub-and-spoke" model illustrated by the London-Bristol alliance, and maybe tomorrow by the Hong Kong–Shenzhen relationship shows the necessary vertical alliance between a hub and allied peripheral cities.

Factors similar to those which contributed to financial dominance in medieval times are still there, but this analysis comes with a twist as we entered the digital age. The catch as it shall be seen later — is about the very meaning of running financial markets operated by algorithms. Information technology has virtually eliminated barriers to the circulation of capital, which [almost] freely flows worldwide to the most efficient markets, but not the need for proper regulation. Technology, electronic trading platforms and communication networks are constantly evolving to make real-time interactions and transactions possible and affordable from virtually anywhere, thus reducing some of the benefits of physical co-location in major financial centres. Straight-through, fully electronic clearing and settlement are becoming the industry standard for futures, options, global bonds and domestic equities in leading markets, although it is still a middle term objective for many others. Virtual networks have gained in importance but financial hegemony is still built on the concentration of power and talents and tends to take the form of compact agglomeration. Technology changes have transformed some of the IFC functions (e.g., no more physical presence of stock markets, which have demateri-alised), but have by no mean challenged for now their dominance as key hubs for international finance. The magnitude of digital infrastructure investments has just raised the barrier to entry and increased the longevity of existing centres. The idea of a possible legal independence for algorith-mic traders has emerged showing that this may be a matter of concern for the future. In July 2000, the American Bar Association panel suggested that courts should turn to "a 'law merchant' for the Internet" in enforcing mandatory, non-binding arbitration clauses, as well as in regulating the activities of automated software robots.[4] This may all be related to the curious phrase "according to law merchant" appearing 730 years ago in the fair court records of St. Ives in Huntingdonshire, following the request of a wine merchant Gerhard of Cologne appearing before a special court established within the fair to hear disputes. Three containers of Gerhard's Rhenish wine had allegedly been seized as collateral in another contro-versy: He was trying to retrieve his property, and he was ready to swear an oath to establish his ownership and get them back. No further proceed-ings in the case are recorded, and Gerhard of Cologne — who probably never did retrieve his wine — might seem to have had little relevance for the future development of the law on financial markets. However, echoes of the possible autonomy of *Lex Mercatoria* based on Gerhard's claim were heard in the report of an American Bar Association panel on "Achieving Legal and Business Order in Cyberspace."[5]

Until the introduction of the common currency in the European Union in 1999, some practitioners would distinguish financial centres by destina-tion, those 'market-oriented' (London and New York) and the others more 'bank-oriented' (Frankfurt, Paris and Tokyo). The consequence of the global financial crisis of 2008–2009 may be a rapid convergence of the two distinctive systems of finance under the competitive pressures of global finance. This crisis also recalls that mismanaged financial institutions can

---

[4] American Bar Association Global Cyberspace Jurisdiction Project, Achieving Legal and Business Order in Cyberspace: A Report on Global Jurisdiction Issues Created by the Internet, 55 Bus. LAW. 1801, 1822, 1933 (2000).
[5] Sachs, Stephen E. From St. Ives to Cyberspace: The Modern Distortion of the Medieval Law Merchant, *American University International Law Review* 21, n°.5: 685–812, (2006).

become dangerous weapons of wealth destruction, and instruments for the application of national power. It is therefore understandable that investment in financial technology companies grew by 201% globally in 2014 to euro 11 billion, compared to 63% growth in overall venture-capital investments, with the U.S. representing 80% of the total. An example of rugged and resilient critical performance provider to IFCs is SWIFT, founded in 1973 and headquartered in Belgium. SWIFT is an international private cooperative company and a global provider of secure financial messaging services. It was founded to replace the telex as a mean of securing international financial transactions. As a cooperative company under Belgian law, it is owned and controlled by its shareholders (financial institutions), representing approximately 3,500 firms from across the world. It transmits orders for transactions worth more than USD 6 trillion and connects more than 10,500 banks, financial institutions and corporations in 215 countries and territories. SWIFT operates internationally with 23 offices located across the world. As a strategic international financial messaging service provider to the financial industry, SWIFT is overseen by the G-10 central banks. Following the announcement of the possible entry of Ukraine into the EC, the annexation of Crimea from Ukraine by Russia in March 2014 and the support by the Kremlin of a pro-Russian armed rebellion in Eastern Ukraine leading to a civil war, sanctions were taken by the West as retaliation. The chief executive of Russia's second largest bank VTB warned that keeping Russia out of the SWIFT banking payment system would be tantamount to "war" as Russia's banks rely heavily on the Belgium-based payments system for both domestic and international payments. "If there are no banking relationships, it means that the countries are on the verge of war, or they are definitely in a cold war." Russia and China are working together to develop their own proprietary platform as an alternative to SWIFT that would remain outside Western influence, a bit like how the Ottoman empire worked in the 16th century to introduce a secondary spice road through the Aleppo hub (Syria).

The use of communication networks is now being pushed to another frontier when it comes to trading. It began when the Rothschilds, who by legend, used a network of carrier pigeons to trade on the outcome of the Battle of Waterloo (1815). As other traders on the London stock exchange braced themselves for a British loss, Nathan Mayer Rothschild went long.

However, the quick outcome of the war between France and England was almost fatal for the Rothschild as they had prepared for a much longer conflict and started to pile up gold to assist England in paying for overseas war supplies. The gold price subsequently depreciated as it was then not so much needed for the supplies payment and the shift in the price of gold resulted in a major loss for the family from which they narrowly escaped. This anecdote exemplifies the critical importance of using advanced information technologies to build competitive information advantage on the market. For roughly a century leading up to 1970, the state of the art in financial communication was the telex and the telephone. Now it is the high-speed server linked to a financial exchange by optic fibre cable as short as physically possible, because each mile adds about eight microseconds of latency — and latency measured in round trip times (i.e., order and confirmation) means money. New York and Chicago, America's two great trading centres are about 3.9 ms at the speed of light, currently about 13 ms using premium fibre. Since Thomas Perterffy, a private stock market trader who fleed Hungary for America in 1965, and invented high frequency trading (HFT) in the early 80s, the race is now open to bring transmission as close to the effective speed of light. If the price of a stock changes in Wall Street, and it takes a few microseconds inside the servers in Mahwah, N.J. to report this, the price of related futures contracts will shift accordingly in Chicago. But it will take 7 ms or more for a report of the stock's price change to reach Chicago. If the news is known faster, high speed trading computers can turn this "latency arbitrage" into profit. It was estimated that USD 21 billion is made with latency arbitrage every year,[6] meaning that a significant transmission speed advantage would allow any player to outrun all the others. There is so much money to be made that any breakthrough in research and infrastructure to shave those microseconds is worth its dollar gold equivalent. These developments create the clear impression that a new arms race is in the offing. However the profitability of HFT declines one year after the other as profitability per trade is eroding. It is likely that most benefits from the current technology have been reaped, and the continuing increased level of regulatory scrutiny or taxation is likely to accelerate this trend.

---

[6] Tabb group, August (2009).

Other strategic financial transmission routes are those connecting the major finance hubs: New York to London and London to Tokyo.[7] Initiatives have been launched for fibre-optic cables under the Arctic Ocean between Europe and Japan. One route skirts the Russian coast and comes ashore north of Murmansk; the other traverses the Northwest Passage through the Canadian Arctic. As they go into operation, they are expected to cut latency by 27–33% from about 230 ms on routes through Asia to between 155 and 168 ms. Meanwhile, providers have begun laying cable for a new USD 300 million New York–London link intended to shave 311 miles off the usual distance and cut the round-trip message time from 65 ms to just under 60. It will do this by taking a great-circle route, traversing the shallow Grand Banks off Newfoundland. A project, such as the 100G Hibernia Express, aims at providing the fastest fibre-optic path between New York and London. Project Express was designed to offer the lowest latency from New York to London and provide HFT with the speed and accuracy they require. Furthermore, it is designed to allow customers to reach other key financial cities and will offer the lowest latency connections between Frankfurt and London and into Chicago, New York City and Toronto. Toronto will now connect to London at sub 70 ms. Express claims to be the shortest route from New York to London which will tighten the Atlantic facilitating New York to London Round Trip Delay at sub 60 ms. This new route is the very first new transatlantic cable in nearly ten years.[8] The race is on and microwave networks can be even faster than their optic fibre counterparts. Signals shot in a straight line between microwave dishes within sight of each other don't have to negotiate the obstacles that lengthen the trip by cable. Electromagnetic radiation travels only about two-thirds as fast in glass fibre as it does in air. Using short-wave radio signals, which follow the Earth's curved surface and can thus travel long distances provide an edge compared to a series of VHF towers positioned every 50 km or so. On the New York–Chicago 1191-km route, a fine tuned microwave route follows the shortest path possible over the Earth's surface. "It can be a 740-mile route, only 4 miles from perfect

---

[7] As trading hours in New York or Chicago don't overlap much with Tokyo, there's less demand for an ultrafast New York–Tokyo link.

[8] Hibernia Atlantic, 30 September (2010) and 21 July (2014).

curvature". This kind of solution should allow a round-trip latency of less than 9 ms. Speed is expected to prevail at the expense of 99.99% reliability. A link that is second or third fastest isn't of much use to keep leading HFT ahead of the pack, even if it is always available. The problem is that the weaponry used for this millisecond war is not bringing much value to non tech market participants, or to the market and society in general. The current race amongst microwave data-link providers only aims at enabling tech companies, such as the microwave link providers to rip-off increasingly super-normal profits, to the detriment of all other financial market participants. Low latency communication through microwave links seems to approach the physical limits. The race to zero is almost over. A cool down in this pylon racing may be necessary to help refocus on more fundamental issues such as better growth, risk assessment and ethics: A solution to stop this addiction to speed could be to move away from continuous electronic trading toward discrete-time quotations, with fixings timed every second or so. Ewald Nowotny, an Austrian economist, member of the board of the ECB, mentioned that "with high-frequency trading there is nothing to be regulated, it is to be banned. There is no really demonstrable net advantage from this (form of trading)"[9] and therefore no practical value.

From a more abstract perspective, network theory has already proven useful in applications ranging from cancer research to the social graph. It is likely that pylon racing in market fibre networks, is fortunately not the most exciting development in finance. Following the Grand Recession of 2008–2009 and the certainty that "the worst is behind us,"[10] analysing the global banking network was recognised as a necessary tool for attempting to better model, visualise and predict interactions between economic agents. At stake is the capacity to assess the resilience of financial systems to systemic risk, especially where traditional analytical methods are weak. Financial interconnectedness has become a concern in macrofinancial regulation, which still remains empirical, and has taken centre-stage in discussions on prudential policies. Initially, the foundation

---

[9] ECB's Nowotny calls for High Frequency Trading ban, Reuters, Hienz-Peter Bader, 13 September (2012).
[10] Richard Fuld, final chairman and CEO of Lehman Brothers in 2008.

of our legal, regulatory and institutional framework was established at times when international trade and investment occurred at low speed, capital mobility was reduced to a minimum and most currencies were inconvertible. As the world has dramatically changed and "expanded", network technologies were much needed to describe the international architecture of cross border financial flows between financial hubs of various importance, to analyse the risk of financial contagion, and monitor the health of payment systems and interbank markets. Contagion refers to the risk that the failure of one financial institution leads to the default of others through a transmission of the crisis in the interbank market, the payment system or through asset prices. Therefore, financial network metrics, represented by cross-border flows of financial capital reflect liquidity conditions in international markets, tend to be unstable and fragile: they can be easily disrupted by violent financial crisis, and the connectivity between centres tends to fall during and after systemic banking crises and sovereign debt crises. Network density expands and contracts, following the cycle of capital flows. The 2008–2009 global financial crisis stands out as an unusually large perturbation to the cross-border banking network, and showed that the structure of international bank linkages is key for the transmission of shocks. Aggregate losses, amplified by a domino effect and default on short term debt to start with, lead to severe disruptions and devastating chain reactions in the real economy. The structure of the interbank network and the banks' role in this network are quantitatively important drivers of the level of systemic risk of individual banks, but they are not easy to monitor as most of them are arranged over-the-counter and often the bilateral counterparty exposures are unknown. The systemic importance of an interconnected financial institution depends not only on the risk it imposes directly on the real economy, but also on the risk it imposes on other peer banks in the system. This risk is then set equal to the expected losses it generates, conditional on systemic events. In other words, each bank and each associated financial hub contributes to systemic risk not only through losses that it imposes on non-banks but also by affecting through its business network the probability and severity of the losses generated by other banks during events of systemic importance. Although we do not have a complete understanding of the forces at work, a key mechanism involves the interaction in the network between loosely anchored perceptions of value and risk as well as attitudes towards risk, on the one hand, and liquidity or financing constraints, on the other.

In a nutshell, bank size, institution-specific probabilities of default and exposures to common risk factors interact in a discrete fashion to determine the systemic importance of financial institutions. This analysis should be completed by the positioning of participants in terms of flows in the global interbank network structure, and within its native financial hub, as a secondary driver of systemic importance, for the long term survival of a financial hub. The relationship between connectedness and the way in which shocks get amplified or diffused must be better known. Little is still known about the structural properties and time-evolution of the network of cross-country financial linkages, which lead to a better understanding of how the global financial system reacts to external shocks, and whether and where systemic risk may emerge. The Quant meltdown of August 2007 concentrated among quantitatively managed equity market-neutral or "statistical arbitrage" hedge funds, showed that interconnection at the speed of light creates new propagation risks that even "power users", those capable of understanding the complex algorithms of the market, are not capable of handling. The partial[11] analysis of the initial losses during the second week of August 2007 suggests that initial losses forced liquidation of one or more large equity market-neutral portfolios, primarily to raise cash or reduce leverage, and the subsequent price impact of this unwinding caused a domino effect on other similarly constructed portfolios which experienced losses. These losses, in turn, caused other funds to deleverage and the shock wave started a chain reaction, possibly magnified by algorithmic trading. Finance has moved from the quiet fireplace to the nuclear age in less than 50 years. Needless to say an earthquake near a nuclear reactor is more likely to trigger catastrophic consequences of potentially systemic magnitude, as seen in Japan in March 2011, than the unpleasant fall of a chimneypot. This is certainly another reason why more time and resources must be dedicated to modelling and understanding the topology of linkages among agents, markets, institutions, countries and financial hubs.

---

[11] Due to the quiet nature of the transactions and lack of communication on the matter, a comprehensive analysis is difficult.

The Derivative Revolution

As far as 3500 A.D., new forms of writing and mathematics already enabled the Sumerians who settled in "the land between the rivers" (Mesopotamia) located in the Tigris and Euphrates river region, to replace the vessels with clay tablets,[12] laying the ground to forward contracts. Contracts for future delivery of commodities spread from Mesopotamia to Hellenistic Egypt and the Roman world. After the collapse of the Roman Empire in 476, contracts for future delivery continued to be used in the Byzantine Empire in the eastern Mediterranean and they survived in canon law in Western Europe. Byzantine traders and Sephardic Jews carried derivative trading from Mesopotamia to Spain during Roman times and the first millennium AD, and, it is probable that Jewish merchants carried derivative know-how to the Low Countries after being expelled from Spain in the 16th century. "By far, the most significant event in finance during the past decades has been the extraordinary development and expansion of financial derivatives."[13] The 17th century brought mathematicians like Blaise Pascal and Pierre de Fermat, who first developed the laws of probability which formed the basis of financial products later capable of dealing with uncertainty on a scientific basis. The Enlightenment also found Edmund Halley, of comet fame, pioneering the first mortality table, which accurately predicted the likelihood of death based on current age. This would be essential for the accelerated development of the asset management industry, especially in the context of life insurance products — which can be traced back to ancient Rome.[14]

---

[12]The most important remnant of this epoch is probably the Hammurapi codex of the Late Old Babylonian Period (ca 1800–1595 B.C.), a basalt stela recording of 282 legal provisions that deal with a range of cases, including those that involve economic transactions and loans. It is housed in Le Louvre Museum in Paris. Among the half million clay tablets recovered, most have been digitalised, translated and more than 200,000 are stored in the London British Museum.

[13]Alan Greenspan, Chairman, FED, speech at a Futures Industry Association conference, quoted by the Financial Enquiry Commission Report, Report on U.S. financial crisis, p. 48, March (1999).

[14]Caius Marius (100 A.D.), a Roman military leader, created a burial club among his troops, so in the event of the unexpected death of a club member, other members would pay for the funeral expenses.

When in 1540, King Charles V, Holy Roman "Emperor, a descendant of the house of Hapsburg, who regulated the affairs of both Spain and the Netherlands, legalised in Antwerp the negotiability of bills of exchange and made by royal decree, contracts for future delivery transferable to third parties, a defining innovation had occurred in the derivative markets. Antwerp practitioners discovered that there was no need to settle forward contracts by delivering the underlying asset, as it was sufficient for the losing party to compensate the winning party for the difference between the delivery price and the spot price at the time of settlement. Contracts for differences were written on bills of exchange, government bonds and commodities. However, these contracts gave traders too much leverage to speculate, and they were banned in 1541. Contracts for differences on bills of exchange, the precursors of modern futures contracts, continued to be common practice in Hamburg, Rouen and Amsterdam as the regulation and practice of derivatives was not uniform throughout a fragmented medieval Europe. After the sack of Antwerp by Spanish troops in 1576, Amsterdam which was already well established as a vibrant trading city took over as a financial centre, and term sales and contracts for difference were nothing new. Forward contracts on listed shares were also authorised, and used as illustrated by the first short selling attack on the capital of a listed company.[15] In 1688, De la Vega, a Portuguese Jew established in Amsterdam, wrote a book[16] about stock trading in Amsterdam and remarked that another form of derivatives was more appealing: "The Dutch call the option business "opsies," a term derived from the Latin word *optio*, which means choice, because the payer of the premium has the choice of delivering the shares to the acceptor of the premium or demanding them from him, [respectively]." Although this account of financial business practice is at times a bit confusing, it shows that the main financial contracts traded today, forwards, call and put options, futures, already existed in Amsterdam in the 1680s. The famous speculative frenzy of 1636 on tulip bulbs, was most probably fuelled by over-the-counter contracts on difference and options, as it sounds unlikely that speculators and intermediaries could

---

[15] A reference to Isaac Le Maire's syndicate short sell of the VOC shares.
[16] "Confusion de Confusiones" remains a milestone for financial history as it constitutes the first accurate description of a stock exchange.

afford to pay the full price of this overinflated commodity. Although, the trading of derivatives was taking place over-the-counter and based on trust and reputation, it is likely that at that time, derivative contracts could be repudiated, as unenforceable, during times of irrational exuberance.

As the English navy was taking the lead over the Low Countries and as English traders started to dominate maritime routes in the 18th century, London became the major commodity trading centre. The financiers of Amsterdam who had followed William III of Orange to England during the Glorious Revolution transferred to the City their knowledge of derivatives trading. The recognition under the English common law of the transferability and negotiability of bills of exchange, about two centuries after the Holy Roman Emperor, in Amsterdam, kicked off the development of the English derivatives market. It developed quickly, possibly too fast, and to the point where it became instrumental in the scandal of the South Sea Company. As a response, the British Parliament passed in 1734 the Sir John Barnard's Act, which declared contracts for the future delivery of securities to be "null and void", meaning that just like in Amsterdam, they could not be enforced in Court but continued to be traded over-the-counter near Exchange Alley on the basis of trust and reputation.

The Wien treaty which ended the Napoleonic wars in 1815 obligated France to substantial reparation payments to the winners. Consequently, the French sovereign debt became the second most important in the world, after England, reaching 4.2 billion francs in 1821. It led to the development of a very healthy derivatives market in Paris of French sovereign bonds. Learning derivatives trading became accessible after the release of the "Manuel du Spéculateur à la Bourse" (Manual of the stock market speculator), written by Pierre-Joseph Proudhon whose best known assertion is that "Property is theft". The author, an anarchist socialist who collaborated with Karl Marx, hated stock markets but needed money. The book was so successful that a revised[17] German version was later published in Zurich. Another valuable contribution to the understanding and development of the market was that of James Moser and Henri Lefèvre, a private secretary of Baron de Rothschild in Paris who published in 1970

---

[17] This sanitized and abridged version published in 1857 did not include some of Proudhon's virulent comments against the stock market.

the first profit charts for options. The government of Louis-Philippe more or less tolerated derivatives trading, but from time to time the police cleared derivatives trading venues to protect the monopoly of the authorised security dealers. In 1885, derivatives contracts finally became legally enforceable in France, although it was still possible to raise the objection against gambling. Germany was also following a prudent path in favour of the acceptance of derivatives and by the turn of the century (1896), future delivery contracts were considered legally enforceable only if the parties had registered as dealers. The information on derivatives markets is scarce since participants were often at the border of legality and preferred to keep a low profile. Records were limited on their transactions. But soon, hedging and speculating were not the only motivations for trading derivatives, they were also used to obtain better financing terms.

The father of financial mathematics, which led to an extraordinary development of derivative products, is recognised as being the French mathematician, Louis Bachelier born in 1870. In 1900, Bachelier defended his thesis *Théorie de la Spéculation* (Theory of Speculation) at the Paris Sorbonne University; his professor, Henri Poincaré, one of the most eminent mathematicians at the time, wrote a favourable report on Bachelier's PhD dissertation. Five years before Einstein's 1905 paper on *Brownian Motion*, in which he derived the equation governing Brownian motion, Bachelier had worked out, for his thesis, the distribution function for what is now known as the Wiener stochastic process (the stochastic process that underlies Brownian motion) linking it mathematically with the diffusion equation. More than 73 years before Black, Scholes and Merton wrote their seminal paper on the pricing of options in 1973, Bachelier had already explained how to price an option where the share price movement is modelled by a Wiener process and derived the price of what is now called a barrier option.[18] The work of Louis Bachelier leads on to the findings of all those who made a defining contribution to pricing complex financial products including Norbert Wiener, who got his PhD at Harvard at the age of 18 (1923), Andrei Nikolaevich Kolmogorov who at the time completed his doctorate had already 18 publications, and later laid the

---

[18] A barrier option is a derivative contract that is activated (knock-in) or extinguished (knock-out) when the price of the underlying asset crosses a certain level (the barrier).

foundation of Markov processes (1931), Kiyosi Itô who contributed to the understand of diffusion processes (1950), and finally Fisher Black, Myron Scholes and Robert Merton (1973) who jointly received the Nobel for Economics in 1997. The shift to options as the centre of gravity of finance, is one of the most noticeable evolution at the end of the 20th century, as every security can now be seen as a package of options, just as every physical object is a package of molecules and sub-atomic particles.

Derivatives enabled market participants to choose the kind of risk bearing they would specialise in and which type of risk they could lay off to other risk bearing specialists. Leading finance hubs received a steroid shot as a large scale derivatives markets took off in the late 1980s; for two decades, the financial sector grew faster than the rest of the economy. This would later have significant consequences on the globalisation of risk and severity of financial crisis. One side of the derivatives market was visible and fully accessible to the public, another side was out of sight of the public and reserved to insiders, as products were traded on the books of a limited number of financial institutions. Soon there would be derivatives on almost anything with a market willing to trade. The derivatives markets got organised as publicly accessible exchanges or as over-the-counter (OTC) markets, although electronic trading facilities tended to blur the distinction between the two compartments. In 1848, a first derivatives exchange was created in Chicago. It was strategically situated, as Chicago was developing as a major centre for the storage, sale and distribution of Midwestern grain. Following the Dojima Rice Exchange in Japan in the 18th century, the Chicago Board of Trade (CBoT) regulated by federal law was playing a leading role in revealing the market's view on the future prices of grain first: Derivatives fostered trade and contracts evolved over history primarily to meet the specific needs of commodities traders. Subsequently other futures contracts and options were developed on commodities or underlying rates, especially since the collapse of the Bretton Woods Agreement ushered in an era of considerable risk in current price fluctuation — risks which could be mitigated through currency futures trading. Another key area of concern in the development of post war economies was the volatility of price of oil, which could equally be better dealt with by derivatives and futures instruments. Almost simultaneously, one of the first market benchmarks was produced in 1896, by

Dow Jones Co. as an index of 12 listed companies, and known as the Dow Jones Industrial Average. An advanced market index was engineered in 1957 on a Burroughs Datatron computer fed by perforated paper tape in a Boston lab located at Melpar, a recent addition to the Westinghouse Air Brake Company. The S&P 500 was the creation of the Paul Babson, the chairman of S&P board and Lew Schellbach of Melpar, a military contractor. Babson had heard that Melpar was capable of producing indices of a massive number of stocks in a matter of seconds. Schellbach and his colleague George Olsen, spent a year refining the concept, and opted for the construction of a stock market index based on 425 industrials, 25 rail stocks and 50 utilities. With the Datatron, the S&P 500 could be recalculated every hour, and within five years, it could be recalculated every five minutes. A new generation of computer based financial products was born.

From the 1970s, the USA has been leading the development of derivatives and complex financial products. Freedom and a favourable regulatory regime constituted key foundation for innovation. The increasing performance of computers and their growing use in financial markets led to a faster and more precise pricing of complex products. The over-the-counter derivatives market flourished even though there was arguably a regulatory and legal uncertainty about its development until 2000. It is estimated that the amount of OTC derivatives reached USD 710 trillion at the end of 2013. OTC derivatives are only traded by large financial institutions, which act as derivatives dealers, buying and selling contracts with customers. Unlike the futures and options regulated exchanges, the OTC market is neither centralised nor regulated. Nor is it transparent, and thus price discovery is limited. No matter which measurement is used — trading volume, dollar volume, risk exposure — derivatives represent a very significant sector of the U.S. financial system. As the OTC market grew following the CFTC's exemption, a wave of significant losses and scandals hit the market. Among many examples, in 1994 Procter & Gamble, a leading fast moving consumer goods company, reported a pretax exceptional loss of USD 157 million, the largest derivatives loss by a nonfinancial firm, stemming from an OTC equity swap bought from Bankers Trust. Procter & Gamble sued Bankers Trust for fraud: the suit was settled when Bankers Trust forgave most of the money that Procter & Gamble owed it. The subsequent failure of Orange County (1994, USD 1.6 billion loss),

Barings (1995, USD 1.4 billion loss), Enron (2001, USD 60 billion loss) and AIG (2008, USD 150 billion rescue package), not to mention others raised some legitimate questions concerning the regulations of derivatives trading and their impact on financial stability. An old problem had resurfaced: The necessary improvements in counterparty risk management on OTC markets and the logical promotion of more transparent exchange-traded derivative markets.

Financial innovation did not stop with derivatives, complex [debt] products included structured products which also contributed to the significant development of financial hubs. In 1987, Michael Milken's Drexel Burnham Lambert, then the hottest firm in investment banking, assembled the first rated collateralised debt obligation out of different companies' junk bonds, a name indicating that they were ranked below investment grade by rating agencies. Pooling a cocktail of bonds of diverse quality reduced investors' exposure to the failure of any one bond, and slicing the securities into rated tranches enabled investors to pick their preferred level of risk and return. Drexel's capacity to raise money on fresh junk new issues became a decisive instrument in the transformation of Western capitalism through take over and leverage buy out, at a time when capitalism was struggling and caught in the middle of the Cold War. Drexel bankers were not shy about asking 3 or 4 times the standard fees of standard bond issues and equity sweeteners (warrants) for themselves. In 1989, the USD 25 billion successful KKR's unsolicited bid on RJR Nabisco, a food and tobacco conglomerate loudly revealed that barbarians were at the gate. But three years later, Drexel L.A.'s most talented and best-paid financier was sentenced to ten years in prison after pleading guilty to six counts of securities fraud. Milken lawyer argued that "Milken's biggest problem was that some of his most ingenious but entirely lawful maneuvers were viewed, by those who initially did not understand them, as felonious, precisely because they were novel — and often extremely profitable." Overwhelmed by the weight of legal battles and a USD 650 million settlement on alleged security fraud, Drexel, became a convenient scapegoat for the Savings & Loans crisis after some thrifts bought junk bonds. The firm collapsed into bankruptcy in 1990, and so did the junk bond market industry. Dealing junks was not a bad idea, provided one clearly knew what to expect from it: The market bounced back in 1993, propelled by the institutional investor's search for yield and the lack of sufficient lending for ventures more risky than average. This compartment for risky financing was to prove resilient and develop to new heights.

Following the conceptual success of the junks, the next step was to spice risk with incremental risk. The fire started after the Federal Reserve cut interest rates in the early 2000s; mortgage rates fell, home refinancing surged, climbing from USD 460 billion in 2000 to USD 2.8 trillion in 2003, allowing people to withdraw equity patiently built up over previous decades and to consume more, despite stagnant income from their daily work. Home sales volume started to increase, and average home prices nationwide climbed, rising 67% in eight years. Money washed through the economy, low interest rates and the injection of foreign capital helped fuel the boom. As households realised they owned an ever appreciating commodity, they felt comfortable pulling cash out of their homes, to send their kids to college, settle medical bills, buy a new car, travel the world or launch new businesses. They also paid off credit cards, even as personal debt rose nationally. Wall Street diligently laboured to exceed consumers' expectations, mortgage marketing reached new heights to convince customers to grab their due share of the windfall. The securitisation machine got to full speed and produced an interesting bestiary of exotic products: Alt-A, subprime, I-O (interest-only), no-doc, ninja (no income, no job, no assets) loans; 2–28s and 3–27s; liar loans; piggyback second mortgages; payment-option or pick-a-pay adjustable rate mortgages (ARM). ARMs variants called "exploding" ARMs, featured low monthly costs at first, but payments could suddenly double or triple, if borrowers were unable to refinance. On the surface, it looked like prosperity, but underneath, it smelt like something was rotten in the kingdom of Denmark. Silently, the lending and the financial services industry had mutated. In the past, lenders were careful to avoid bad loans, but now because of the growth of securitisation, it was not even clear who the lender was, and in terms of P&L signing the client was more important than making sure he could afford to buy. The mortgages would be thoroughly processed, sliced, repackaged, insured and sold as incomprehensibly complicated debt securities to a large cross section of investors looking for yield. Wall Street firms would package the loans into residential mortgage-backed securities that would mostly be stamped with AAA ratings by the rating agencies.

In many cases, the securities were repackaged again into collateralised debt obligations (CDOs) and sold to other market participants. Some investors would buy credit default swap (CDS) to protect against the securities' defaulting. The instruments grew more and more complex; CDOs were constructed out of CDOs, creating CDOs squared. When firms ran out of real product, they started generating cheaper-to-produce synthetic CDOs composed not of real mortgage securities but just of bets on other mortgage products. Each new permutation of this "spaghetti" construction was built on the boiling real estate market and created an opportunity to extract more fees and trading profits. Most of these miracle mortgage end-users were unable to understand the risk attached to the contracts they had signed, until they reached the early steps of default often followed by foreclosures and the destruction of their family life.

Leveraged loan issuance more than doubled from 2000 to 2007 in the United States fuelled by soaring real estate prices, but the rapid growth was in the longer-term institutional loans rather than in short-term lending. From 1978 to 2007, the amount of debt held by the financial sector soared from USD 3 trillion to USD 36 trillion, more than doubling as a share of gross domestic product. As the market for leveraged loans continued to grow, credit became looser and leverage increased as well. After the housing bubble had burst in 2007, a staggering USD 11 trillion in household wealth has vanished, with retirement accounts and life savings had vanished. However despite the severity of the crisis, New York managed to tame it and keep its rank as world leading international financial centre.

Welcome to the Machine

To date, international financial centres split mostly between New York, London and Tokyo. The most active competition for dominance is going on in Asia between Tokyo, Hong Kong[19] and Singapore. Behind the traders running the show in the market, the critical infrastructures supporting IFCs should not be forgotten. This new chapter of their development is burnt into space age silicon as human traders have left the floor and have

---

[19] And its possible associated mainland China centre, Shanghai or Shenzhen, provided that confidence in Hong Kong's stability is not questioned too much.

been replaced by algorithms embedded into highly secured computer vaults. Algorithms, including support vector machine and reinforcement learning, have been quite effective in tracking the stock market and helping to maximise the profit of stock option purchase while keep the trading risk low. At the time market pricing systems involved only chalkboards, shouting, hand signals and large paper limit order books in a face-to-face market. The structure of a human operated open outcry market was well known, comprehensible for any participant, and rigidly prescribed: traders had designated functions, used common gestures to trade, wore jackets of certain colours, and could be found in specific locations on a trading floor. The regulatory bodies had a clear simultaneous mission to protect investors, maintain fair and efficient markets, and promote capital formation. The introduction of electronic market systems has slightly rewritten this organisation. The structure of financial markets started to change drastically in 1976, when the NYSE introduced the Designated Order Turnaround (DOT) system, the first electronic execution system. Since then, there has been a significant growth in alternative trading systems (ATS). In the United States, for example, there are eleven equity exchanges and over sixty Alternative Trading platforms. Many large exchanges now have their own off-exchange trading platforms and dark books, responding to this investor demand.

BATS-Direct Edge is now headquartered in Kansas City, and the New York Stock Exchange (NYSE) was acquired by the Intercontinental Exchange, an Atlanta-based futures and options exchange, is now little more than a television studio, with its servers relocated to New Jersey, USA. Equity markets headquarters are slowly distancing themselves from mainstream cities. It seems quite remarkable that no city has emerged as a financial centre on the North American west coast. By far the most liquid markets today are the Forex market, the interest rate derivatives, insurance and bond markets, the essential lifeblood of the global financial system. As mergers go on between "physical" market infrastructures, resulting new exchanges become more integrated and more powerful. The world's financial markets infrastructure continues to shift to more technology oriented platforms, so does the money as an increasing portion of the profits from intermediation to entities outside the financial sector. Trading floors have been replaced by server vaults, market gestures by message protocols, traders by algorithms often operating with little or no human oversight, with still human regulators having a hard time analysing and qualifying transactions happening in milliseconds.

Unlike in the time of Venice, wealth or threats are now not only coming from the sea or from inland. Those seeking to harm an IFC do not need to travel thousands of miles to carry out an attack, they are just a few keystrokes away with a computer. In the 21st century, cyber defence capacities will be part of the credibility of modern IFCs. There is no doubt that the computer integrity of IFCs will be challenged, possibly breached, and there is no doubt that the better prepared will prevail. One of the top priorities remains to promote the sharing of cyber threat data among the IFC key players and governmental institutions to not only defend but counter strike against cyber-attacks and encourage better coordination. Improving the IT security of the most critical IFC infrastructure is comparable to Venice clearing the sea of piracy in the Middle Ages. Weaknesses in cybersecurity can put at risk the electrical grid, financial markets, emergency response systems and citizens' personal information, which is enough to cause serious damage to any IFC. Henry Ford once famously noted that "It is well enough that people of the nation do not understand our banking and monetary system, for if they did, I believe there would be a revolution before tomorrow morning." Nevertheless, the market's ability to continue operating during periods of extreme stress and volatility during the Great Recession, and to recover speedily from serious glitches — such as the Flash Crash of 2010 or the Knight Capital malfunction in 2012, are testament to the resilience of modern market structures.

Safe, efficient and convenient security settlement systems have a direct impact on the international competitiveness of securities markets. For example, to be globally competitive, Europe perhaps needs a single, integrated, low risk and low cost post-trading system for the benefit of its users. This objective has been shared by the securities industry and public authorities since the beginning of the decade. Estimated aggregate excess costs of post-trading of between euro 2 and 5 billion per annum emphasise the importance of achieving efficient post-trading in Europe. Moreover, replacing a highly fragmented structure with a single, integrated post-trading system will significantly improve the liquidity and resilience of European securities markets. Clearstream, now part of the German stock exchange operator, Deutsche Börse, is a European leader in post-trade securities services with more than euro 12.2 trillion in assets under custody, processing 122 million transactions annually in all asset classes, making this firm one of the world's largest settlement and custody firms for domestic and international securities. As an international central securities depository (ICSD) headquartered in Luxembourg, Clearstream provides the post-trade infrastructure for the Eurobond market and services for securities from 54 domestic markets worldwide — for approximately 2,500 financial institutions in more than 110 countries. As a central securities depository (CSD) based in Frankfurt, it provides the post-trade critical infrastructure for the German securities industry, offering access to a growing number of markets in Europe. Clearstream also offers such services for the Luxembourgish market via LuxCSD, a CSD which is jointly operated by Clearstream and the Banque Centrale du Luxembourg. The firm has consistently high credit ratings (AA) which testify to its robustness and reliability. Three market disrupting technologies: dark pools, cognitive systems and topological quantum computing are likely to continue changing the way market operates. Just like in the higher middle ages, security will remain a long-lasting concern as threats will be standing at the gate, ready to take advantage of possible loopholes in the system. As with the ruling Princes of the Champaign fairs, the current incumbent will see how valuable was the provision of safe conduct insurance to those merchants travelling on his main roads.

It is still early days for cryptocurrencies, perhaps one should call them synthetic currencies, but following the extraordinary multiplicity of currencies in the High Middle Ages, they are an interesting development in the digital world of international finance.[20] They may have the capacity to reflect that the ultimate reserve unit may well be the Common Good and by extension the net national wealth, the actual and expected difference between total assets and total liabilities, in a nutshell the difference needed to build a future for humanity. The concept of "cryptocurrency" was first described in 1998 by Wei Dai on the cypherpunks mailing list, suggesting the idea of a new form of money that uses cryptography to control its crea-

---

[20]The reason for this goes beyond the focus of the book, but relates to the connection of such currency to the life supporting assets on this planet (and it is unlikely to be gold!).

tion and transactions, rather than a central authority. Bitcoin was subsequently created in 2009 by a pseudonymous developer named Satoshi Nakamoto, as a medium of exchange, just like currencies issued by sovereign states, but designed for the purpose of exchanging digital information through a process made possible by certain principles of cryptography. Bitcoins are cryptographic token alternatively considered a commodity, a mania comparable to tulip bulbs in the 1600s or a currency in limited supply. Some heterodox view may be that Bitcoin is a commodity just as money at large is a commodity. It is, above all, a digital version of barter, but it may have the capacity to become a more financial tool. Bitcoin differs from conventional money in that it lies in a decentralised system with no central authority, fully built on trust and fully independent from state organisation. A group of 100,000 people called miners own the bitcoin infrastructure which is a financial cooperative. No institution controls the Bitcoin network and it is not issued by a sovereign Central Bank. The ownership of bitcoins is achieved through digital signatures. With the development of virtual currencies, something even more important is at stake: the monopoly of emission held by central banks, traditionally considered as a regalian attribute of sovereignty.[21] Payments with Bitcoin are less expensive than those made on banking card alliances, 1% on average compared to 2.5% for the leading banking card players. The entire network is maintained by individuals and organisations referred to as "Bitcoin Miners", on the basis of an open-source model. Bitcoin miners process and verify bitcoin transactions through a mathematical algorithm based on the cryptographic (hence the name cryptocurrency) hash algorithm SHA256. Bitcoins are created by miners who contribute to processing transactions. Miners process and secure the network using specialised hardware that "mine" for new bitcoins. As "payment" for their contribution, they are awarded new bitcoins, this is how new bitcoins are created. The rhythm of creation of new bitcoins is decreasing, until a "cap" of 21 million units is reached in 2140 — around 14.8 million units exist today. Their creation by miners is backed by an open source mathematical formula accessible to everybody. This "organized scarcity" is also the

---

[21] French Senate, "Public authorities and the development of virtual currencies," (English abridged version), p. 3. August (2014), see reference.

condition of its success. It is supposed to guarantee bitcoin holders against a devaluation of their assets: artificial "bitcoin pumping" is simply not possible. Bitcoins are not based on gold or silver like sovereign currencies in the past. However, these coins can be divided into smaller parts, the smallest divisible amount is one hundred millionth of a bitcoin and is called a "Satoshi". The benefits of this rather volatile and speculative digital currency are; independence, confidentiality, liquidity and low transaction fees. However as a community, Bitcoin has not been always easy to manage as there are tensions between centralisation and decentralisation, independence and alliances with groups capable of protecting and helping the system to evolve. For now, the bitcoin is just another interesting experiment which does not represent any threat to the global financial stability or any significant opportunity for an international financial hub, given its negligible money stock, just worth a few billions of dollars, as opposed to several trillions of dollars for the leading international currencies. Bitcoin, or one of its clones,[22] may fail or succeed as a widely accepted new international currency, or hypothetically as a replacement currency for countries experiencing monetary turmoil,[23] and develop a full suite of high value added services related to the (re)construction of the common good. Alternatively it may scale, or expand, to a size where it can be used as a new international settlement network, as the bitcoin technology, has proven to be an open-source, decentralised and very secure validation protocol for contracts. Banks are currently testing the power of the blockchain technology, a digital ledger distributed by a network of computers developed to secure Bitcoin transactions, in a belief that it could radically transform the way the industry works, but as usual terminate some legacy business. Each participant must approve the transaction and as the ledger is shared and transparent between participants it is impossible to temper with it. Cutting edge blockchain technology has a potential for a very broad spectrum of applications and can be used, among other things, from handling payments to notarise client identities, from

---

[22] There were over 530 cryptocurrencies worldwide as of January 2015. Other popular ones include for example, Liberty Reserve and e-Gold.
[23] However, Bitcoin did not perform that role in the recent cases of Venezuela or Greece.

executing contracts to clearing and settling trades[24] involving the most sophisticated financial products. The safety of bitcoin and cryptocurrencies still come with safety challenges after Mt. Gox, the most popular bitcoin exchange, filed for bankruptcy in 2014 after being hacked, losing around 850,000 coins. Wallet-stealing is already a threat for bitcoin owners, and the possibility of something called a "51% attack"[25] in which members of powerful mining pool successfully "double-spend" their coins cannot be totally discounted.

Mastering innovative trading and clearing tools can be compared to sailing a strong navy in the Middle Ages. All of them are already being experimented with at various level of maturity. Nevertheless, legacy technology and the difficulty of deploying new technology fast at an industrial scale, is also a big part of the issue when it comes to innovation. Semiconductor innovation has led users and consumers to come to expect a continuous stream of faster, better, and cheaper high-technology products. But for outsiders, changes in the finance industry have been very slow compared with Moore's law.[26] Non-commoditised activities, meaning the finance "value-added" and "tailor made" activities, will likely remain in the academic and business clusters that financial centres nurture. Clustering has historically been essential not only for financial innovation but also for developing a nationwide emulation to go beyond the known world. The connection of innovative nodes through a heuristic network capable of emulating a collective ambition to become a centre of excellence is probably one of the critical features of the emergence and of the development of financial centres, however face-to-face contact between diverse communities will remain a vital part of the human economic experience, especially when it comes to designing and exchanging

---

[24] Santander, Oliver Wyman and Anthemis estimate that the operating gains of the technology could reach USD 15–20 billion by 2022.

[25] This is a possible attack vector that can appear when one entity or a pool of miners has control over a large percentage of the overall network hash rate.

[26] Gordon E. Moore was Intel's co-founder, his simple observation published in 1965 in Electronics Magazine prophesized that circuit densities of semiconductors had and would continue to double on a regular basis, and this even appeared in a mathematical form: (Circuits per chip) = 2(year-1975)/1.5. Moore was then a Director of R&D at Fairchild Semiconductor.

innovative non-standard services. The term community means that some of their critical components was not only geographical locations but also the influx of talents from the outside world capable of interacting with the hub natives on the basis of shared cultural reference. This analysis would apply to the banking elite from Florence travelling all over Europe in the middle ages, the Jewish community capable of transferring critical expertise from Amsterdam to London, today from Berkeley, Stanford, UCLA to Silicon Valley and to Asian technology centres. Gary Becker's analysis[27] that human capital represents "as a rule of thumb 75–80% of total capital" put to work seems empirically consistent with that organisation. These differentiating value added components include senior 'strategic' management and front office, product innovation, client facing and deal-making activities. But ultimately, the capacity to attract and manage large volumes from international origins, and master visible and complex transactions, such as sovereign debt issues or large IPOs, does indeed makes a difference. Alfred Marshall (1890) devoted a whole chapter in his Principles of economics to "The concentration of specialised industries in particular localities", but that subject was barely touched on in the standard economics curriculum until the end of the 20th century.

Dark Pools and the Algo War

These names resound loudly like something George Lucas would have possibly thought up for his *Star Wars* series. Technological advances and regulatory changes have emulated competitive forces that created faster and more fragmented markets as a response. The prospect of a future in which autonomous stealth trading computer programmes exercise their power over humans raises a host of additional concerns. Their introduction also creates serious international division, between those capable of affording them and those who cannot. The "Algo club" weakens the role and rule of international law — and in the process undermines the international financial stability. For the members of the club, such technological

---

[27] Gary Becker (1930–2014), Economy Nobel 1992, conversation with Pr. Edward Lazear, HR and Management economics, Stanford University, senior fellow at the Hoover Institution (2003).

advances represent legitimate financial advances, which help to make larger contribution to GDP and create better liquidity on the market. The new landscape has challenged established exchanges playing a central role in facilitating the funding of firms and promoting investment and wealth creation, to maintain their central role. Their role has been challenged specifically in the price discovery process. New solutions, such as peer-to-peer venues and automated market making destinations, have the potential to further erode the exchanges' standing. Dark pools were started in the 1980s when a handful of institutional investors got together to trade in private market places not accessible to the public to download quietly large quantities of stocks without affecting the market and thus get better execution prices. "Dark pools are dark for a reason: buyers and sellers expect confidentiality of their trading information."[28] Some of the success-ful names in this space include Turquoise Dark, or Liquidnet H2O and Bats Chi-X. One additional benefit they provide is cost efficiency on trad-ing costs. They get their business in great part from the computers of HFT firms, mainly quant hedge funds like Renaissance and others. High-frequency traders are a subset of quants, buying and selling shares extremely quickly with the aim of getting into and out of a stock before its price moves in response to a stimulus. They make only a fraction of a cent at a time, but multiplied by hundreds of shares, tens of thousands of times a day. The result is that HFT accounts for 60–70% of the market volumes over the last years only emphasising the declining role of broker-dealers.

The most obvious motivation for algorithmic trading is the impressive sequence of breakthroughs in quantitative finance that began in the 1950s with portfolio optimisation theory. In his pioneering PhD thesis (1952), Harry Markowitz showed that an investor should allocate his wealth over a portfolio of n securities so as to optimise his expected utility of total wealth. He demonstrated how this was, under certain conditions, equiva-lent to maximising the expected value of a quadratic objective function of the portfolio's return which, in turn, yields a mean–variance objective function. The key of this asset management optimisation problem may be considered the very first algorithmic trading strategy. The second

---

[28] Robert Khuzami, Director of the SEC's Division of Enforcement. http://www.businessinsider.com/what-is-a-dark-pool-2012-10#ixzz3W986oEs6.

significant milestone in quantitative finance was the development of the Capital Asset Pricing Model (CAPM) by Sharpe (1964), Lintner (1965) and Mossin (1966) in the 1960s, and the intense empirical and econometric it launched in the following decades. The third breakthrough was introduced by the publication of the Black and Scholes (1973) and Merton (1973) articles on the pricing of options and other derivative securities. Another influential idea to come out of this research program was Merton's insight that under certain conditions, the frequent trading of a small number of long-lived securities can create new investment opportunities that would otherwise be unavailable to investors.

With the development of powerful computer systems and an increasingly complex international financial system, all conditions were met for algorithms to start at the beginning of the 1990s, as powerful decision tools for institutional investors. They were developed concurrently by a handful of people who were generally not aware of each other. Even motivations were different: some wanted to make money by keeping themselves in the market at all times, others wanted to create the illusion of dealer trading activity to encourage other dealers to trade. Decimalisation, direct market access, full electronic exchanges, pressure on commissions and exchange fees, the creation of new markets led to an explosion of algorithmic trading at the beginning of the decade. Algorithms have proven extremely effective to look for the best venue in which to trade, in case more than one venue is available, and later to execute statistical arbitrage, i.e., comparing the return of stocks to the corresponding sector Exchange Traded Funds (ETF) at even higher speed. Algorithmic trading can be defined as "placing a buy or sell order of a defined quantity into a quantitative model that automatically generates the timing, the size and the location (venue) of orders based on goals specified by the parameters and constraints of the algorithm." Algorithms are now widely recognised as one of the fastest moving bandwagons in the capital markets.

The last fifteen years have represented a revolution from Cantor (voice) trading to Photonic (light speed) trading in terms of the way traders execute client orders around the world. The electronic trading revolution began quietly as a payroll reduction strategy, but quickly it became clear that the key advantage to participants was not lower commissions, but a new family of trading strategies, and lower mispricing risk on hundreds of bond, forex and swaps simultaneously. Furthermore, algorithms prove extremely useful when clients need to trade larger amounts of stocks than what the market could absorb without impacting the price. Since Credit Suisse launched in 2001 a powerful product suite, the offer has evolved from simple automation tools into full-fledged execution strategies that behave like a trader, operating on its leading proprietary dark pool. The bank[29] also produced a companion programme; Guerilla was the first mass-marketed computer-trading algorithm capable of trading stocks aggressively and minimising market impact without displaying bids or offers. It had the capacity to evade detection from other algorithms and anti-gaming techniques and started what was then called the Algo war. On 13 January 2010, the NYSE inflicted a financial fine on the Swiss bank following the lack of monitoring of a market algorithm which generated 600,000 orders in 20 min and disrupted the market. A few month later, the 6 May 2010 Flash Crash[30] revealed that the risks associated with algorithmic computing were far more important than initially assumed. Automated algorithm wildly hunting for yield, a sell and run game among high-frequency traders, cross-market arbitrage trading, and a practice by market makers to keep placeholder bid-offer "stub quotes" all conspired to create an extreme and sudden period of volatility.[31] When the prices of some of the largest and most actively traded companies in the world crashed and recovered in a matter of minutes, it was clear that machines had created new challenges as well as new opportunities for the financial industry at large and its regulators. The marketplace was now under the constant scrutiny of automated systems equipped with sophisticated algorithmic sensors trolling the market. They would immediately detect changes in volatility of the stock price and initiate selling, enhancing volatility and

---

[29] For the avoidance of doubt, all the major financial institutions developed their own e.g., *Ambush* and *Razor* for Bank of America or *Dagger for* Citigroup, just to mention a few well-known names.

[30] The Dow Jones Industrial Average lost about 800 point in a matter of minutes.

[31] Kirilenko, Kyle, Samadi, and Tuzun (2011) found that a rapid automated sale of 75,000 E-mini S&P 500 June 2010 stock index futures contracts worth about $4.1 billion over an extremely short time period created a large order imbalance that overwhelmed the small risk-bearing capacity of financial intermediaries, in particular high frequency traders and market makers.

starting a self-fulfilling downward vortex. The party stopped when the regulators started to lay boots on the ground to avoid a larger disaster, but it was still not certain that circuit breakers and shock absorbers would be sufficient to prevent an overall panic given the interconnection of the world markets across the board. After the crisis, Nanex, an American market data provider revealed that some market places provided more than 5,000 prices in a second for a single security, in the absence of any rational reason. In a context of the full automation of trading techniques, in particular related to the management and the processing of market orders, the management of operational risks has become a growing concern, possibly of systemic importance. New trading strategies enabled by electronic trading platforms can potentially cause disruptions to market liquidity in the face of shocks. HFT algorithms for example are providing professional market players with tools susceptible of manipulating the markets.[32] These advanced technologies are complicating the task of the regulating authorities who need to follow the innovation path and ensure that all market players are fairly treated.

When a major institutional investor launches an order to buy a large number of shares, systems trolling the market become alive aggregating as much as shares as possible on a profit, and slightly move the prices up. Non transparent segments of the market would then be created to minimise costs. Dark pools are trading systems where there is no pre-trade transparency of orders in the system (i.e., there is no display of prices or volumes of orders in the system). Technically, any off-exchange marketplace that executes shares anonymously (without quoting) could be considered "dark" in that it provides limited opportunity for information disclosure. Dark pools can be split into two types: systems such as crossing networks that cross orders and are not subject to pre-trade transparency requirements, and trading venues such as regulated markets and MTFs that use waivers from pre-trade transparency not to display orders.[33] They are electronic market places where "dark" orders are suddenly sprayed across multiple destinations in very deliberately complicated patterns produced

---

[32] Autorité des marchés financiers (AMF, France), Risques et tendances n°9, May (2010) (page 52).
[33] Banking and finance, European Commission.

by algorithmic models that are patented by their owners. "Dark pools" aim at capturing very large buy orders and the sell orders to execute blocks of stock. The biggest hazard in dark pools is that the participants are not informed on how they operate or who's operating inside them. Through MIFID 2, the European Union has come up with a rule to be implemented in January 2017 to cap dark pool transactions to 4% of trading in an individual security and 8% of total volume per stock. It is estimated that the dark pool share of the European trading market is over 11%. In the United States, dark pools have been suspected in some cases of giving an unfair edge to high-frequency traders and that their staff did so in an attempt to boost their revenues and bonuses.

This certainly was a news item that in February 2011, "Watson" defeated Brad Rutter and Ken Jennings in the popular Jeopardy Challenge. At the "Jeopardy!" classic television game show created by Merv Griffin, the answers are given first: The contestants are requested to supply the questions. In the late 90s, IBM Research was looking for a major research challenge to rival the scientific and popular interest of Deep Blue, the computer chess-playing champion,[34] that also would have clear relevance to IBM business interests. Cognitive computing is a new field in computer science that combines proven technologies with advanced analytical algorithms, natural and machine based learning coupled with massive computer processing power to yield probabilistic response to user questions. This is a specifically needed field in finance or economy. One can easily think of the analysis of moving factors in financial markets for the prevention of asset bubbles or critical data needed to pilot central bank intervention, especially in a so called "non classical environment", meaning markets not responding to classic incentives following a deep crisis.

The IBM "Watson" team undertook the challenge to build a computer system that could compete with human champions in real time on Jeopardy. The extent of the challenge included fielding a real-time automatic contestant on the show, not merely a laboratory exercise. After three years of R&D by a core team of about 20 researchers, Watson performed at human expert levels in terms of precision, confidence, and

---

[34] Feng Hsiung Hsu, *Behind Deep Blue: Building the Computer that Defeated the World Chess Champion*, Princeton University Press (2002).

speed at the Jeopardy quiz show. The goals of the IBM Research team were to explore new ways for computer technology to impact science, business, and society. Advances in question-answering (Q&A) technology can help support professionals in critical and timely decision making in many areas and notably economics and finance. The open-domain Q&A problem is very challenging in the realm of computer science and artificial intelligence, as it requires a synthesis of information retrieval, natural language processing, reasoning, knowledge representation, machine learning and computer–human interfaces[35] for final delivery. Research in artificial intelligence has been around for five decades, and when judiciously applied to cognitive sciences, it can find patterns in data, but only as a preliminary step to problem solving. Cognitive systems are developed on the assumption that machines can gather and dig out a massive amount of structured or unstructured information, assemble evidence and develop logical hypothesis, come to insights not reachable by conventional analytics thus improving expert's ability to make better decisions. Like a human brain, knowledge, experience, and pattern understanding are necessary in addition to data processing power if complex decisions are to be made. This breakthrough technology, has ushered finance, and possibly one day risk analysis preventing bubbles to a world in which man and machine are harnessed together to attack problems that neither can attempt alone. Humans have a limited ability to systematically analyse information and derive a methodological action plan. Yet robots have limitations in other respects as compared to humans. The resolution of a crisis will continue to require human judgement, common sense, appreciation of the larger picture, understanding of the intentions behind people's actions, and understanding of values and anticipation of the direction in which events are unfolding. It is unlikely that strict logic can serve a one size fits all purpose but rather help in defining the route closer to theoretical optimum.

---

[35] David Ferrucci, Eric Brown, Jennifer Chu-Carroll, James Fan, David Gondek, Aditya A. Kalyanpur, Adam Lally, J. William Murdock, Eric Nyberg, John Prager, Nico Schlaefer and Chris Welty, *Building Watson: An Overview of the DeepQA Project*, AI Magazine Fall (2010).

The high speed trading race

Stock exchanges as physical trading places belong increasingly to the past: the open outcry systems are now relics of the late 20th century, and many buildings housing the stock exchange have been transformed in museums or conference venues. Stock trading via public exchanges may be supplanted by "professional only" equity exchange, as most trading is now electronic. Wall Street, has become more a brand name than a physical location, as the hub of U.S. stock trading. In fact, the real action takes place along a busy state highway in a 24,000 people city about 50 km away, in a huge, windowless heavily guarded datacentre in suburban Mahwah, N. J. and across the Atlantic in Basildon, Essex (UK). These are the places where market participants can co-locate servers to access the most direct route to NYSE market data and trading venues. Customers who colocate in Basildon are afforded the most direct route to ICE and Euronext exchanges housed at that location.

Charles Babbage, Lucasian Professor of Mathematics at Cambridge from 1828 to 1839, plans for a digital computer, called the Analytical Engine, were not seen at that time a very attractive project. He never completed his difference engine but wrote on economy.[36] A bit more than a century later, just after WWII, a decommissioned ENIAC started to revolutionise finance. In a keynote address at CalTech in May 1981 and published later in International Journal of Theoretical Physics, Richard Feynman expressed his belief that in the near future quantum computers will be able to simulate quantum processes. In nature, there are two types of quantum particles; Bosons and fermions. Einstein predicted that when bosons are kept near absolute zero (−273°), bosons would draw closely together into a single, indistinguishable entity. This ultracold quantum gas made of bosons with exactly the same quantum behaviour is called a Bose–Einstein Condensate, (BEC).[37] This state creates a versatile quantum

---

[36] A difference engine was built after his death, using parts found in his laboratory and among other things, he published "On the Economy of Machinery and Manufactures" (1832).
[37] The first BEC was produced in a laboratory in 1995, and it won Eric A. Cornell, Wolfgang Ketterle and Carl E. Wieman the Nobel Prize in Physics in 2001 "for the achievement of Bose–Einstein condensation in dilute gases of alkali atoms and for early fundamental studies of the properties of the condensate." *Source*: Nobel Foundation.

system that can be precisely controlled, and one of the essential requirements to quantum technology computing. Initially considered a "crazy idea", especially coming from the most unconventional physicist ever, the Feynman quantum computer is now probably operational. Another massive revolution has arrived and poised to set new standards. Binary code, a method of storing information as a series of ones (1) and zeros (0), is the basis for all "conventional" computers. But bits do not exist in the abstract, each depends on its reality on the physical state of the processor or the memory. Quantum computers utilise "qubits," a unit of information that can be a "1," a "0," or both a "1" and a "0" at the same time. Qubits have been created using two quantum phenomena called superposition and entanglement which are based on quantum mechanics principles that describe the dual particle-like and wave-like behaviour of matter and energy on an extremely small scale. Other competing particles, anyons,[38] acting as qubits may also be used — provided their existence is confirmed. The braiding and fusion of anyonic excitations in quantum Hall electron liquids and 2D-magnets are modelled by modular functors, opening a new possibility for the realisation of quantum computers. This approach is currently championed by Microsoft and Dr Michael Freedman,[39] as it would be immune from [topological] errors, providing much better conditions for very high speed calculations.

Physical states at the quantum level are not as clear cut as classical textbooks pretend. The quantum bits, or qubits, on which quantum computers deliver their performance, are expressed as a superposition state of particles which are extremely fragile making the system highly sensitive to outside interferences. Qubits do not have a defined value. Qubits possible states — zero or one can be superposed, meaning that they are in one of these states and to some degree in the other, with the probability of being in one state or the other rising or falling with time. In quantum computer physics, the term "magic" refers to a particular approach to building noise-resistant quantum computers known as magic-state distillation. One complexity lies in the fragility of this process of entanglement.

---

[38]In mathematical terms, these are unitary topological modular functors. They underlie the Jones polynomial and arise in Witten's Chern–Simons theory.
[39]Awarded Fields Medal in 1986 for solving the long-standing Poincaré conjecture in four dimensions.

Identifying these magic states as contextual, helps clarify the trade-offs involved in different approaches to building quantum devices. The production of qubits requires a stable physical system with two opposite quantum states, such as the direction of a spin of an electron orbiting an atom nucleus. Contextuality was first recognised as a feature of quantum theory almost 50 years ago. These results led to the design of new algorithms that better exploit the special properties of these magic states. The algorithmic difficulty in building a quantum computer seems to be now solved by topological quantum computing.[40] Topological quantum computer is based on the simple idea that topological properties of an object remain unchanged under deformations.

The computation with a topological quantum computer is nothing more than braiding the non-abelian anyons in a predefined series of clockwise and counterclockwise moves. The braid of stock prices has a remarkable connection with topological quantum computing. Using pairs of quasi-particles, called non-abelian anyons, having their trajectories braided in time, topological quantum computers can effectively simulate the stock market behaviour encoded in the braiding of stocks. In a typical topological quantum computation process, the trajectories of non-abelian anyons are manipulated according to the braiding of stocks and the outcome reflects the probability of the future state of stock market. The probability depends only on the Jones polynomial of the knot formed by plat closing the quantum computation. The Jones polynomial of the knotted stock market acts, making a parallel with the common financial literature, in a topological quantum computation as a counterpart of a classical technical indicator in trading the stock market. The type of knot stock market formed is an indicator of its future tendencies. Trading stocks at the stock exchange is compared to a process of writing a quantum code and the topological quantum computing will help assessing the most probable outcome for the market in any instance.

Quantum computers need a new generation of algorithms to help them deliver their promises. New algorithms, such as the Shor's algorithm

---

[40] Ovidiu Sorin Racorean, Decoding Stock Market Behaviour with Topological Quantum Computers. *Working paper, Applied Mathematics in Finance Dept*, SAV Integrated Systems, Academy of Economic Studies, 25 June (2014).

which factorises any nonprime number, can break problems into parts and calculate the most probable solution, to provide the most likely answer. In 2013, a quantum computer performed a complex mathematical calculation 3,600 times faster than the best of three leading algorithms running on a high-end traditional desktop computer. However, "Ninety-nine percent of quantum computing will be correcting errors," explained Yale physicist Rob Schoelkopf, Sterling Professor of Applied Physics and Physics. Qubits are so fragile that searching for errors can result in more errors. "Demonstrating error correction that actually works is the biggest remaining challenge for building a quantum computer." New machines will be able to run advanced portfolio optimisation algorithms, and they are likely to introduce another dimension in what defines perfect markets in the future. Trading stocks with a quantum computer, the HFT of today is going to be the very low frequency trading of tomorrow. This new generation of machine will not be good at all the tasks that our current computers are performing but they are likely going to be unparalleled in analysing and structuring critical information extracted from "data soup". One can easily imagine the impact for financial markets dominance, for example in areas such as risk management and stock market analysis.

The structure of markets has profoundly changed as institutional investors, in particular, have become the dominant market participant in the market. Households increasingly delegate their wealth management needs to professional investors. The initial market model behind the existing structure in both the United States and Europe was designed with the assumption of many small and heterogeneous participants interacting. In reality, the retail investor volume that remains has been successfully segregated by broker-dealers, and no longer directly participates in the price discovery process on exchanges. Large asset management institutions make fewer, but larger trading decisions than a heterogeneous set of retail investors holding the same number of shares. This means that the likelihood of two matching natural orders appearing at the same time is lower than in a world of many small investors. And a number of quiet algorithmic sentinels are trolling the market to take advantage of these moves. Alternative ways of trading, such as block-crossing venues, the increasing attractiveness of end-of-day auctions, and changes in the intraday volume distribution are all an expression of the need of all market participants for liquidity at a fair price. It is precisely to fulfil those needs that some pricing platforms have announced the introduction of mid-day batch auctions. This is certainly an encouraging sign that responses are available when potential market threats are identified. The 2008 Great Recession was "the result of human action and inaction, not of Mother Nature or computer models gone haywire. The captains of finance and the public stewards of our financial system ignored warnings and failed to question, understand and manage evolving risks within a system essential to the well-being of the American public."[41] To keep their position in the top league, leading hubs need to keep on their guard and adjust timely to threats while responding to changes in market structure and investor needs. This also means resisting over regulation and constantly eliminating the red tape that prevents businesses from forming. As always, this requires not only talent and persistent work but also independence and courage to read the weak signals and start adjusting the trajectory before it is too late.

Barbarians at the Gat.Exe

Parallel to the development of highly sophisticated financial infrastructure and sentient trading programmes, new threats developed when we thought we had them understood. Malware emerged as a possible threat to financial hubs. The network connectivity that the leading financial hubs have used to tremendous advantage, have made them more vulnerable to cyber disruptions. As such "machine health" is an area of concern. The theoretical foundational work on computer viruses goes back to John Von Neumann who developed in 1948 the theory of self-reproducing automatons, a complex mathematical model for elementary biological functions. By 1949, those ideas evolved into his series of lectures on "self-reproducing automata," given at the University of Illinois. Von Neumann's breakthrough theories mentioned "cellular automata" ideas applied to microbes, such as biological *viruses*. From there, partly based on his experience with ENIAC, he imagined "self-reproducing automata" that could be an entity

---

[41] Final report from the National Commission on the Causes of the Financial and Economic Crisis in the United States, January (2011).

embedded in those new "computing machines." However, the details of the technical implementation were not conceivable at this time. Primitive viruses for Apple II computers were exchanged within a small circle via diskette. Due to an error, the virus caused program crashes, and it was fixed in later versions. As the first "in the wild" Apple/DOS 3.3 virus, the "Elk Cloner" virus plagued users with spoonerisms, inverted or false displays and clicking noises. It spread via floppy disks, with which other operating systems — probably inadvertently — were made unusable. In 1971, Bob Thomas was a computer programmer in Cambridge (MA), who worked on a timesharing program called TENEX. He wanted to test if a self-replicating program could be written. His machine was connected to ARPAnet, the very first packet-switched network and direct ancestor of the Internet. His program was called Creeper, and it is considered to be the very first computer virus but it did not replicate. Soon, Brain developed in Pakistan, by the Farooq Alvi brothers did replicate through infecting the booting sector of every inserted floppy disk. The Indonesian Denny Yanuar Ramdhani used his virus "Den Zuk" to detect and remove the "Brain" virus. The "Brain" virus did no harm and the authors signed the code, but this would not last as malware became assembled with the purpose of being destructive. The Omega, Walker or Michelangelo viruses would start harming computers by intentionally deleting code. Viruses got more comprehensive attributes when they received the capacity to morph following the contribution of a Bulgarian hacker dubbed Dark Avenger. The first antivirus, the Reaper, acting in fact as a Creeper killing virus, was released to clean machines from Creeper but the actual removal of viruses using antivirus technology did not begin until the late 1980s. The word "virus" was not used as the official name of a computer invasion of this type until it was coined by American computer scientist Frederick B. Cohen in 1983. After the Reaper experience, the first removal of a computer virus is believed to have been performed by Bernd Fix in 1987. Around the same time, the Atari Corporation developed its own antivirus software. In 1975, science fiction writer John Brunner theorised a new type of computer threat known as worms in *The Shockwave Rider.* Possibly after reading the novel, Jon Hepps and John Shock from the Xerox Alto Research Centre, programmed the first worms. They were used for distributed calculations and spread independently in the network

in an uncontrolled manner, which after a short time crippled the computers of the centre. The first worm invasion can probably be attributed to
Robert T. Morris Jr., a doctoral student at Cornell University, who on
2 November 1988, released a worm, capable of spreading over the internet. The intention was not malicious but the program infected around
6,000 university and military computers, including NASA's computers
where it completely paralysed the machine's work. The most destructive
internet worms were introduced with the purpose of breaching the security
of real systems (banks, factories, power plants, airports and other transportation systems) and starting actions of virtual sabotage. As an example,
the "Iloveyou" worm attacked tens of millions of Windows personal computers and it cost an estimated USD 15 billion to clean the mess. Melissa
and later Blaster, Slammer and Sasser also left a durable and costly mark.
After the Slammer attack, Bank of America ATMs ceased to function,
14,000 post offices in Italy were closed, and online stock market trading
suffered severely. It certainly came as a surprise that the first RootKit was
engineered by a leading MNC, Sony Entertainment, and had quite a devastating impact. RootKits are malware capable of modifying the existing
computer operating system so that an attacker can keep access through a
backdoor and hide on the machine. The Sony BMG RootKit was ready by
2005, with the objective of protecting the copyright of their music.
It started from the idea that the firm had to do something against piracy
through detecting and disabling illegal copies of their property. But things
went out of control when Thomas Hesse, Director of global sales in Sony
BMG made the following statement "Most people, I think, don't even
know what a rootkit is, so why should they care about it?." This declaration infuriated the public and had a devastating impact on Sony's corporate image. The generation of malware continued to morph, new rootkits
became capable of infecting computers while surfing with the objective of
stealing confidential information from users to blackmail them. "Malware",
a general term used to refer to a variety of forms of hostile or intrusive
software, reached a new stage in 2010, as cyber-threats became officially
a matter of national security. Cyber-weapons had already emerged on the
agenda of security discussions between heads of states. Aurora or Stuxnet
were chillering illustrations of what can be achieved. Aurora which possibly originated from China, sought to retrieve sensitive information and

source code from over 34 commercial companies in the financial, technology and defence sectors using unprecedented tactics that combined encryption, stealth programming and an unknown hole in Internet Explorer. This attack involved very advanced methods with several pieces of malware working in concert to give the attackers full control of the infected system, at the same time it attempted to disguise itself as a common connection to a secure website and covertly gathered all the wanted information without being discovered. Stuxnet was created to destroy or at least slow down the Iranian nuclear program in sabotaging turbines for uranium enrichment by changing rotation frequencies. This was done with a level of sophistication that was never seen before. The military grade device which was capable to self-destruction left a chilling illustration of what could possibly happen to inadequately protected financial IT infrastructure.

From 1990, virus creation became a mundane hobby; things all changed in 2006 when the first underground criminal hack kits were made available on the underground market. ZeuS was the first one and quickly became a very popular tool. It compromised over 74,000 FTP accounts on websites of companies such as Bank of America, NASA, Monster.com, and many more. The success of the kit triggered competition and in 2009 SpyEye entered the market with a cheap entry version which became a commercial success on the malware market. Soon others appeared on the market, Carberp of Russian origin which not only was sold to users but was used itself to target banks in the North of Europe and later Russia, but most of the gang key members were arrested in 2012 following a Russian police dawn raid. In 2010, ZeuS announced that it had ceased development and had handed over its product to SpyEye developers. The reason for the move was the conclusion that ZeuS developer, Slavik, was making more money in working for a different set of malware producers exclusively focused on large commercial accounts. In 2011, the entire ZeuS malware manufacturing code leaked into the internet, and was made available for free. As a result many players appeared on the market and SpyEye stopped developing its initial product and worked on a brand new serviced version of its initial software. The founder, however, was arrested by the FBI on 2013. A 25-year-old Russian Alexander Panin pleaded guilty to authoring SpyEye. From 2011 to 2014, peer-to-peer ZeuS, P2PZeuS version, was immensely popular and used by many criminal groups to launch their own attacks. The platform proved very resilient and difficult to bring down but the identity of Slavik was released together with an FBI bounty of USD 3 million. The 30-year old Russian–Ukranian Evgeniy Mikhailovich Bogachev was now a celebrity appearing on the FBI's Most Wanted list. He was accused of being the mastermind of the criminal gang behind the Gameover ZeuS botnet and the creator of the original Zeus Trojan which infected tens of millions of computers and harvested huge volumes of sensitive financial data.

In this context, financial cybersecurity has emerged as one of the key priorities for the world's financial hubs, as they can be listed as national economic assets of strategic significance. Cyberattacks running silent programmes, vacuuming up data from the shadows have been targeting sensitive infrastructure. Other worrying problems have emerged such as the highly invasive undisclosed installation of original manufacturer software on some high-end smartphones capable of reporting or modifying detailed personal information without the user's consent. In addition, the concept of hardware modification is so prevalent that criminal elements routinely attempt to insert modified hardware to steal customer information from automated teller machines (ATMs), and other commercial activities. In the 2013, an ATM located in Kiev, Ukraine, started dispensing cash at random times during the day without anybody being around. As money was piling up on the pavement, the bank staff realised that this was only the tip of a much more serious problem. Months earlier, the bank computers had been breached by criminals from various origins who studied the way their staff operated through screenshots, video and recording. After the gang was comfortable enough with the operation's mode, it started to proceed with massive cash transfers into dummy accounts set up all over the world. Over 100 financial institutions were hit in 30 countries. This is possibly one of the largest known cyberattack recently performed on the financial sector with consequent losses of over USD 1 billion. Recently, Western companies and administrations are becoming concerned that so far over 90% of the cyber-intrusions are seemingly emanating from China.[42] The breach of

---

[42] Thomas E. Donlon, President Obama's security national advisor quoted in the New York Times, on 6 May 2013, "U.S. blames China military directly for cyberattack."

sensitive information led by various foreign military units and their affili-
ated groups, is thought to have targeted a broad spectrum of strategic companies including financial institutions, power transmission lines, oil
pipelines and power generation facilities to name but a few. Another Cold
War, a bitwar, which has been theorised by cyberpunk science fiction
author William Gibson in 1984,[43] has started and is likely to create even
more damage than the past one, if it does not cool down. The most unforeseen consequences may then be expected in economies and financial stability, especially since learned fools are greater fools than ignorant ones.

---

[43] William Gibson, Neuromancer, published by Ace, in July 1984. Gibson was the first
winner of the science-fiction "triple crown" — The Nebula Award, The Philip K. Dick
Award and the Hugo award.

Chapter 6

UNINVITED GUEST
TO THE PARTY

Some may object to mentioning uninvited guests to the party. It would be a momentary lapse of reason to forget that from John Law to John Maynard Keynes, the longstanding relationships between finance and gambling have been ambiguous and dangerous liaisons, often at the expense of their unfortunate victims. The three devils of finance may well be greed, gambling and finally cheating, and as history has shown it never took long for them to follow the money. In this context, rating certainly acquired a pivotal role in better assessing financial risk.

Mirror, Mirror or the Tyranny of Index Rating

By the time of John Moody's bond rating innovation in 1909, Dutch investors had been buying bonds for three centuries, English investors for two, and American investors for one century, all the time without the benefit of agency ratings. John Moody is credited with initiating agency bond ratings, in the United States in 1909. By the time he started to rate bonds, the American corporate bond market was several times larger than that of any other country. It seems quite puzzling that for much of the preceding nine century history of the construction of financial hubs, the question of a debt rating system had not surfaced earlier in an industry where reputation was the cornerstone of dealings. This was probably related to the dominance of close knit communities who knew each other locally, and where participants had to get themselves recognised as merchants and members of a guild. It was only centuries later when leading Italian merchant bankers recommended to their staff to keep in writing and share their observations on the business standing of their clients, that this started to be organised as an independent practice. In 1841, Lewis Tappan, a New York merchant, decided to specialise in the provision of commercial information. Tappan founded the Mercantile Agency, which gathered commercial information through a network of agents and sold reports on the reputation and creditworthiness of businesses all over the United States. His company, the Mercantile Agency became R.G. Dun & Company in 1859. About 600 miles West of New York, John Bradstreet founded a similar firm in Cincinnati, and by 1857 was publishing what was possibly the world's first commercial rating review. The Dun and the Bradstreet companies merged in 1933 to form Dun & Bradstreet. In 1962, Dun & Bradstreet acquired Moody's Investors Service, the bond rating agency founded by John Moody.

As railroad corporations were America's and indeed one of the world's first large industrial businesses, leading to the creation of the world's largest corporate bond market, more trusted information was needed on their expansion. By 1832, the industry was reported on by a specialised publication, The American Railroad Journal. The journal became a reference publication in the industry and then for investors under the management of Henry Varnum Poor, publishing comprehensive information on the ownership of railroads, their assets, liabilities and income. After the American Civil War, Poor and his son started a firm to publish Poor's Manual of the Railroads of the United States, an annual volume that first appeared in 1868. The book was widely recognised as the authoritative source on the industry's economics for several decades. After Henry Poor's death in 1905, and after John Moody began his ratings of railroad bonds in 1909 and U.S. state and local government bond a decade later, the Poor company entered the bond rating business as a natural extension of its publishing business, and made its first rating in 1916, and S&P credit rating publishing grew to over 1 million as of 2012. The company merged with Standard Statistics, another information and ratings company, in 1941, to form Standard & Poor's (S&P). S&P was a recognised brand and was later acquired in 1966 by McGraw Hill, the publishing giant. The publishing house had previously acquired Platts, the leading information provider in commodities, founded in 1909 by Warren Cumming Platt, a young journalist fascinated by the oil business. Platts' published oil prices was established as a reference for oil contracts. In 2012, the Company launched S&P Dow Jones Indices, the world's largest provider of financial market indices, in a joint venture with CME Group. Nearly a century later, Moody's and S&P, the original ratings agencies, remain by far the world's largest rating agencies. Fitch, the other world leading rating agency, was founded in 1913 by John Knowles Fitch. In 1924, the firm introduced the AAA through D rating system that is the basis for ratings throughout the industry. Fitch is now part of the Hearst group, one of the largest private diversified communications companies in the United States. Although these three firms were non-financial participants, they certainly represented extremely powerful forces in establishing and strengthening New York's position as a leading financial centre. A newcomer to the rating industry is the Beijing based Dagong agency created in 1994 upon the joint approval of The People's Bank of China and the former State Economic and Trade Commission. The Chinese rating agency's ambition to compete with the established U.S. agencies on the basis of a new methodology examining the way debtors repay their loans, is in contrast with many Western rating agencies' method of analysing whether a loan is being repaid.

Ratings created a common language to assess and compare risk but a burning question remains to understand how effectively these ratings have performed in assessing probabilities of defaults in the state and local debt markets, especially during financial crises of systemic importance. The facts are slightly surprising. During the Great Depression, "The proportionate totals ... show that 78 per cent of the defaulted issues were rated Aa or better in 1929. The defaulting issues rated Aa or better in 1929 constituted 94.4 per cent of the total dollar value of the 264 issues".[1] And

---

[1] George H. Hempel, The Postwar Quality of State and Local Debt, New York: National Bureau of Economic Research, p. 108, (1971).

during the Great Recession of 2008–2009, "financial institutions and credit rating agencies embraced mathematical models as reliable predictors of risks, replacing judgment in too many instances. Too often, risk management became risk justification."[2] The three credit rating agencies were key enablers of the financial meltdown, and were probably overconfident in feeding their macroeconomic models without seeing the need to step back and assess what was ongoing at a microeconomic level on the housing market. The mortgage-related securities at the heart of the crisis could not have been marketed and sold without their seal of approval. A probably excessive view, would be to consider that rating agencies are in the business of facilitating business in "selling regulatory licences". A more balanced view would probably be to consider that the loopholes on the regulatory net, blinded warning signals as fragmented regulatory bodies failed to question, understand, and manage evolving and more complex risks. The agencies maintained that claims that they kept subprime ratings high when they knew they should be lower are fallacies, as ratings were based on verifiable information available to the rest of the market.

In a world of competition, ratings and rankings are powerful tools of branding and influence. Designed to simplify a complex reality and catch the general public's attention, they make information easy to process for the benefit of society at large. Rankings today influence the opinions and decisions of a wide range of stakeholders. The central issue with respect to ranking is whether they contribute to improved overall market quality, thus allowing participants to make more educated choices on human and financial asset allocation. One must understand how the rankings work and how sometimes the numbers can get skewed. With hundreds of financial centres to choose from, rankings are a useful way to narrow down the options: but as usual the leaders and market movers will get the lion's share.

Imagine if an institution decided to create a table ranking the world's cities. Interesting questions would be raised such as: Is New York better than Sydney, would Hong Kong squeeze in above Milan, or is Bangkok above Madrid? It would be a nonsensical exercise suitable for another great Jose Luis Borges' novel. There is no doubt that simple numbers

---

[2]Conclusions of the Financial Crisis Enquiry Commission, p. xix, p. xxv, January (2011).

cannot capture every aspect of an international financial centre's (IFC) degree of excellence and the question arises whether rankings serve any use at all. Generally accepted criteria for ranking encompasses: i) the role an IFC is supposed to play in the international financial system, ii) the volume or the intensity of financial assets traded. IFC rankings have possibly garnered too much attention from the media and market players, possibly with pernicious effects, as the need to adjust financial practices, for example, to mitigate systemic risk, can hardly be captured by an index. No wonder rankings are also known to be influential in shaping new laws and policy making. In June 2003, the Corporation of London published "Sizing up the City — London's ranking as a Financial Centre."[3] The Global Financial Centres Index surveys global business leaders in order to rank the world's commerce centres. The index, which was first published in 2007, takes into account five broad areas including the business environment, finance, infrastructure, human capital and reputation. The surveying team asked 3,246 finance professionals twice a year to give their take on the world's commerce centres. On a 1,000 point scale, they anointed the following cities with the precious top 3 spots: New York (786), London (784) and Hong Kong (761). Is this the coming age of "*vox populi, vox dei*" or another media-based coup to establish a poll based franchise. Opinion polls are, by definition, subjective, and the fact that a world class index relies on reputational indicators to this degree has led to healthy scepticism. The detailed ranking and the answer are not so important; what really matters is that with a negligible difference, the top two cities of New York and London have emerged as world leading business centres, closely followed by China's SAR city-state of Hong Kong. Rankings seek both to measure how perceptions of IFCs and competitive edge change from time to time, and to expand the scope of the exercise by embracing a wider range of factors and a greater number of centres. Respondents consistently believe that the availability of skilled personnel and the nature of the regulatory environment are the two most important competitive factors affecting IFC. However, this "on-the-field" perception may not be sufficient to sustain and strengthen a top position.

---

[3] A report written by the Centre for the Study of Financial Innovation based on a survey of City opinion of London's competitive position as an international financial services centre.

The report highlighted that London's reputation was under scrutiny, especially following the several scandals that hit the City, from the rigging of Libor to that of the foreign exchange market. The latter has engulfed several banks in the UK, with the Bank of England also being dragged into the investigation after it suspended one of its own officials amid fears that some of its staff had been possibly compromised in or knew about currency market manipulation. Additional scandals including British banks abusing their clients by selling unneeded insurance, manipulation of financial benchmarks and trading losses and uncertainties regarding the remaining of Scotland in the Union have combined to damage the City's standing. New York's seven-point rise in its rating to the top spot after London suffered a 10-point decline, the largest swing of any centre in the top 50, and is indeed a meaningful and strong wake-up call. The London financial centre which has made a point of being outside of Eurozone is not backed by large integrated economies comparable to the USA or PRC, and therefore is possibly more fragile.

The IFC index ranking proved to be a very useful instrument for surveying over several years the dynamics of the top ten cities involved in international finance; however, some have refused to participate and provide data on the basis that the dices were loaded since inception. Caution is needed as some rankings may reflect idiosyncrasies; for 1905 and 1910 St. Petersburg (Russia), and Montreal (Canada) briefly moved higher than Hong Kong in ranks, before the situation was corrected. A decline in rank does not necessarily indicate a reduced role for an IFC. Instead, temporary moves into the top ten of outsider financial centres (such as San Francisco or Chicago), combined with small differences in significance among the significant centres may exaggerate the seeming decline of one or the other. Any ranking is controversial and no ranking is absolutely objective. Compiling the indices involves significant efforts to ensure the values are accurate. The process can hardly be automated, due to possible deficiencies in the survey databases. The controversy really arises from the question whether the leadership of a financial centre can be measured precisely by mere numbers, and beyond that what numbers and for what weighting as everything cannot be put on the line. To continue the parallel made with education, universities and professors continue to score students on a scale without any significant changes in methodology; however, the students are regularly informed that they will not be judged by scores absolutely, as the university and potential employers will have the capacity to make more sophisticated, independent judgements.

Competing indices jostle in the intellectual marketplace, and one can be sure that one of the first things that an aspiring IFC will study is precisely the index positioning. Unfortunately this is sometimes based on the well-known principle of "defining the problem and dictating the solution," especially since some advisors may be willing to do that for a fee. There are many ways of concocting a spurious index when the numbers are on your side; one can chose what to put in the index, but this is no guarantee that free market players will buy it. A composite measure has the ability to summarise multi-dimensional issues in a simple manner in the form of a ranking or single number, making it possible for policymakers to get a tractable and representative sense of the situation in a given country relative to others. The regular publication of an index over years comes with the identification, the production and the update of critical data for the users and it not only facilitates communication within a group of professionals and the public but also shows a global international commitment to follow a particular set of critical development challenges. Indexes act as success accelerators for established leaders and may generate useful signals on the emergence or decline of financial centres. However, since the creation of financial centres, the deep and long term trends affecting the global landscape of world finance are emerging slowly and take time to crystallise: money relates to confidence and the best place to handle it cannot be established by decree or polls. Every index is a delicate combination of a survey and a number of discretionary chosen indexes without full transparency on how each country's calculation is performed. There are major differences in the ranking methodologies used, although everybody recognises that league tables only give a glimpse of a synthetic answer to a complex reality; similar issues can be experienced, for example, for the methodologies of ranking universities. Combining a survey of qualitative measure with quantitative indexes is particularly difficult, and likely to trigger many objections. Several institutions have produced various models and methodologies to try to prove their point and deliver better rankings. Consequently, a ranking of the rankings has emerged as a first result of the multiplications of the claims to publish reliable indicators, usually on an annual basis. Even if annual rankings have merit, they do need to be reviewed within a long period of time to be really meaningful. Rankings have been used too often for marketing purposes to promote aspiring global financial centres and fuel a debate between the respective merits of the leaders. This is healthy but this must be reviewed in the face of financial reality with a critical eye.

Indexes must first be built on a selection of representative variables, which then are weighted one to the other to form the pixels of a possibly accurate picture of what is measured and benchmarked. The "fuzzier" the concept and the more subjective the available data, the more likely it is that only a large pool of indicators can accurately capture the construct in question. "Crooks already know these tricks. Honest men must learn them in self-defence," wrote Darrell Huff in 1954 in "How to Lie with Statistics," a guide to getting figures to say whatever you want them to. One of the dangerous by-products of index ranking is the risk that either established or emerging centres may focus on improving the index rather than excelling in the real world; this may lead to perception bias and wrong decisions which ultimately may shape market player behaviour. Given the contribution of trading volumes to a number of ranking indexes, what is the incentive to forbid High Frequency Trading, even if HFT is not contributing anything to the quality of an international finance centre. Since banning HFT would result in trading volume decline, and lower trading ranking for those banning such practices compared to those authorising HFT, the incentive is obviously low. Measuring Service quality or financial innovation are very subjective matters, especially on a large scale. One particular problem is that rankings perpetuate a single definition of quality and excellence at a time when financial institutions, and regulations — or more precisely property rights,[4] are quickly evolving. The introduction of block chain technology used to develop Bitcoin, is one of the vivid examples of the possible revolution related to future notarisation of such rights.

Ranking is usually organised by clusters to ensure better clarity in the critical factors. The long history of the use of composite indicators in the social sciences has led researchers to develop a range of statistical

---

[4]This point has been extensively developed by Vernon L. Smith, Economy Nobel 2002, Chapman University, Orange, California.

diagnostic tests designed to assess construct validity and indicator reliability. These include tests designed to help identify outlier indicators, assess the degree to which indicators reflect a single underlying dimension, and identify redundancies or assign weights among the indicator set. Notably, techniques such as confirmatory factor analysis, cluster analysis, and calculations of statistical leverage and influence are standard practices in the process of index design and analysis. Nevertheless, professionals, the general public and many public policymakers often see rankings as just another way of assessing quality; informed professionals know that the assessment of finance centres cannot be reasonably held in a single number, although some policymakers have clearly become obsessed with rankings. In the competitive IFC marketplace, policymakers cannot afford being insensitive to marketing and market changes; but one should guard against excessive commercialisation of financial rankings. How rankings influence a decisive pool of talents willing to join a leading financial centre in their decision process is of the essence to foster dominance and innovation, and this may well be the ultimate reason for publishing annual rankings.

Stakeholders also refer to rankings when considering which marketplace offers the best brand image and global return-on-investment. This may even influence asset pricing, as the endorsement from an international centre may have a different impact on investors, especially for new products such as IPOs, than a lower ranked financial centre. Rankings affect stock markets decisions, and pricing, for their international partnerships and mergers. Such partnerships have become strategically important for attracting new customers, talents including high-achieving students and high-skilled labour, research, academic programmes. Clearly, less static means of evaluating the quality of an IFC in its different components should be sought, especially since web and mobile based instruments and user feedback can provide much better and more precise measurements. Rankings have placed a new premium on status and reputation, with a strong bias towards long-established marketplaces. IFCs are complex constructions with strengths and weaknesses across various markets and product lines. Excellence can be defined differently depending upon the criteria or indicators and weightings that are used. By aggregating the score across the various indicators, rankings reduce the complexity of each centre's value proposition to a single digit score, and exaggerate differences, or level of excellence. Hence, global rankings must be treated with caution, not only because some algorithms or methodologies have prompted some respondents to provide erroneous or twisted data as a large fraction of the proposed ranking is the combined assessment of a finance centre's reputation by peer finance professionals from rival institutions, and also because some important uninvited guests to the party may have been unaccounted for. Rankings may change from one year to the other but, in the real world, little has changed, as the scale of observable movement from one year to the other is hardly perceptible. In the absence of dramatic events, such as war or systemic disaster, the relative strengths of one centre to the other vary only marginally and incrementally year on year.

Gambling "Financial Centres": Place Your Bets ...

All laws against gaming never hinder it,[5] therefore establishing a well-defined economic compartment for "gambling" can be considered a rational idea. Before the middle of the 19th century, the frontier between finance and gambling was very thin. Nevertheless, problems associated with gambling still create immense costs to society, individuals and their families. Investment in some respect is a distant but fully assumed and rational cousin in risk, reward and probabilities. Conversely, as gamblers move from stage to stage, and more and more into the powerful grip of betting, their perception of money starts to change. It no longer holds its traditional value. Money for the compulsive gambler has only one value: To enable him to keep gambling, to stay "in action." This form of addiction is similar to being hooked on cocaine or other psychotropics, as neuro science has shown. Gambling is one of the earliest forms of entertainment that has ever taken place in human history. Evidence points to the earliest forms of gambling taking place in China back around 2300 A.D. Dice were even thought to have decided territory. Back around the year 1020 A.D., King Olaf of Norway and King Olaf of Sweden met at Konungahella (Norway) to peacefully resolve a conflict as to who should own the

---

[5]Adam Smith, Lectures on Justice, Police, Revenue and Arms, Part III, of revenue, §4 of stock-jobbing, (1763).

District of Hising. The Swedish King rolled back to back double sixes to win the territory. China is also thought to be the origin of playing cards. The deck of cards as it is known today was developed because once cards reached the Mediterranean countries, the cards were made to be distinguished by the royal ranks of nobleman. The French altered the deck by pulling out one of the men and adding a queen. The Chinese developed paper, which led them to develop paper money. Once card and paper money were put together, playing cards were invented, and gambling thrived. The Chinese learned how to shuffle paper money, and this is possibly where the practice of shuffling cards came from.

Just before 79 A.D., on a famous painting in Italy from the Tavern of Salvius, via di Mercurio, in Pompeii, two men sat opposite each other on stools, holding a gaming table on their knees and on it arranged in various lines are several latrunculi (The game of soldiers) of yellow, black and white. They are rolling dices and get into an argument about who has won. The man on the left watched by two other men is exulting "Six" meaning he has won, "No" says the other player loudly it is not a three, it is a two. In this famous scene mentioned by Ovid, they both know that they are playing on chance and taking both a money and fistfight risk that they presumably understand as the innkeeper is pushing them into the street after the dispute turns into a fight. Gambling and finance still entertain this ambiguous relationship. But what both players do not realise is that, behind the uncertain outcome of their own game, a bigger risk is lurking.[6] In effect we do not know what happened to those two after the Vesuvius volcano erupted and engulfed on 24 August, this very year, the flourishing roman towns of Pompeii and Herculaneum, when the lives of both towns came to an abrupt and catastrophic end. The scene can be easily translated to the context of the 14th century just before the Black Plague unexpectedly struck Europe in a matter of hours in 1348, triggering the collapse of the Florentine banking system.

The theory of gambling owes much to Girolamo Cardano, a 16th century Italian mathematician, who published in 1565, his treatise *Liber de Ludo Aleae, The Book of Games of Chance,* which founded the elementary

---

[6]Pr. Amartya Sen, Lecture on Oxford Martin Programme on Resource Stewardship, 11 July (2012).

theory of gambling. His interest in gambling not only enabled him to survive during difficult times but also laid the theoretical ground for probabilities and the random walk hypothesis. Despite the bitter lesson learned from John Law de Lauriston's practices in the 18th century, a convicted gambler who ruined the ailing French royal public finances, the temptation to outsmart the odds has continued until now. Many continue to play the stock market and, unfortunately, approach it with a gambling mentality. Day trading is a patent example. Day traders buying and selling stocks, currencies or commodities dozens, even hundreds, of times a day, often knowing nothing about the fundamentals of what they are trading, are just playing numbers, glued to their computers much like a gambler is glued to on-line poker. The vast majority of day traders are not making any income, and they can even lose all their assets. Gambling is known to be dangerously addictive and possibly devastating when one cannot refrain from playing: drawing a clear line between the real world, finance and gambling has sometimes proven a difficult task. The 2008–2009 subprime crisis which nearly put the world financial system to its knees more or less proceeded from a similar logic, in a coded way. Signals were sent to market intermediaries that gambling time was back, and suddenly the line between gambling and finance became blurred. After the Glass–Steagall legislation, which separated retail banks and investment banks was abrogated in 12 November 1999, by the Financial Services Modernization Act, the change allowed banks, whose deposits were guaranteed by the FDIC, i.e. the government, to engage in highly risky investments: money was available for nothing, and chips were almost free. Simultaneously, interest rate went down, and asset managers were hunting for yield. Lightly regulated derivatives and "innovative" mortgage products emerged to address a booming real estate market: 2/28 adjustable-rate mortgages, interest-only loans, piggy-bank mortgages (simultaneous underlying mortgage and home-equity lines) and the notorious negative amortisation loans (borrower's indebtedness goes up each month). These loans defaulted in vastly disproportionate numbers to traditional 30-year fixed mortgages, and we know the rest. In the early and mid-2000s, high risk mortgages were available to people who had difficulty in borrowing money for housing, due to insufficient revenues or poor credit history. The reason for this change was the repackaging of risky mortgages into pools that were sold to investors as a quality composite material. Private-label mortgage backed securities (PMBS) provided most of the funding of subprime mortgages. The resulting demand predictably bid up real estate prices, and this was good news for lenders as the value of their collateral assets[7] appreciated. However, as soon as too many of those borrowers defaulted on their loans, the real estate bubble deflated. The value of real estate collateral shrunk, financing became tighter and the whole construction started to tank: it seems that the riskiness of PMBS was more a gamble than the result of a proper risk analysis. The problem was that the whole market was on steroids, hungry to generate lucrative revenue streams with another type of junk bonds for a long chain of intermediaries. In 2007, the five major U.S. investment banks were operating with extraordinarily thin capital. By one measure, their leverage ratios were as high as 40:1, meaning for every USD 40 in assets, there was only USD 1 in capital to cover losses. Less than a 3% drop in asset values could wipe out a firm. This was aggravated by short-term financing, in the overnight market: borrowing had to be renewed each and every day and complex derivatives difficult to unwind. Critical components of the financial system such as, the multitrillion-dollar repo lending market, off-balance-sheet entities, and the use of over-the-counter derivatives, were hidden from view of the regulator in the shadow banking system, opaque and laden with short-term debt that rivalled the size of the traditional banking system, without the protections designed to prevent financial meltdowns. The system was back to its Florentine origins.

The crisis began with the bursting of the USD 8 trillion housing bubble: the collapse of the subprime lending fuelled a downward spiral in housing prices and provided a major impetus for the Great Recession of 2008–2009. The resulting destruction of wealth translated into cutbacks on consumer spending, and a chaos on the stock market. Subsequently, business investment dried up and the resulting crisis was the longest post war recession. It lasted 18 months in the USA compared to 10 months on average for the other recessions. As consumer spending and investment dried up, massive job loss followed. In 2008 and 2009, the American market lost 8.4 million jobs, the most dramatic contraction since the Great Depression. Europe also got contaminated right after the USA. As a

---

[7]The value of the piece of real estate used as a guarantee to the loan.

consequence of the crisis, jobs, marriages and lifetime savings were ruined, to a level unseen since the Great Depression. "When one is unemployed for six months or a year, it is hard to qualify for a lease, so even the option of relocating to find a job is often off the table. The toll is simply terrible on the mental and physical health of workers, on their marriages, and on their children."[8] A possibly slower but disciplined economy is healthier than a gamble oriented economy, experiencing crash and booms. However, as pointed out in the late 1990s by U.S. Federal Reserve Chairman Alan Greenspan, "there is a fundamental problem with market intervention to prick a bubble: it presumes that you know more than the market ... identifying a bubble in the process of inflating may be among the most formidable challenges confronting a central bank, pitting its own assessment of fundamentals against the combined judgment of millions of investors." Looking back, pricking a bubble may seem the obvious thing to do but looking forward this gamble of last resort of the central bank, equally comes with huge risks, especially since the tools of monetary policy are too broad to be really effective: tighter monetary policy may ultimately be the reason for an even more severe market crash.

Over ages, lotteries have been considered a more respectable way to play the odds, and occasionally a convenient instrument for managing public finance. Scholars disagree on who started the ancient tradition of lotteries, but there are undisputable early references. In Chapter 26 of the Book of Numbers (52–56), Moses (1391–1271 B.C.)[9] used a lottery to award land west of the Jordan River. Other evidence for the early use of chance can be found in Greek mythology. But chance also played an important role in other cultures. In Japan and China, it was used to predict the future, while Muslim religion explicitly forbids gambling and lotteries, thereby acknowledging their existence. In 100 A.D., the Han Dynasty in China, after opening the Silk Road to foreign trade, created Keno. Cheung Leung (2nd century A.D.), a Chinese Han dynasty emperor, was then tied up in a long war which was depleting the city's funds. He could not get any more money

---

[8] Janet L. Yellen, A Painfully Slow Recovery for America's Workers: Causes, Implications, and the Federal Reserve's Response, at the "A Trans-Atlantic Agenda for Shared Prosperity" conference.

[9] According to rabbinical Judaism calculations.

from the city residents and came with this idea for a new money game, Keno. Years later Keno was used again to finance the building of the Great Wall of China which started in the 7th century A.D. and lasted for about 500 years. According to historical records, the official Chinese lottery was not licenced until the 1800s, so whether there is any truth to these legends is not known for sure. When Keno was first invented, it was played with 120 Chinese characters rather than 80 today. Nevertheless, the game was an immediate success when it was first brought to the shore of San Francisco by Chinese sailors in the 20th century.

Real lotteries were first used at dinner parties hosted by the Roman emperors, and their format was similar to their contemporary avatars: Augustus distributed small presents to his party guests by means of a lottery and raised funds for repairs to the city of Rome, and Nero had thousands of tickets thrown to the public, and mega prizes included slaves, real estate, and ships. After a period of oblivion, the first public lottery reappeared in the 15th century in Flanders, in the Dutch seaport of Sluis (1434), situated 6 km away from Bruges. The Dutch were the first to shift the lottery to monetary prizes alone. One out of four tickets would be a winning one. A decade later, lotteries flourished in numerous towns of Flanders including Ghent, Utrecht and Bruges. Lottery was used to finance dikes and fortifications and assist those in need. Already in the 13th century it had been common practice in Brussels to allocate market space randomly by lottery. The English word lottery is derived from the Dutch word *loterij* which stems from the Dutch noun *lot* meaning fate. On the other side of the world, Japan Tokugawa shogunate, issued in 1615 a 17 article set of "Regulations for the Imperial Palace and Aristocracy, *daimyo*" cautioning that "addiction to sex and indulgence in gambling were the foundation of ruin."

The association of finance and games of chance does not bear a futile heritage: it is tightly connected with balancing public finance on large projects, enduring political power and enticing people to beat the odds to become richer than they can possibly imagine. Funds raised by lotteries were used for defence, primarily to finance large projects. In Europe, instruments for mitigating risk coexisted since the Middle Ages with instruments of risk taking: gambling in all its shapes and forms was extremely popular. The commonalities between gambling and finance made gambling equally suspicious to the Catholic Church as smelling of usury. A gambling compartment helped clarify how and where gambling and finance had to separate. Indeed the gambling capitals of this world, Macau and Las Vegas, are not claiming the title of IFC, but may have a legitimate claim for international financial recreational centres as the assets under their management and proceeds are far from negligible. In the 15th century, the Low Countries pioneered the use of lotteries for the financing of public works. In addition to the simple lottery ticket, they creatively developed the multistage or 'Dutch' lottery, in which winners in each stage participated in subsequent stages with ever greater prizes. The provincial government, presumably under Hapsburg pressure, prohibited all lotteries in 1526. Public lotteries spread to Florence and to England in the 16th century and the use of lotteries and lottery bonds were to become an important element of public finance in the 17th and 18th centuries. It was not until the 16th century that the first English lottery was chartered by Queen Elizabeth I (1566) and drawn in 1569. It was organised as a fund raising event for the "reparation of the heavens and strength of the Realme, and towards such other publique good workes". This lottery was special in the sense that every ticket was more or less a winning one and the total proceeds from the lottery would be refunded as prizes. This means in financial terms that this specific state lottery was an interesting innovation, very close to subscribing to a government bond with a random yield for the investor. After the success of this first public lottery, the government sold the right to sell lottery tickets to brokers, who in turn hired intermediaries to sell them to the public. In 1693, the Million Adventure in England, famously offered on top of a 10% coupon a chance to win a prize worth up to a hundred times the initial investment. Lottery tickets were sold through brokers until Parliament declared the final lottery in 1826. During this time, private lottery tickets were also sold as a mean of raising money to fund risky ventures such as the financing of the settlement of Jamestown, the first permanent one in America. After the success of this initial pitch to the public, lotteries continued to play a significant part in the financing of the British colonies, especially in America. Records show that over 200 lotteries were organised between 1744 and the American revolution (1765). Benjamin Franklin organised a lottery to raise money to purchase cannons for the defence of Philadelphia. Many American institutions including Columbia or Princeton universities, churches, libraries, bridges and other public buildings were financed this way. In the United States, the financial panic of 1837 resulted in the accelerated development of mutual life insurance companies. A cultural shift away from preachers who demonised life insurance as "gambling" and legal changes allowing women to purchase life insurance created a boom period for life insurance companies. The difference between gambling and sparing money to protect over an uncertain future was gradually being clarified in the market. In the 19th century, a number of fraudulent schemes erupted, notably in Louisiana, and the reputation of lotteries became tainted with scandals and suspicion, and Congress finally halted this means of financing in 1900. In France in July 1927, the NGO "Les Gueules Cassées", organised a nationwide lottery to assist the wounded veterans of the Great War, and in particular the disfigured ones who did not have the resources to pay for long term medical care. The success was such that it later led in 1933 to the creation of the French National Lottery.

The three gambling capital of this world: Monte Carlo, Macau and Las Vegas

It is not a coincidence that the Monte Carlo simulation widely used in finance[10] is named after the city of Monaco, where the primary attraction is games of chance. Iconic high end gambling capital, Monte Carlo is a rebel and distinct offspring of the Genoese financial powerhouse. In 1162, Genoa's authority over the Ligurian coast was recognised by the Emperor Frédéric I Barberousse, from Porto Venere as far as Monaco. In 1191, the Holy Roman Emperor Henri VI, a member of the Hohenstaufen dynasty, finally conceded the Rock of Monaco to Genoa city state, together with its port and adjacent lands. Among the Guelph families of the Genoese aristocracy, one of the most brilliant was the Grimaldi; its most illustrious

---

[10] Any method which solves a problem by generating suitable random numbers and observing that fraction of the numbers obey some properties. The method is used for obtaining numerical solutions to problems which are too complicated to solve analytically, such as early computational models for a thermonuclear reaction. It was named in 1946 by the mathematician Stan Ulam from Los Alamos in honour of a relative having a propensity to gamble.

known ancestor was Otto Canella, "Doge" of Genoa in 1133, whose son was called Grimaldo. After three centuries of struggle, this branch of the Grimaldi family was to gain sovereignty of the 2.02 sq. km Monaco. In 1215, the Genoese Ghibellines led by Fulco del Cassello, well aware of the strategic importance of the place and convinced of the advantages of the harbour, landed on the Rock to lay the first stone of the Genoese fortress. In 1296, as a result of party quarrels, the Guelphs and with them the Grimaldi were expelled from Genoa and temporarily took refuge in Provence. They had assembled a small army and took the fortress of Monaco by surprise. On 8th January 1297, the Guelphs led by Francô Grimaldi started the Grimaldi dynasty, under the sovereignty of the Republic of Genoa. Monaco, first secured the recognition of its independent sovereignty from Spain in 1633, and later from France (1641). Prince Charles III, successor to Prince Florestan 1, initiated the creation of a less pastoral life for the Principality. The press announced that "The new Casino launched by the Société des Bains de Mer will soon rise from the ground in monumental proportions. Around the Casino, fine hotels will be built, having nothing to fear by comparisons with those that have been opened in Paris, London or New York." Five years after the first stone was laid, the Casino was inaugurated, in the spring of 1863. It was to carry off a brilliant success. The Plateau des Spélugues on which the Casino was built used to be a simple piece of land near the sea used to cultivate traditional Mediterranean species: Orange, lemon and olive trees. Less than 600 years later, the Monte Carlo legendary casino became a reference for all players in the world and French Roulette won its letters of nobility from 1863. Monaco is largely the dream of Rainier III, the prince who ruled it from 1949 until his death in 2005. Despite an annoying crisis with France in 1962 under President Charles de Gaulle fed up with French citizens taking residence in Monaco to evade paying income tax, and a lighter row in 2000, Monte-Carlo kept its independence and status as an exclusive meeting-place for the high rolling international high society.

With an equally long gaming history stretching back for more than 500 years, Macau was renowned as the "Monte Carlo of the Orient" and "Las Vegas of the East". Contrary to the West, gambling is a socially well accepted practice in China and beyond in Asia. It is still the pillar industry of Macau, although the new Chinese leadership called for more diversification of its economic resources. The Macau gaming industry can be traced back to the 16th century, when the city state first opened its harbour to foreign visitors. At that time, gaming was specifically popular among the construction workers who emigrated from Mainland China, harbour coolies and domestic helpers. They had little to lose and much to win if they managed to get the most valued prizes. Since no gaming regulation was implemented, the gambling stalls were spread over streets and lanes and were operated by the bankers themselves, another clear evidence of the unlikely DNA convergence between finance and gaming. In 1847, the Macau's Portuguese government led by the enclave's governor Isidoro Francesco Guimares, legalised games of chance for the first time, in an effort to find new fiscal resources and diversify the city's economy. By 1850s, there were more than two hundred "Fantan" traditional Chinese game stalls operating in Macau. Towards the late 19th century, Macau gaming industry started booming and became a legend, thus, making gaming tax as the main income for the government. In 1937, the Macau gaming industry had undergone a revolutionary uplift. The Macau's Portuguese government passed a Decree Law to move forward and integrate the operations of different games. The casino monopoly concession was granted to the "Tai Heng Company". It converted the "New Central Hotel" in Avenida Almeida Ribeiro into its flagship casino and introduced Baccarat, the most popular game at the present time, and many new western game types. In February 1961, the 119th Governor of Macau Jaime Silvério Marques designated Macau as a "permanent gaming region" and officially positioned Macau as a low taxation region and regarded gaming and tourism as its major economic activities. Marques had also better defined gaming as "Any game with results that are unpredictably and randomly generated and won purely by one's luck is called games of fortune."

Before Macao was returned to Mainland China's sovereignty in 1999, there were numerous discussions and studies under different perspectives on the practicality of liberalising the gaming industry. In fact, the Portuguese Macao Government had made considerations and preparations on over-ruling the monopoly system in the gaming industry. An international tender was launched in 2001, and on 2002 three new concessions were granted. The former Portuguese enclave has become the world's largest gambling hub, which has seen gaming revenues increasing from

USD 24 billion in 2010 to USD 44 billion in 2014, dwarfing the Las Vegas Strip. A large part of the success of Macau owes much to its opening to Mainland China high rollers who have been flooding the place. From a total of 31 million visitors in Macau in 2014, 21 million originated from Mainland China. Macau casinos have become extremely reliant on the Mainland VIP high-roller sector, which accounts for more than 70% of revenues. By enrolling with a VIP room promoter known as junket operator, VIP Mainland China visitors can access all sorts of goodies while visiting Macau, use their non-freely convertible quota of Renminbi to buy casino chips, and cash out their winnings in foreign currencies. Macau's junkets have attracted increasing attention because of fears that their funding channels may have their roots in China's underground lending market, a legal grey area but a key financing channel for China SMEs. It does not come as a surprise that Hong Kong wanted to build a bridge as a mean of faster and direct connection with its sister gambling city, currently accessible by ferry. However, 2014 has been challenging for Macau as the Beijing anti-corruption crack down kept VIPs away from gaming tables and this led to a 2.60% drop in gaming revenues. Nevertheless, Macau should keep its privilege position as it remains the only place in China where gambling is legal.

The gaming revenues in Vegas Strip peaked in 2007 with revenues of USD 6.8 billion, then declined to USD 5.6 billion in 2009. The casino industry at the Strip was worst hit by the economic slowdown and resulting lower household disposable income. Since then, it has still been unable to reach the pre-recession levels. Meanwhile, other states legalised casinos, which further weighed over the casinos in Nevada: Pennsylvania, Delaware or Massachusetts recently legalised casino table games like poker and blackjack. Gaming in Nevada, and Clark County in particular only started to rebound slightly in 2010: Las Vegas revenues grew to USD 6.5 billion in 2013. Las Vegas was founded as a city a bit more than a century ago, on 15 May, 1905, when 110 acres of land situated between Stewart Avenue on the north, Garces Avenue to the south, Main Street to the west, and 5th Street (Las Vegas Boulevard) to the east, were auctioned off by the railroad company. Nevada, now the reference gambling state in the USA and beyond, actually made it first a felony to operate a gambling game in 1910. Twenty five years later, in 1930, the first gaming license in

Nevada was issued to Mayme Stocker at the Northern Club. The Pair-O-Dice Club opened in 1931 three miles south of Las Vegas on the Los Angeles Highway, today's Strip. In 1941, the western-style El Rancho Vegas Hotel and Casino, the first themed resort opened on the Strip. Today the Nevada gambling authority supervises five cities including Carson City, Elko, Laughlin, Las Vegas and Reno. It is not a surprise that 87% of the gaming (fiscal) income, comes from Clark county, home of Las Vegas. The largest possible market change may be coming from Japan if the liberalisation process goes through. Japan could well become the next very big market for gambling. It would certainly make sense for local and international casino operators to create a new and advanced gambling hub here, as all the conditions for success seems to be met. Picking a smart and entertaining location for a new gaming hub will remain a critical success factor.

Exactly like stock exchanges, technology played its part in keeping gambling safe. In the first half of the 20th century in the U.S., horse-race results were sent out over Western Union's telegraph network, but when that company cut off this service to what it deemed shady customers, others with fewer scruples stepped in. On their private wires, race results were sent from the tracks to illegal bookmakers before the public at large learned of them, allowing bookies to accept bets on horses that had already lost and turn down wagers on horses that had already won. For decades, bookmakers paid handsomely for those wire services, helping to support some notable Chicago mobsters. In fact Cicero[11] criticises exactly this: the whole system of peering into the future by means of lots [or reward] was the invention of tricksters who were only interested in their own financial welfare. Access to a fast wire carrying breaking results from the track was an offer that bookies could not refuse. A 1951 report of the United States Senate Special Committee to Investigate Crime in Interstate Commerce noted, "The wire service is as essential to a bookmaker as the stock ticker to a stockbroker."

The gambling centres of Macau, or Monte Carlo are closely associated with the benevolence of a nearby Offshore Financial Centre (OFC), and Las Vegas residents benefit from the hospitable income tax climate

---

[11] De Divinatione [5, page 433].

which prevails in the state of Nevada. OFCs have the objective of providing relaxed tax regulation and burden, mostly based on limited income tax. Such a favourable environment may also create a tempting base for the development of money laundering and sheltering doubtful financial flows. Gambling centres therefore require careful monitoring from regulatory authorities to keep the place clean. They are usually well insulated and somehow distant from leading financial hubs, as is not sustainable to have an economy where too much of the growth is based on "a casino mentality."[12] Since the 12th century, it has been recognised that those banks that are too big or too complex to be managed, and had succeeded in cleverly evading the financial regulatory system are also the ones whose performance has been dismal. "Zombie banks — with little or no net worth, but operating as if they were viable institutions — are always likely to 'gamble on resurrection.' If they take big bets and win, they walk away with the proceeds;"[13] if they fail, they pass the bill to the taxpayer and their failure shakes the entire financial system, destroying years of trusted practices. Adam Smith[14] already warned that "Persons who game must keep their credit, else nobody will deal with them." Too Big to Fail (TBTF) arises when the uninsured creditors of systemically important financial institutions expect government protection from loss when these financial institutions get into financial or operational trouble, after pushing financial risk beyond manageable limits. While safety net expansion has increased TBTF concerns, the essence of the problem and underlying cause of TBTF remain clear: Policymakers support large-bank creditors to contain or eliminate spillover effects, but the support creates an incentive for renewed gambling in the future. A direct way to discourage activities that generate spillovers is to put a price on them, money cannot come for nothing and chips cannot come for free: a market that favours Fremont Street[15] over Wall Street and Wall Street over Main Street ends up hurting everyone.

---

[12] United States President Barrack Obama, Remarks by the President on the Economy — Northwestern University, 2 October 2014, referring to a "casino mentality on Wall Street".
[13] Joseph Stiglitz, America's socialism for the rich, The Guardian, 12 June 2009.
[14] Adam Smith, Lectures on Justice, Police, Revenue and Arms, Part III, of revenue, §4 of stock-jobbing, (1763).
[15] A famous casino street in downtown Las Vegas.

Gambling cannot be understood in the context of finance hubs without referring to speculation and one of its most sulphurous avatars; cornering or gaming the markets. Both gambling and speculation proceed from the same origin with a twist. There is always an element of bet in both cases, but a fundamental divergence stands from the difference between educated and calculated risk taking and compulsive gambling. The remaining bit, manipulating or cornering the market has always been the logical criminal undesirable offspring of both gambling and speculation, especially when market regulation and justice enforcement were weak. As the CBOT developed, the gold forward market became the speculator market of choice in New York in the 19th century, especially during the Civil War. The traders' behaviour on the NYSE was so harsh that it fostered the first set of legislation on futures. Alongside the NYSE a side market was held on the Coal Hole in William Street, for more dodgy transactions, where all sort of people were trading in gold. The frantic behaviour of the NYSE gold traders infuriated Abraham Lincoln who "wish every one of them had his devilish head shot off." The infamous Jay Gould who later masterminded the cornering of the gold market was named one of those chiefly responsible for the 1873 recession in the United States, and became one of the most hated businessmen in America. Conversely, speculation on the CBOT pits on wheat coincided with Midwest farmers claiming that market manipulation was responsible for price instability, overall declining farm income and dire consequences for their livelihoods. The response was that, following the end of the Civil War, there was simply too much supply of wheat for price manipulation, and market conditions were such that prices were indeed unstable. This provided a fertile ground for the development of conspiracy theories and an abundant number of pamphlets[16] on the manipulation of American agriculture by Wall Street bankers.

Exceptional outbursts of collective speculative fever are of interest in the study of financial centres due to moral collapse, deception and the fluctuations in fortunes that they induced. Max Weber took aim at the

---

[16] Such as the "Seven financial conspiracies that have enslaved the American people" by Sarah E.V. Emery (1887), "the people are awakening but the money power is on guard, they have entrenched themselves at every available point" (excerpt from the conclusion).

bucket shop customers, these small market speculators "armed with practically nothing beyond good lungs, a little notebook and a pencil" whom he describes as unsuited for stock trading since they lack both the capital to survive and a robust knowledge of the market. At the other end of the spectrum lie the contemporary hyper sophisticated hedge funds, capable of crunching a phenomenal amount of economic data before taking educated, but still risky, bets on market moving information. Under the limelight of the much publicised standard of living of some happy few participants, finance is then transformed into a spectacular form of popular entertainment, where the frontier between professional speculations, in the sense of risk taking, and games of chance is blurred. Spectacular speculation has always created through hysteria and euphoria, the ideal conditions for finance to be perceived as one of the strongest stimuli for the pleasure of feverish imagination and greed. This remains a dangerous stage in the development of IFC as it undermines the credibility of their markets and challenges the legitimacy of the market economy. Walter Bagehot, editor of the Economist between 1860 and 1877, argued that the most destructive financial panics occurred when the "blind capital" of the public flooded into unwise speculative investments. Concentrating efforts on strengthening corporate reporting discipline, prosecuting cases of fraud and the dissemination of misleading information has always been a good starting point to keep the market healthy.

OFCs Revisited

Other prominent and quiet guests to the global financial centre party belong to the comprehensive OFCs' family, also called "specialised financial centres" due to their tradition of confidentiality and low tax rate designed to attract capital from non-residents borrowers and depositors or foreign-owned legal entities. Some are also known as tax havens — as opposed to tax hells. OFCs developed as businesses became multinational but fragmented with income coming from a variety of jurisdictional sources around the world. The maintenance of historic and distortionary regulations in the financial sectors of industrial countries during the 1960s and 1970s was a major contributing factor to the success of offshore banking and the development of OFCs. In this context, leading OFCs managed to offer tax-neutral or low-tax jurisdictions, together with trust and financial expertise as additional advantages. Every Fortune 500 company, most Fortune 1000 companies, and thousands of other enterprises including family firms and trusts have taken advantage of the facilities offered by small islands and purpose-made IFCs around the world. In 2006, the IMF started an assessment programme with a view to enhancing its understanding of 46 jurisdictions, which, according to its initial evaluation were considered to be acting as OFCs. Only 16 of the presumed OFCs submitted information, and five declined and explained that they would not report any information, as they already reported to the BIS or contributed to other compilation initiatives (FSI). A better understanding is needed of the nearly 50 identified OFCs worldwide, which are mostly in Europe and the Caribbean.

Although information it is still limited, there is strong evidence that OFCs have captured a significant amount of global financial flows and function both as partners and back doors to leading financial centres especially since the 70s. In a sample of G7 countries, OFCs banking assets showed a wide dispersion ranging from just above USD 100 million to over USD 1 trillion compared with banking assets close to USD 10 trillion. The USD 1 trillion league include countries such as Ireland and Switzerland, with Singapore being most likely somewhere in between. A similar analysis of the OFC insurance industry shows that gross insurance premiums range from about USD 10 million to USD 100 billion. However, based on the data available, most of the markets' aggregate gross premiums are either below or about USD 1 billion. Apart from Bermuda[17] which has quietly and remarkably established itself as one of the world's largest insurance and re-insurance services hubs in 1947, OFCs vary significantly in their development and in the range of products offered. Bermuda continues to be a centre for innovation in the insurance market and has developed a sophisticated services and business infrastructure where many of the world's leading underwriters live and work. This is far from the simplistic vision of paper entities with no physical or actual presence in offshore jurisdictions. This place has long been

---

[17]Behind New York and ahead of London in re-insurance.

recognised as the domicile of choice for the world's captive[18] insurance industry and other sophisticated insurance products.

OFCs differ from Regional Financial Centres, in that they developed financial markets infrastructure and intermediate funds at an international level, but have relatively small domestic "real" economies and limited resources to support their banking intermediation services. Since the failure of BCCI and Meridian Bank, it is difficult for a bank incorporated in a jurisdiction with limited domestic markets to carry on business in major economies. Regional feeders for global financial centres include Luxembourg and Panama; they usually have strong expertise, a significant economic base and recognised world class specialties. Their specialist role, alongside major centres, has been in existence since the development of the medieval financial centres. What makes their definition slightly complicated is that offshore centres come in different flavours: (i) primary centres, usually regional finance centres since they have not yet become IFCs, (ii) booking centres, channelling outside funds to the global financial system with a limited infrastructure (e.g. Bahamas), (iii) funding centres, channelling outside funds into a precise area (e.g. Panama), (iv) collection centres, aggregating funds for investment abroad (e.g. Bahrain) and finally (v) host centres, a magnet for international banking activity with some OFCs gathering several of these features. Offshore means in any case that these financial jurisdictions have developed a specific edge compared to conventional financial, which gives them a specific competitive advantage: The more obvious is the tax effective provision of financial services to non-residents and the less acceptable is wide eligibility — which opens the door to money laundering. This shows that the OFC is a generic term for a broad family of constituents. The result is that they deliver these services at a scale incommensurate with the size of their economy.

The term "offshore" does not only mean an island somewhere in the Caribbean, the Pacific or the English Channel. A number of jurisdictions

---

[18]A captive insurance company is a 'do-it-yourself insurance company', which insures the risks and exposures of its parents and affiliates. It started in the United States in 1955 and developed in Bermuda in the 1960s. Traditionally, captives were established to provide customised solutions to risk financing needs which were not available in the commercial insurance markets.

are firmly anchored in a mainland location, but for some purposes, fall within the scope of offshore jurisdictions. In Canada, for example, the province of British Columbia, has established itself as a captive domicile giving special regulatory treatment to offshore companies; in the United States of America, the states of Delaware, Vermont and Nevada offer similar derogatory regimes and in Europe, Luxembourg and Dublin, are clearly physically onshore, but they have legislative facilities, which treat certain transactions differently from other major industrial jurisdictions. But for some reasons, "offshore" still carries a perception of dubious or nefarious activities. There are reputable OFCs that actively aspire to and apply best internationally accepted practices, and there are some legitimate uses of OFCs including providing a positive competitive stimulus for their neighbours' financial sectors, and for this very reason their symbiotic presence with leading hubs resulted in them been called symbionts.[19] Notwithstanding the contradictory perceptions of offshore jurisdictions, they are major players and a key element in international finance. OFCs that have successfully attracted non-resident financial activity usually offer some clear advantage, such as lower tax rates, less onerous regulatory burdens, special facilities for company incorporation, or highly protective secrecy laws for those who participate in international capital markets. Some claim the title of having the most secretive and tax efficient jurisdictions and have rankings of their own starting with the OECD's Committee on Fiscal Affairs' list of uncooperative tax havens. The OECD 1998 report identified four distinctive features to help define uncooperative tax havens: (i) no or low effective tax rates, (ii) ring fencing of regimes (when tax regimes are fully insulated from the domestic economy to protect them), (iii) lack of transparency of the origin of the funds and (iv) lack of effective exchange of information. This methodology produced a list of 47 potentially harmful regimes in 20 OECD countries. The outcome of the reviews of these regimes was reported in 2004, which concluded that regimes had either been abolished in the meantime or were not harmful. No jurisdiction is currently listed on the OECD's uncooperative tax haven list any more, even if some still continue to struggle with reputation and regulation. This shows that the majority of OFCs have been

---

[19]A term coined by Rose and Spiegel (2005), cf bibliography.

working seriously to raise standards in order to improve their trustworthiness and market image. Problematic OFCs allow some financial market participants to engage chiefly in regulatory arbitrage and clearly constitute weak links in the supervision of an increasingly integrated financial system.

Another term cannot be dissociated from OFCs: Special Purpose Vehicles (SPVs) have been at the very centre of the financial magic for decades. SPVs smell like the proverbial "skunk works" in finance terms. They are legal structures based on confidentiality and designed to capture a higher return on investments, in exchange for services fees paid to the host jurisdiction. SPVs are used for different purposes including as asset holding vehicles, to park and isolate valuable or toxic assets; as collective investment and derivatives trading vehicles, to take advantage of tax incentives or to undertake risky investments which are difficult to implement under onshore regulation; as asset protection schemes, to circumvent inheritance taxes or potential expropriation; to levy financing (bond issuing and syndicated loans) while keeping the liabilities "off balance sheet"; and as trade vehicles, to keep export receipts offshore.[20] OFCs are a domicile of choice for the incorporation of any special purpose vehicle for insurance derivative transactions, also referred to as alternative risk transfers (ARTs). ARTs work to transfer risks to the capital markets in the form of cat bonds and other securitisations, derivatives, swaps and in some ways, finite insurance. Shell companies, trusts and SPVs, banks, security dealers, mutual funds, hedge funds, insurance companies, pension funds and nonfinancial corporations, also frequently perform custody functions. Assets are booked offshore, while in most cases the management is located elsewhere, often onshore. All these categories, which represent the major part of offshore business, engender a change in the domicile of assets and may be used as a way to evade the radar screens of both auditors and regulators.

In addition to declared OFCs, established financial centres must compete with a burgeoning number of self-declared IFC, in particular, those designated as special economic zones, or free zones capable of leveraging

---

[20] IMF Working Paper Monetary and Capital Markets Department Concept of Offshore Financial Centers: In Search of an Operational Definition Prepared by Ahmed Zoromé, April (2007).

tax and regulatory advantages, in order to incentivise business activity, especially as it relates to the financial sector. The history of financial free zones, in their early days is associated with the Roman empire, when the island of Delos, a small island of the Cyclades Archipelago in the Mediterranean, was returned to Athens in 167 A.D. Trade on this island was free of taxes and free of customs duties. The place quickly became a very successful transit haven for slaves, ivory, silk, wine and spices. The island was repopulated by Athenians and foreigners after its original inhabitants were expelled by a decision of the Roman senate. After the 8th century, the Republic of St. Peter was an autonomous region within the Carolingian empire, which lasted over 1000 years: it is often earmarked as the first offshore centre. The popes became rulers over one of the oldest continuously functioning states of Europe, the Papal States, with a population of 1.7 million stretching from Rome and its environs north-eastward to the Adriatic Sea, including a number of scattered territories. The most populous cities were Rome and Bologna; among those of middling rank were Orvieto, Spoleto, Perugia, Ancona and Ravenna. The principal ports of Civitavecchia on the Tyrrhenian and Ancona, Rimini and Pesaro on the Adriatic coast, were convenient low tax haven. The idea of fiscal competition was also deeply rooted in the mindset of the Hanseatic League members, an economic bund of 50 cities at its height. In Champagne (France) in medieval times, fair taxes were considered a substantial incentive for merchants participating in the fairs. The first free tax fair, "Foire du Lendit"[21] in Saint-Denis near Paris which started on the second Wednesday of June and went on until 24 June, the feast of St. John the Baptist, can be traced back to the rule of King Dagobert of France in the 7th century. In the North of Europe, the Channel Islands developed as a privileged tax haven from the English invasion expedition of William the Conqueror (1066). In contemporary terms, OFCs and Eurocurrency centres are a response of international banks to government policies in many advanced

---

[21] The Lendit is a Christian day, meaning « announced », derived from the Latin *indictum* or *indicere*. The day relates to the opening of the holy relics in St. Denis on 9 June 1053, which coincided with the display of relics of the Passion of Christ (one nail and part of the Crown of Thorns). Exceptional spiritual graces were granted to those visiting St. Denis Cathedral on this very day.

countries in the 1960s and the 1970s to control capital flows through restrictive regulations. The shift of financial activities to Eurocurrencies accelerated after 1966, when the U.S. money market rates rose above the interest rate ceilings on dollar deposits allowed by Regulation Q. The resulting credit crunch forced U.S. banks to seek funds in the Eurodollar market whose growth was spectacular, from USD 18 billion at the end of 1966 to USD 310 billion ten years later (1977).

OFCs range from those with regulatory standards and infrastructure similar to those of the major IFCs, such as Hong Kong and Singapore, to those where supervision is non-existent. Cayman, Anglo-Norman Islands and the Bahamas have retained a strong lead in specialised financial services. A more practical definition of an OFC is a centre where the bulk of financial sector activity is offshore on both sides of the balance sheet, where the transactions are initiated elsewhere and where the majority of the institutions involved are controlled by non-residents. They span from respectable well-developed financial markets and infrastructure, where a considerable amount of value is added to transactions undertaken for non-residents, to centres with smaller populations, such as some of the Caribbean centres, where value added is usually limited to the provision of professional infrastructure. In some micro-financial centres, where the financial institutions have little or no physical presence, the value added may be limited to the booking of the transaction. In addition to banking activities, other services provided by offshore centres include fund management, wealth management, special purpose vehicles sheltering, insurance, trust business, tax evasion, IBC[22] activity,[23] tax evasion and when things go really wrong, criminal money laundering. The maintenance of historic and distortionary regulations in the financial sectors of industrial countries, and the need to manage windfall opportunities during the 1960s and 1970s were major contributing factors to the development of that last category of OFCs. In Europe, their development coincides with high inflation and the central banks' imposition of reserve requirements, interest rate ceilings, restrictions on the range of financial products that supervised

---

[22]International Business Corporations (IBCs) are limited liability vehicles registered in an OFC. They may be used to own and operate businesses, issue shares or bonds, or raise capital in other ways.

[23]IMF, OFCs, background paper, Monetary and exchange affairs department, 23 June 2000.

institutions could offer, capital controls, and high effective taxation in many OECD countries. In the Middle East, Bahrain for example began to serve as a collection centre for the region's oil surpluses during the mid 1970s, after passing banking laws and providing tax incentives to facilitate the incorporation of offshore banks.

Panama, which was used since the 16th century as a strategic transit centre for the Peruvian gold by Spanish merchants, is also a vivid example of the connection between a strategic sea path and a leading financial centre. Panama City fell under the U.S. protection in the 18th century following the collapse of precious metal prices which sent its economy into chaos. In the context of the mid-19th gold rush in California, the Panama Rail Road Company, connecting the Atlantic to the Pacific Ocean was a leading stock on Wall Street. The economy which owes the majority of its revenues to the Canal and related infrastructure was fully dollarised, thanks to a treaty signed between Panama and the U.S. in 1904. The territory which had always been a specific administrative zone for international trade, gradually shifted to OFC status in the 1970s working in synergy with Wall Street's time zone. The ousting in December 1989 of General Noriega, who was fostering the development of a narco-state, managed to refocus the local economy on its core assets. Over the past decade, Panama has been one of the fastest growing economies worldwide. Average annual growth was 7.2% between 2001 and 2013 and growth is estimated to be 6.2% in 2015.[24] Panama's economy continues to grow strongly, buoyed by the Panama Canal's expansion and large public infrastructure projects. In 2016, an additional new Canal lane will open to accommodate ships that are 250% larger than the maximum sized ship that can cross using today's Panama Canal. These new ships will be able to carry 12,500 containers whereas the current canal can only accept ships carrying 5,000 containers. It will result in significant enhanced revenues for the city state. Panama, which is reminiscent of European and Asian City States, and which is now home to 3.6 million people, has developed a sound,[25] stable and growing banking hub, the largest in Central American

---

[24] World Bank, Country overview, updated 18 August 2015.

[25] The Mossack Fonseca Panama Law firm at the center of a massive leak of offshore financial data in April 2016 has shed a crude light on the shadowy financial arrangements related to offshore companies.

region, and possibly the leading one in South America, with consolidated assets over three times Panama's GDP.[26]

Altogether, the British Crown dependencies and overseas territories, keep a strong leadership in the tracks of their parent, London. In the past, the growth of London itself as the largest offshore banking centre can be directly connected with regulations imposed on the U.S. banking sector: capital controls implemented through the Interest Equalisation Tax of 1964, the Foreign Credit and Exchange Act of 1965, cash reserve requirements on deposits imposed in 1977 and a ceiling on time deposits in 1979. By establishing foreign branches to which these regulations did not apply, U.S. banks run their business in a more cost effective way. While OFCs are usually perceived to be small paradise island states, the cases of London, Tokyo (e.g. Japanese Offshore Market, JOM) or certain U.S. states such as Delaware or Nevada highlight that even advanced countries have succeeded in attracting very large concentrations of non-resident business by offering competitive economic incentives either throughout their jurisdiction or in special economic zones (e.g. flags of convenience).

Offshore shell banks and booking offices have been a matter of concern for regulators and the tracking of illegal financial operations. A shell bank maintains just a registered agent in its country of incorporation, with the agent having little or no knowledge of the day-to-day operations of the bank, and simply providing an address for legal service in the jurisdiction. Such shell banks have been frequently involved in illegal or suspicious financial activities. The term "booking branch" refers to the branch of a foreign bank which has no meaningful mind and management in the jurisdiction in which it is licensed. Often, such branches are nothing more than "brass plates", with simple administrative services being supplied by a local housing agent who may provide "caretaking" services to a number of banks. The real management of the branch may be located in an office in the home jurisdiction of the head office or in an office located in a third jurisdiction, which may or may not be an office subject to supervision.

---

[26] IMF, Panama: Assessment of Financial Sector Supervision and Regulation. 15 February 2007.

The key distinction between booking branches and shell banks is that the former are part of an existing bank that is regulated by a home country supervisor. The benefit of establishing booking branches is to allow a bank to conduct certain types of non-resident business in a foreign jurisdiction without the expense of establishing a full foreign branch. Many banks operating in the USA maintain booking branches, mainly in the Bahamas and Cayman Islands, which lie in the same time zone. It is understood that their reason for doing so is to provide so-called "sweep accounts" to corporate customers. Sweep accounts are used because, under U.S. law, banks are not permitted to pay interest on U.S.-based commercial checking accounts. In order to be able to do so to their corporate customers, available customer funds are wired at the end of every business day from their U.S. account to an offshore booking branch account. The funds stay in the booking branch account overnight, and they are moved back to a U.S. account the next day. Such business is almost pure offshore banking involving no local operations in the branch, thus emphasizing the somewhat artificial existence of such institution. In some cases, international banks have also established "booking subsidiaries". Such operations are used mainly for private banking or fiduciary relationships. The purpose of incorporating a subsidiary is to segregate the risk of the locally incorporated entity from that of the parent institution. It is rather unhealthy from a risk management standpoint if they are permitted to be managed from a jurisdiction other than the home or host, as there are increased operational and legal risks.

For centuries, finance specialists have exploited legal loopholes to obtain fiscal competitive advantages that enable them to make greater profits than their rivals. Gaming the system was too often considered acceptable even sometimes necessary due to the increasing shareholder's value creation constraint, but sheltering serious criminal activities,[27] which had always been a tempting alternative due to potential high profits, jeopardises economic stability as a whole. The appropriate qualification is somewhat subtle and the line may be thin. One of the key attributes of the best

---

[27]Defined by the BIS (1996) as terrorism, theft, kidnapping, drug-trafficking, extortion, money-laundering or fraud.

financial hubs is precisely to define limitations to what is acceptable and make sure the rules are enforced; inevitably borders will be tested. Ultimately, it depends on the magnitude of the problem created by those who will try to game the system. Perhaps the most notorious case of tax evasion and fraud via offshore subsidiaries involved the Enron Company which for decades devised ways and means of diverting funds to branches abroad simply to avoid paying tax. It is usually bad news when a string of problems align and quietly develop in a loophole of the regulatory system. In the banking crises in Venezuela (1994) and Argentina (1995), the failure of parent banks to oversee effectively the activities of offshore establishments exacerbated the weaknesses of the domestic financial sector in the wake of external shocks. Even if OFCs cannot be considered responsible for major crises, concerns about offshore centres have intensified in the context of initiatives undertaken by the international community to strengthen financial systems, in response to systemic financial crises.

Trustworthiness from the Early Days of Finance to the 21st Century

Finance is certainly the most talented, but turbulent, daughter of economics, which itself proceeded from philosophy. This is not an innocuous parenthood as this led economists to go beyond the comfortable belief that human psychology remains fundamentally the same at all times and in all places; and that the present is determined by the past according to invariant laws. Moving forward the evolution stays not only with economic knowledge itself but more importantly with the methodology used to absorb information on the outside world, the latter being slower than the economic "mining process" itself. Finance today has not only associated itself with mathematics but also with neurosciences and computer sciences, and remains a young science. Coincidently, the concept of childhood, and its associated maturation process, only emerged in European culture in the 15th century, in the High Middle Ages as the commercial revolution was spreading in Europe. Philosophers hardly even considered finance as an illegitimate offspring as philosophy reluctantly reflected upon the purpose of mercantile relationships. There is no doubt that it would certainly be beneficial if they ventured more often into this field and regard openly the consequences of "maternal deprivation" as a risk to the child's development. Parents approach the task in many ways, and they value and consider their children very differently in different cultures. However, children left to themselves have only show limited capacity to develop to their full potential.

Interestingly, philosophy is a meditation on what knowledge is available, but it is also a critique of illusions, of prejudices and ideologies.[28] In this respect, economists do have a duty to keep thinking about the purpose of their science beyond the noise of existing theories and the sophistication of scientific instrumentation, and this is by the way, what great economists are doing. The knowledge which is relevant to an economy is dispersed in "bits of incomplete and frequently contradictory knowledge which all the separate individuals possess"[29] and can hardly be centralised in mathematical models only. A sound economy needs a fully functional, transparent and probably bustling financial system. There is no doubt that large swings in asset markets are detrimental to the stability of the real economy — possibly in a systemic way. This has been demonstrated, for example, when the credit market gets contaminated to the point that liquidity is affected. This is not be confused with innovative "Schumpeterian" bubbles which are absolutely needed to rejuvenate the system, as growth is a function of experimental entrepreneurial unstability. This means that equity market bubbles, limited in time, are likely a "brownian creative unstability", part of the economy development process. As such they may not be as harmful as generally considered: a swing in asset value is locally a painful reset in the price discovery process but a rational adjustment of unsymmetrical anticipations, with globally little impact over the long run on the real economy. A typical example is the 1630s Tulip mania. Systemic crashes are different in the sense that they may result from the long term self-feeding of a series of adjacent bubbles, for exemple on a key class of "household supporting" assets and credit with widespread diffusion in the economy, typically real estate. The resulting adjustment crash so broad and deep that it can impair the needed trustworthiness in the normal

---

[28] André Comte-Sponville, *The Little Book of Philosophy*, Vintage books, London, (2011).
[29] Friedrich August von Hayek, The use of knowledge in society, *The American Economic Review*, 35 (1945).

functioning of almost all the compartments of the financial system, and in particular credit and liquidity. The magnitude and depth of the 2008–2009 crisis demonstrated that deep swings of that type could be momentarily worse than anticipated, with 93 countries recording decline in their GDP. Meanwhile, the stock of worldwide traded financial assets has expanded from USD 7 trillion (71% of world GDP) to USD 163 trillion (226% of world GDP) between 1980 and 2012, and may increase to possibly USD 400 trillion by 2050. One implication of the rising importance of capital markets is that wealth and financial accelerator effects may be amplified, fuelled in part by institutional innovations that make it easier to monetise asset price gains through increased consumption and borrowing.[30]

Many still argue that from a rational point of view only money talks — especially at bonus time. Already in 1705, Mandeville's[31] recounted this Fable of the Bees — or Private Vices, the decadence of a swarm of bees. Having been a thriving community based on deceit and vice, the bees condemned their own behaviour and became honest and virtuous. Their society then collapsed and died. His thesis was that individual vices can indeed generate public benefit, and a moral illustration of the invisible hand. Mandeville provides a plausible explanation to what may have inspired Jeffrey Skilling, President of Enron, which was bankrupted in 2001 because of the biggest case of accounting fraud in history at that time, to say shortly before its downfall: "We are doing something special. Magical. It isn't a job — it is a mission. We are changing the world. We are doing God's work." Cheating becomes "Magic" or "a mission," stealing becomes "pinching" and "freeloading." By labelling things differently, the perception of the environment is reset and adjusted, the whole thing may even become a "game"[32]. Once the ethical sting is taken out and neutralised, things become acceptable, normal or even desirable, if organised in a way to establish ones status. Fraudulent practices do prosper

---

[30] See IMF, Asset Bubbles, Brad Jones, working paper in reference.

[31] Bernard Mandeville (1670–1733) was born in Holland in a family of physicians and naval officers. He received his degree of Doctor of Medicine and wrote several political economics works.

[32] It has been extensively described as such in Liar's Poker, a best-selling semi-autobiographical book by Michael Lewis describing the author's experiences as a bond salesman on Wall Street during the late 1980s.

behind decriminalising terms such as "earnings management", "income optimization," "pragmatic arbitration" or "creative accounting." A similar dialectic helps to minimise consequences afterwards nurturing a widespread culture of irresponsibility. Quietly, under the radar of regulators, this is also how lending and the financial services start mutating to set themselves free from supervision.

The latest avatar in 2008–2009 in a long string of financial crisis has hopefully strengthened this seemingly obvious perception that the complex machinery of financial markets must be built on something bigger than a collection of rogue individual interests, especially since systemic risk, not to be confused with episodical market crash, can trigger disasters of the magnitude of those of the 14th century and the Great Depression. The latest 2008–2009 crisis has exposed the human factor in the inner workings of organisations as never before: "Part of the reason this crisis occurred is that everyone was living beyond their means — from Wall Street to Washington to even some on Main Street. CEOs got greedy. Politicians spent money they didn't have. Lenders tricked people into buying homes they couldn't afford and some folks knew they couldn't afford them and bought them anyway."[33] Aside from greed and hubris, the failure to account for human weakness was relevant to this crisis. We still do not understand from an economic perspective why human beings get caught up in self-reinforcing expectations of rising prices. In the context of investment managers being compensated over the short term on the upside, and not penalised on the downside, and on volumes — as part of the fee structure is related to the amount of funds under management, it seems fully rational for them to run bubbles, especially since participants get their fees upfront with little or no due diligences. Furthermore, the risk of not riding the bubble is far greater both for their individual total compensation and their risk of being early terminated. This is in itself a game theory dilemma, but unfortunately with a seemingly punitive payback for those who may choose to withdraw too early from the game. This is as long as there is no individual incentive to keep "honest" and contribute pricking a bubble, meaning to go against the market unless you are an edge fund. The capacity to prick a bubble over the long run, may prevent

---

[33] United States' President, Barack Obama's speech on the economy, October (2008).

a heated market situation from degenerating into a bubble whilst the desire to immediately prick a bubble may result in a market crash. The crisis that followed the subprime Great Recession is, among other things, a crisis of trustworthiness which is extended by a doubt on the real value of banks' balance sheets. In 2011, the Edelman Trust Barometer reported that trust in banks had declined tremendously over the last three years, while at the same time trust in other industries and government has not undergone significant change. Banks, the study concludes, had become "the most distrusted global industry." This is not new and it explains numerous attempts to gradually close the gap, first on specific financial functions such as payment, and develop peer-to-peer payment systems based on cryptographic proof instead of trust — such as bitcoin, allowing any two willing parties to transact directly with each other without the need for a trusted third party.

John Maynard Keynes, who had a keen interest in psychology and psychiatry, observed in his 1936 work "The General Theory of Employment, Interest and Money" nearly 80 years ago that economic decisions were due more to "animal spirits" than carefully weighed probabilities, and that financial markets operated more like beauty contests than efficient price-discovery platforms. The matter was even temptatively explored earlier by Adam Smith who unfortunately lacked the conceptual tools to push this intuition further into the economic field. It seemed logical that a better understanding of the brain must lead to a better understanding of how humans get educated and make decisions both individually and collectively in financial markets. However, as interesting as scientific advances were made to the brain's function, they made very little impact on the field of economics. The brain is not only complicated to map and understand, but it is also extremely difficult to examine while functioning. Research in neuroscience uncovered, for example, that patients treated with L-DOPA, a chemical which would be converted to dopamine in the brain, often became addicted to gambling, an interesting conclusion for better understanding financial markets. This was one of the very first clues that dopamine was involved in the brain's reward system, which is key to better understanding greed. Other researchers discovered that addictive drugs such as cocaine and methamphetamine also flooded the brain with dopamine through the mesolimbic pathway, releasing it into the nucleus accumbens. It was best known as a precursor to adrenaline until the Swedish researcher Arvid Carlsson showed in 1957 that it was in fact a neurotransmitter, a discovery for which he was awarded the Nobel Prize for Medicine in 2000. Carlsson gave reserpine, a drug known to deplete neurotransmitters, to rabbits, which then fell into a catatonic state. By injecting the rabbits with L-DOPA, a chemical which would be converted to dopamine in the brain, Carlsson was able to awaken them. The neurologist Oliver Sacks (1974) then started to treat patients suffering from sleeping sickness with L-DOPA. One peculiarity of patients treated was that they often developed afterwards an addiction to gambling. This was one of the first clues that dopamine was involved in the brain's reward system. As far as finance was concerned, this highlighted that an imbalance in an individual's dopamine system can easily lead to greater risk-taking. If risk-taking activities are, on average, associated with financial gain, a potentially destructive positive-feedback loop can easily emerge from a period of monetary gains. Conversely, the aversion to sure loss, which triggers fraudulent gambling to evade losses, is a potential risk that lies deep in the heart of every major financial institution. The case materialises when a trader loses more than he expected, but rather than owning up to the loss and moving on, he chooses to hide it and increases his bet, hoping to make it up on the next trade, after which all might be forgiven. Of course, this rarely happens, and the "doubling down" process continues, usually until the losses become so large as to be impossible to recover. It is usually known as the rogue trader syndrome, but expands beyond this limited definition to investors and even regulators into game theory frameworks, especially when gambling becomes the culture of a whole financial institution or a whole market. In such situations, gamblers tend to synchronise culture, and the virus spreads to the point where moral blindness aligns with regulatory loopholes, making increasingly bigger bets unstoppable, inflating into a bubble until the crisis emerges.

The English philosopher Thomas Hobbes (1588–1679), considered that people are wolves for each other, "*homo omini lupus (est)*"[34]: the

---

[34] «man is a wolve for others» published in Hobbes' Latin work De Cive, "On the citizen", in 1642, but extracted from Asinaria, a comic play, translated as the One with the Asses, written by Plautus in 495.

bestial nature of man means that we are purely focused on our own interest while French philosopher Jean-Jacques Rousseau (1712–1778) considered that people have a preference for good: "Man is by nature good
and happy; it is society which destroys original happiness." According to
Rousseau, it is the corrupting influence of society, which incites man to
do wrong and therefore makes him unhappy. Moral cognitive neurosciences provides additional insight into the deliberation, affect and emo-
tion leading to the human decision making process. We now know for
certain that our cognitive system must work through the affective system:
options and consequences defined by our cognitive system are weighted
by our affective system, and to further complicate the matter our brains
work in a different mode according to what is at stake. A more sophisticated view of the role of emotions in human cognition is that they are
central to rationality. This research seriously mitigates the original classical Cartesian view of decision-making as a purely rational, emotion-free
process. A critical reason why massive financial market failure has proven
so difficult to resolve is the associated collapse of trust as a foundation
for economic action and as a means of mediating risk: Moral sanctions
hardly work in the perspective of fat corporate bonuses and pay checks.
The degree of competitiveness of financial markets and the much publicised rewards that accrue to the "fittest" traders suggest that Darwinian
selection is profiling successful investors. The result is that we now live in
this so-called "new normal" environment, in which tail risks not only happen more frequently than before but may also happen in many layers of
the financial world at the same time.

The understanding of economic mechanisms has made huge progress
since Venice established itself as the world leading finance hub in the High
Middle Ages, but the cause of financial problems have remained remarkably similar. In spite of centuries of experience, the ability to evade rules
has always been faster than the capacity to effectively regulate markets,
when good practices were not shared as the *modus operandi* between participants. Very few economic analyses of ethics have had mainly macroeconomic implications, and this reflects the harmful century-long separation
between two sides of economics: the quantitative side and the ethical heritage. This needs not be the case. Recognising economics as a unified
whole, where macroeconomic elements are firmly rooted in their microeconomic foundations still represent a challenge. The term responsible

economics was coined as a legacy of philosopher and economist E.F. Schumacher's (1911–1977) utopian paradigm, but remains largely in the most obscure sphere of economics, specifically when it comes to finance. The highly abstract nature of social relationships involving money in its various forms makes these relationships remarkably difficult to understand and the corresponding theoretical treatment of them particularly complex.[35] In 1265 in Florence, the popular encyclopaedist Brunetto Latini already declared "Money wants you to be its slave," and followed with this advice "Therefore, if you really wish to be free, diminish your covetousness." Later humanists would go even further, claiming that as poverty is the basis of virtue, then it must have been the ultimate source of the ancient Roman Imperium. Some healthy house rules are needed and they must be enforced by the best leaders in the interest of the common good, keeping in mind that some sort of self-interest always plays a role,[36] even when we help others — and there is nothing wrong about it. Finance people support trustworthiness not only because they think this is a just and moral cause, but also because of the glow they get from the idea of being trusted, and for some because they realise that ultimately the market can only build on trust. This is the expression of a preference that the works of economist Gary Becker can explain. But as a few hundred years of banking history has shown, trustworthiness comes first as the foundation of any longstanding financial hub. Trust may not be always so immediately valuable as it can be easily misplaced. It is indeed striking that in the long history of the emancipation of finance as an autonomous discipline, stern advice had been provided on what should be the foundation of the common good and social responsibility. The risk that both economist and finance people otherwise take is so great, that some tectonic forces could lead to a significant portion of their art becoming outdated and useless.

Ancient Chinese writings, from Guan Zhong, Shan Mo Gong, Fang Li or Ji Ran, showed that economics was in itself a specific matter of interest as early as the 7th century A.D., especially from a political perspective to induce proper policy. Guan Zhong was a strategist and a politician before becoming the prime minister of the house of Qi. Guan advocated that the

---

[35] Jesus Huerta de Soto, Bank, *Credit and Economic Cycle*, p. xxii, Ludwig von Mises Institute (2002).
[36] Such as being in peace with one's conscience.

ruler should care for the economic prosperity of all social classes and ensure that the people were willing to serve the ruler. Guan Zhong believed that the four pillars of a state were decency, justice, integrity, and conscience. The ruler should live according to these principles and be an exemplar of virtue. Guan Zhong[37] also believed that the people's welfare was the foundation of a state. Well-fed people would be easily educated with decency and etiquette, and be more amenable to being regulated by rulers.

In the West, Aristotle (384–322 A.D.), is recognised as the first economist although the preceptor of Alexander the Great was a reluctant supporter of this new discipline. His economic ideas are developed in "Politics", "Nicomachean Ethics", "Rhetoric", "Economics" and "Rhetoric to Alexander". His work on money was the backbone of medieval thinking about commerce even if his economic thought, especially his value theory, is insightful but occasionally contradictory and inconsistent. Aristotle failed to fully appreciate that both financial markets and money-making activities could provide a mechanism through which order in society could be produced through economic agents pursuing their own ends. The most problematic Aristotelian legacy is that ethics and economics are supposed to be competitors over the same ground, as rival source of reasons for decision-making in the public realm, and as such cannot be reconciled. He believed that the individual human action of using wealth is what constitutes the economic dimension. One of the great economic policy questions has been to properly define wealth and then how it separates from greed, not only at a microeconomic level but more importantly in a sociological context. Aristotle who was Plato's prized student was certainly correct from a philosophical point of view but failed to detach himself from the idea that economy was something other than a gathering of people who had lived, chained in a cave all of their lives, facing a blank wall. In the 14th century, the chasing of Lombard bankers in the streets of Paris and the looting of their mansions after the Jews had been expelled from the French Kingdom shows that this philosophical dimension has to be taken seriously. The purpose of economic action is to use things that

---

[37] Guan Zhong is credited as the author of *Guan Zi* (管子), one the earliest known book that covers politics, economy and philosophy.

are necessary for life (i.e. to keep alive) and for the "good life" (i.e. flourishing). The "good life" is the moral life of virtue through which humans attain happiness. Aristotle taught that economics is concerned with both the household and the *polis* and that economics deals with the use of things required for the good (or virtuous) life. As a pragmatic or practical science, economics is aimed at the good and remains fundamentally moral. Though wealth must constitute not only the strength but also the ambition of a City State it must also be accompanied by virtue. And it is only the joining of wealth and virtue which gives to economics the character of a moral science. It is probably fair to say that after deviating from this dual path under the influence of David Ricado, economics, and its offspring financial economics, elected to be almost exclusively associated with wealth, technical innovation and probabilities.

Aspiring financial centres are doing their best to build respect, inspire confidence and exalt freedom in the marathon to become eligible for an international role, but beware of those who come in sheep's clothing but inwardly are ravenous wolves. Allurement, muscle or sworn oaths have never been sufficient factors to inspire trust. Professionals have a wide range of venues for checking on each other's word and veracity. This means relying on a consistent and predictable regulatory environment, with a single point-of-contact, that preserves high ethical standards, affects all markets, both primary and secondary, and participants, both current and potential. Regulatory clarity, even for complex matters, and enhanced predictability also helps participants enter the "game" on the right foot and manage regulatory risk more effectively through proper training and monitoring of their staff. Enforcement has a strong value of exemplarity and should be promptly and fairly taken if there is a material impact on either the specific institution or the financial system in general. The open sharing of information based on a notarised electronic platform between regulated entities and regulators certainly fosters a regulatory environment emphasising collaborative rulemaking and enforcement rather than retributive punishment. Doing so would also alleviate the probability that problems posing a significant systemic risk could proliferate in the shadow, unnoticed and unchecked due to a failure to share critical information between market participants and the regulator. There is no doubt that such a candid recommendation may lead the most impatient participants to smile or shrug, but endurance comes with a price and those who have been cutting corners on safety nets have always paid the price. The 2008–2009 crisis has shown that sticking to sound principles and discipline is a lifeline to recovery and growth. Those who greedily believed that finance is a casino, forgot that ultimately the house is merciless and wins by design.

"History never repeats itself" observed Voltaire, "Man always does". Untrustable business models thrive in finance largely because being untrustworthy makes the implicit promise of being extremely profitable, at least in the short term, and our individual life is short, and many businesses are managed almost entirely for short-term results and on bonus time. Furthermore, when the expected benefit of an unethical or even fraudulent transaction far exceeds the expected penalty, one does not need to be a games theory specialist to predict the outcome since economics is divorced from ethics. Under David Ricardo's recommendation; "it is not the province of the Political Economist to advise: He is to tell you how to become rich". In his Instrucción de mercaderes (Instruction to merchants) published in Medina del Campo in 1544 Luis Saravia de la Calle criticised bankers harshly, calling them "voracious gluttons who swallow everything, destroy everything, confuse everything, steal and soil everything, like the harpies of Phineus." Fortunately marketing people have helped economists understand better the constituents of intangible value and the price sensitivity of reputation, as a promise of quality, when it comes to differentiating customer services. Trustworthiness in business is a combination of both objective and judgmental factors, including integrity (honesty, ethics), commitment (good faith, professional attitude), competence (intelligence, capabilities) and perceptions (reputation, interpersonal communication skills, fear).

Over the past two decades, successive financial boom and bust cycles have thrown up extraordinary examples of both economic achievement, such as the capacity to extract millions from poverty, and ethical failure. An industry does not pay USD 139 billion in fines to American regulators between January 2012 and December 2014 if its behaviour is exemplary. From 1999 to 2008, the U.S. financial sector spent a reported USD 2.7 billion in federal lobbying expenses; individuals and political action committees in the sector made more than USD 1 billion in campaign contributions. But those were too often regarded as an operating cost to business as usual, rather than as a structural problem. Financial institutions that engaged in widespread mis-selling rarely went out of business. As several finance practices were wasteful if not fraudulent, the contribution of finance to the "real economy" was again deeply challenged. Despite this string of events, incumbent leading financial hubs have resisted and proven to be extraordinarily resilient. It seems that the reassessment of trust did not come so much from the level of severity of the crisis than from how it had been dealt with. Historically, trusted relations have been at the core of the development of financial markets, most classically in the old City of London's culture in which a broker's word was his "bond". Political or repeated large scale behavioural crises anger the markets most and deliver the biggest hits on reputation and value; a house of thieves cannot pretend to be a house of trust. Unreliable information or corporate malfeasance "may change not only the distribution of expected payoffs, but also the fundamental trust in the system that delivers those payoffs." The impact of a financial crisis is first felt gradually in the market but accelerates quickly, possibly to systemic scale in the most severe cases.

As a contrast to the slightly dated *homo economicus* paradigm, or purely rational economic agent behaviour, George Akerlof and Robert Shiller[38] address five, more or less distinct, "spirits": confidence; concern for fairness; corruption and other anti-social behaviour; money illusion and the role of "stories" in shaping economic behaviour. In the development of international hubs, one can add the capacity to attract and retain talented individuals from diverse cultural background and swiftly regulate the business environment in an equitable and unbiased fashion. Ethics finally meets with psychology and reconciles with rationality to serve a much more ambitious social objective incorporating the development of the common good. The very meaning of trustworthiness is to supplement and give a weight, a direction and a positive charge to rationality. Ultimately, the processing of critical financial information is likely be based on trust rather than purely rational information. In the absence or failure of reliable mechanisms of confidence, one resorts to trust in order to make decisions and in an attempt to deal with risk. It is also clear that

---

[38] Akerlof GA, Shiller RJ: Animal Spirits: How Human Psychology Drives the Economy, and Why it Matters for Global Capitalism, Princeton, NJ: Princeton University Press (2009).

from time to time trust can be blind when based merely on competence or charisma. An example of this was the trust placed in Mexico's Finance Minister Jesus Silva-Herzog Mexico before August 1982 and the irrational belief he would be able to serve his country's sovereign debt. This is an area where the competition, or the association with advanced information processing tools, capable of extracting rational information from unstructured data, will be of interest, especially to finance hubs.

Almost a millennium after the first trading hub emerged, current leading finance hubs can hopefully continue to be these lighthouses for fostering international exchange provided that they can deliver a compelling value proposition beyond the dated Ricardian wealth accumulation paradigm. If political benevolence becomes necessary for operating in a leading financial hub, only the type of finance that enjoys sufficient rents to lobby heavily, not to say corrupt, and ensure the permeability of regulation to its wealth creation objectives, may survive. The coexistence of two irreconcilable cultures, the need to maximise wealth on the one hand and the will to show that such participants are trustworthy and reputable parties to deal with on the other hand — and the resulting schizophrenia — is very deeply rooted in modern economic and managerial practice and theory. These approaches run into the problem raised by St Augustine, who proclaimed "Lord, give me chastity, but not yet." This is ultimately the most dangerous and cynical type of financial practice: the non-competitive, plutocratic and clubbish one[39] driven by blind shareholder value. If the only goal is the enrichment of a financial hub, there is a significant risk that abuses and fraud become not just a distortion, but a continuation of the core strategy by other means, to the point where it becomes generally unacceptable. When incentive structures are at odds with the requirements of decent ethics, it is inevitable that the softer more fragile side, ethics, becomes the casualty. Leading finance hubs need wise impartial protection to design and support competition on a level playing field. They must show by example, through regular and measurable initiatives that they are capable of developing strategies and implementing actions capable of differentiating in the long run between enhancing the common good and predatory rent-seeking practices. Florence or Venice would never be what

---

[39]Zingales, Luigi, Harvard University, cf bibliography, January (2015).

they are, 700 years later, without the sometimes obligated but necessary "generosity" of their merchant bankers during the High Middle Ages. Aside from fear of divine justice and pride in showing ones magnificence, the willingness to leave behind a fine architectural legacy to future generations could be seen as a clear manifestation of a desire to give back to society.

Since the Great Recession has shown the limitations of our system of incentives, retaining a talented, well trained, open-minded and ethical workforce is essential for the sustainability of a financial services sector based on trustworthiness and fair practices. This resorts in emphasising again the paramount importance of human capital in the formation of total capital as the need for increased returns on knowledge economy. The reason for capital investment in permanent education in neglected sensitive ethical areas, as a consumer intangible durable for example, is fully consistent with the desire of increasing returns in fostering a sound knowledge economy. The diffusion of new knowledge at the beginning of the Enlightenment offered the opportunity to access a new form of education better suited to fit the challenges needed for the improvement of the whole world. This orientation toward curiosity and continuous education is not only a matter of policy, but also a matter of responsibility of the civil society, which may compete from time to time with the development of a leisure oriented society. It shall not be confused with the multiplication of rules. A legal framework is indeed useful; especially to ensure clarity and consistency in what is permissible. In the first instance rules lead to certainty, but too many rules have the opposite effect and are an impediment to making judgment and taking responsibility. In this respect blindly following rules cannot be interpreted as a synonym for trustworthiness and responsibility. To continue developing, the system needs more, it does need to keep some breathing space and the cases when the rules had to be superseded must be seriously reflected upon, in a rigorous but benevolent spirit. The most lethal blows can be inflicted on any organisation when management leaves aside common sense and relies rigidly on the rules. There is not only one route and it is not a coincidence that the best financial hubs have been those capable to associate cultural diversity, flexibility, perspective and a capacity to prune the unnecessary rules and balance the necessarily biased wisdom sponsored by the hub participants. In spite of pressure for profitability and monetary performance, a concluding paradox is that short term money cannot be the only metric in the world of finance. It should come with a visionary policy dedicated to attracting the finest talents, with a clear ethical intention of separating the wheat from the chaff. As finance is about incentives, the professional curriculum should emphasize more not only financial performance but also a significant contribution by participants to the common good. Already by 13th century, one of the partners of the Compagnia dei Peruzzi was "Meissei Domnedio", the Lord himself, who got attributed one share of capital, together with the corresponding dividends which were distributed to charitable organisations. In this field, individual and team effort, healthy competition and careful rating can remain a sure means for improving standards. Some will argue that this is better than nothing, others will have a point when they emphasize that in the absence of ethical values cynicism will flourish. In this respect, a long term oriented policy fostering responsibility will produce deeper and more durable results than hypocritical short term efforts to capture a quick fix with using the best mercenary experts available. Even if regulation has been tightened to ensure a culture of compliance, when too many of those on the trading floors regard themselves as hired guns, who are borrowing the bank's capital to support their personal pursuit of profit, then there is a systemic risk lurking in the background. The challenge for leading financial hubs is to make sure that sufficient resources are dedicated to innovative training, not only technical training in mathematics, statistics and economics applied to finance but also shared and applied training in humanities as a sound discipline to remind all the participants that the fragile ecosystem of the best financial hubs depends on both individual and collective trustworthiness. Friedrich A. Hayek observed that an economist who is only an economist cannot be a good one, this observation can be extended to finance hubs at large in their capacity to deliver good finance. We have a brain and a "heart" which jointly participate in the way we act as supposedly rational economic agents. Adam Smith in his "Theory of moral sentiments" (1759), possibly the most important book on moral philosophy, written prior to "An inquiry in the nature and causes of the Wealth of nations" (1776), analysed our somewhat unpredictable decision making process as an economic experimental process defined as the learning to humble the arrogance of our self-love and bring it down to what other people will go along with. Contemporary thinkers are rediscovering the depth of Smithian analysis especially as it connects ethics to economics, and where as humans we come from when we intend to focus on wealth accumulation. Long term success comes with a price: economic responsibility cannot be replaced by placebo codes and stringent regulation, especially when sometimes participants are permitted to pick their preferred regulators in what may become a race for the weakest supervisor. Collectively, we have powerful brains but individually a weak heart, as our emotions, including the addictive pay-off resulting from greed, are prompt to hijack our genuine desire to maximise long term utility for an immediate enhanced level of individual recognition. The aggregation of irrational preference may then build as a strong psychological inference engine, specifically at time of deep economic transformation, such as the impact of the digital revolution on the job market, where anxiety is challenging the rationality and need for trustworthiness. Beyond our individual level of consciousness this may finally crystallise in negative income anticipations leading to large macroeconomic swings, financial irrational exuberance and possibly secular stagnation. Then, leading financial hubs have this unique responsibility to help move away from pessimism and funnel monetary resources to innovation at large, which remains one of the best cure to economic depression.

CONCLUSION

"We are in the middle of very ancient waters,
In the middle of a history which, seemingly, has no age,
we may suddenly roll back two or ten centuries,
and, at a glance, eyewitness these remote times."[1]

Five thousand years ago, presumably 75% of the world trade was taking place within a radius of 20 km. The development of long haul shipping in the 15th century and trade finance has helped push the limits beyond the horizon of the known world, and a specific dynamic resulted from this curiosity. Surprisingly, it took some time for geography to become a main stream concern within economics. For centuries, seaports bundled with finance centres acted as nodes of economic, political and social change in Europe first — and beyond later. Across oceans, financial hubs saved on transaction and information cost and delivered the knowledge needed for the development of lively markets. This evolution coincided with the free circulation of goods, ideas and talents under the rule of law. As such, it has been essential for the structuring of contemporary economic space. In this context, the concentration of population, plus the centripetal nature of

---

[1] Fernand Braudel, La dynamique du capitalisme, Arthaud, p. 14, (1985).

maritime complexes set port zones apart from inland areas, as the seed of international financial hubs. Civilisations who decided to purposefully close their borders could not match the path of such progress, as freedom and competition proved to be necessary ingredients for fostering innovation.

Being bold at crossing borders

The rise and fall of Genoa during the medieval commercial revolution provides an enlightening illustration of (i) the success and failure of what, in the same vein of Walter Bagehot, Joseph Schumpeter called the "gales of creative destruction", a memorable phrase borrowed from Werner Sombart, and (ii) the role of international financial markets in that economic transformation.[2] A vision of general economics on the one side and financial markets on the other side only promotes a schizophrenic interpretation of the world. In 1873, Bagehot, then chief editor of The Economist, wrote a thoughtful book, "Lombard Street", about the role of finance and markets in the so-called "industrial revolution". This process of change as the only constant in the evolution of the most dynamic economies was not a mechanical one; it was rather the result of the leadership of a handful of inspired and powerful merchant families, involved the government of their cities at various degrees. Being successful required both macroeconomic and microeconomic acumen of fluctuations of somewhat unperfect markets, and a keen appreciation of the contextual equilibrium between temporal and spiritual forces. Medieval merchant bankers and their supporting powerhouses were praised for their sagacity, foresight and capacity to make fair but rapid emotionless decisions. One of the most vivid renderings of this state of mind is probably reflected in what was virtually the final painting of Frans Hals: The group portrait of the Regentesses of the old men's Almhouse, ca. 1664. "Hals did in pictorial terms what Balzac did two centuries later in literature."[3]

---

[2] Joos de ter Beerst, Didier, Crisis of contracts for merchant in crisis institutions, corporate finance and growth in Genoa (11–17th) paper presented at the Eighth Conference of the European Historical Economics Society (EHES), Geneva, 4–5th September (2009).

[3] Frans Hals museum, Haarlem. At the time of painting, Hals was a destitute old man dependent on the charity of people whose portraits he now painted (cf. John Berger, *Ways of Seeing*, Chapter 1, Penguin books, 1977).

Maybe it should have been expected that Haarlem, the thriving centre of the Dutch textile industry in the first half of the 17th century, should have produced Hals — one of the greatest painters of personalities to have lived, reflected in the tones within darkness of black silk, Utrecht's velvet or needle lace. He was also one of the great painters of the human hand. The Regentesses' old men's Almhouse situated at the right of the picture depicts an extraordinary, "shrivelled claw that her merciless gaze almost challenges the viewer to inspect,"[4] as a metaphoric illustration of financial dominance.

The emergence of international financial centres is not just an accidental occurrence related to the pit and the pendulum of human history and the vanity of Princes. The dominance of countries over international finance arose both from the need to satisfy domestic demand and the capacity to provide value added services for other countries to create wealth. But it is the latter activity that truly reflected the role of a city acting as an international financial centre. The past 1,000 years showed that the emergence of a financial hub capable of becoming a single anchor point for international finance across time and geography is also certainly related to policy, visionary political leadership, based on a simultaneous triple set of technical, geopolitical and ethical conditions. Leadership as self-proclaimed evidence surely is totalitarism and despair, and in such context neither the conditions needed for trustworthiness nor innovation can flourish, nor can it lead to the development of a world acclaimed centre of excellence. The illusion of strength can be created through the consolidation in a single point of nationwide financial activities, but the ability of such a centre to act as a genuinely international magnet will be limited. Therefore, it shall not come as a surprise that the emergence of international financial centres is supported by talents and the existence of deep, liquid, transparent markets operating under the rule of law that is enforceable irrespective of the participants' position and country of origin. Small changes in the parameters of the economic framework may have large effects on its qualitative behaviour. That is, when some index that takes into account freedom-innovation, institutions and revenues

---

[4] Andrew Graham Dixon, The fabric of everyday's life, *The Independent*, 16 January (1990).

anticipations crosses a critical threshold, talents will start to clusterise; once started, this process will feed on itself.

Understanding the conditions of global leadership

We possibly overconfidently believe that leading financial centres have emerged from a combination of precise centripetal (market size, labour market, external economies) and centrifugal forces (institutions, land rents, external diseconomies) affecting geographical concentration, as opposed to mere luck. A first set of technical conditions relates to (i) innovation in finance and the capacity and freedom for bankers and traders to find and implement solutions to better accompany international trade, (ii) an institutional mechanism on which the debtor cannot renege on its debt, (iii) the presence of a single bank above the others, like the Wisselbank in 1609 modelled on the Venitian Banco di Rialto of 1587, capable of gradually acting as the institution accountable for the management of sovereign debt, and later economic stability. Another set of conditions is related to geography, and more precisely to the quality of the hinterland. All the major international financial hubs were connected to trading roads of good quality, a powerful harbour and a rich industrial environment. In short, the presence of a strong hinterland and vorland, have been and remain a key condition for success. As late as 1990, international economists took virtually no notice of trade within countries, or of the location of production in space. A large part of the explanation of this factor is the centrality of increasing returns to geographical patterns: nobody really thinks that Silicon Valley owes its existence to exogenously given factors of production or Ricardian comparative advantage. A final set of conditions complements the first two sets as technical criteria would be too shallow if it were not anchored into trustworthiness, a multifaceted factor which not only encompasses virtues (honesty, integrity, accountability), but also political stability (political endorsement, military force, stable fiscal and legal business oriented environment) and freedom for the players to innovate within the framework of a fairly regulated environment. This factor is challenged and evaluated over a long period of time more from a practitioner's point of view than from a theoretical basis. For example, a great legal arsenal without a clear proof of its capacity to be enforced is not very useful and chances are that it will be challenged and defeated, and conversely a capacity to over litigate for dubious reasons creates transaction costs capable to curb the development abilities of a financial centre. The arrival of new talents to replenish the international financial centres energy has been seen as a decisive factor in their 900 year history, and clearly some aspiring cities are not as inspiring as London and New York: over the long run, freedom, justice, moderation especially from the fiscal side, acceptance of multiple cultures and a healthy environment in which to settle are crucial conditions to attract, nurture and retain talents. One of the key challenges of this century is the ability for hub regulators to keep up on with the extraordinary (r)evolution of tools used by finance masters and their followers. This probably involves the need to redesign the controlling instruments to bring the regulatory framework into the digital age. Most probably the leading finance centres will be at the forefront of this initiative to provide enhanced trading quality to their participants. Surveillance, audit, regulation and enforcement of the market practices will become more dependent on cyber agents or speed and innovation will need to be temporarily restrained. This triple helix of factors spins around each other to make the very fabric of safe trading practices, which gradually evolved across time and geographies, and inspired generations of bankers and merchants. The *lingua franca* of international finance centres is trustworthiness, expertise, freedom and stability. Uncertainty is the other essential factor in finance that cannot be properly incorporated in the conditions of the trade if there is no systemic benchmark to characterise the probabilities assigned by a given model and no choice of a model among a family of models to assess risk. As a conclusive analysis, it is necessary to cut through the complexities of the real world and focus on a more limited set of centripetal and one centrifugal forces. Krugman[5] summarised that from a conceptual standpoint the geographical structure of an economy depended on a few key parameters: (i) transportation costs, (ii) economies of scale and (iii) factor mobility. This is a sort of door-opener for economists to better explain with simplified but still powerful representations of the reality, cute mathematical models, the formation

---

[5] Krugman, Paul R. Increasing returns and economic geography, *Journal of Political Economy*, 99, 483–499 (1991b).

of financial hubs and reconcile this process with both history and geography.

Keep sailing beyond the known world

"This is no time, to be making new enemies" conceded Voltaire on his death bed. It is indeed desirable that competition always exist to create this innovative tension, to the point that it may occasionally lead to conflicts as in the Middle Ages, but afterwards some kind of cooperation will ultimately prevail, as global wars and chronical unrest have proven to be one of the most lethal threats to the resilience of international financial centres. We are prone to overestimate our understanding of the world as it looks and to underestimate the role of chance in the occurrence of defining events capable to modify this perception. Every time the sea cities could not continue to assert their freedom and entrepreneurial independence, their power started to dwindle, as they got integrated into larger predatory political unified systems. Over the last 1,000 years, international financial centres have proven to be extremely resilient and capable of resisting to a variety of unpredictable external assaults. However, a conjunction of catastrophic events, including severe financial crashes related to market manipulation, or internal political meltdown have led to the disappearance of some — or the lack of emergence of others, while the most adverse factor of all being possibly external war. The security challenges have switched from sea piracy and overland thieves in the Middle Ages to cyberspace data theft and hacking, deviant algorithmic trading on autopilot, and massively organised destruction scenarios. The 11 September 2001 attacks on New York's financial district have already provided a hint of what is imaginable. Extreme social inequalities are probably responsible for the most disruptive economic shocks, and today a price is likely to be paid for the inequalities between the wealthiest citizens of this world and the "bottom billion". Education bears this unique burden to remain the sure bridge to decent living and a rampart against extreme poverty.[6] More than any other factors, external large scale wars, the default on sovereign debts, failed faith, corrupt governments and

---

[6]The international standard of extreme poverty is set to the possession of less than 1$ a day (UNESCO).

zombie states together with consistent bad economic policy have been the cause of major and often serious disruptions not only for IFCs but also for the world economy in general. In about 2.8 million years of human history, human (or pre-human) brains have grown 3.5 times from 400 cc. for australaupithecus, to 800 cc. the pre-human Homo habilis and 1,400 cc. for Homo sapiens.[7] At the level of the changes in human history, this evolution is not so impressive. Kiyosi Itô, one of the fathers of the probabilistic tools used to price finance game-changing tools, coined the word "Homo sapiens sapiens sapiens", referring to the human species living in the forest 20,000 years from now.[8] He continued explaining that the forest people have a new and simple set of values: they believe that the value of sapiens, is true wisdom. This is something to meditate, as we think we want to move forward in financial economics.

As a consequence of the sharp increase of the earth population in the last millennium, the next step in our evolution is probably going to reorder a number of priorities including our relationship with wealth and money in the face of the vulnerability of our life-supporting resources and abilities to truly express the best of our human capacities. "Seek what suffices, seek what is enough, and don't desire more. Whatever goes beyond that, produces anxiety not relief: it will weight you down, instead of lifting you up."[9] Frugality of the spirit does not consist in not having things or in searching for excellence but rather in keeping away from greed, which leads to no other perception of our environment but what serves for immediate pleasure and consumption. One of the duties for finance masters to guide humanity towards a better future is likely to be avoiding that greed and trust collide together. And for this to happen, not only most ambitious and talented, but also wise and humble people should lead.

---

[7] Pr. Yves Coppens, Collège de France, interview with François Lestavel, 13 June (2011).

[8] Speech delivered for the reception of the Kyoto Prize in Basic Sciences from the Inamori Foundation in June 1998.

[9] St. Augustine.

MAPS

1. Early European financial centres
2. The Champaign fairs
3. Venetian trading routes
4. The Silk roads
5. Main exploration sea routes in the 15th and 16th century
6. Dutch East India Company trading routes in the 17th century
7. The world in 2015 according to free float market capitalisation

1. Early European international financial centres

Source: Maverlinn

Note: Florence and the Hanseatic League are mentioned for reference due to their very significant influence on the development of finance hubs in the medieval times and beyond, but are not strictly international financial hubs.

2. The Champaign Fairs and the Kingdom of France around 1200

Source: Adapted from Stanford Geographical Establishment (Stanford), London, Cambridge University Press, and Georges Duby, The Middle Ages, Hachette, 1998.

3. Principal commercial galley routes in the Mediterranean (15th century)

Source: Adapted from Frederic C. Lane, Venice, *A Maritime Republic*, John Hopkins University Press, 1973, map 9.

4. Principal Silk Roads from China to the West

Source: Adapted from Stanford University and the Oriental Institute at Chicago University.

5. Main exploration sea routes in the 15th and 16th century

Source: Adapted from Dr. Gayle Olson-Raymer, Humboldt, California State University.
Note: This map reproduces a selection of routes for illustration purposes, many other routes and expeditions are well worth studying for those interested by long distance naval exploration, in particular da Verrazano, Cabral, Dias, Cabot.

6. Dutch East India Company (VOC), trade network in the 17th century

Source: Adapted from Dr. Jean-Paul Rodrigue, *The Geography of Transport Systems*, Dept. of Global Studies & Geography, Hofstra University.

7. The world in 2015 according to free float equity market capitalisations

Source: Adapted from Bank of America Merrill Lynch and Market Watch, August 2015.
Note: The size of each country is proportionate to its equity free float market capitalisation. The map excludes China A-Shares, the shares only available for purchase to Mainland China citizens. If these restricted shares were included in the calculation, the size of the People's Republic of China would swell by tenfold from USD 0.9 trillion to approximately USD 9 trillion.

GRAPHS

1. Global financial assets worldwide in 2014
2. CARG of global financial assets worldwide in 2005–2014e
3. Split of the worldwide sovereign debt

1. Global financial assets worldwide in 2014

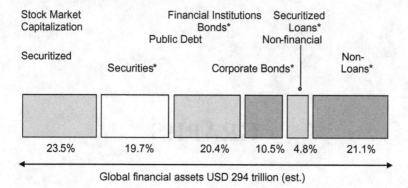

Source: Adapted from McKinsey Global Institute, Hover, BIS, DB, Maverlinn.
Note: *Outstanding.

2. CAGR* of global financial assets worldwide in 2005–20a14e (in USD, trillion)

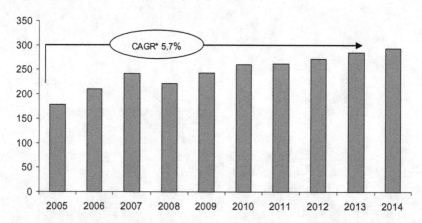

Source: Adapted from McKinsey Global Institute, Hover, BIS, DB, Maverlinn.
Note: *Compound Annual Growth Rate, CAGR.

3. Split of the worldwide sovereign debt (in USD trillion)

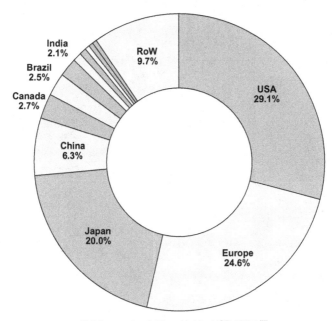

Total sovereign debt worldwide: USD 59.7 trillion

Source: Adapted from Visual capitalist by Jeff Desjardins (August 2015).

ACRONYMS

ACU — Asian currency unit
ADM — Asian dollar market
ARM — Adjustable rate mortgage
ART — Alternative risk transfer
ATM — Automated teller machines
ATS — Alternative trading system
CAGR — Compound annual growth rate
CAPM — Capital asset pricing model
CAT bond — Catastrophe bond
CDOs — Collateralized debt obligations
CFTC — Commodity futures commission
CSD — Central securities depository
DNA — Deoxyribonucleic acid (figurative, i.e. distinctive characteristics)
DOT — Designated order turnaround
ECB — European central bank
EIC — British honourable East India company
ENIAC — Electronic numerical integrator and computer
ETF — Exchange traded funds
FDI — Foreign direct investment
FDIC — Federal deposit insurance corporation
FED — Federal reserve board
FSA — Financial services authority
FTP — File transfer protocol

GDP — Gross domestic product
HFT — High frequency trading
ICDS — International central securities depository
IFC — International financial centres
IFRS — International financial reporting standards
LTCM — Long-term capital management
MAS — Singapore monetary authority
MIFID — Markets in financial instruments directive
MTF — Multilateral trading facilities
NGO — Non-governmental organization
NYSE — New York stock exchange
OFC — Offshore financial centres
OTC — Over-the-counter
OTS — Office of thrift supervision
P&L — Profit & Loss
PMBS — Private-label mortgage backed securities
PRC — People's Republic of China
RMB — Renminbi or Chinese yuan
ROE — Return on equity
SPV — Special purpose vehicles
SOX — Sarbanes–Oxley act
SSA — Sub-Saharan Africa
SWF — Sovereign wealth fund
SWIFT — Society for worldwide interbank financial telecommunication
TBTF — Too big to fail
USA — United States of America
USD — United States dollar
VIP — Very important personality
VHF — Very high frequency
VOC — Dutch East India company
WWI — World War I
WWII — World War II

BIBLIOGRAPHY

Agoston, Gabor and Masters, Bruce, *The Encyclopedia of the Ottoman Empire*, Facts on file (2008).

Aho, James, *Confession and Bookkeeping*, State University of New York Press (2005).

Akerlof, G.A and Shiller R.J, *Animal Spirits: How Human Psychology Drives the Economy and Why it Matters for Global Capitalism*, Princeton University Press (2009).

Alessandrini, Pietro, Fratianni, Michele and Zazzaro, Alberto, *The Changing Geography of Banking and Finance Springer*, Springer Science & Business Media (2009).

Astuti, G., *Origini e Svolgimento Storico Della Commenda Fino al Secolo 13*, S Lattes & Co. (1933).

Atack, J. and Neal, L. (eds.), *The Origin and Development of Financial Markets and Institutions from the Seventeenth Century to the Present*, Cambridge University Press (2009).

Bell, C. Brooks and Moore T.K, Accounts of the English Crown with Italian Merchant Societies, *1272–1345*, (ed.) Kew, *The List and Index Society*, (2009).

Balard Michel, Rome-Genoa (12th to 15th century), Bibliothèque des Écoles Françaises D'athènes et de Rome, (1978).

Battutah Ibn, *The Travels of Ibn Battutah*, Macmillan Paperback, 1 June (2003).

Becker, Gary, Crime and punishment: An economic approach, *Journal of Political Economy* 76: 169–177, (1968).

Braudel, Fernand, Afterthoughts on Material Civilisation and Capitalism, *The John Hopkins Symposia in Comparative History*, John Hopkins University Press, March (1979).

Braudel, Fernand, Civilization and Capitalism, *From the 15th to the 18th Century*, Vol. III, Harper & Row (1982).

Braudel, Fernand, Grammar of civilisations, Champs Flammarion, Arthaud, Paris (1987).

Boulnois, Luce, Mayhew, Bradley, The Silk Road: Monks, warriors and merchants, Odyssey Illustrated Books (2012).

Bourquelot, Felix, History of Provins, Volume 1, Lebeau (1839).

Bowsky, William M., A medieval Italian commune, Siena under the nine: 1287–1355, University of California Press (1981).

Carlos, Ann M. and Neal, Larry, Amsterdam and London as Financial Centres in the Eighteenth Century, LSE, Cambridge University Press (2011).

Cassis, Youssef, Capitals of Capitals: A History of International Financial Centres 1780–2005, Cambridge University Press (2007).

Cassis, Youssef, Bussière, Eric, London and Paris as International Financial Centres in the Twentieth Century, Oxford University Press (2005).

Cercle of economists, The war of capitalism will come, Chap. V, *The Great Threat of Sovereign Funds*, Perrin (2008).

Coppens, Yves, Bourdial, Isabelle, Homo Sapiens, Flammarion Père Castor (2006).

Chancellor, Edward, *Devil take the Hindmost: A History of Financial Speculation*, Macmillan (1999).

Chaudhuri, K. N., *Trade and Civilisation in the Indian Ocean: An Economic History from the Rise of Islam to 1750,* Cambridge University Press (1985).

Chernow, Ron., *The House of Morgan: An American Banking Dynasty and the Rise of Modern Finance*, New York: Grove Press (1990).

Chapin, Elizabeth, *The Cities of the Fair of Champagne from their Origin to the Begining of the 14th Century*, Paris, Champion (1937).

Christaller, Walter, *Central Places in Southern Germany*, Jena: Fischer Verlag (1933).

Crawcour, E.S., The Premodern Economy. In *An Introduction to Japanese Civilization,* (ed.) Arthur E. Tiedemann, Columbia University Press (1974).

Crowley, Roger, *The City of Fortune: How Venice Ruled the Sea*, Random House (2013).

Dash, Mike, The Tulipomania: The Story of the World's Most Coveted Flower, Broadway books, (2001).

De Roover, Raymond, *Money, Banking and Credit in Medieval Bruges — Italian Merchant Bankers, Lombards and Money Changers — A Study in the Origins of Banking*, The Medieval Academy of America (1948).

De Roover, Raymond, *The Evolution of the Bill of Exchange from the 16th to the 18th Century*, Librairie Armand Colin (1953).

De Roover, Raymond, *Business, Banking and Economic Thought in Late Medieval and Early Modern Europe*, University of Chicago Press (1976).

De Roover, Raymond, *The Rise and Decline of the Medici Bank: 1397–1494*, Beardbooks (1963).

Deal, William E., *Handbook to Life in Medieval and Early Modern Japan*, Oxford University Press (2006).

Dehing, Pit, and 't Hart, Marjolein, Linking the Fortunes: Currency and Banking, 1550–1800, in *The Financial History of The Netherlands*, (eds.) P. Dehing, J. Jonker, and J. van Zanden, Cambridge University Press, pp: 37–63 (1997).

Duby, Georges, *The Middle Ages*, Pluriel, Hachette (1987).

Dunn, Ross E., The Adventures of Ibn Battuta, a Muslim Traveler of the Fourteenth Century Paperback, 12 October (1989).

Favier, Jean, *Gold and Spices: The Rise of Commerce in the Middle Ages*, Holmes & Meier Pub, 1st US edition, 1 July (1998).

Favier, Jean, The Plantagenêts: Origin and Destiny of an Empire, XI–XIVe, Fayard, 6 October (2004).

Ferguson, Niall, *The Ascent of Money: A Financial History of the World*, Penguin books (2009).

Fox, Edward Whiting, *History in Geographic Perspective: The Other France*, Norton (1971).

Fratianni, Michele, The evolutionary chain of international financial centers, Chapter 12, in *The Changing Geography of Banking and Finance*, Springer (2009).

Galbraith, John Kenneth, *The Great Crash 1929*, Mariner books, reprint edition, September (1929).

Gelber Harry G., *Opium, Soldiers and Evangelicals England's 1840–1842*, Palgrave Macmillan (2004).

Gjerstad, Steven and Smith, Vernon, *Monetary Policy, Credit Extension and Housing Bubbles: 2008 and 1929*, Routledge, vol. 21 (2009).

Heers, Jacques, The Medicis, Tempus, Perrin (2012).

Huff, Darrel, *How to Lie with Statistics*, W. W. Norton & Company (1954), reissued in (1993).

Hunt, Edwin, The Medieval Super-Companies: A Study of the Peruzzi Company of Florence, London: Cambridge University Press (1994).

Hsu, Feng Hsiung, *Behind Deep Blue: Building the Computer that Defeated the World Chess Champion*, Princeton University Press (2002).

Garber, Peter, Famous First Bubbles, in *Speculative Bubbles, Speculative Attacks, and Policy Switching,* (eds.) Robert Flood and Peter Garber, MIT Press: Cambridge MA (1994).

Geisst, Charles R., *Wheels of Fortune: The History of Speculation from Scandal to Respectability*, Wiley (2002).

Institute for International Economics, *Japan's Financial Crisis and Its Parallels to US Experience*, (eds.) Ryoichi Mikitani and Adam S. Posen, Special Report, 13 September (2000).

Jardines, *175 Years of Looking to the Future*, corporate eBook (www.jardines.com).

Jehel, Georges, The Genoese in West mediterranean from the end of the 11th century to the begining of the 14th century. Draft strategy for building an empire, Centre d'histoire sociale, Presses de l'Université de Picardie (1993).

Jensen, Marius B., *The Making of Modern Japan*, Harvard University Press (2002).

Kaptein, Muel, Why good people do sometimes bad things? 52 reflections on ethics work, KPMG and Erasmus University Rotterdam: School of Management (2012).

Kindleberger, Charles P, *Economic and Financial Crises and Transformation in the 16th Century*, Princeton University Press, June (1998).

Kindleberger, Charles P, *Manias, Panics and Crashes: A history of Financial Crises*, Wiley (2000).

Lambert, Nicholas, *Planning Armageddon: British Economic Warfare and the First World War*, Cambridge, MA: Harvard University Press, (2012).

Landes, David S., *The Wealth and Poverty of Nations*, W.W. Norton & Company, (1998).

Lane, Frederick C., *Money and Banking in Medieval and Renaissance Venice*, Johns Hopkins University Press (1985).

Le Gall, Jean Marie *et al., The Capitals of the Renaissance*, Presses Universitaires de Rennes (2011).

Le Goff, Jacques, *Merchants and Bankers in the Middle Ages*, Que-Sais-je, Presse Universitaires de France (2001).

Levathes, Louise, *When China Ruled the Seas: The Treasure Fleet of the Dragon Throne, 1405–1433*, Oxford University Press (1996).

Lee, Alexander, The ugly renaissance, Random House, Hutchinson (2013).

Lynch, Martin, *Mining in World History*, Reaktion books Ltd, (2002).

Mackay, Charles, *Extraordinary Popular Delusions and the Madness of Crowds*, Start Publishing 2012, originally published in (1841).

Madden, Thomas F., *Venice: A New History*, Penguin Books, (2013).

Mahan, Alfred Thayer, *The Influence of Sea Power upon History: 1660–1783*, Dover publications (1987).

Mann, Michael E., The little ice age, Volume 1, The Earth system: physical and chemical dimensions of global environmental change, pp. 504–509, *Encyclopedia of Global Environmental Change*, John Wiley & Sons, Ltd, Chichester (2002).

McClain, James L., *Japan: A Modern History*, New York W.W. Norton (2002).

McGraw Hill, One proud legacy, two powerful companies, *125 Years of Powerful Intelligence*, McGraw Hill (2013).

Mohlo, Antony, *Marriage Alliance in Late Medieval Florence*, Harvard University Press (1994).

Moser, James, *Die Lehre Von Den Zeitgeschäften Und Deren Combinationen*, Julius Springer (1875).

Munro, John H., The medieval origins of the 'Financial Revolution': usury, rentes, and negotiability, Department of Economics, University of Toronto February (2002).

Miyazaki Hirokazu, *Arbitraging Japan: Dreams of Capitalism at the End of Finance*, University of California Press (2013).

National Commission on the Causes of the Financial and Economic Crises in the United States, *Financial crisis inquiry report*, January (2011).

Neal, Larry, *I am not Master of Events. The speculations of John Law and Lord Londonderry in the Mississippi and South Sea Bubbles*, Yale University Press (2012).

Nelson, Kenrad E, *Epidemiology of Infectious Disease: General Principles*, Johns Hopkins University, Jones & Bartlett Learning (2014).

Noble, F.X. Thomas, *The republic of St. Peter: The Birth of the Papal State 680–825*, University of Pennsylvania Press (1991).

Norwich, John Julius, *A history of Venice*, Vintage Books, (1989).

O'Flanagan, Patrick, Port Cities of Atlantic Iberia, c. 1500–1900. Aldershot: Ashgate Publishing (2008).

O'Malley, John W. How the First Jesuits Became Involved in Education, in *The Jesuit Ratio Studiorum: 400th Anniversary Perspectives*, Vincent J. Duminuco, S.J., Ed. New York: Fordham University Press, pp. 56–74 (2000).

Patterson, Scott, *Dark Pools: The rise of the Machine Traders and the Rigging of the U.S. Stock Market*, Crown Business (2013).

Phillips, John, *A General History of Inland Navigation: Foreign And Domestic*, (eds.) I. and J. Taylor, London (1792).

Poitras Geoffrey and Majithia Asha, Isaac Le Maire and the Early Trading in Dutch East India Company Shares. Published in Pioneers of Financial Economics: Vol 1, Cheltenham: Edward Elgar (2006).

Pufendorff (de), Introduction to the general and political history of the universe, published by Zacharie Chatelain, Amsterdam (1743).

Puttevils, Jeroen, Merchant and trading in the sixteenth century, the Golden Age of Antwerp, Perspective in economic and social history n°38, Routledge (2016).

Raynal (Abbé), Philosophical and historical history of European settling in the two Indies, T.1., T.6., Elibon Classics Series (1773).

Racorean, Ovidiu Sorin, Decoding stock market behavior with topological quantum computers. Working paper, Applied mathematics in finance dept, SAV Integrated Systems, Academy of Economic Studies, 25 June (2014).

Rémond, René, Introduction to Contemporary History, Book III ("Introduction à l'histoire de notre temps", le XXe siècle), Seuil/Points, (1974).

Rothbard, Murray N. An Austrian perspective on the history of economic thought, Ludwig von Mises Institute, (2006).

Scott, Tom, The city states in Europe 1000–1600, Hinterland-Territory-Region, Oxford University Press (2012).

Sframeli, Maria, Nitti, Patrizia, The treasures of the Medici, Skira-Flammarion, (2010).

Shorto, Russel, Amsterdam, A history of the world's most liberal city, Doubleday; First Edition, 22 October (2013).

Sombart, Werner, *The Modern Capitalism*, Duncker & Humbolt, Munich and Leipzig (1928).

Stäheli, Urs, *Spectacular Speculation*, Stanford University Press (2013).

Stanton, Charles D, *Medieval Maritime Warfare*, Pen & Sword Maritime (2015).

Tuchman, Barbara W, *A Distant Mirror: The Calamitous 14th Century*, Random House (1987).

Tracy, James D. *et al., The Rise of Merchant Empires: Long Distance Trade In The Early Modern World*, Cambridge University Press (1990).

United States Senate, Permanent sub-committee on investigations, Wall Street and the financial crisis, Anatomy of a financial collapse, 13 April (2011).

Van Der Wee, Herman, The rise of merchant empire, Cambridge University Press (1990).

Van Der Wee, Herman, Monetary, credit and banking systems, in *The Organization of Early Modern Europe*, The Cambridge Economic History of Europe, vol. V, Rich (E.) & Wilson (C.) (eds.), Cambridge University Press, (1977).

Vega (de la), Joseph, Confusion de confusiones, published by M.F.J. Smith/G.J. Geers bron. Joseph de la Vega (1688).

Velde, François R., French public finance between 1683 and 1726, Federal Reserve Bank of Chicago, 20 July (2006).

Victoria County History (VCH), A History of the County of Hampshire: Volume 5. Originally published by Victoria County History, London (1912).

Villani Giovanni (Cronica di) (XII. 54), Rerum italicarum Scriptores, L.A. Muratori, t. XIII, col. 934–935 (1845).

von Thünen, J., *The Isolated State*, London: Pergamon (1826).

Wallerstein, Immanuel, *World-Systems Analysis: An Introduction*, Duke University Press, 27 August (2004).

Wilson, Charles, *Queen Elizabeth and the Revolt of the Netherlands*, University of California Press (1979).

Zorzi, Elise, *History of Venice*, Tempus (1979).

Zyen, The Competitive Position of London as a Global Financial Centre, November (2005).

Further Reading

Abraham Jean-Paul, Bervaes Nadia, Guinotte Anne. The competitiveness of international financial centers, In: *Revue d'économie financière*, n°21, (1992).

Allaire, Gloria, Review of Edwin S. Hunt, The Medieval Super-Companies: A Study of the Peruzzi Company of Florence, London, University of Kentucky, Cambridge University Press, 1994, in Heliotropia — An online journal of research to Boccaccio Scholars, volume 2, article 4 (2004).

Allen, Franklin and Babus, Ana, "Networks in Finance," in P. Kleindorfer and J. Wind (eds.), Network-based strategies and competencies, pp. 367–382, Wharton School publishing (2009).

Allen, Franklin, Douglas Gale, Bubbles and Crises, *Economic Journal*, 110: 460 (2000).

Ante, Spencer E., *Creative Capital: Bloomberg business*, 2 April (2008).

Arrow, Kenneth J. *Some Development in Economic Theory Since 1940: An Eyewitness Account*, department of economics, Stanford University, Annual review of economics (2009).

AMF, Map of risk and trends on the financial markets and asset management in 2010, Risques et tendances n°9, Mai (2010).

Appleby, Guide to the Bermuda insurance market (2007).

Aumann Robert J., Nobel Prize Lecture, 8 December (2005).

Bosworth, Michael L, The rise and fall of 15th Century, Chinese Seapower, doctoral working paper (1999).

Baker, Gerard, *The Wall Street Slide*, The International Economy, Spring (2007).

Balard Michel, Roma-Genoa (from 12th century to the 15th century), *Bibliothèque des Écoles françaises d'Athènes et de*, Rome (1978).

Balard Michel, Insurance and maritime trade in Genoa in the second half of the 14th century, *Annale de Bretagne et de l'Ouest*: 273–282 (1978).

Bellhouse, D.R, The Genoese lottery, Statistical Science, *Institute of Mathematical Statistics*, 6(2): 141–148 (1991).

BIS, Shell Banks and Booking Offices, Basel Committee on banking supervision, January (2003).

BIS, The supervision of cross-border banking, Report by a working group comprised of members of the Basle Committee on Banking Supervision and the offshore group of banking supervisors, Basle, October (1996).

Bishop, Jennifer, Naughty money: clippers and coiners in 16th century England, University of Cambridge, Faculty of history, Research features, 12 April (2014) http://www.cam.ac.uk/research/features/naughty-money-clippers-and-coiners-in-16th-century-england

Blundell-Wignal, Adrian, Hu Yu-Wei and Yermo Juan, *Sovereign Wealth and Pension Fund Issues*, Financial Market Trends, OECD (2008).

Borio Claudio, James Harold and Shin Hyun Song, The international monetary and financial system: a capital account historical perspective, BIS Working Papers No 457, Monetary and Economic Department August (2014).

Borst Nicholas, The rise of Asian Sovereign Wealth Funds, Federal Reserve Board of San Francisco, March (2015).

BRA, History of Boston's economy, growth and transition, 1970–1998, Report from the Boston redevelopment authority (BRA), Report #529, November (1999).

Breiter, Hans C., Aharon, I., Kahneman, D., Dale, A., and Shizgal, P, Functional imaging of neural responses to expectancy and experience of monetary gains and losses, *Neuron*, 30: 619–639 (2001).

Burke, Joseph, *Money for Nothing: The Sin of Usury*, Ave Maria University, November (2008).

Byham, William C. Business networking: a necessary third millennium skill, White paper, DDI (2009).

Carlos, Ann M. and Neal, Larry, Amsterdam and London as financial centers in the eighteenth century, LSE, Cambridge University Press (2011).

Carmel, Stephen M., Globalization, security and economic well being, *Naval War College Review*, 66(1), 41–55: (2013).

Cheng, Hang-Sheng, The U.S. West Coast as an International Financial Center, Economic Review, Federal Reserve Bank of San Francisco, pp. 9–19, Spring (1976).

Choi Sang Rim, Park Daekeun, Tschoegl Adrian E., Banks and the World major banking centers, Financial Institutions Center, Wharton University, July (2002).

City of New York and United States Senate, "Sustaining New York's and the US' Global Financial Services Leadership," research by McKinsey & Company and New York City Economic Development Corporation (New York: Office of the Mayor) (2006).

Cochrane, Sarah, Explaining London dominance in international financial services, 1870–1913, Discussion paper series, Oxford University (2009).

Collective, Robin Cosgrove Prize, Trust and Ethics in Finance (2015).

Davis, Donald, and Weinstein, David, *Empirical Testing of Economic Geography: Evidence from Regional Data*, Harvard University (1997).

De la Vega, Joseph, Confusion de Confusiones, 1688, Portions Descriptive of the Amsterdam Stock Exchange, introduction by Hermann Kellenbenz, Baker Library, Harvard Graduate School of Business Administration (1957).

De Roover, Raymond, Money, Banking and Credit in Medieval Bruges — Italian Merchant Bankers, Lombards and Money Changers — A Study in the Origins of Banking, The Medieval Academy of America (1948).

van Dillen, J.G. Isaac Le Maire and the trading of the shares of the Compagnie des Indes Orientales, Revue d'Histoire Moderne (1935).

Drehmann, Mathias and Tarashev, Nikola Measuring the systemic importance of interconnected banks BIS Working Papers No 342, Monetary and Economic Department, March (2011).

Economist Intelligence Unit, The role of trust in business collaboration, The Economist (sponsored by Cisco Systems) (2008).

(The) Economist, Quantum computers, A little bit, better, June (2015).

(The) Economist, The Drexel Burnham Lambert's legacy, Stars of the junkyard, 21 October (2010).

Elliott, Catherine, Notes on "A treaty of Commerce" (1601), The University of Massachusetts Amherst (date unknown).

Elster, J, Emotions and economic theory, *Journal of Economic Literature*, 36: 47–74 (1998).

Engelen Ewald, Amsterdamned? The uncertain future of a financial center, *Environment and Planning A*, 39: 1306–1324 (2007).

ESSF, A Vision for Integrated Post-Trade Services in Europe, White Paper, August (2009).

European Commission, Green paper, Shadow banking, Brussels, 19 March (2012).

European Commission, Final report, High level expert group on reforming the structure of the EU banking sector, chaired by Erkki Liikanen, Brussels, 2 October (2012).

Evans, Allison Celia, Interpreting the success of the Antwerp tapestry market in the 1500s, Department of Art, Art history and Visual studies, Graduate School of the Duke University (2012).

Fachbereich Planen und Bauen Lübeck plant und baut, Heft 107/November (2011).

Felloni, Giuseppe (and Guido Laura), A profile of Genoa's "Casa di San Giorgio" (1407–1805): a turning point in the history of credit, Professor Emeritus, University of Genoa, http://www.giuseppefelloni.it/en/writings.php

Feynman, Richard, Simulating physics with computers, *International Journal of Theorical Physics*, 21: 467–488 (1982).

Fidler, David P., Hacking the wealth of nations: Managing markets amid malware, *Turkish Policy Quarterly*, 14(2): 43–53 Summer (2015).

Financial Stability Forum, Report of the Working Group on Offshore Centers, Chair: Andrew Crockett, 5 April (2000).

Foa, Roberto, Department of Government, Harvard University, Tanner, Jeffery C. Pardee RAND Graduate School, Methodology of the indices of social development, Harvard University, working paper funded by the World Bank, January (2011).

Fratianni, Michele and Spinelli, Franco, Did Genoa and Venice kick a financial revolution the Quattrocento, ONB, working paper 112, September (2005).

Fratianni, Michele, The evolutionary chain of financial centers, Indiana University, Università Politecnica delle Marche, Department of Economics, Mofir working paper, 6 October (2008).

Freedman, Michael H. Kitaev Alexei, Larsen Michael J. Wang ZhengHan, Topological quantum computation, *Bulletin of the American Mathematical Society*, 40(1): 31–38 (2002).

French Senat, Public authorities and the development of virtual currencies, English summary, 4 August (2014).

Freshfields Bruckhaus Deringer, Knowing the risks, protecting your business, Crisis management, White paper, September (2012).

Fujita, Masahita, Krugman, Paul, When is the Economy Monocentric: von Thünen and Christaller Unified, *Regional Studies and Urban Economics*, 25: 505–528 (1995).

Gelber Harry G., China as "Victim"? The Opium War That Wasn't, Center for European Studies Harvard University Working Paper Series #136, (2006).

Gordon, John Steele, A short (sometimes profitable) history of private equity, WSJ, 17 January (2012).

Goujon, Patrick S.J. Jesuit humanism today, Etudes, Tom 413, November (2010/11).

Grais, Wafik, Islamic Finance, A Development Opportunity for Egypt, CASAR, 30 October (2012).

Gruyet, Gustave, Lorenzo the Magnificent, Revue des deux mondes, Tome 7, page 758 (1875).

Hew, Denis, Singapore as a financial center, Institute for South East Asian Studies, 7–8 March (2002).

Huat Tan Chwee, Lim Joseph and Chen Wilson, Competing International Financial Centers: A Comparative Study between Hong Kong and Singapore, paper for Saw Centre for Financial Studies and ISEAS Conference — Singapore as a Financial Centre: Development and Prospects, November (2004).

Hui Chun Hing, Huangming zuxun and Zheng He's Voyages to the Western Oceans, *Journal of Chinese Studies*, 51: 67–85 (2010).

IMF International Monetary Fund, Mauro Mecagni, Daniela Marchettini, and Rodolfo Maino, Emerging bank trends in Sub-Saharian Africa, African Department, September (2015).

IMF International Monetary Fund, Brad Jones, Asset bubbles, rethinking policy for the age of asset management, Monetary and Capital Market Department, February (2015).

IMF International Monetary Fund, Working Paper, Al-Hassan Abdullah, Papaioanmou Michael, Skancke Martin, Sung Cheng Chih, Sovereign Wealth Funds: Aspects of Governance Structure and Investment Management, November (2013).

IMF International Monetary Fund, Laura E. Kodres, What is shadow banking? Finance & Development, Monetary and Capital Market Department, April (2013).

IMF International Monetary Fund, Working Paper, Udaibir S. Das, Adnan Mazarei, and Han van der Hoorn, *Economics of Sovereign Wealth Funds* (2010).

IMF International Monetary Fund, Working Paper, Monetary and Capital Markets Department Concept of Offshore Financial Centers: In Search of an Operational Definition, April (2007).

IMF International Monetary Fund, Offshore Financial Centers, The Assessment Program — A Progress Report Prepared by the Monetary and Financial Systems Department, 8 February (2006).

IMF International Monetary Fund-World Bank, Informal Funds Transfer Systems, An analysis of the informal hawala system, Mohammed El Qorchi, Samuel Munzele Maimbo, and John F. Wilson, Working paper, August (2003).

IMF International Monetary Fund, Wilson, John F. Hawala and other Informal Payments Systems: An Economic Perspective, Senior Economist, Middle Eastern Department, IMF. Seminar on Current Developments in Monetary and Financial Law, (2002).

IMF International Monetary Fund, Offshore Financial Centers, Monetary and Exchange Affairs Department, June (2000).

Jackson, Gordon, Early modern European seaport studies: highlight and guidelines, European seaport systems in the early modern age, *International Journal of Maritime History*, XIII n°2, December (2001).

James, Harold, Lessons in financial preparations in the lead-up to first world war, Princeton University, July (2014).

Jarrow Robert A., Protter, Philipp, A dysfunctional role of high frequency trading in electronic markets, *International Journal of Theoretical and Applied Finance*, 15(3) 1–15: (2012).

Joos de ter Beerst, Didier, Crisis of contracts for merchant in crisis institutions, corporate finance and growth in Genoa (11–17th) paper presented at the eighth Conference of the European Historical Economics Society (EHES), Geneva, 4–5 September (2009).

Jorion, Philippe, The Story of Long Term Capital Management, University of California, Canadian Investment Journal, Winter (1999).

Kirilenko, Andrei A. and Lo, Andrew L. Moore's Law versus Murphy's law: Algorithmic trading and its discontents, *Journal of Economic Perspectives*, 27(2): 51–72 (2013).

Kindleberger, Charles P. The formation of financial centers: A study in comparative history, Princeton studies in international finance n°36, November (1974).

Kohn, Meir, Risk instruments in the medieval and early modern economy, Working paper, Department of Economics, Dartmouth College, February (2009).

Kosmetatos, Paul, A portrait of a banking calamity, Faculty of history, University of Cambridge, Research discussion, 14 March (2013). http://www.cam.ac.uk/research/discussion/a-portrait-of-a-banking-calamity

Krueger (H.C.), Genoese merchants, Their Partnerships and Investments, 1155 to 1230, in Studi in honore di Amintore Fanfani, Multa Paucis (1962).

Krugman, Paul, Princeton University, Nobel Lecture, The increasing returns revolution in trade and geography, 8 December (2008).

Krugman, Paul, Increasing returns and economic geography, Journal of Political Economy 99: 484–499 (1991a).

Krugman, Paul, The new economic geography, now middle-aged, prepared for a presentation to the Association of American Geographers, 16 April (2010).

Krugman, Paul, The role of geography in development, prepared for a presentation to the Annual World Bank Conference on Development Economics 20–21 April (2008).

Kummer Steve, Pauletto Christian, The History of Derivatives: A Few Milestones EFTA Seminar on Regulation of Derivatives Markets, Zurich, 3 May (2012).

Lefèvre, Henri, Physiology and social interactions, *Journal des Actuaires Français* 2 (1873).

Lewis, Michael, Flash Boys: A Wall Street Revolt, W. W. Norton & Company, March (2014).

Liang Qichao, Biography of Our Homeland's Great Navigator, Zheng He, [publisher] (1904).

Leung, Cynthia and Unteroberdoerster Olaf, Hong Kong SAR as a Financial Center for Asia: Trends and Implications IMF Working Paper Asia and Pacific Department, Authorized for distribution by Jahangir Aziz, March (2008).

LMG — London Market Group, BCG — Boston Consulting Group, London matters, the competitive position of the London Insurance Market, November (2014).

Lo, Andrew, Fear, *Greed and Financial Crisis: A Cognitive Neurosciences Perspective*, MIT School of Management, October (2011).

Lo, Andrew, Repin, D. and Steenbarger, B., 2005, Fear and greed in financial markets: An online clinical study, *American Economic Review*, 95: 352–359 (2005).

Luo, Raph, Shanghai as an International Financial Center — Aspiration, Reality and Implication, *Undergraduate Economic Review*, 8(1) (2011).

Mankad Shawn, Michailidis George, Kirilenko Andrei, Discovering the ecosystem of an electronic financial market with a dynamic machine-learning method, *Algorithmic Finance*, 2(2): 151–165 (2013).

Marsilio, Claudio, The Genoese exchange fairs and the Bank of Amsterdam: Comparing two Financial Institutions of the 17th Century, working paper, Università Commerciale "L. Bocconi" — Milano (2009).

McKinsey, Day of reckoning? New regulation and its impact on capital-markets businesses, Working papers on risk n°29, October (2011).

Meikle, Scott, *Aristotle's Economic Thought*, University of Glasgow, Clarendon Press (1997).

Meir Kohn, Merchant Banking in the Medieval and early modern history, Department of Economics, Dartmouth College, working paper, February (1999).

Menon, Ravi, Keynote address by the Managing Director of the Monetary Authority of Singapore, at the Investment Management Association of Singapore's (IMAS) 14th Annual Conference, Singapore, 13 March (2013).

Meyer David R, Hong Kong's transformation as a financial center, Olin School of business, Washington University in Saint Louis, Brown University (2009).

Miller, Merton H, The history of finance, an eyewitness account, *Journal of Applied Corporate Finance*, 13(2): 8–14 (2000).

Milošević, Nikola, History of Malware, Digital Forensic Magazine, Issue 16, August (2013).

Minoiu, Camelia and Reyes, Javier A. A network analysis of global banking: 1978–2009, IMF Institute, Working paper, April (2011).

Miyajima Shigeki, Weber Warren E. A Comparison of National Banks in Japan and the United States between 1872 and 1885, Institute for Monetary and Economic Studies, Bank of Japan, August (2000).

Mukherji, Biman, China's Metal-Backed Finance Finds New Asian Homes, *The Wall Street Journal*, 11 June (2015).

Munro, John H., The medieval origins of the 'Financial Revolution': usury, rentes, and negotiability, Department of Economics, University of Toronto, February (2002).

Munro, John H. The financial origin of the financial revolution, Department of Economics, University of Toronto, February (2002).

Nakamoto, Satoshi, Bitcoin: A Peer-to-Peer Electronic Cash System, working paper published on bitcoin.org

Nakasawa, Katsumi, Antwerp, Emporium of the European Economy in the Sixteenth Century, Hitotsubashi University (1992).

National Endowment for Financial Education, Problem gamblers and their finances, A guide for treatment professionals (2000).

Niepmann, Friederike, Banking across borders, Federal Reserve Bank of New York, Staff reports n°576, revised version October (2013).

Norges Bank, The role of exchanges in well-functioning markets, [an] asset manager perspective, February (2015).

Okumura, Ariyoshi The future role of Tokyo's financial market, as part of the Distinguished Lecture Series at Columbia Business School, November (2004).

Olivier, Alex, De Bruin, Boujewijn, Trust me, I am a banker, Faculty of philosophy, University of Cambridge, October 14, (2014) http://www.cam.ac.uk/research/features/trust-me-im-a-banker

Petram, Lodewijk, The world's first stock exchange: How the Amsterdam market for Dutch East India Company shares became a modern securities market, Academisch Proefschrift, University of Amsterdam (2010).

Pezzolo, Luciano, The Rise and Decline of a Great Power: Venice 1250–1650, University of Venice, May (2006).

Pavoni, Silvia, London leads again, IFC rankings, The Banker, October (2013).

Polónia, Amélia, European seaports in the Early Modern Age: concepts, methodology and models of analysis, Cahier de la Méditerranée, n°80, pages 35–39, June (2010).

Puga, Diego, Trefler, Daniel, International Trade and Institutional Change: Medieval Venice's Response to Globalization, NBER Working Paper No. 18288, August (2012).

Raphael, Freddy, Werner Sombart and Max Weber, Werner Sombart seminar, *Les Cahiers du Centre de Recherches Historiques* (1988).

Rapp, Richard T. The Unmaking of the Mediterranean Trade Hegemony: International Trade Rivalry and the Commercial Revolution, *The Journal of Economic History*, 35(3): 499–525, (1975), Published by: Cambridge University Press on behalf of the Economic History Association.

Reed, Howard Curtis, The Ascent of Tokyo as an International Financial Center, *Journal of International Business Studies*, 11(n°3): 19–35, Winter (1980).

Reszat, Beate, Evolution, Spatial Self-organisation and Path Dependence: Tokyo's Role as an International Financial Center, working paper, Hamburg Institute of International Economics (2000).

Rolnick, Arthur J., Velde, Francois R., Webe, Warren E., The Debasement Puzzle: An Essay on Medieval Monetary History (p. 8), Federal reserve bank of Minneapolis, Fall (1997).

Rose, Andrew K. Haas and Spiegel, Mark M. Offshore Financial Centers: Parasites or Symbionts? School of Business University of California,

Berkeley and Federal Reserve Bank of San Francisco, Working paper, May (2005).

Rubel, Robert C., Command on the Sea, An Old Concept Resurfaces in a New Form, *Naval War College Review, Autumn*, 65(4): 21–33 (2012).

Sachs, Stephen E., The "Law merchant" and the fair court of St. Ives, 1270–1324, Thesis submitted to the Department of History, Harvard University, Cambridge, Massachusetts, 21 March (2002).

Sachs, Stephen E., From St. Ives to the cyberspace: The modern distorsion of the "Law merchant", *American University International Law Review*, 21(5): 686–812 (2006).

Saito Osamu, A very brief history of Japan's Economic and Social History Research, XVIIth World Economic History Congress, in Kyoto, Japan 3–7 August (2015).

Saitou Tsutomu, Takahashi Teruhiko, Nishikawa Yuichi, Chemical Study of the Medieval Japanese Mochu-sen (Bronze Coins), Institute for Monetary and Economic Studies, Bank of Japan, November (1998).

Santander Innoventures, Oliver Wyman and Anthemis, The Fintech 2.0 paper: rebooting financial services, (2015) http://santanderinnoventures.com/wp-content/uploads/2015/06/The-Fintech-2-0-Paper.pdf

Sayous, André-Emile, The financial transactions of Italian bankers in Italy and at the Champaign fairs in the 18th century, ("Les opérations des banquiers italiens en Italie et aux foires de Champagne, pendant le XIIIe siècle"), Revue Historique, (1932).

Securities and Exchange Commission (SEC), Can the U.S. be an International Financial Center? Remarks at Women in Housing & Finance Public Policy Luncheon, Commissioner Daniel M. Gallagher, Washington, DC, 13 January (2015).

Securities and Futures Commission (SFC), Hong Kong as a Leading Financial Center in Asia, Research Paper No. 33, Research Department, Supervision of Markets Division (Hong Kong SAR) (2006).

Schoon, Natalie, Islamic finance — a history, Financial service review, August (2008).

Shiller, Robert J., Speculative asset prices, Nobel Prize lecture, December (2013).

Shiller, Robert J., Searching for economic stability, on Bubble economy: hot market concerns, The Economist — The Buttonwood Gathering, 29–30th October 2013, New York City, December (2013).

Silla, Richard, A Historical Primer on the Business of Credit Ratings, Department of Economics, Stern School of Business (2001).

Spufford, Peter, From Antwerp to London: the decline of financial centers in Europe, NIAS, Ortelius Lecture 4, (2005).

Smith Kuznets, Simon, The Doctrine of Usury in the Middle Ages, transcribed by Stephanie Lo, an appendix to Simon Kuznets: Cautious Empiricist of the Eastern European Jewish Diaspora, E. Glen Weyl (2007).

St Giles, Winchester Planning Document adopted as a Supplementary Planning Document by Winchester City Council's (LDF) Committee on 28th September (2011).

Stern Gary, Addressing the too big to fail problem, Testimony before the Committee on Banking, Housing, and Urban Affairs, U.S. Senate, Washington D.C., 6 May (2009).

Strikwerda, Carl, Legacy of World War I Conference, Chestnut Hill College, The First World War in the History of Globalization, 14–15 November (2014).

Taylor, Brian, The rise and fall of the largest corporation in history, Global Financial Data, 6 November (2013).

Unknown, The taste of adventure, the history of spices is the history of trade, the Economist, 17 December (1998).

Ventana Research, Cognitive research redefine business potential, White paper, (2012).

Vernon L. Smith, Constructivism and ecological rationality in economics, Nobel Prize lecture, 8 December (2002).

Warburg, Paul M. Address Of Hon. Paul M. Warburg of the Federal Reserve Board before the Twin City Banker's Club of St. Paul and Minneapolis at the Minnesota Club, St. Paul, 22 October (1915).

Weber, Ernst Juerg, A short history of derivative security markets, Business School University of Western Australia, August (2008).

Willmann, Gerald, The History of Lotteries, Department of Economics, Stanford University, working paper, 3 August (1999).

Wolff, Hans-Georg, Moser, Klaus, Affects of networking on career success: A longitudinal study. *Journal of Applied Psychology*, 94(1): 196–206 (2009).

World Economic Forum (in collaboration with PwC), The evolution of trust in business: From deliveries to values, January (2015).

Yamagushi Kenjiro, Onuki Mari, The Gold and Silver Wraps of the Edo Period — A Unique Form of Gold and Silver Coins, Institute for Monetary and Economic Studies, Bank of Japan, November (1997).

Yee, Colin, The formation of American financial centers, Honors thesis, Williams College, 9 May (2006).

Yellen, Janet L. A Painfully Slow Recovery for America's Workers: Causes, Implications, and the Federal Reserve's Response at the "A Trans-Atlantic Agenda for Shared Prosperity" conference sponsored by the AFL-CIO, Friedrich Ebert Stiftung, and the IMK Macroeconomic Policy Institute, Washington, D.C. 11 February (2013).

Zingales, Luigi, Does Finance Benefit Society? Harvard University, NBER, and CEPR, January (2015).

Other References

Accessed on December 31, 2015

On medieval finance:

http://www.reading.ac.uk/economic-history/ceh-research-credit-finance.aspx
https://www.clio.fr/BIBLIOTHEQUE/les_lombards_et_le_commerce_de_l_argent_au_moyen_Age.asp
http://www.thepublicdiscourse.com/2013/12/11099/

On Troyes:

http://www.jschweitzer.fr/les-comtes-de-champagne
http://vieuxtroyes.free.fr/t/indfoir.htm

On Amsterdam:

http://www.iamsterdam.com/en/visiting/about-amsterdam/history-and-society
http://www.amsterdam.info/netherlands/history/
http://www.theguardian.com/books/2013/oct/23/amsterdam-liberal-city-russell-shorto
https://www.rijksmuseum.nl/en/explore-the-collection/timeline-dutch-history/1600-1665-amsterdams-prosperity

On Florence:

http://autourdelombreduconnetable.com/aux-sources-de-la-richesse-de-florence/#_edn2

On Lübeck:

http://www.luebeck-tourism.de/culture/history.html
http://www.metro-handelslexikon.de/en/special_topics/ts_2a_short_history_of_
trade.html

On Japan:

http://aboutjapan.japansociety.org/content.cfm/the_british_isles_and_japanese_
archipelago_a_comparison_of_environmental_basics
http://aboutjapan.japansociety.org/content.cfm/japans_medieval_age_the_
kamakura__muromachi_periods

On Adam Smith:

http://videos.econlib.org/archives/2015/04/will_the_real_a.html

On the 2008–2009 subprime crisis:

http://www.federalreservehistory.org/Events/DetailView/55
http://www.federalreservehistory.org/Events/DetailView/65

On insurance:

https://www.lloyds.com/lloyds/about-us/history/corporate-history
http://www.lifehealthpro.com/2013/09/09/a-brief-history-of-life-insurance?
t=life-products

On computer security:

https://www.rsaconference.com/events/us15/agenda/sessions/1627/a-short-
history-of-attacks-on-finance
http://anti-virus-software-review.toptenreviews.com/what-was-the-first-antivirus-
software.html
http://resources.infosecinstitute.com/history-malware-part-one-1949-1988
https://www.gdatasoftware.com/securitylabs/information/history-of-malware/
1988-1994

https://www.gdatasoftware.com/securitylabs/information/history-of-malware/
1996-today
http://ftp.cerias.purdue.edu/pub/doc/morris_worm/worm.paper
http://arxiv.org/ftp/arxiv/papers/1302/1302.5392.pdf

On maps:

http://www.brown.edu/Departments/Italian_Studies/dweb/images/maps/decworld/
france-growth.jpg
http://archive.silkroadproject.org/tabid/177/defaul.aspx
http://oi.uchicago.edu/sites/oi.uchicago.edu/files/uploads/managed/feature_
blocks/Silk%20Road_map.pdf
https://people.hofstra.edu/geotrans/eng/ch2en/conc2en/map_VOC_Trade_
Network.html
http://www.lasalle.edu/~mcinneshin/251/wk03/images/global-trade-routes-
1400-1800.png

INDEX

algorithm, 168, 205, 212, 222, 225, 229, 230, 231
animal spirits, 282
annuities, 118, 125
annuity contract, 30
art collection, 53

back doors, 269
back office, 188
bad loans, 178
bank runs, 154, 156, 162
bankruptcy, 26, 33, 42, 48, 85, 107, 119, 125, 132, 160, 219, 227
bills of exchange, 32, 48, 64, 84, 98, 102, 116, 136, 137, 214
black plague, 38, 39, 47, 51, 136
blockchain, 226
bourse, 89
Brokerage, 135
bubbles, 41, 112, 155, 221, 233, 139, 257, 258, 279, 281, 283

cable, 144
capital investment, 195
cartographers, 70

central banks, 121, 153
city-state, 31, 65
claim, 124, 125
clearing house, 90, 101, 102, 174
climate, 37
cloth, 87
clustering effect, 188, 227
coaling station, 181
coffee, 77
cognitive computing, 233
cognitive revolution, 91
coinage, 26, 27, 62, 107, 171
colonial empire, 60, 135, 144, 157
commercial revolution, xx, 19, 21, 27, 190
commercial routes, 62
commodities, 86, 104, 149, 152, 168
common good, 132, 285, 289, 292
common law, 215
contracts for difference, 214
corporate bond, 151
corruption, 140
courier, 202
crash, 42, 125, 151, 159, 258, 281
credit crunch, 40, 274

credit instruments, 106
criminal, 267
crisis, 116, 140, 154, 157, 163, 182,
    185, 206, 211, 217, 221, 234, 257,
    278 280, 281, 289
crusader, 59, 62
cryptocurrencies, 224
cybersecurity, 243
cyber threat, 223
czarist bonds, 131

dark pool, 231, 224, 229
debasement, 26, 85
default, 40, 91, 132, 192, 211, 247
depression, 151, 155, 162
derivatives, 86, 160, 213, 216, 257
diamond, 84, 88
digital, 206, 225, 226
dividends, 109, 111, 292
dowries, 64
dowry fund, 36, 54, 196
draft banks, 79

ecosystem, 183, 184, 292
education, 92, 104, 291
enforcement, 148
enlightenment, 42, 55, 61, 91, 132, 291
equity market, 135
ethical principles, 48, 164, 205, 210,
    280, 284, 286, 288, 289, 290, 292,
    293
eurodollar, 182, 274
exchange fair, 101
exploration, 74

fair, xxi, 2, 3, 6, 7, 9, 30, 42, 98, 100,
    101, 107, 170
feeders, 129, 270

finance masters, xviii
financial crash, 124
financial crises, 119, 121
financial engineering, 23
financial instruments, 17, 28, 30, 89,
    103, 144, 188
financial markets, 169, 177, 286
flyboat, 106
forced loans, 34
framework, 15, 21, 164, 298
free cities, xxi, 115, 120
freedom, 180, 186, 218, 287, 296,
    298, 300
free market, xvii, 251
free spirit, 110
free trade, 172
fund, 66, 260

galley, 63, 65, 66, 110, 118
gambling, 115, 123, 190, 245,
    254–256, 259, 261, 262, 283
gateway, 186, 187
genocide, 59, 93, 127, 192
gold, xxii, 27, 62, 67, 69, 74, 88, 98,
    101, 110, 121, 122, 124, 126, 130,
    139, 146, 159, 168, 190, 191, 208,
    267, 275
goldsmith, 137, 144
government bonds, 63, 197
guild organization, 13, 28, 43, 201

handbook, 34
hawala, 190
hedge funds, 268
high speed trading, 208
holding companies, 54
human capital, 228
hydrocarbon, 196, 197

incentives, 16, 291, 292
index, 218, 252
indicators, 253
innovation, 30, 71, 73, 100, 115, 123, 138, 140, 146, 148, 152, 160, 167, 192, 218, 219, 245, 253, 296, 297
insurance, 100, 141, 142, 145, 149, 152, 213, 250, 261, 269, 272
interest, 19, 22, 23, 35, 144, 170, 190, 192, 256, 274
international payments, 56

Jews, 6, 21
joint stock companies, 65, 150
junk bonds, 219, 257

knowledge, 76, 91, 203, 204, 291
known world, 132, 201, 227, 295

Lex Mercatoria, 5, 206
liquidity, 99, 153, 183, 211, 212, 229
loan sharks, 23, 24
lotteries, 86, 88, 102, 258

malware, 240, 241
Marine Insurance, 49, 100, 142, 147
marine routes, 94
mathematics, 216, 235
medieval fairs, xix
mega companies, 30
meltdown, 248
mercenaries, 111
merchant banker, xviii, 18, 28, 32, 33, 98, 101, 120, 129, 246, 296
merchant banking, 26, 54, 64, 78, 84, 202
microfinance, 45
military, 58

mint, 27, 62, 123
mobile money, 194
monetary stability, 108
money changers, 12, 19, 26, 85, 173, 176
money laundering, 270
monopoly, 111, 128, 136, 139, 174, 181, 216
mortgage, 220, 221
multinational company, 108

navigation, 60
navy, 58–60, 65, 67, 73, 75–77, 80, 117, 127, 155, 201, 215, 227
network, 147, 171, 194, 203–205, 207, 211, 239
nutmeg, 67, 111

offshore, 179, 182, 183, 185, 187, 265, 268, 270, 274, 276, 277
oligarch, 65, 68
onshore, 189
open market, 109
opium, 79–81, 181, 185
option, 214, 216
option market, 112
outrage, 80
over-the-counter, 114

panic, 145, 153, 155, 156, 232, 261
papal finances, 50
papal States, 273
paper money, 78, 121, 124, 255
partnership, 22, 33, 44, 45, 52, 86, 192, 253
passport, 12
patriotic bonds, 146
perpetual bonds, 63, 118

perpetual debt, 100
pestilence, 6, 7
piracy, 18, 67, 83, 107, 112, 119,
 145, 223, 241, 300
pirate, 58, 180
Ponzi scheme, 54, 164, 193
poverty, xvi, 288, 300
precious metal, 88, 90, 114, 122,
 275
private equity, 67, 194, 195
property rights, 14–15, 252
public bank, 96, 99, 128, 136
public debt, 36, 41, 99
public finance, 34, 55, 63, 89, 102,
 118, 256, 259, 260

quantitative easing, 130
quantum computers, 235, 236
quantum computing, 224, 237

rankings, 179, 248, 252
rating, 125, 152, 163, 179, 220, 245,
 246
regulation, 183, 290, 292, 293
regulator, 148, 163, 189, 231, 232,
 276, 281
regulatory, 167, 168, 218, 222, 249,
 266, 278, 287, 299
relationship, 29, 145, 202, 204, 285,
 301
remittance, 143, 191
reputation, 29, 215, 246, 250
reserve bank, 107
reserve currency, 37
reward, 22, 32
rice voucher, 173
riots, 120
rule of law, 187

run, 55
rural markets, 42

safe harbour, 7, 117
scandal, 124
seafarer, 72, 126
sea loan, 94
seaport, 4, 8, 26, 75, 77, 117, 127,
 128, 150, 151, 168, 180, 187, 196,
 295
sea routes, xxii
secret accounts, 50
securities markets, 29
shadow banking, 165
shareholders, 109, 111, 135, 207
shift out, 184
shipping routes, 59
shock, 212, 232, 300
silk, 31, 42, 43, 56, 57, 68, 74, 75,
 87, 97, 120, 143, 172, 273
Silk Road, 190
social capital, 97
sovereign debt, 99, 135, 137–139,
 215, 228
sovereign loans, 89
sovereign wealth funds, 196, 197
special economic zones, 272
special purpose vehicle, 272
speculation, 140, 267, 268
spice, 34, 42, 50, 57, 65, 66, 75, 77,
 85–87, 90, 106, 110, 111, 120, 181,
 192, 207, 273
stability, 146, 150, 160, 165, 194,
 219, 244, 279
stock exchange, 87, 123, 191, 235
stock market, 64, 116, 124, 130, 161,
 237
subprime, 161, 248, 256, 282

subscription market, 142
sukuk, 193
super companies, 33, 48
systemic, 232, 249, 278, 279, 281, 287, 289, 292
systemic risk, 210

talent pool, 183
taxes, 16
tax havens, 268, 271
ticker, 265
Too Big to Fail, 266
trading model, 93
trading strategies, 230
treasure fleets, 75
treasury, 61, 98
trust, 37, 121, 145, 204, 205, 215, 225, 282, 285, 287, 289

trustworthiness, xvii, 4, 279, 285, 288, 289, 291, 293, 297, 298
tulip bubbles, 114
tulip bulb, 113, 214

usury, 10, 19–21, 23, 25, 28, 29, 35, 49, 61, 64, 260

vertical alliance, 205

war, 6, 17, 18, 40, 44, 47, 59, 61, 62, 72, 81
warehousing, 105
waterway, 118, 119, 149
wealth pool, 187
wraps, 172

zombie banks, 266